SATHER CLASSICAL LECTURES
Volume Thirty-three

SALLUST

SALLUST

by Ronald Syme

UNIVERSITY OF CALIFORNIA PRESS
BERKELEY, LOS ANGELES, LONDON

UNIVERSITY OF CALIFORNIA PRESS
BERKELEY AND LOS ANGELES, CALIFORNIA

UNIVERSITY OF CALIFORNIA PRESS, LTD.
LONDON, ENGLAND

© 1964 by The Regents of the University of California
Second Printing, 1974
ISBN: 0–520–02374–9
Library of Congress Catalog Card Number: 64–17069

Printed in the United States of America

PREFACE

It was the rule among the classic historians of China to keep their personal statement for the end. They preferred the facts to speak. Nor need a preface be long, unless the author has been abnormally incompetent or expects dull readers.

Sallust was a senator before he became a writer. It is expedient to provide the social and historical setting of his life and works in some detail. Of the writings, most space goes to the *Bellum Catilinae,* for two reasons: Sallust was close in time to that transaction, and the abundant testimony on other record permits one to assess his accuracy and his integrity.

Sallust was able at the same time to admire both Cato and Caesar. He detested the Triumvirs and passed censure on their rule, sharp and courageous. On that count he here earns a favourable presentation. Perhaps too favourable, as can happen when one believes that a historian has been maligned or misunderstood.

None the less, I should not have been bold enough to take on Sallust had there not come an impulsion as amicable as it was urgent—the invitation to deliver the Sather Classical Lectures. Not that this book bears much resemblance to the six discourses presented in the autumn of 1959. It is an equivalent, in a different mode of exposition. Indeed, Chapters XII–XV were not finished until the year's end, being composed in that ambience of industry tempered with ease and elegance which visitors to Berkeley recall with affection. To friends in the Department of Classics in Dwinelle Hall, and to many others in the vicinity, the volume can thus be dedicated, in full and especial propriety. Further, I am happy to acknowledge advice and help accruing in the sequel to the manuscript of *Sallust*, on both sides of the water, notably from Ernst Badian, Herbert Bloch, and Isobel Henderson.

Oxford,   R. S.
March, 1962

CONTENTS

I

THE PROBLEM

Sallust conquered a new domain for the literature of the Latins. Fortunate in the vicissitudes of his life and career, he elected to write history, with the decline and fall of the Roman Republic as his general theme, and he discovered the suitable style and manner: plain and abrupt, hostile to eloquence, ostensibly archaic but in truth artful, insidious, innovatory. Two monographs and an uncompleted history, that was enough. Sallust created a fashion, and his fame grew with the years.

A sober and judicious critic brings confirmation. For Quintilian, Sallust stood without a rival, the greatest of the Roman historians. Further, Quintilian went so far as to match him with Thucydides. What can have been in his mind and meaning? He is not pronouncing a verdict that derives from some personal whim. The Romans, it appears, put Sallust on a level with Thucydides for certain qualities of style—he was brief and rapid, concentrated and majestic. Moreover, Sallust himself resorted to imitation of the classic Greek historian. His act was deliberate and undisguised.

Quintilian's claim comes as a shock. The monographs of Sallust betray all manner of disquieting features; and, even if Sallust's mature and major work, the *Historiae,* had survived, there is no reason to suppose that it came anywhere near the *History of the Peloponnesian War* for diligence, integrity, and depth.

The Roman estimation of Sallust is exorbitant. That is not in dispute. But it can be understood: Roman historiography developed canons all of its own, and Quintilian is writing as a

1

literary critic. That question need not detain. The modern perplexity about this historian is of a different order. Three opinions
have had their advocates.

Sallust invented a style, careful and subtle. Is he to be regarded
first and foremost as a literary artist? That view is narrow and
imperfect. Sallust was a Roman senator, tribune of the plebs,
praetor and governor of a province. History at Rome had its
origin in life and strife, not in belles lettres or erudite investigation; and for a long time history was kept as the proper preserve
of the governing class. Sallust, like certain other senatorial writers,
took up the pen only when the career of action ended, for refuge
and for consolation. His writing is also a continuation and a kind
of revenge.

The monographs disclose an author with strong views about
men and affairs. Some critics therefore hold him little better than
a political pamphleteer, advocating the interests of a leader or
arguing the doctrine of a party. Sallust had in fact espoused the
cause of Caesar. Yet a closer inspection raises doubts. Sallust is
very far from being a defender of Caesar or apologist of any sort.
He attacks. And, for all his bitterness against birth and the
oligarchy, a Roman and a patriot might somewhere be expected to
rise above partisanship when he contemplated the tragedy of the
Republic.

Some go much further along the path of rehabilitation, discovering in Sallust a moral and political historian of the first
rank, an author inspired by plain and unimpeachable sincerity.
What he says in the prologues to his monographs is taken to be
convincing testimony; and the thesis has been supported by appeal
to other documents. Hence large claims for Sallust, lavishly expounded in the recent age (but not conceded everywhere).

Exclusive attention to any one of these three aspects cannot fail
to have harmful results. Sallust is at the same time an artist, a
politician, and a moralist—the elements so fused and combined
that he seems all of one piece. Yet changes and a development
might perhaps be allowed for, brief though the span of years be
from the pioneer monograph to the mature achievement. And
finally, the enigma of the historian's character: are the man and
the author the same person? The style is marked, the manner

uniform, the opinions coherent—so much so that it was easy to
imitate or parody Sallust. What lies behind the style and attitudes?
Who was Sallust?

Such is the challenge of Sallust's writings, sharp and not to be
evaded. But there are risks and complications.

When Sallust turned to historical composition, he was well past
forty. Curiosity asks (and it is a legitimate question) whether
something cannot be glimpsed or divined of the earlier man in his
life and occupations. The facts on record are scanty, but imagination demands its rights, or a little licence—and scholarship has a
plain duty to extend the debatable frontiers of knowledge.

One direction seemed open and inviting. Recourse was had to
certain pamphlets surviving from antiquity, but generally held in
no esteem at all, either passed over or flatly condemned. Those
documents have been elevated to a place of predilection in Sallustian studies during the last half century.

The *Epistulae ad Caesarem senem,* as they are entitled, are
ostensibly a pair of missives giving advice to Julius Caesar. These
Suasoriae became a fashion for a time, and a creed, with weighty
names in support, among the most authoritative and illustrious,
whether in the study of history or of style and language. Distrust
and the contrary arguments tended to be ignored or overridden.
Confidence, however, was premature. The tide now sets the other
way. For various reasons, it will be safe and wiser to discard these
productions.[1]

Benefit and clarity can accrue from abstention. Nothing is
known for certain about the style, doctrines. or standpoint of the
historian before he wrote his first monograph. Many questions,
however, have to be asked concerning the earlier and hidden
existence of C. Sallustius Crispus before he emerges in open day
as tribune of the plebs in 52 B.C., a year that nobody predicted
dull and tranquil. There are also his actions in the sequel, until

---

[1] For the *Suasoriae* see further p. 299 and Appendix II. There is also the
Invectiva in Ciceronem (p.298), with the dramatic date of 54 B.C. Some hold
it not only contemporaneous (a tall order), but even Sallustian. Another
pamphlet, "Cicero," *In Sallustium,* has deceived nobody. But items thence
derived find admittance to standard and recent works.

he gave up the pursuit of public honours and discovered his true vocation. The task entails sundry hazards, and speculation cannot be avoided if one tries to put Sallust in his proper setting: origin and education, ideals and allegiance—and perhaps opportunism.[2]

---

[2] The *testimonia* for Sallust's life and writings are registered in the edition of A. Kurfess (Teubner, ed. 3, 1957), not adequate everywhere. In estimating Sallust's career, much demolitionary work has to be done on the "tradition," both ancient and modern. Items must be eradicated that have crept in from sources dubious or spurious. Further, it will be expedient to question certain assumptions about Roman political and social life, and also to go against the persistent habit of treating the history of the period in terms of the biography of Cicero or of Caesar.

II

SALLUST'S
ANTECEDENTS

A man's rank in society and local origin might be worth inspection for light on his conduct and career. The city, people, and region have to be scrutinised with a vigilant eye: Italy was heterogeneous, still a name, not a unit or a nation. On broad definition (which is at the same time precise and legal) Italy had long presented a double aspect—on the one side the communities belonging to the Roman Commonwealth, on the other the autonomous allies. In 91 the peoples of the Abruzzi seceded and created a federal "Italia," with rebellion all the way from Picenum down to Samnium and Lucania. Hence a murderous war, heralding a whole decade of chaos, for civil strife supervened on the *Bellum Italicum*. And, although the final settlement brought the rebel Italici—and indeed all Italy south of the river Po—into the Roman franchise, there was no concord yet, no sense of unity or identity throughout the peninsula, and little loyalty or trust in the Roman government. At Rome they spoke loudly and warmly of "tota Italia." An aspiration, not a fact.

Even in tracts such as the Sabine and Volscian countries, incorporated long since in the Roman State and not exacerbated by persistent feuds or recent damage, local solidarity and attachments might persist, profound and genuine. A municipal man who transferred his ambitions to the metropolis and entered the governing order could still proclaim that his town was his "germana patria." Cicero bears witness, speaking of Arpinum and the Tullii. "There

is our origin," he says, "a most ancient stock, there our family and
worship, and many memorials of our ancestors." [1]

Some of the cities boasted an antiquity that went back before
Romulus; and, like the Roman patricians, their aristocratic *gentes*
claimed descent from kings and gods. Families of substance and
repute contracted alliances by matrimony, built up large estates,
and secured domination over a town or a whole region. But these
magnates, "domi nobiles" as they are designated, count for nothing at Rome in their own right. The way was hard, they came
under dispraisal as ignoble and upstart—and some preferred to
stay in their own place, enjoying ease and the dignity of municipal
honours.

It is true that local and even regional support might muster usefully at the polls. Defending Cn. Plancius of Atina, Cicero extols
his popularity through a wide zone (it included Arpinum) and
produces an eloquent panegyric—"that rough and mountainous
land, loyal to its own sons and frank and true." [2] He can also exploit the theme in invective against a political enemy. P. Vatinius
had failed to win the votes of his own tribe, the "Sergia," in which
some of the old Sabines were enrolled along with the Marsians
and the Paeligni. What a rebuff! Nobody since the founding of
Rome, the orator exclaims, had lost the "Sergia." [3]

P. Vatinius was not discommoded. He got his praetorship, and
he vowed he would end as consul (which seemed over-bold). What
the *novus homo* needed at Rome was a leader and patron, not a
collection of rustic voters. Conversely, great houses in the *nobilitas*
were eager to extend their *clientela* throughout the land of Italy;
and the traditional devices which the *nobiles* exploited in the
struggle for honour and power were annexed and enhanced in
the fatal sequence of the dynasts: Marius, Sulla, Pompeius, Caesar.

A question therefore arises that concerns Sallust, also some
other sons of municipal Italy. How far is origin relevant to sentiment, allegiance, and behaviour? It might matter a lot, if one
knew, or very little. The phenomenon is not paradoxical that men

---

[1] Cicero, *De legibus* I. 3.

[2] *Pro Plancio* 22. And, for Cicero himself and his brother, "agri ipsi prope
dicam montesque faverunt" (ib. 20).

[3] *In Vatinium* 36. For the town and origin of Vatinius see p. 27.

transcend or deny their antecedents, all for Rome and the free play of ambition or talent. The question touches the great *novus homo* from Arpinum. Also, a generation later, a new Roman deriving from the recesses of rebel Italy, Asinius Pollio, the consular orator and historian. Pollio belonged to the first family at Teate of the Marrucini.[4]

Not only senators are involved, but poets—and with them one of the central problems in the literature of the Latins, often neglected or misconceived. Some fancy that the ancestry of Lucretius goes back to the patrician *gens Lucretia* of early Rome. A careless assumption, or a delusion. Those Lucretii had perished centuries before. Conjecture for conjecture, it would be better to suppose him Sabine or Umbrian. Again, Asisium in Umbria is the home of Propertius: what does that mean? As for Ovidius Naso, scattered items in the poems proclaim (with external evidence to confirm) that he came from Sulmo of the Paelignians, far from Rome. Otherwise, matter, expression, and sentiment would declare a sophisticated product of the metropolis, urban and urbane.

C. Sallustius Crispus came from Amiternum (near the modern Aquila) in the heart of the Abruzzi, more than thirty miles east from Reate. The Sabine land, though acquiring a certain unity from the Via Salaria (Rome to Reate and thence to Asculum in Picenum), which traversed it from southwest to northeast, covers a wide expanse and falls into separate parts. On the southwest there was no sharply defined frontier against Latium—there could be none. Ancient legends agree with the facts of geography and economic life—Sabine kings and the migration of baronial families, such as the Valerii and the Claudii. Though Numa Pompilius and Titus Tatius may be figures of myth or constructions of erudite fantasy, no doubts can impair the provenance of the *gens Claudia,* which a Roman emperor, the last of his line, was proud and happy to parade—"maiores mei, quorum antiquissimus Clausus, origine Sabina." [5]

---

[4] That origin emerges only indirectly. Catullus addressed Pollio's brother as "Marrucine Asini" (12. 1); and there was a "Herius Asinius praetor Marrucinorum" killed in the *Bellum Italicum* (Livy, *Per.* LXXIII).

[5] Tacitus, *Ann.* XI. 24. 1.

Like Nursia in the north (which is close to Umbria and Picenum), Amiternum belongs to the back country. Amiternum
faces eastwards, being separated from the basin of Reate by the
watershed between the Tyrrhenian Sea and the Adriatic. The
route eastwards from Reate, leaving the Salaria at Interocrium,
has a difficult course and must cross a mountain pass over three
thousand feet above sea level before it descends to the upland
plain of Amiternum. That plain is watered by the Aternus, which
flows eastwards through the lands of Vestini, Paeligni, and Marrucini to the Adriatic; and the boundary against the Vestini is only
a few miles east from Amiternum. To the north stands the massif
of the Mons Fiscellus (Gran Sasso), to the south the mountains of
the Marsian country.

The Sabines earned universal commendation as a people of
hardy mountaineers, plain and parsimonious, austere and god-
fearing, tenaciously attached to the ancient ways. Some will have
it that Sabines were prone to mysticism.[6] That notion can do little
harm if it be added that they also had a tendency to emigration,
liked money, and were good with donkeys.

Rustic and Sabine virtue is a theme regularly invoked by ser-
monisers or poets in rebuke of frivolous and degenerate Romans.
The idea did not fail to appeal to respectable men who advertised
reverence for the past without needing to practise frugality, who
took up the newest methods of economic exploitation, and who
enjoyed all the plentiful comforts of a refined and tranquil existence.

Especially if they happened to be Sabine themselves. M. Terentius Varro of Reate is a commentary in his own person, and, along
with Varro, those proprietors who speak, or are spoken about, in
the dialogue *De re rustica*. Various masters of rural science hold
discourse about their special aptitudes and so disclose precious
pieces of information.[7]

There was a tract near Reate, the "Rosea rura" (Le Roscie), a
reclaimed lake bottom—the richest soil in all Italy, fabulous for

---

[6] E. Bolaffi, *Sallustio e la sua fortuna nei secoli* (1949), 23: "quella terra di
montanari . . . proclivi al misticismo." Also ib. 75.

[7] Varro's friends (Sabine and others) are a subject that repays exploration.

its productivity.[8] It had passed into the hands of a few big proprietors, and was used for pasture. Varro grazed horses there.[9] But
donkeys were the fame and pride of Reate, known the world over
and even eclipsing Arcadia. They commanded a high price (40,000
or even 60,000 sesterces each), being used as stud animals for
the breeding of high-class mules.[10] It is Murrius of Reate who
speaks for donkeys in Varro's dialogue; but the Sabine senator
Q. Axius earned the lasting notoriety. He had purchased one of
these animals. It was a prize exhibit at the elegant country house
where he once entertained the consul Ap. Claudius Pulcher.[11]

Amiternum could not, it is true, enter into competition of
wealth and fame with Reate. A pleasing fancy evokes the young
Sallust in the salubrious air and stern upbringing of a Sabine hill
town.[12] Some hesitations are in place. Sallust's town lies on a
low elevation beside the river Aternus in the middle of a broad
plain that was noted for the variety and excellence of its products.[13]
Nor did every *municipium* of Italy answer to the conventional
pattern of decent and archaic simplicity. Life among the better
sort at Larinum of the Samnites, as portrayed in Cicero's oration
Pro Cluentio, is a warning. Torpor and parsimony eke out the
slow years in a municipal existence. The alternative might be a
bout of criminality: vice and forgery, poison or the dagger. That
is what they preferred at Larinum.

The Sallustii, it will be assumed without discomfort, belonged
to the nobility of office at Amiternum. The *nomen*, with its un-

---

[8] It was described as "sumen Italiae" (Pliny, *NH* XVII. 32). For the ancient
evidence see *R-E* IA, 1128; H. Nissen, *Italische Landeskunde* II (1902), 473.
[9] Varro, *Res rusticae* II, praef. 6.
[10] ib. II. 1. 14; 8. 3; III. 2. 7.
[11] ib. III. 2. 3; 7; 9. For his tribe, the "Quirina," ib. 2. 1, cf. *SIG*³ 747.
Cicero also stayed with Axius in 54, the occasion being one of the recurrent
disputes with the people of Narnia about the drainage of Rosea (*Ad Att.* IV.
15. 5; *Pro Scauro* 27).
[12] G. Funaioli, *R-E* IA, 1915: "die reine Luft einer Landstadt"; 1918:
"seine Bergstadt."
[13] The site is San Vittorino, about five miles northwest from Aquila. For
the agriculture and products of the region, see the *testimonia* in *R-E* I,
1840 f.

common termination, in "-ustius," had not been heard of before. Amiternum, according to Varro, was the ancient cradle of the whole Sabine folk; and the inscriptions of Amiternum duly furnish a splendid crop of rare or archaic names.[14]

By a peculiar coincidence this generation also produces Cn. Sallustius, the friend of Cicero, and a kinsman called Publius. The latter is mentioned only once; but the former crops up several times in the space of twenty years—generally without the *praenomen*.[15] No link is discernible with the man of Amiternum; but it will be recalled that ambition, politics, or disagreements about property cut across families, the municipal no less than the aristocratic.

This Sallustius attached himself to Cicero at an early date—he is discovered in certain transactions of the year 67. Nine years later, when Cicero departed for exile, this faithful friend was with him on the journey and was the first to be apprised of Cicero's dream about Marius and a triumphant return; he went to Brundisium, if not further across the sea to Macedonia. In a letter to his brother Quintus in February of 54, Cicero, after a brief verdict on the poems of Lucretius, adds a reference to the *Empedoclea* of Sallustius: you need to be a hero to read that work.[16]

Who then wrote the *Empedoclea*? That a man who ends as a senator and a historian may have previously dabbled in doctrines or composed a philosophical poem is not in itself a wild paradox. It might elicit approbation or a smile of tolerance rather than a movement of incredulity. The notion has indeed been seized with avidity by the curious or the uncritical.[17] There are strong reasons against.

---

[14] The early inscriptions are fairly numerous, *CIL* I². 1846–1889. Among the rare *gentilicia* observe "Apisius," "Fadenus," "Lacutulanus," "Mitsionius," "Oviolenus," "Teibanus," "Tettiedius."

[15] F. Münzer, *R-E* IA, 1912 f. Apart from *Ad Att.* XI. 11. 2, where the *praenomen* is needed to distinguish him from Publius, he is styled "Cn. Sallustius" only in *Ad fam.* XIV. 11.

[16] *Ad Q. fratrem* II. 9. 3: "virum te putabo si Sallusti Empedoclea legeris, hominem non putabo."

[17] A. Rostagni. *La letteratura di Roma repubblicana ed augustea* (1939), 265; E. Bolaffi, *Sallustio e la sua fortuna nei secoli* (1949), 87 ff.; E. Paratore, *Storia della letteratura latina* (1950), 281; L. O. Sangiacomo, *Sallustio* (1954), 21.

Cicero's friend has the prime and patent claim to the *Empedoclea*. A man of principle, he was not afraid to give Cicero the benefit of his opinions, literary as well as political. In October of 54 he urged that Cicero ought to prosecute Gabinius.[18] And, about the same time, at a recitation of the first two books of *De re publica*, he came out with a decided view: the author ought not to bother about characters from ancient history in the dialogue: his own person would carry greater weight.[19]

Cn. Sallustius was not on Cicero's staff in Cilicia (in 51–50). Perhaps for a good and decisive reason. A letter sent by Cicero to an official in Syria in the summer of 50 is addressed to a Sallustius, with the title "pro quaestore."[20] Some assume (or would like to believe) that this Sallustius is none other than C. Sallustius Crispus.[21] Not very likely. Inspection of the letter (and of the historical context) will suggest that the man was not a *legatus* acting as quaestor, but a quaestor of the previous year.[22] He had been quaestor in 51, going out with M. Calpurnius Bibulus, the proconsul of Syria, and he was now about to leave. That is to say, not somebody who had been a tribune of 52.

Nor, for that matter, is it certain that the Syrian quaestor is identical with Cicero's friend. The tone of the missive is distant, censorious, and testy. Cicero makes it clear that he does not want to have this man's company on the journey back to Italy.[23]

---

[18] *Ad Q. fratrem* III. 4. 2.

[19] ib. 5. 1.

[20] The superscription of *Ad fam.* II. 17 has "canini salustio proq." Orelli proposed "Cn. Salustio," followed by some recent editors such as Sjögren (Teubner, 1925), also Constans and Bayet (Budé, 1950), Mommsen, however, suggested the *praenomen* "C.," i.e., the historian. Broughton in *MRR* II prudently registers the man as "†Anini Sallustius." And might he not have been a Caninius Sallustianus, as Münzer once thought (*R-E* III, 1479)?

[21] Thus, after Mommsen, F. Münzer, *R-E* IA, 1913; G. Funaioli, ib. 1919; L. Pareti, *La congiura di Catilina* (1934), 203; O. Seel, *Klio*, Beiheft XLVII (1943), 112 ff.; E. Paratore, *Storia della letteratura latina* (1950), 283.

[22] A provincial quaestor in the second (calendar) year of his tenure is properly and officially styled "pro quaestore," but otherwise and normally "quaestor." And this man is the anonymous quaestor referred to in *Ad Att.* VI. 5. 3.

[23] *Ad fam.* II. 17. 1. Note further that Cicero's friend, already mentioned in 67 (*Ad Att.* I. 3. 3; 11. 1), would be well above the normal age if quaestor in 51.

Cn. Sallustius opted for Pompeius and the cause of the Republic. He was once again with Cicero at Brundisium, this time in 47. He secured pardon from Caesar.[24] After that, nothing more is heard of "Sallustius noster."

To return to Amiternum, and earlier wars. Sallust's family may (or may not) have incurred damage and impoverishment in the ten years of tribulation which began with the secession of the Italici and went on through civil war to dictatorship and proscriptions. Amiternum itself was exposed to harm, being on the edge of the insurrection (Vestini, Picentini, Marsi). And, like other *municipia*, Amiternum might have stood with the party of Marius. Sabine Nursia was the home of the famous Sertorius.[25]

Confederate Italia was defeated, and many of the leading families among the peoples of the Abruzzi were despoiled or brought low.[26] The next generation shows a Vettius Scato (his name recalls a Marsian general) who took up the profession of a house agent at Rome.[27] Also Ventidius the Picentine, operating a team of mules.[28] The grandfather of Asinius Pollio fell in battle when leading his people, the Marrucini, against the Roman legions; but there is no sign that young Pollio was reduced to the expedient of earning a livelihood.

The partisans of Marius and Cinna also suffered loss. Many towns had been active in that allegiance, or slow to discern the better cause when Sulla came back from the East to restore the rule of the *nobiles*. Sallust may have had sharp and personal

---

[24] *Ad Att.* XI. 20. 1: "etiam Sallustio ignovit." This passage was unwisely included by A. Kurfess in the Teubner edition of the historian: which has deceived some.

[25] Plutarch, *Sertorius* 2. For a full and generous account of the Sabine milieu see A. Schulten, *Sertorius* (1926), 17 ff.

[26] cf. *Rom.Rev.* (1939), 91. For the Italian generals, see E. T. Salmon, *TAPA* LXXXIX (1958), 159 ff.

[27] Scato, born among the Marsians (*De domo sua* 116), to be identified with the Vettius of *Ad Att.* IV. 5. 2; VI. 1. 15. Observe *Phil.* XII. 27: "cum P. Vettio Scatone, duce Marsorum."

[28] Gellius XV 4. 3.

reasons for nourishing a grudge against Sulla and the aristocracy
—and against the "Sullani homines" who benefited from the
proscriptions by acquiring wide domains.[29]

Sallust's birth falls in the decade of troubles, and he lived to
within four years of the Battle of Actium. The dates are 86 and
35, furnished by the *Chronicle* of Jerome—at least with a small
but necessary adjustment, be it observed.[30] The first item happens
to stand as the year corresponding to 87. The second is 36, but it
registers at the same time the historian's decease as falling "quadriennio ante Actiacum bellum." That is to say, 35. The contradiction can be abolished, but there is no base of certitude in the
standard solution. The particulars about literary history in
Jerome derive from Suetonius ultimately, but the compiler was
cursory and careless. There are internal discrepancies—or independent facts that contradict. Jerome cannot be accepted on
Lucretius and Catullus. Further, he may well be in error with his
dates for Livy's life (59 B.C.–A.D. 17). Here the original item can
simply have been a rough estimate or vague tradition that Livy
was seventy-five when he died; and there is the chance that the

---

[29] Cicero refers to "Septimiis, Turraniis ceterisque Sullanarum adsigna-
tionum possessoribus" (*De lege agraria* III. 3). These persons are not registered in *R-E*. For Sabine Septimii, note C. Septimius T. f. Quir. (*Ad fam.*
VIII. 8. 5), and, later, T. Septimius Sabinus (*ILS* 5921); and a P. Septimius
was Varro's quaestor (*De lingua latina* V. I. 1). A Septimius was among the
proscribed (Appian, *BC* IV. 21. 96 f.). As for Turranii, Varro dedicated the
second book of *Res rusticae* to Turranius Niger, an important grazier (II,
praef. 6).

[30] Jerome, p. 151 H: "Sallustius Crispus scriptor historicus in Sabinis
Amiterni nascitur"; p. 159 H: "Sallustius diem obiit quadriennio ante Actia-
cum bellum." There are also the data in the *Chronicon Paschale* and the
Consularia Constantinopolitana (reproduced among the *testimonia* in the
Teubner edition): here we have Sallust's birthday asserted (October 1), and
the day of his decease (April 29).

For the sorting-out of the dates (to produce 86 and 35), see G. Funaioli,
R-E IA, 1914; R. Helm, *Philologus*, Supp. XXI. 2 (1929), 39 f. Helm assumes
that the precise date of the historian's birth was on record; and he further
suggests that Sallust himself had referred to it in the *Historiae*—which is not
at all plausible.

span of Livy's life reached from 64 B.C. to A.D. 12, more or less.[31]
Similarly, one ought to begin to wonder about Jerome's precise
figures for Varro (116–27). They furnish the ninetieth year as the
term of his life—attractive no doubt but unverifiable. And
Jerome in fact says "prope nonagenarius." [32]

It may have been assumed or conjectured that Sallust died at
fifty. The birth dates of persons more eminent than Sallust could
be liable to variants or controversy.[33] The year of decease might
have better attestation. It is therefore not excluded that Sallust
was born two or three years earlier than the seventh consulate
of C. Marius.

Jerome states that Sallust was born at Amiternum. That is only
his way of indicating the "patria" of the historian. The infant
might have seen the light of day at Rome, his parents having
come there for refuge on the outbreak of the *Bellum Italicum*—
or already established at the capital. One should therefore be
chary of deductions about infancy and boyhood, though nothing
forbids the notion that some part of Sallust's boyhood was in
fact spent at Amiternum, or on a country estate, if the notion be
thought helpful. But, as nothing is known about father, mother,
or kinsfolk, the topic is best abandoned.[34]

---

[31] cf. the arguments adduced in *Harvard Studies* LXIV (1959), 40 f.
Jerome brackets Livy and Messalla Corvinus under 59 (p. 164 H.). That is
patently too late for Corvinus (*cos.* 31): perhaps 64. The full corollary is to
shift Livy's birth as well—and also his decease.

[32] Jerome, p. 164 H.

[33] Thus Pompeius Magnus (Velleius II. 53. 4) and Tiberius Caesar (Suetonius, *Tib.* 5).

[34] The foregoing remarks were designed not to explain Sallust but to provide a background and to reveal (as is expedient) something of the Italian
and municipal aspect of Roman social history. It is salutary to recall that,
but for Jerome's notice, the "patria" of Sallust would not be known. Where
would we be without it? It may be contended that the manner of the historian
and his opinions both can and should be estimated without recourse to
inferences from his local origin—inferences which are likely enough to be
superficial, conventional, or fallacious. It is not clear that Sallust would have
been a different sort of historian if the Sallustii came from somewhere else,
for example from Arpinum.

On the other side, most modern writings about Sallust neglect unduly the
Sabine country and the municipal milieu. For example, not a word in L. O.

Sallust's youth and prime of manhood were passed in the thirty years of precarious peace under the system of the oligarchy which Sulla restored. At Rome for his education, he was perhaps in time to witness the more or less peaceful revolution of 70, when the consuls Pompeius and Crassus overthrew some of the ordinances of Sulla. He saw the turbulence of the middle sixties: tribunes' bills and the prosecution of tribunes, fierce competition at the elections, and violence threatened. Then came the conspiracy of Catilina, the return of Pompeius Magnus from the eastern lands, the dynasts' pact in 60, the consulship of Caesar.

Sangiacomo, *Sallustio* (1954); and K. Büchner allocates only a sentence, which, however, imports the adventitious notion that the memory of Cato the Censor was still verdant in that region (*Sallust* [1960], 14). Some scholars in brief mention, with conventional prepossessions in favour of a Sabine birth place, manifest their lack of real interest through positive errors. Thus E. E. Sikes, discussing Sallust, adds Horace to Varro as Sabine (*CAH* IX [1932], 767); and, to M. L. W. Laistner, Sallust "came, like Marius and Cicero, from the Sabine hill country" (*The Greater Roman Historians* [1947], 47).

The most peculiar aberration was that of E. Schwartz, condoned in the sequel or covered up, who assumed that Sallust was a Roman of Rome—"der bis ins Mark verdorbene Sohn der Hauptstadt, geistvoll, charakterlos, ein echter Revolutionär" (*Hermes* XXXII [1897], 582 = *Ges.Schr.* II [1956], 306). With Sallust is contrasted Livy, "der biedere Provinziale." It would have been more instructive to adduce the difference in the season of their writing—and the fact that Sallust was a senator, Livy a rhetorician.

III

THE POLITICAL SCENE

The fashion persists of condemning and deploring the last epoch of the Roman Republic. It was turbulent, corrupt, immoral. And some speak of decadence. On the contrary, it was an era of liberty, vitality—and innovation. Political strife brought oratory to perfection; and the master of eloquence, in seasons of eclipse or disappointment, turned his abundant energies to refining the Latin language, which he converted into a suitable medium for theoretical disquisition. Other writers went in for verse, with new and splendid achievements of vigour or elegance.

Roman life was coming to feel to the full the liberating effects of empire and prosperity. In the aftermath of the Punic Wars, cult and ritual lapsed, and law was separated from religion (the process and agents are obscure). In various other ways good sense or chicanery were able to abate or circumvent the "antiquus rigor," the "duritia veterum." The quality of a civilisation can be estimated on various criteria. One of them is art and letters, which posterity tends to rate highly, for interested reasons. Another is the position of women in relation to husband and property. Ancient custom kept the woman in strict tutelage. *Tutela* was never abolished, only disregarded in practice; and women (at least of the better sort) acquired a large measure of liberty. That was not all. Divorce was easy and normal, the initiative not always coming from the husband. The classical law of marriage eschewed

16

rigour or formality. It was perhaps the most imposing achievement of the Roman legal genius.[1]

This liberal and humane evolution is seldom appraised as it deserves. Sallust himself is partly to blame. Not that he wasted words or regrets on the decay of religion.[2] But he wrote in revulsion from his own time. He interpreted a process of economic change and political adjustment in terms of morals; and he fell an easy prey to conventional notions about old Roman virtue. The distortion was enhanced in the next epoch, eager to escape from the memory of recent freedom and turbulence, and complacent in its own type of felicity—that is, liberty but not licence, discipline but not despotism. Political fraud and Augustan romanticism conspired to embellish the venerable past—with unhappy consequences for historical study ever after.

Sallust is also in part to blame for the prevalence of another doctrine, namely the belief that Rome had a regular two-party system, Optimates and Populares. The origin of this persuasion in the modern world can plausibly be traced to false and schematic views about parliamentary England in the eighteenth century; and its subsequent fortunes are a topic of no little instruction.[3]

There were two sources of power at Rome, it could be held, the *libertas* of the People and the *auctoritas* of the Senate; while senators and *populus* or *plebs* stand in patent contrast. In the attempt to describe political actions, however, there was a danger of simplification or confusion. Sallust, in a digression on Roman politics before the Jugurthine War in fact refers to two parties in the State—the *nobilitas* and the *plebs*.[4] Terminology has to

---

[1] It is so styled by F. Schulz, *Classical Roman Law* (1951), 103.

[2] P. 247.

[3] H. Strasburger, *R-E* XVIII, 773 ff. For the social basis of Roman political life see M. Gelzer, *Die Nobilität der römischen Republik* (1912) = *Kl.Schr.* I (1962), 17 ff.; F. Münzer, *Römische Adelsparteien und Adelsfamilien* (1920); L. R. Taylor, *Party Politics in the Age of Caesar* (1949).

[4] *Jug.* 40. 5 ("nobilitas" and "plebs"); 41. 5 ("nobilitas" and "populus"); 43. 1 (Metellus as hostile to the "populi partes"). See further p. 171. Note also *Cat.* 37. 10: "quicumque aliarum atque senatus partium erant." For Sallust's use of political terminology, cf. K. Hanell, *Eranos* XLIII (1945), 263 ff.; L. R. Taylor, o.c. 9 ff.

be watched. Not all senators are *nobiles,* for that term is restricted
to the descendants of consuls; and *nobiles,* as Sallust reveals,
might be advocates of the People's cause. But Sallust does not
countenance the belief in an organised Popular Party.

There were "populares," it is true. The term, more often one
of depreciation or abuse than of praise, can apply to a man or a
measure, to an attitude and even a tradition.[5] But there is no
sign of a party designated as the "Populares." An individual might
adopt a "popular" line to further his career or his feuds. It is
always expedient to see where such a "popularis" stands at the
end (if his career has not been abruptly cut short).

Sallust (it is relevant) avoids the term altogether in its political
application. With him "popularis" is restricted to a member of a
common nation or an ally in a common enterprise.[6]

He does not use "Optimates" either—the nearest he allows
himself is "boni." [7] That avoidance is highly instructive for his
sentiments. "Optimates" cannot fail to convey or imply approval.
Instead, Sallust operates with "potentia paucorum," or with
"factio." That is not at all a friendly term.[8] Cicero eschews "factio"
in his orations.

On a favouring interpretation, the leaders of the governing
clique will be styled "principes optimatium." Thus Cicero in an
oration designed to promote harmony.[9] His treatise *De re publica*
presents the other aspect: "When a group dominates the Commonwealth through riches and birth and other resources, they are
in truth a *factio,* but they are called *Optimates.*" [10]

---

[5] Cicero describes Caesar as having followed "viam quae popularis habetur"
and credits him with an "animus vere popularis" (*In Cat.* IV. 9). Not so
polite is the allusion to Crassus: "de istis qui se popularis haberi volunt"
(ib. 10).

[6] The one use, *Jug.* 7. 1 (and six other cases). The other, *Cat.* 22. 1; 24. 1;
52. 14. The reading in *Jug.* 41. 1 is a matter of dispute.

[7] *Cat.* 19. 2.

[8] *Jug.* 31. 1: "opes factionis"; 41. 6: "ceterum nobilitas factione magis
pollebat"; *Hist.* III. 48.8 (ed. Maurenbrecher): "C. Cotta, ex factione media
consul." For a full discussion of "factio," L. R. Taylor, o.c. 9 ff.

[9] *Pro Sestio* 138.

[10] *De re publica* III. 23, cf. I. 51: "opulentos homines et copiosos tum
genere nobili natos esse optimos putant. hoc errore vulgi cum rem publicam

Oligarchy is a plain and solid fact. Though secret in many of its operations, or subject to rifts and discord, the "factio" cannot evade detection. It is the group which, after resisting Pompeius Magnus in a long and tenacious struggle, finally came to terms and a distrustful alliance, which precipitated the Civil War.[11]

Pompeius and Crassus, after their consulate, went different paths for a time—rivals but with common enemies. Pompeius enjoyed a preponderance with the People, and through tribunes' bills he got great commands abroad. In the five years of his absence his name hung over Rome like a heavy cloud. What would be the manner of his return? Crassus had abundant influence in the Senate.[12] Nor did he neglect in due course to strengthen his ties with other aristocratic houses, such as the Metelli.[13] He was elected censor in 65; and, lacking any large and clear policy, might have seemed destined to end as a valuable conservative statesman. For the present, however, he was content to stir up trouble and annoy the government, inconclusively.

Caesar was turning the complicated situation to advantage. Instead of serving as legate under Pompeius in the East, as did certain other young *nobiles* (notably the two Metelli, Celer and Nepos), and gaining more experience of warfare than he needed, he chose to stay at Rome. The record of the years 66 to 63 links his name to sundry abortive intrigues or proposals that fell flat. The appearance of failure is delusive.[14] Caesar had his consulship in view, and he was moving in a straight line—curule aedile in 65, praetor in 62. Moreover, in 63, after a notable contest with leaders of the Optimates, he was elected *pontifex maximus,* demonstrat-

---

opes paucorum non virtutes tenere coeperunt, nomen illi principes optimatium mordicus tenent, re autem carent."

[11] *Rom.Rev.* (1939), 20 ff.; 43 ff.

[12] Plutarch, *Pompeius* 22.

[13] By the marriages of his two sons, the elder to the daughter of Metellus Creticus (*ILS* 881), the younger to Cornelia, the daughter of the P. Scipio adopted by Metellus Pius.

[14] P. 99. Anecdote, biography, and the impact of later events have produced misconceptions about Caesar's career previous to his consulship. Cf. H. Strasburger, *Caesars Eintritt in die Geschichte* (1938).

ing his command of voters and securing an office with resources of
superior patronage.

Harrying the creatures of Sulla, reviving the Marian cause, and
championing the rights of the People, Caesar by a nice calculation
was careful not to go too far and wreck his career. At the same
time, none of his activities were to the detriment of Pompeius
Magnus. On the contrary. In 63 and 62 he is discovered working
with certain tribunes—agents whom Pompeius had sent back from
the East to protect his interests and cause trouble.[15]

When Caesar returned from Spain in the summer of 60, it was
a season for momentous decisions. A "popularis" crowned with
success (or wanting the consulate) might be persuaded to see the
better course, and, after a stormy career, find a safe haven at last.
And the Optimates, it could be argued, ought not to repel a convert to political sanity.[16]

In the event, Caesar's past actions, bitter and justified rancour
in certain of the "principes," and Cato's hostility (which was
sharpened by personal motives) proved too strong. Caesar's price
was high—and Pompeius needed a sharp and ruthless consul for
59. Caesar reconciled Crassus to Pompeius; and thus, to manage
and control Roman politics for a space of years under the predominance of Magnus, was established the famous and fatal
compact of the three dynasts in the consulate of Metellus Celer
and L. Afranius.

Such in brief outline was the setting. When Sallust looked back
and reflected on his first steps in politics, he fell into the language
of stern and melancholy condemnation. The way, he said, was
far from easy; virtue and integrity were not wanted; men had to
be bold, lavish, rapacious.[17]

Instead of moaning and moralising, the author might have

---

15 P. 98.

16 For the type of argument, cf. De prov.cons. 38: "qui si ex illa iactatione
cursuque populari bene gesta re publica referunt aspectum in curiam atque
huic amplissimae dignitati esse commendati volunt, non modo non repellendi
sunt verum etiam expetendi."

17 Cat. 3. 3: "mihi multa advorsa fuere. nam pro pudore pro abstinentia
pro virtute audacia largitio avaritia vigebant."

counted himself fortunate for several reasons. His was a generation that benefited manifestly from the casualties in the Ten
Years War. There were many gaps in families of the Roman
nobilitas; the oligarchy was hard put to it to find consuls in the
seventies and sixties; and not all of the immediate seniors of
Sallust were conspicuous for talent or energy.

As his close coevals, born in the decade 90 to 80, there stands a
whole cluster of sons from consular families, a promising generation, but doomed. Notable among them are Faustus (the son of
Sulla), the two sons of M. Crassus, the three Antonii, Decimus
Brutus, Marcus Brutus, C. Cassius, M. Aemilius Lepidus. For
each and all the consulate could with confidence have been
predicted. But the wars came again. Only two of the ten became
consuls. And, as it happened, only those two outlived Sallust,
namely M. Antonius and M. Lepidus.

Opportunity beckoned also to men from the *municipia.* Augmented by Sulla, the Senate now comprised six hundred members.
The *nobiles* were only a fraction. Behind and beneath was a
voiceless mass without name or consequence, casually emergent
or in total obscuration, for all the abundant documentation of
this period.[18] If entrance to the Senate was easy, the praetorship
demanded an effort, and the *nobiles* tried to keep a monopolistic
grasp on the consulate. It was a scandal and a pollution if a *novus
homo* got so far.[19] The *municipalis* without alertness, capacity,
and a powerful patron was condemned to languish and vegetate
under the contemptuous label of "parvus senator."

Ready speech was requisite even for a modest measure of success
in Forum or Senate, and consummate oratory won splendid prizes:
money, influence, and station. The aspirant applied himself to
some notable practitioner, for this was not an art to be learned
in any school. Cicero had come quickly to the fore and into
fashion, attracting many disciples. Among them will be observed
(for the contrast of their subsequent destiny), M. Caelius Rufus,
a banker's son (his town of origin is not quite certain), and
L. Munatius Plancus, who belonged to an office-holding family

---

[18] *BSR Papers* XIV (1938), 23; *Rom.Rev.* (1939), 10 f.

[19] *Cat.* 23. 6: "quasi pollui consulatum credebant si eum quamvis egregius
homo novos adeptus foret." Similarly, *Jug.* 63. 7.

at Tibur.[20] Caelius, a powerful and bitter speaker, acquired classic
rank when young; while Plancus developed a smooth and be-
guiling style without much forensic fame or opportunity (because
of his active career).

Speculation might ask whether Sallust applied to Cicero—and,
if so, whether he liked the experience or profited from that great
exemplar. Cicero for his part may not have discerned that this
was a young man worth encouraging. Similarly, a lack of sympathy
towards Asinius Pollio might be suspected.[21]

Some of the younger men, such as Marcus Brutus and Licinius
Calvus were coming to find the style of Cicero too redundant and
diffuse and pompous for their liking. Their predilection went to
a plain, vigorous, and concentrated manner. Sallust, like Pollio,
may have been drawn to that company.

The pace of public life was rapid and ruthless. Fame accrued
through prosecution in the courts of law, a speaker's earliest
laurels being a historic event, or at least likely to pass into the
annals of Roman eloquence.[22] In 59 young Caelius Rufus came to
sudden notoriety through the prosecution of the consular C. Antonius; in the next year Licinius Calvus attacked Vatinius; and
Asinius Pollio was not much over twenty when he made his debut
in 54. The game was hazardous. A *nobilis* took pride in his feuds
(often inherited) or commanded immunity, but a *novus homo*
without especial talent or protection might have to walk warily
and confine his forensic efforts to speaking for the defence. For
one reason or another, Sallust escaped prominence as an orator
before the exciting opportunities he was unable to resist when
tribune of the plebs.

The *novus homo* could not make his way alone. No matter—
party leaders looked for useful recruits, while noble houses had a

---

[20] Caelius has often been assigned to Tusculum, but "Praetuttiani" can be
read in *Pro Caelio* 5, cf. the strong arguments of R. G. Austin in his edition
(ed. 3, 1960), 146 ff. For the "patria" of Plancus, *Horace, Odes* I. 7 and a
Munatius magistrate at Tibur (*CIL* I.² 1496 = *ILS* 6231).

[21] The references to Pollio in Cicero's letters are few, late, and insignificant.
Pollio's own missives, from Spain, belong to spring and summer of 43 (*Ad
fam.* X. 31–3).

[22] Tacitus, *Dial.* 34. 7.

plain duty to promote their clients, and a clear advantage. Alliance through marriage was a factor in political calculations, whatever a man's rank. The *nobiles,* often impoverished, did not look askance at new money, but were not always eager to surrender their daughters to the rising class. It is much to be deplored that there is no hint anywhere of a wife for Sallust.[23]

Where was he to look for support or a leader in the sixties? While Pompeius was away in the East, the great master of patronage M. Crassus had plenty of scope, assiduous in the law courts (he would defend anybody) and ready to disburse for an electoral contest or to pay off debts. The hand of Crassus was suspected in sundry intrigues in 66 and 65, subsequently magnified.[24] Sallust in the first monograph alludes to the distrust he incurred: it was the habit and practice of Crassus to embarrass the government through his "patrocinium malorum."[25]

Then there was Caesar, cleverly steering his course towards the consulate. It is not clear, however, that he had already won a large following for himself. A number of his most notorious or constant adherents were only acquired later, on the eve of the breach with Pompeius, and some of them joined him for personal or adventitious reasons.[26]

The patrician demagogue L. Sergius Catilina, by his personality and programme, was able to attract the young and energetic and the various enemies of the Optimates. Cicero at a later date, when

---

[23] Apart from a late fable (p. 284).

[24] P. 93.

[25] *Cat.* 48. 8: "ne Crassus more suo suscepto malorum patrocinio rem publicam conturbaret." That Sallust was an adherent of Crassus has been suggested by K. Büchner, *Römische Literaturgeschichte* (1957), 253; *Sallust* (1960), 16, cf. 34 f.

[26] The persistent notion that Sallust must have been an early adherent of Caesar depends on sundry assumptions about both. It can produce strange results. L. Pareti speaks of a "ventennale devozione" (*La congiura di Catilina* [1934], 205)—and further suggests that Catilina in 63, described as "il già seguace di Cesare," must therefore have been in relations with Sallust (ib. 200). In the view of E. Bolaffi, Caesar since 66 was "capo del partito populare in Roma," and, in 63, may have exercised a restraining influence on his ardent young friend (*Sallustio e la sua fortuna nei secoli* [1949], 26 f.). The author engagingly concedes that this conclusion can be reached "solo a lume di logica."

seeking to excuse or palliate certain early activities of Caelius
Rufus, was not afraid to concede the seduction exercised by this
enigmatic character. His seeming virtues had taken in many excellent men—Cicero himself for a time had nearly been deceived.[27]
Further, a number of municipal aristocrats are reported in the
party of Catilina.[28]

The patrician Claudii by old tradition were notable experts in
the device of extraneous *clientela*. Sabine themselves—but the
evidence does not avail to prove that they were able to keep up
a strong connection in that region. It is not enough to adduce
Ap. Claudius Pulcher visiting the Sabine senator Q. Axius; or,
for that matter, a person from Reate among the gang leaders of
P. Clodius.[29]

Three Claudian brothers faced the challenge to ancestry and
dignitas. Only one achieved his consulship. This was the eldest,
Ap. Pulcher, consul in 54, a strong Optimate but veering towards
Pompeius at that time. The second brother, Gaius, praetor in
56, succumbed to a prosecution after his governorship of Asia—
which cannot but excite surprise. The Claudii were opportunist
in politics. The youngest, P. Clodius, was early on show. After
service abroad in the armies commanded by consular relatives,
he came forward in 65 with an abortive prosecution of Catilina.[30]
Indeterminate for a time in his politics, but brought by accident
into conflict with the Optimates, he struck out on an independent
line, developing urban *clientela* (but that too was very much in
the Claudian tradition), and serving the interests of Pompeius,
of Crassus and of Caesar, from time to time, for his own ultimate
ambitions.

Clodius had manifold gifts. The gay and turbulent tend to
congregate in his vicinity—the "perdita iuventus" of Rome.[31]
The group (if such it should be called) claimed young men like
M. Antonius, Scribonius Curio, and Caelius Rufus. Some suppose

---

[27] *Pro Caelio* 12 ff.

[28] Sallust, *Cat.* 17. 4: "ad hoc multi ex coloniis et municipiis, domi nobiles."

[29] *Pro Sestio* 80: "Titio Sabino, homini Reatino." Cf. F. Münzer, *R-E* VI
A, 1554.

[30] Asconius 78, etc.

[31] *Ad Att.* VII. 7. 6.

that C. Sallustius Crispus can be assumed a typical member of this set. If not, he might perhaps have been discovered somewhere on the fringe or outskirts. Others in this ambience are the son of a consul, L. Gellius Poplicola (a disreputable character),[32] and the youthful Sempronius Atratinus—who prosecuted Caelius Rufus in 56, when he was aged only seventeen.[33]

Clodius had three sisters, consigned in matrimony at an early age for the advantage of the family. Alliance was thus secured with the eminent and opulent Licinius Lucullus, with Q. Marcius Rex, with Q. Metellus Celer. Absent husbands, pride of birth, or the love of luxury and competition produced scandalous conduct in the Clodiae; while, on the other hand, wit and talent were far from being disdained. Hence the opportunity for a *municipalis* like Valerius Catullus, who came from Verona in the Transpadana—of a good local family, perhaps in the *clientela* of the Metelli.

Marriage, divorce, or adultery in the *nobilitas* seldom failed to be items of political consequence. The affair between Caelius Rufus and the violent Clodia who married Metellus Celer (she was now a widow, it is true) issued in discord; and so Clodia was behind the prosecution engineered against Caelius in 56, which transactions made him diverge from the path of P. Clodius.

Debarred from public life but enjoying the social prestige of family or husband, the daughters of the *nobilitas* could not be cheated of the real and secret power that comes from influence. They count for more than does the average senator, they might effect nothing less than an ex-consul achieved by the quiet exercise of *auctoritas* in the conclave of his peers—and they suitably foreshadow the redoubtable princesses in the dynasty of Julii and Claudii. The notable example is Servilia, Cato's half-sister, the mother of Brutus—and, for a season, the mistress of Julius Caesar. Her influence survived his removal—in June of 44 Servilia can undertake to get a decree of the Senate modified.[34]

One of these political ladies only comes into history because a

---

[32] F. Münzer in *R-E* VII, 1003 ff.

[33] ib. II A, 1366 ff.

[34] *Ad Att.* XV. 11. 2.

historian decided to pay her the honour of a full-length portrait.[35] It is Sempronia, the wife of a consular well on in years and deficient in prestige, D. Junius Brutus (*cos.* 77): she is said to have given some help to the associates of Catilina. A bold woman and well educated, with the gift of affairs and a taste for intrigue, Sempronia did not stop at crime; in her ardent pursuit of pleasure, no meaning attached to good fame and modesty; she seldom waited to be asked and courted.

Sallust terminates with a handsome tribute to the intelligence of Sempronia, to her cultivated grace and personal seductions. Sallust, it is no hazard to affirm, knew this woman—and others of the type. Not all as senior as Sempronia, whom the author introduces as one among a group of society ladies who had run into debt and were no longer able to turn their charms to financial profit.

Notorious for her amours, but not, so far as known, a force in politics, was Fausta, the daughter of Sulla the Dictator. She lacked constancy or care for social rank in the choice of her lovers (her brother Faustus mocked her behaviour).[36] Married to C. Memmius (the patron of Catullus and of Lucretius), she no doubt took full advantage of his absence when he went to Bithynia in 57. In 54 Memmius divorced her. She then married T. Annius Milo. There is no word of Fausta subsequent to her husband's condemnation and exile two years later. Her decease will more readily be supposed than a lapse to chastity and an orderly life.

With the passage of years it would need abnormal care and erudition to catalogue the lovers of Fausta Cornelia and verify their credentials. Malice had free scope, or honest error. Varro was able to come out with a startling allegation against Sallust. Taken in adultery by Milo, Sallust was flogged and compelled to buy himself off.[37]

The story has a piquancy that makes it suspect—Sallust was an enemy of Sulla's cause, and an enemy of Annius Milo. Further, when old Varro impugned the morals of Sallust, he was moved

---

[35] *Cat.* 25, see further p. 133.

[36] Fausta suitably had simultaneous paramours: Fulvius the son of a dyer and Pompeius Macula. Hence her brother's joke (Macrobius II. 2. 9).

[37] Gellius XVII. 18. Discussed and estimated on p. 278.

by loyalty to the memory of his patron and friend, Pompeius
Magnus.

Posterity for good reasons honours M. Terentius Varro as the
prime product of the Sabine country in that age. For political
importance and for success he was surpassed by P. Vatinius,
tribune of the plebs in the year of Caesar's consulate, and praetor
in 55.[38] Endowed with good sense and good humour, loyal,
courageous and capable in the field, this partisan of Caesar got to
the consulate in the end. It may be added that the history of the
fifties nowhere discloses Vatinius on a different side from Clodius.

Other senators from the Sabine country can be identified in this
age. From Amiternum itself, perhaps only one, and he of no
known significance.[39] Nothing emerges for Sallust. And, in any
event, local links may not have been decisive in his advancement.

There is another question. How soon did Sallust make his
choice of a vocation? Did he begin with literary aspirations (and
perhaps some modest performance), haunting the salons of the
fashionable world until some turn of fortune or sudden opportunity spurred his ambition? Apparently not. Sallust in the first
monograph, while avowing an early affection for the things of the
mind, affirms that he had political ambitions from the beginning,
with emphasis on his youth.[40]

Access to the Senate lay through the quaestorship. Before that
point the aspirant to honours might have sought experience or a
patron abroad in the provinces; and, at the least, he might have

---

[38] Vatinius' town of origin is a problem. The "Sergia" was his tribe—
"severissimorum hominum Sabinorum, fortissimorum virorum Marsorum et
Paelignorum" (In Vatinium 36). His town, however, has generally been
assumed to be Reate (cf. De nat. deorum II. 6), which was enrolled in the
"Quirina." There is a difficulty here, touching persons called "Vatinius" and
"Vatienus," cf. L. R. Taylor, The Voting Districts of the Roman Republic
(1960), 262 f. That scholar suggests that Vatinius was a Marsian. Note, however, that whereas the bulk of the Sabines belong to "Quirina," Cures and
Trebula Mutuesca are in "Sergia."

[39] Amiternum yields the freedman of a C. Attius Celsus, presumably the
praetor of 65 (CIL IX. 4436, "litteris antiquioribus").

[40] Cat. 3. 3: "sed ego adulescentulus initio sicuti plerique studio ad rem
publicam latus sum."

been a military tribune. The case of Cn. Plancius is instructive, a
banker's son from the small town of Atina who was quaestor in
Macedonia in 58. A decade earlier Plancius had been on the staff
of a proconsul of Africa as his "contubernalis," after which he
saw service under Q. Metellus in Crete; and he was a military
tribune in Macedonia in 62.[41]

If 86 is in truth the date of Sallust's birth, he could have been
quaestor in 55, under the second consulship of Pompeius Magnus
and M. Crassus. However, his quaestorship lacks direct attestation. There is a faint chance that Sallust never held the office.
The tribunate of the plebs before it was curbed by Sulla carried
a seat in the Senate (in virtue of the *Plebiscitum Atinium*), which
a man would keep until or unless removed by a censor at the next
scrutiny of the roll. When Sulla's restrictions were finally swept
away in 70, this privilege ought to have come into force again.[42]
It is worth noting that tribunes enter the Senate under the dictatorship of Caesar (Asinius Pollio and P. Ventidius acquired rank
that way), under Augustus, and under his successors.[43]

However that may be, nothing, it must be repeated, can be recovered of Sallust's career and vicissitudes before he stood for the
tribunate in the summer of 53. There was a story here, a theme
of perennial interest in any age: merit asserting its rights, a *municipalis* invading the society of the metropolis.

---

[41] *Pro Plancio* 27 f.; 61.

[42] This possibility after 70 appears not to be noticed by G. Niccolini, *Il
tribunato della plebe* (1932), or A. Lengle, *R-E* VI A, 2486. For the general
and long persistent difficulty of making the quaestorship compulsory, cf.
Mommsen, *R.Staatsrecht* I[3] (1877), 533 f.

[43] *BSR Papers* XIV (1938), 9.

IV

SALLUST'S CAREER

Whatever his occupations until then, Sallust enters history as tribune in 52 in a blaze of notoriety. More important, with adequate documentation. The historical introduction and commentary which the careful Asconius devoted to Cicero's oration *Pro Milone* not only registers the activities of Sallust, several times: it discloses his associates.[1] These items (which have not always earned proper attention) permit a guess at his political allegiance—or, at the least, will serve to challenge and perhaps demolish the common assumption that Sallust was always and inevitably a partisan of Caesar.

Pompeius Magnus dominated the political scene. He had acquired the two Spains as his province, but, declining to go there after his second consulate, he installed himself in the suburban vicinity of Rome, to curb or subvert the processes of civil government. Magnus was promoting anarchy to achieve monarchy, so Cato said.[2]

Events quickly turned propitious in the electoral season of 54, Ap. Claudius Pulcher and L. Domitius Ahenobarbus being consuls. The features of political life that recently became normal were now enhanced—open bribery (the rate for cash advances doubled suddenly), secret intrigue, the mob and the armed bands, the use of the state religion for deceit or obstruction.[3]

---

[1] Asconius mentions Sallust in five places (33, 39, 43, 44, 45). It is unfortunate that Kurfess in his *testimonia* (ed. 3, Teubner, 1957) registers only the first of them.

[2] Plutarch, *Cato* 45.

[3] The main evidence for the electoral scandals and disorders in 54 and 53 comes from Cicero's letters to Atticus and to Quintus.

One of the candidates, Aemilius Scaurus, had first to face a prosecution, but not unaided: six advocates (among them Cicero and Clodius), and nine men of consular rank submitting their earnest testimony.[4] Scaurus was acquitted, but dropped in the sequel by Pompeius. Two others, C. Memmius and Domitius Calvinus, struck a bargain with the consuls, involving money and mutual benefits. The elections were postponed until September. Memmius, under persuasion from Pompeius, now revealed in the Senate the infamous compact. And eager prosecutors saw their opportunity. Before long, all three candidates, and a fourth, Messalla Rufus, were indicted. But still no elections.

The second half of the year also produced a whole crop of trials not in direct relation to consular contests and scandals, but arising from feud, ambition, or various cross currents. Asinius Pollio now emerged to fame, prosecuting in a case where Licinius Calvus was advocate for the defence.[5] And Calvus, renewing his assaults on Vatinius for the last time, found himself confronted by the eloquence of Cicero, and baffled, for all his vigour and sincerity.[6] Cicero was now in total subservience to the masters of Rome. At the end of the year, under direction from Pompeius, he spoke for Gabinius, the proconsul of Syria. That was the supreme ignominy, to public opinion, and felt as such by the orator himself—even if he had not been writing in these months about his ideal commonwealth and the "optimus civis."

Since the summer, rumours of a dictatorship had been loud and persistent. And, before the year was out, a strong hint about the tribune who would propose it, namely Lucilius Hirrus (a kinsman of Pompeius).[7]

The next year thus opened without consuls or praetors. The tribunes kept on blocking the elections. Finally, Scaurus and Memmius having been discarded, Domitius Calvinus and Messalla Rufus secured election, but not until July. Meanwhile, the agitation for a dictatorship had not abated. It evoked some reaction

---

[4] Asconius 18; 24 f.

[5] The prosecution of C. Cato (Tacitus, *Dial.* 34. 7), Calvus defending (Seneca, *Controv.* VII. 4. 7).

[6] For his speeches against Vatinius, H. Malcovati, *ORF*[2] (1955), 494 ff.

[7] *Ad. Q. fratrem* III. 8. 3.

from defenders of the constitution—Cato threatened to have the tribune Lucilius Hirrus deposed from office. Among the fomentors of disorder was one at least of the ten tribunes designated for 52, namely Q. Pompeius Rufus—he was sent to prison by order of the Senate.[8]

There were no consuls at the beginning of 52 either, but three candidates competing in lavish bribery and open violence.[9] The Optimates put their trust in T. Annius Milo, ruthless and brutal, with his well-organized gangs. Pompeius' efforts went to Q. Metellus Scipio and P. Plautius Hypsaeus; his candidates had strong support from P. Clodius Pulcher, himself standing for the praetorship; and two of the tribunes were active, Q. Pompeius Rufus and T. Munatius Plancus Bursa. Not much had been heard of Clodius since his reconciliation with Pompeius in 56. This aristocratic demagogue was a political force in his own right, with high ambitions and an eye on that future consulship which his ancestry claimed.[10]

On January 18 Clodius was killed on the Via Appia by Milo's band. His body was brought to Rome and displayed in the Forum, while tribunes delivered harangues hostile to Milo. They incited a riot, and the mob set fire to the Curia.

The learned Asconius in his introductory narrative names Pompeius Rufus and Plancus Bursa.[11] Later, however, in comment on a passage in the *Pro Milone* it is C. Sallustius Crispus who is registered along with Pompeius Rufus, and the author appeals to the evidence of the *Acta*.[12]

---

[8] Dio XL. 45. 2.

[9] Asconius 26.

[10] The assumption seems to prevail that Clodius at this time was primarily an adherent of Caesar, cf. J. Carcopino, *Histoire romaine* II (1936), 794: "il gardait à sa dévotion Clodius." Neither here nor in *CAH* IX, 624 f. is there record of Clodius' strong support of Pompeius' candidates, attested by Asconius 26 (cf., for Hypsaeus, 42). Cicero, to be sure, asserts that Clodius was really an enemy of Pompeius—"fuisse illum sibi inimicum, familiarem Milonem; in communi omnium laetitia si etiam ipse gauderet, timuit ne videretur infirmior fides reconciliatae gratiae" (*Pro Milone* 21).

[11] Asconius 29.

[12] ib. 43: "sunt autem contionati eo die, ut ex *Actis* apparet, C. Sallustius et Q. Pompeius, utrique et inimici Milonis et satis inquieti. sed videtur mihi Q. Pompeium significare; nam eius seditiosior fuit contio."

Disorder continued. The Senate passed the ultimate decree and instructed Pompeius to hold military levies throughout Italy. Further, after renewed clamour for a dictatorship, Pompeius was made sole consul on February 25, with the reluctant approbation of Cato (the proposal came from Calpurnius Bibulus, his son-in-law).

The prosecution of Milo was now set on foot. The three tribunes had not confined their attentions to Milo. They attacked Milo's champion Cicero, who in his oration exclaims with indignation that "abiecti homines ac perditi" called him a brigand and assassin.[13] No names, it is true. Asconius supplies them—Pompeius Rufus and Sallustius Crispus.[14]

Rufus was Clodius' closest friend, an open and declared partisan (so Asconius affirms);[15] and Plancus Bursa was an ape of Clodius, a "simiolus," according to Cicero.[16] What is to be thought about the third tribune in relation to P. Clodius—and also to Pompeius Magnus? [17]

Caesar was far away, but Caesar cannot be left out of account. He must have secured partisans somewhere among the ten tribunes. Only two other names are on record, M. Caelius Rufus and a certain Manilius Cumanus—both, however, strong for Milo.[18] Later in the year, a bill of the ten tribunes was passed, permitting Caesar to stand for the consulate in absence. The only other item about this tribunician college is scandalous. A minor official gave a banquet in honour of Metellus Scipio (now consul as colleague of Pompeius) and the ten tribunes. The entertain-

---

[13] *Pro Milone* 47: "me videlicet latronem et sicarium abiecti homines et perditi describebant."

[14] Asconius 44.

[15] ib. 45: "qui fuerat familiarissimus omnium P. Clodio, et sectam illam sequi se palam profitebatur." Rufus was a grandson of Sulla on the maternal side and brother of Pompeia, Caesar's second wife. The family of Pompeia, the second wife of P. Vatinius (*Ad fam.* V. 11. 2), is not attested.

[16] *Ad fam.* VII. 2. 3.

[17] Not everybody can stomach the notion that Sallust was a partisan of Clodius. L. O. Sangiacomo assigns his behaviour to opportunism, rejecting "ogni innaturale affinità di vedute e di intenti fra il torbido demagogo e il futuro storico moralista" (*Sallustio* [1954], 27).

[18] Asconius 32.

ment was staged in the form of a *lupanar*, with ladies of birth on exhibit.[19]

To revert to Clodius and his partisans, known or surmised. Pompeius had insisted that Clodius be avenged—or rather, that Milo be condemned. Having established order in Rome and his own predominance, he could already be moving towards an accommodation with the faction of the Optimates. Pompeius had a bad name for ingratitude and duplicity, and his new role of defender of the public peace offered a pretext to discard his former allies and agents. Magnus refused to help Plautius Hypsaeus (once his quaestor), who was on trial for bribery, spurning his plea and supplication with harsh contempt.[20] It is not clear that Magnus would care to exert himself overmuch for all adherents of dead Clodius.

The tribunes were immune until their term of office expired. Then Cicero tasted a slight revenge, but welcome for his humiliations, by securing the condemnation of Plancus Bursa, despite a testimonial sent by Magnus in his favour;[21] and Pompeius Rufus succumbed, the prosecutor being Caelius Rufus, his former colleague in office.[22] Pompeius Rufus retired to a drab and impoverished existence in Campania, but Bursa went for sustenance to the proconsul of Gaul.[23]

Of Sallust there is no word, no hint to explain how he managed to evade the fate of his associates in violence.[24] It would be worth knowing what kind of protection he enjoyed, or was able now to acquire. Perhaps Pompeius had nothing against him, perhaps Caesar intervened, insisting that Sallust be not discarded. The respite was brief and fallacious. In 50 Sallust was thrown out of the Senate.

The censors were L. Piso (the parent of Caesar's wife), an excellent man who had not wanted the honour, and Ap. Claudius

---

[19] Valerius Maximus IX. 1. 8, cf. p. 135.

[20] Plutarch, *Pompeius* 55.

[21] *Ad fam.* VII. 2. 2; Plutarch *Pompeius* 55.

[22] Valerius Maximus IV. 2. 7.

[23] *Ad fam.* VIII. 1. 4.

[24] Nothing can be got from a statement in Asconius referring to events before the actual prosecution of Milo—"postea Pompeius et Sallustius in suspicione fuerunt redisse in gratiam cum Milone ac Cicerone" (33).

Pulcher. Piso held aloof, avoiding trouble. But Ap. Pulcher was
eager to satisfy pride, ambition, and rancour. According to the
historian Cassius Dio, all sons of freedmen were struck off the
roll, but also many persons of good standing such as Sallust.²⁵ No
other name is on record save that of C. Ateius Capito, the tribune
of 55, whom Ap. Pulcher (no mean authority on ritual) incriminated for having announced *auspicia* mendaciously.²⁶

To justify an expulsion, reasons or pretexts were normally put
forward of public or personal misbehaviour. In view of the allegations of loose living that came later to adhere to the memory of
Sallust, it will be salutary to observe that Dio has nothing to contribute. Not that this Greek of Nicaea would be eager to shield
the fame of an earlier historian, still less if that historian happened to be one of the classic glories of Latin literature. That is
clear from a passage about Sallust's subsequent career and conduct, half a dozen years later.²⁷ However, if Dio had paid close
attention to the events of 52, he might there have happened on
the tribune Sallust, and, if so, might be moved to find a cause for
his ejection. That would have demanded some research, for the
tribunate of Sallust did not occur in the standard historians used
by Dio.²⁸

The censorship offered a useful weapon in party strife, though
it had not thus been employed recently—at least no purge is on
record since that of 70, or even a single name. Ap. Pulcher was
the front and hinge of the coalition now forming against Caesar

---

²⁵ Dio XL. 63. 4: ὁ γὰρ Πίσων οὔτ' ἄλλως πράγματ' ἔχειν ἐθέλων καὶ πρὸς τὴν τοῦ
γαμβροῦ φιλίαν πολλοὺς θεραπεύων αὐτὸς μὲν οὐδὲν τοιοῦτον ἐποίησεν, ἐκείνῳ δὲ οὐκ ἀντέπραξε
πάντας μὲν ἐκ τῶν ἀπελευθέρων, συχνοὺς δὲ καὶ τῶν πάνυ γενναίων, ἄλλους τε καὶ τὸν
Κρίσπον τὸν Σαλούστιον τὸν τὴν ἱστορίαν γράψαντα, ἀπελάσαντι ἐκ τοῦ συνεδρίου.

²⁶ *De div.* I. 29—where it is said that Appius acted "non satis scienter." If
Clark's reading "C. Ateio" be accepted (Asconius 34), he was one of the
prosecutors of Milo. Writing to L. Munatius Plancus in 47 or 46, Cicero
asserts "semper Caesarem Capito coluit et dilexit" (*Ad fam.* XIII. 29. 6).
Perhaps a slight (and expedient) exaggeration.

²⁷ Dio XLIII. 9. 2.

²⁸ Asconius, it must be emphasized, is the sole source extant. If Livy had
this detail, it might have emerged somewhere in writers hostile to Sallust, or
curious.

—one of his daughters was married to Marcus Brutus, Cato's nephew, another to the elder son of Pompeius Magnus.[29] Not a figure to be ignored or depreciated. Ap. Pulcher tried to expel Scribonius Curio, tribune in this year, a vigorous orator who had been won and purchased by Caesar: he was frustrated by his colleague (not otherwise active). Appius also turned against Caelius Rufus, a friend of Curio, and the quarrel was enlivened by mutual charges of unnatural vice.[30] Appius the censor proved detrimental to his allies; and others in the oligarchy (such as the proud and stubborn L. Domitius Ahenobarbus) helped by their feuds to augment the party of Caesar. Asinius Pollio went that way, he affirmed, because of a powerful enemy on the other side.[31]

For the Optimates, the expulsion of Sallust meant revenge for Milo; and Appius may have decided that the former partisan of Clodius was deficient in respect to the *gens Claudia*. For Sallust the only succour was the proconsul of Gaul, whatever his own previous attachments, whatever his opinions about state and society. Like others he looked to reinstatement, if the compact held between Caesar and Magnus. If not, desperate hazards, but a rich reward from victory. Caesar did not subject any ally to anxious scrutiny.

Caesar's following was like an epitome of the last forty years of history—the causes of Marius and of Italia resurgent; the proscribed and the dispossessed; enemies of Sulla and of the oligarchs; partisans of Catilina and of Clodius; the failed and frustrated men, and the various victims of political justice at Rome. In short, and on unfriendly estimate, a ghastly crew.[32] Inspection of names and persons helps to redress the balance.[33] Birth, youth, and energy were not lacking on Caesar's side; while the monied interests and the holders of property were not unduly alarmed—or soon regained assurance.

---

[29] *Ad fam.* III. 4. 2.

[30] ib. VIII. 12. 1; 14. 4.

[31] ib. X. 31. 2.

[32] Described by Cicero as a "colluvies" (*Ad Att.* IX. 10. 7), by Atticus as a νέκυια (IX. 18. 2).

[33] *Rom. Rev.* (1939), 61 ff.; 78 ff.; D. R. Shackleton Bailey, *CQ* X[2] (1960), 253 ff.

The war began with a daring invasion of Italy (the only strategy) and spread to the four quarters of the world. Caesar had a splendid company of generals—most of the legates in the Gallic campaigns stood by him. But active employment also offered to men whose military experience lay far back in the past, or was negligible. Thus, in notable contrast, two Cornelii: P. Sulla, who was about sixty (a consular candidate in 66), and the youthful P. Dolabella.

Sallust is discovered in early operations of the Civil War at the head of the Adriatic. The Pompeians held and easily retained command of the sea. P. Dolabella, Caesar's admiral, suffered a defeat, C. Antonius was forced to capitulate on the island of Curicta, and the army on the mainland could give no help—a pair of legions commanded by Sallust and Minucius Basilus.[34] The narration of the disaster has fallen out of the text of the *Bellum Civile*, but a later reference shows that Caesar felt acutely the loss in men and ships.[35]

The name of C. Sallustius Crispus does not occur in the *Bellum Civile*. For the best part of two years he fades out of history while Caesar goes on, one campaign after another—Dyrrhachium and Pharsalia, Egypt, Pontus. Asinius Pollio, Sallust's junior by a decade, had been with Caesar at the crossing of the Rubicon, and shared in almost every action down to Thapsus and Munda.

Sallust's reëmergence is in no way glorious. The troops gathered in Campania in the late summer of 47, in preparation for the invasion of Africa, were fractious and truculent. Sallust (now praetor designate) was sent to appease them, and barely escaped with his life.[36] He was lucky. The mutineers killed two other envoys, senators of praetorian rank, and marched on Rome. It took all of Caesar's arts and authority to abate the disturbance. Sallust's

---

[34] Orosius VI. 15. 8. For the scene of operations, G. Veith, *Strena Buliciana* (1924), 267 ff.

[35] Caesar, *BC* III. 10. 5.

[36] Appian, *BC* II. 92. 387; Dio XLII. 52. 1 f. For the year of the praetorship (46, not 47), cf. T.R.S. Broughton, *TAPA* LXXIX (1948), 76 ff. Dio's statement is explicit—στρατηγὸς γὰρ ἐπὶ τῷ τὴν βουλὴν ἀναλαβεῖν ἀπεδέδεικτο. It is therefore peculiar and disturbing that a number of scholars should state that Sallust entered the Senate again through the quaestorship (their names need not here be registered). The item of the iterated quaestorship comes from "Cicero," *In Sallustium* 17 and 21.

failure, however, does not have to be put down to any kind of incompetence. P. Sulla and the consular Messala Rufus had no success with the legions in Sicily.[37] The troops threw stones at Sulla—yet Sulla had fought with distinction at Dyrrhachium and had commanded Caesar's right wing at Pharsalia.

Sallust earned employment in Caesar's African campaign, but not (so far as known) any command in battle. Caesar used the smooth Munatius Plancus for diplomacy (in an attempt to win by words a Pompeian commander), Sallust for transport. Supplies were short. Caesar sent Rabirius Postumus (a banker and business-man) to Sicily, while Sallust went with a part of the fleet to collect foodstuffs at Cercina. He performed the task with expedition and success.[38] That is all. What surprises is the sequel.

Caesar after his victory annexed the greater part of Juba's Numidian kingdom and turned it into a Roman province, Africa Nova. By its area and function, extremely important—three legions for garrison against one for the old province that had existed now for a century. For the first governor he chose Sallust. Other men were available, with a long experience of warfare, legates in the Gallic campaigns such as Munatius Plancus (since 54) or T. Sextius (since 53). Sextius had to wait and be Sallust's successor in Africa Nova (Sallust, so far as known, had never seen an army before 49).[39]

The motives behind Caesar's choice are a theme to tempt speculation, and perhaps to baffle enquiry. An engaging fancy will have it that Caesar wished high ideals to have a chance to demonstrate their validity in the governing of a province.[40] Caution is in place. Caesar was under no illusions about anybody who

---

[37] *Ad Att.* XI. 21. 2; 22. 2. Cf. *Bell.Afr.* 28. 2.

[38] *Bell.Afr.* 8. 3; 34. 1; 34. 3. Sallust remained there "pro consule" (ib. 97. 1).

[39] Sallust might, however, have been *tribunus militum* or quaestor in some province (cf. p. 28). Not therefore a complete novice when put in charge of a legion in 49 (Orosius VI. 15, 8). It is wanton to style him "il teoretico" (L. O. Sangiacomo, o.c. 31).

[40] It was for that reason that Caesar "in seiner tiefen Menschenkenntnis dem idealistischen Mahner die neue afrikanische Provinz verliehen hat" (E. Meyer, *Caesars Monarchie und das Principat des Pompejus*[3] [1922], 587).

had been tribune of the plebs in 52. He was accessible, it is true, to favouritism (birth, literary art, or social graces), he was generous and conniving. The aristocrat who proclaimed that he would reward thugs and brigands if they had stood in defence of Caesar's *dignitas* had a duty to requite allies of standing and education.[41] But there was a limit to his indulgence—and complete freedom of decision. Caesar was not so remiss as to consign three legions and a province of the first rank to greed, torpor, or incompetence. He must have discerned ability in Sallust. Battle is the least part of warfare. [Sallust, though nowhere signalised in the field, proved his value in supply and transport.] The first governor of Africa Nova needed some capacity for organisation.

Sallust's neighbour in Africa Vetus was C. Calvisius Sabinus, who had commanded a column for Caesar in 49 (his earliest appearance).[42] On his western flank was the Campanian adventurer P. Sittius, established by Caesar at Cirta with a vast domain as a kind of principality. Sittius, no stranger to the African territories (and vaguely incriminated long ago for complicity in subversive or Catilinarian designs) had brought valuable aid to Caesar in the recent campaign.[43]

Caesar before leaving Africa imposed fines and confiscations. Plenty of tasks were left for the proconsul, opportunities of traffic and sources of enrichment—above all, the royal estates, castles, and depositories of treasure in different parts of Numidia, art collections, and libraries. Tribunes of the plebs and enemies of the oligarchy were apt to rail at rapacity and corruption in aristocratic proconsuls. Sallust was now in a position to emulate their normal and traditional licence. According to Cassius Dio, he pillaged the province.[44] There can be no way of correctly estimating the behaviour of Sallust. Equity and malice are alike baffled. When in later years Sallust looked back on Numidia, he may have

---

[41] Suetonius, *Divus Iulius* 72: "professus palam, si grassatorum et sicariorum ope in tuenda sua dignitate usus esset, talibus quoque se parem gratiam relaturum."

[42] Caesar, *BC* III. 34. 2.

[43] *Bell.Afr.* 25. 2, etc. On Sittius see further p. 100.

[44] Dio XLIII. 9. 2: ἀμέλει καὶ ἐδωροδόκησε πολλὰ καὶ ἥρπασεν ὥστε καὶ καταγορηθῆναι καὶ αἰσχύνην αἰσχίστην ὀφλεῖν.

wondered (as others in a like situation) whether he ought the more to regret his weakness or marvel at his moderation.

On his return from Africa Sallust had to face charges of malversation.[45] A matter not without embarrassment for Caesar. When consul he had carried the *Lex Julia de repetundis;* and further, parading strict justice when dictator, he removed from the Senate men convicted of extortion.[46] Sallust's misdemeanours, so it appears, were hushed up. Cassius Dio, narrating events of the year 45, furnishes a hint, if not a clue. When certain persons accused of corrupt practices (bribery in this instance) were let off, public rumour had the answer: Caesar had taken money from them in return for that indulgence.[47] It could perhaps be guessed that Caesar waived the extortion and discreetly mulcted Sallust, annexing a share of the Numidian profits. The delinquent was thus spared the supreme indignity, forefeiture of his seat in the Senate, but was left with slight prospect of further employment and honours.

What had happened was a misfortune. It is not easy to assess the measure of Sallust's disappointment. However, this *novus homo* had no reason to hope for a consulate in any near or previsible future. The autocrat, making his disposition for a long absence abroad, had other candidates in view or already designated, among them three *nobiles* (D. Brutus for 42, M. Brutus and C. Cassius for 41).

A leader who has had recourse to civil war on no better plea than his own *dignitas* and the rights of the tribunes, with no clear principle and with a heterogeneous following, can hardly fail to disappoint or antagonise a number of his adherents when he confronts the duty of rebuilding a government. Several personal grievances happen to be attested. The patrician Ser. Sulpicius Galba, Caesar's legate long ago in Gaul, wanted the consulate—he had failed as Caesar's candidate in 50.[48] Caesar thought

---

[45] Dio, ib.

[46] Suetonius, *Divus Iulius* 43. 1.

[47] Dio XLIII. 47. 4. Cf. E. Meyer, o.c. 424; W. Allen, *Studies in Philology* LI (1954), 7 f.

[48] Hirtius, *BG* VIII. 50. 4, cf. Suetonius, *Galba* 3. 2.

otherwise, and may have had valid reason. Minucius Basilus had fought in Gaul, on the Adriatic, at Dyrrhachium. Caesar made him praetor in 45, but excluded him from a provincial governorship, offering a sum of money instead.[49] There must have been something highly unsatisfactory about Minucius Basilus.[50]

Rancour or envy account for Galba, Basilus, and others. But no grudge or setback explains why Decimus Brutus joined the conspiracy of Republicans and Pompeians. With the proconsul continuously in Gaul from 56 if not from 58, Decimus appears to have been treated with especial favour in the Civil War, being selected for tasks where he did not have to fight against fellow citizens.[51]

History or legend awards the primacy to Marcus Brutus, Cato's nephew, for the heroic decision and deed. The plot itself originated with Cassius, who had once been an adherent of Caesar.[52] Perhaps Decimus Brutus, Caesar's marshal, was a factor no less potent in the enterprise, and a more valuable clue than either to the motives that induced honourable men to assassinate the Dictator.

The Ides of March, so some are bold enough to assert, meant a shattering catastrophe for Sallust. Not only a loved leader basely slain but a bright hope and faith destroyed.[53] A more sober approach is to be enjoined. Dismay and apprehension was not a monopoly of fervid Caesarians. Men of understanding who saw

---

[49] Dio XLIII. 47. 5.

[50] Basilus was murdered by his slaves in the summer of 43 (Orosius VI. 18. 7; Appian, *BC* III. 98. 409).

[51] This fact is properly emphasised by F. Münzer, *R-E* Supp. V. 373.

[52] Cassius described Caesar as "veterem et clementem dominum" (*Ad fam.* XV. 19. 4). For Cassius as the originator, cf. Plutarch, *Caesar* 62; *Brutus* 8 and 10; Appian, *BC* II. 113. 470 ff. He is named first, before Marcus and Decimus, in Suetonius, *Divus Iulius* 80. 4.

[53] According to F. Klingner, Sallust's faith depended on Caesar and was "mit dessen Tod zusammengebrochen." *Hermes* LXIII (1928), 189. It was "die Katastrophe seiner Gläubigkeit" (O. Seel, *Sallust von den Briefen ad Caesarem zur Coniuratio Catilinae* [1930], 32). And further, "was musste es bedeuten, wenn die Stütze des einzigen, woran Sallust glaubte, wegfiel, Cäsar. Der Zusammenbruch seiner ganzen Welt musste die Folge sein" (K. Büchner, *Sallust* [1960], 90).

but deplored the need of ordered government and feared the
return of ruinous liberty could have echoed the sentiments expressed by Caesar's friend Matius—"if Caesar with all his genius
could not find a way out, who will now?" [54]

On the other hand, there was time to conceive doubts about the
autocrat before his tragic end, if Sallust reflected upon Caesar's
ruthless pursuit of "gloria" and "dignitas" or the barren fruits
of ambition. Nor could he fail to acknowledge the quality of the
Liberators. They took their stand for a principle and a cause. Not
something to be found in books and doctrines, but the dignity
and privilege of their order—"virtus," "fides," "libertas."

Sallust was a *novus homo*; he had fought against the faction of
the Optimates; he had enemies among the *nobilitas*. That did not
debar him from sympathy with the aristocratic ideal, which was
bound up with the majestic past of Rome. Old-fashioned sentiments held a wide sway over men from the *municipia*; and a
recent arrival, however brief or unfriendly his experience in the
Senate, quickly acquired the feeling for tradition.

The Ides of March may have reinforced in Sallust an inclina-
tion that had already been prompted by the outcome of his proconsulate—the retreat from politics, and farewell to that kind of
ambition. What followed swift and sharp in the course of 44 was
enough to decide him, irrevocably—concord soon disrupted,
Caesar's heir and his private army levied against the consul
Antonius, the march on Rome, new compacts and a new civil war,
with D. Brutus besieged by Antonius at Mutina. If Sallust wanted
action and hazard and a consulate, Antonius would not have disdained his services. Adequate evidence reveals the kind of partisans he was ready to welcome. Less is known about the earliest
associates of Octavianus—and worse can be surmised.[55]

The next year saw Antonius defeated near Mutina but retriev-
ing his position (the generals in the western provinces, Lepidus,
Plancus, and Pollio were persuaded to desert the ambiguous
cause of the Republic), Octavianus marching on Rome again,
this time to seize the consulate, and the coalition of the Caesarian
leaders. Antonius was forced to ally himself with Caesar's heir,

---

[54] *Ad Att.* XIV. 1. 1.
[55] *Rom.Rev.* (1939), 132 f.

and they seemed to need Lepidus. On November 27 the Triumvirate was established by law, and the Proscriptions began.

The list of those proscribed was not confined to political enemies. Rather than blood or revenge the Triumvirs needed money
for their war against Brutus and Cassius, who meanwhile had
acquired the armies and resources of the eastern lands. The
Proscriptions resemble a levy on capital, and took the form of a
vendetta against the rich, whatever their station or allegiance.
Private enmities and local feuds in Italy now came into play. For
example, it is not idle to suppose that the lists included a number of holders of *latifundia* in the Sabine country.[56] Varro was
one of them. Proscribed, he owed his life to the intercession of an
Antonian partisan, but he lost some of his estates.[57] Other persons
of conspicuous wealth had devised protection in advance (the
astute Atticus kept relations of amity with all parties), or now
purchased immunity. It would have been criminal negligence to
let Atticus be killed.

There is no sign that Sallust was molested. Perhaps they persuaded him to make some contribution to the war chest of the
Triumvirs. However, it is a fair surmise that Sallust could appeal
to powerful friends among the Caesarians, who remembered old
ties or bore no malice for his present neutrality—perhaps M. Antonius himself.[58]

The wars went on, and the Republic was crushed at Philippi.
Sallust had escaped from the turmoil. He discovered a refuge, and
a vocation: he exploited his past misfortunes, creating from them
benefit and success. He was writing history.

---

[56] These proprietors may have been alarmed on an earlier occasion, after
Caesar's invasion of Italy in 49. Observe the enigmatic notice in *Ad Att.* IX
8. 1: "de Reatinorum corona quod scribis, moleste fero in agro Sabino
sementem fieri proscriptionis."

[57] Appian, *BC* IV. 47. 202 f. His libraries were pillaged (Gellius III. 10. 17).
For his estates, observe the tense of the verb in *Res Rusticae* II, praef. 6:
"et ipse pecuarias habui grandes, in Apulia oviarias et in Reatino equarias."

[58] For the notion of Sallust as an Antonian, cf. W. Allen, o.c. 10 ff.

V

FROM POLITICS
TO HISTORY

When a man who has held office and emolument chooses to give up the career of honours (or is thrust aside), it will be expedient for him to signify his retreat gracefully—no rancour, but motives above reproach. He is done with ambition, and he is happy to be liberated at last for literary pursuits, which were no doubt his true or postponed vocation; and, if the senator turns to the recording of recent or contemporaneous transactions, it is manifest that, having nothing to hope and nothing to fear, he can tell the truth, and he will tell it, without regard for any cause or allegiance.

Such is the explanation that Sallust puts out in his first essay (*Cat.* 3. 3 to 4. 2). No paradox, but normal enough in any epoch or even predictable. It concludes his prologue which, from a general discussion of what is worth while in the life of man, leads on to the paramount value of history (3. 1 f.).

The author might have enforced his thesis by a pertinent argument. Roman annals had their origin in the Roman aristocracy of government. History, being a prolongation of public life, was a laudable task for the statesman in retirement, who benefited the community by his experience and wisdom. And some composed memoirs of their lives, without incurring any imputation of arrogance.

Sallust eschews the appeal to named and illustrious predecessors. Instead, he inserts a subsidiary reason, on a note of scorn and indignation. He refuses to pass his remaining years in sloth and idleness—and he will not go in for farming or hunting. Those

43

occupations, he exclaims, are despicable and degrading, only good enough for slaves—"servilia officia" (4. 1).

One must pause and ask a question or two. This is a peculiar outburst. Manual pursuits could be styled servile. But who would expect a senator in this refined epoch to take a spade in his hands or capture wild animals for food? Where does the explanation lie?

In the first place, hunting. Sallust's disdain could not fail to evoke surprise and protest in antiquity.[1] And it continues to puzzle. It might be that the author merely took over an obsolete and conventional notion, without thinking. Prejudice, however, is more likely than total inadvertence. Emotional language or a slight incoherence can sometimes disclose strange revelations about historians.[2]

Hunting was princely and aristocratic, being first commended at Rome by the high example of Scipio Aemilianus.[3] In the time of Sallust, it came to acquire definite if not deleterious connotations. Interest in wild life ceased to be a vigorous pastime. Tired, baffled or discontented, the great Optimates Lucullus and Hortensius turned from Senate or Forum to the indulgence of tranquil and opulent leisure. Their fish ponds on the Bay of Naples made them notorious, and "piscinarius" became a joke or a term of reproach.[4] Something could have been said about their game parks.[5] When guests dined with Hortensius on his estate at Laurentum, they enjoyed a sylvan and mythological spectacle— herds of deer and boars and other animals mustering to the sound of a trumpet, and a huntsman dressed up as Orpheus.[6]

Sallust's scorn for cynegetics can pass. With agriculture, a paradox and a scandal. How could one admire Cato the Censor with-

---

[1] Symmachus, *Epp.* V. 68. 2: "interea recuso sententiam quae rem venaticam servile ducit officium. statuerit hoc scriptor stilo tantum laudandus, nam morum eius damna non sinunt ut ab eo agendae vitae petatur auctoritas."

[2] Thus Tacitus, rebuking those who praise political martyrs to excess (*Agr.* 42. 5), or angry at the neglect of Arminius, with adventitious blame of the Greeks (*Ann.* II. 88. 3).

[3] J. Aymard, *Essai sur les chasses romaines* (1951), 43 ff.

[4] *Ad Att.* I. 19. 6; 20. 3.

[5] J. Aymard, o.c. 68 ff.

[6] Varro, *Res Rusticae* III. 13. 2 f. Varro himself had just such a park at Tusculum (ib. 13. 1).

out extolling the land, the farmer, rustic virtue? The highest
praise among the ancients, he said, was to call a man "bonum
agricolam bonumque colonum."[7] And he made loud boast about
hard labour on rocky soil when he was a young man (he had inherited a Sabine farm).[8]

The contemporary scene again offers a hint: agriculture praised
and exploited by the wrong people. No pursuit, says Cicero, is
more ample and delicious, none more worthy of a free man.[9] As
he engagingly explains, commerce and banking become highly
respectable, if practised on a large scale, and if the profits go
into the land. Hence the creation of *latifundia,* with a wide range
of intensive exploitation. The prime document is Varro and the
friends of Varro, agronomic experts, and owners of large estates
in the Sabine country. Italy, so it was proclaimed to men who
had travelled everywhere, had now no rival in the world—it was
like one great garden, beautiful and profitable.[10] For the benefit
of the few, it could be added, for gain and recreation and luxury.
These were the men (ancient families or new recruits to the
oligarchy) whom the descendant of Cato might properly denounce.
They cherished their mansions in town or country, their collections of sculpture and paintings; they did not love the Commonwealth.[11]

There may be something else. In the early spring of 44 Cicero
published a homily on old age, the *Cato Maior.* The Censor, here
paraded as a bland, innocuous and amiable character, holds discourse on the delights of gardening in a lyrical vein, with choice
and precious language.[12] The idealised and horticultural Cato
cannot have been much to the liking of the former governor of
Africa. Perhaps some friend, well-meaning or malicious, pointed
to the *Cato Maior* and assured Sallust that the farm or the garden

---

[7] Cato, *De agri cultura* 1. 2.

[8] Nepos, *Cato* 1. 1, cf. H. Malcovati *ORF*² (1955), 51.

[9] *De officiis* I. 151: "nihil est agricultura melius, nihil uberius, nihil dulcius,
nihil homine libero dignius."

[10] Varro, *Res rusticae* I. 2. 3: "vos, qui multas perambulastis terras, ecquam
cultiorem Italia vidistis?"

[11] *Cat.* 52. 5: "vos ego appello, qui semper domos villas signa tabulas vostras
pluris quam rem publicam fecistis."

[12] *Cato Maior* 51 ff.

was just the thing for declining years and a senator in retirement, salubrious for both body and soul.

Intellectual pursuits, therefore. And history, precisely: not, as with some, legal or antiquarian studies. And the season was propitious. Senators were the first writers in that field. But, despite the excellence which the governing order acquired in oratory and in law, history was slow to reach maturity and assert rank as a branch of literature.

Defeat, eclipse, or anger indicated history as a consolation or a weapon. Cicero was tempted, intermittently, over a long period. However, the first of his major works elicited by disappointment was the treatise *De oratore*, in 55. It was arranged in the form of a dialogue between prominent speakers in the autumn of 91, on the eve of the *Bellum Italicum*. He went on before long to produce another dialogue (set in the year 129), on the best form of government. That is, patently, the primacy and rule of an enlightened aristocracy, in which due honour would be accorded to a new man endowed with eloquence, high ideals and political wisdom. *De re publica* was finished in 51. The natural sequel was *De legibus* (and it came quickly), expounding the institutions of a well-ordered state. It was the ancestral constitution modified in certain respects: more power for the Senate, tribunes curbed, and the censorship converted into a permanent office. Those proposals were not alien to the author's experience or aspirations.

The dialogue *De oratore* conveys a verdict on the Roman annalists. History among the Greeks exhibited writers of genius. At Rome, only the register of events, year by year—"annalium confectio." Prose style was not sought or needed. Enough if the recorder was accurate and truthful; and the sole credit he could aspire to was praise for brevity. Cato, Fabius Pictor, and Piso are named as examples. With a grudging exception conceded for Coelius Antipater, there were no historians, only "narratores rerum." Rome was patently far behind the Greeks. A reason could be adduced. At Rome talent and eloquence had gone into public and forensic oratory.[13]

The treatise *De legibus* is more explicit and revealing. The

---

[13] *De or.* II. 51 ff.

great orator holds converse with his brother Quintus and his friend Pomponius Atticus. The setting is near Arpinum, beside a famous tree which evokes the memory of Marius and the veracity of history, primeval as well as recent. To demonstrate that Rome has no history that deserves the name of literature, Atticus briefly retails a select catalogue of annalists, concluding with the latest writers, Licinius Macer and Cornelius Sisenna.[14]

There is no word of Valerius Antias. That omission causes perplexity, and has moved some enquirers to toy with an extreme hypothesis: the histories of Antias were published subsequent to the year 50.[15] Unnecessarily. An easy explanation offers. Atticus was exact and scholarly, with a passion for the documentary; and, like Cicero, who was highly sceptical about early Roman history, Atticus would dismiss much of Valerius Antias as romantic fiction.

As for Licinius Macer, Atticus damns him for "loquacitas."[16] Sisenna, to be sure, easily outdistanced all predecessors, but that was not saying much. He achieved "puerile quiddam" as an imperfect emulator of the Greek Clitarchus.

The passage gives no sign of the scope and subject of their writings. In fact, diverse and contrasted. Macer went to the history of the early Republic.[17] He had recourse to documents, the enigmatic "libri lintei."[18] But Macer was anything but an antiquarian researcher. By bitter attacks on the aristocracy he sedulously imported into his narrative the conflicts of his own life and times. Macer played a notable part as tribune of the plebs in 73. Cicero disliked him intensely, as is shown by the estimate of his person and his oratory in the *Brutus*.[19] Macer ended ignominiously. He duly reached the praetorship, but was prosecuted for extortion in 66 after governing a province (Cicero, then praetor, was president of the tribunal). Condemned, though

---

[14] *De legibus* I. 6 f.

[15] cf. the four writers cited by H. Volkmann, *R-E* VII A, 2313 f.

[16] *De legibus* I. 7: "cuius loquacitas habet aliquid argutiarum, nec id tamen ex illa erudita Graecorum copia, sed ex librariolis Latinis."

[17] For his career and writings see H. Peter, *HRR* I[2] (1914), CCCXLVIII ff.; F. Münzer, *R-E* XIII, 419 ff.

[18] R. M. Ogilvie, *JRS* XLVIII (1958), 40 ff.

[19] *Brutus* 238: "huius si vita si mores si vultus denique non omnem commendationem ingeni everteret, maius nomen in patronis fuisset."

the great Crassus spoke for him, Macer could not stand the unexpected shock and died forthwith (some spoke of suicide).[20]

L. Cornelius Sisenna had been a partisan of Sulla.[21] After his
praetorship in 78 he governed the province of Sicily. He was a
friend of Lucullus and Hortensius; he is suitably discovered among
the advocates for the defence when Verres stood trial; and, serving
as a legate under Pompeius, he died in Crete in 67. Sisenna chose
contemporary history: he narrated the Italian insurrection and the
ensuing civil war. He might have stopped with the victory of
Sulla and the *nobilitas* in 82; but he may have gone on as far
as Sulla's abdication—or even Sulla's death and funeral. As for his
style, the parallel with Clitarchus is significant. Further, something may be gleaned from the fragments—he was diffuse, sometimes precious, and prone to unusual words or forms.[22] Cicero accords him merit as a man and a speaker—"doctus vir et studiis
optimis deditus, bene Latine loquens, gnarus rei publicae." [23]
But, Cicero goes on to say, Sisenna did not take sufficient pains,
and a similar failing can be discovered in his history. It will perhaps be pertinent to add that Sisenna translated a Greek erotic
novel and did not shun the scabrous in his annals.[24]

Sisenna, it was agreed, was the best that Rome could show so
far. Atticus appealed to Cicero. It was his plain duty to redeem
history and exalt it to the level attained by the Greeks. Style and
composition is needed—"quippe cum sit opus, ut tibi quidem
videri solet, unum hoc oratorium maxime." [25]

That notorious verdict echoes a statement in *De oratore*—
"videtisne quantum munus sit oratoris historia." [26] It is liable to
be misunderstood. What is there affirmed is not the identity of
history and oratory. Rather the need for the kind of prose composition that is practised by a master of public discourse.[27] One is

---

[20] *Ad Att.* I. 4. 2; Valerius Maximus IX. 12. 7; Plutarch, *Cicero* 9.

[21] For Sisenna, *HRR* I², CCCXXXIV ff.; E. Badian, *JRS* LII (1962), 50 f.

[22] P. 259.

[23] *Brutus* 228.

[24] Ovid, *Tristia* II. 443 ff.: "vertit Aristidem Sisenna nec obfuit illi/historiae
turpis inseruisse iocos." For the fragments of his *Milesiae, HRR* I², 297.

[25] *De legibus* I. 5.

[26] *De or.* II. 62.

[27] cf. G. Boissier, *Tacite* (1903), 59.

inspired by the passion for truth, one builds on facts, and "exaedificatio" is requisite.[28]

Nor is it any mystery how Cicero would have written. He furnished a formula in *De oratore*: the genre calls for a smooth, flowing, and copious style.[29] Among the Greeks, it is explained, the admired exponents of that manner began with the study of rhetoric. The school of Isocrates was a noble institution, a kind of Trojan Horse—from it issued "meri principes," such as Ephorus and Theopompus.[30] Further, and in confirmation, one observes the high rank Cicero assigns to a historian junior to Theopompus and Ephorus: Timaeus earns praise for "magna eloquentia." [31]

What of the language? Some of the Roman orators artfully paraded an old-fashioned manner (as implying simplicity and honesty) and went in for archaic turns of speech.[32] It was not easy to condemn them out of hand. Furthermore, the writing of history already exhibited deviations from standard prose usage in the direction of the poetic, the archaic, the picturesque.[33] As for archaism of forms and vocabulary, various reasons contributed. Some of the writers were old men, intent to extol the ancient ways and arraigning the irreverence of a new generation; if annalists wrote about the distant past, they would wish to reproduce something of its quaintness or primeval majesty; and students of antiquities reflected the language of the old documents, unconscious or deliberate.

An infusion of the old Roman manner might have something to commend it. Much depended on the theme. It is not likely that Cicero would make many concessions to archaism in a narration of contemporary transactions, himself a large part therein.

---

[28] *De or.* II. 63.

[29] ib. 64: "genus orationis fusum atque tractum et cum lenitate quadam aequaliter profluens." Cf. *Orator* 66: "tracta quaedam et fluens expetitur, non haec contorta et acris oratio."

[30] ib. 94, cf. 57 (an "officina"); *Orator* 207.

[31] ib. 58.

[32] ib. III. 42; 153. A rustic accent might also be assumed (*Brutus* 137).

[33] cf., on Sallust's predecessors, E. Skard, *Symb.Osl.,* Supp. XV (1956). And further, p. 258.

There is another thing to be considered. Narrative by its nature
is different from argument and persuasion. When Cicero had to
send in official reports from Cilicia, he couched his despatches in
a manner that resembles the *Commentarii* of Caesar.[34] In the
Brutus Cicero pays a handsome tribute to those *Commentarii* for
their plain unadorned eloquence—"nudi enim sunt et recti et
venusti."[35] *Commentarii*, however, are only the material on
which historians would draw. That, Cicero adds, is a pity. Nobody in his senses ought to try to improve on Caesar—"nihil est
enim in historia pura et inlustri brevitate dulcius."

One is tempted to echo the regrets of Cicero, especially in view
of Book VII of the *Bellum Gallicum*, which goes a long way beyond a proconsul's despatches. For example, it presents the speech
of a Gallic rebel in direct discourse.[36]

The Romans had their own standards of style and literary
genres. Caesar's name does not stand on the roll of their historians,
and his *Commentarii* find no mention in Quintilian anywhere,
not even as suitable reading matter for the very young. Fate dealt
unjustly. Such was the classic rigour of Caesar's style that the
grammarians and glossologists, eager for the anomalous, hardly
cite him.[37] They delighted in Sallust; and, but for their curious
zeal, few fragments of Cornelius Sisenna would have been preserved.

Averse from Cicero's precepts, and ambitious to outdo Sisenna
(without resembling him too closely), where was Sallust to turn
for guidance? And, a larger question, how far could any theory
help?

History had moved on since the pupils of Isocrates. The age
after Alexander saw the development of a vivid, rhetorical, and
dramatic manner. Some of its exponents are known (more for
blame than praise), and various characteristic features can be
diagnosed. Further, it has been claimed that those historians

---

[34] *Ad fam.* XV. 1 f.

[35] *Brutus* 262.

[36] Caesar, *BG* VII. 77.

[37] Only two instances against more than four hundred from Sallust in the
Grammatici Latini of H. Keil.

wrote according to a prescribed theory; and a whole doctrine of historiography has been discovered and labelled as "Peripatetic."[38] In this result, scholarship tended to acquiesce, with joy and confidence.

The notion was vulnerable on various counts.[39] For one thing, insufficient attention to the atmosphere of the times and the conditions of literary production. It was a dramatic epoch—sudden turns of fortune and great actors parading on the stage of the world. And the reading public had its demands, few tragedies being written now, and the novel in a rudimentary condition.

A general (and sometimes pervasive) influence of Hellenistic historians on the Romans need not be denied. How far is it relevant to Sallust? He seems to go on another track. He puts personality at the centre of events; but he avoids most of their deplorable habits such as lavish pathos, harrowing horrors, the trivial, the erotic or the supernatural, the invocation of dreams, omens, and oracles.[40]

More perceptible, the imitation of the austere Thucydides. Why should that be? Theory again? A doctrine is postulated that went back to Thucydides for precedent and justification.[41] To establish the doctrine is another matter. No evidence avails before what is furnished by Dionysius of Halicarnassus, writing under Caesar Augustus. He refers to certain professors who admitted Thucydides as a model for history, but not for oratory.[42] That will not take one very far.

---

[38] The notion was launched by E. Schwartz, *Hermes* XXXII (1897), 560 f.

[39] For criticism, B. L. Ullman *TAPA* LXXIII (1942), 25 ff.; F. W. Walbank, *Historia* IX (1960), 216 ff. Also the discussion (largely negatory) following the paper of K. v. Fritz in *Histoire et historiens dans l'antiquité* (Fondation Hardt, Entretiens IV [1958], 85 ff.). However, a strong case can be made out for the importance of Theophrastus Περὶ ἱστορίας, cf. N. Zegers, *Wesen und Ursprung der tragischen Geschichtsschreibung* (Diss. Köln, 1959), 76 ff.

[40] E. Schwartz, o.c. 562 f.; K. Latte, *Neue Wege zur Antike* II. 4 (1935), 41 f.; K. Bauhofer, *Die Komposition der Historien Sallusts* (Diss. München, 1935), 127 ff.; V. Paladini, *Sallustio* (1948), 103 ff.; K. Büchner, *Sallust* (1960), 345.

[41] E. Schwartz, o.c. 564 f.

[42] Dionysius, *De Thuc.* 50. On which cf. A. D. Leeman, *Rev.ét.lat.* XXXIII (1955), 197 f.

System and doctrine have more charm and value for students of historiography than for writers of history. Who needs them? [43] Sallust had to find his own way and forge his own style, with effort. One of the components is Thucydides.

Thucydides suffered the fate of a classic, to be praised and not read.[44] Cicero in *De oratore* makes his bow and duly produces a safe and standard appreciation.[45] There is no sign that he was familiar with the text. War and disturbance, however, bring men to Thucydides in different ages, for recognition, instruction, and grim comfort. Cicero's letters to Atticus contain only two citations from this author. Their occurrence is perhaps worth noting—the first in October of 50, from Athens on the way back from Cilicia, the second in May of 49.[46] It is early in the year 46 that the name of Thucydides bursts into sudden notoriety. Not through civil war and the contest now being fought out in Africa between Caesar and the last champions of the Republic. Thucydides comes into debate and polemics about Roman oratory in the *Brutus*.

Cicero had quickly annexed the first place for eloquence. Not without rivals or recalcitrant disciples who found his manner too ample and ornate. They desiderated a plain, vigorous, and concentrated style: "sanitas" and "integritas" were the watchwords.[47] Dissent arose in practice, and it was able to invoke a theory, conveniently labelled "Attic." [48] Letters which M. Brutus and Licinius Calvus addressed to Cicero conveyed some of their criticisms. The Attic tendency claimed illustrious names. In a

---

[43] Compare Cicero's view—"neque eam [sc. historiam] reperio usquam separatim instructam rhetorum praeceptis: sita enim sunt ante oculos" (*De or.* II. 62).

[44] For his influence at Rome, cf. H. G. Strebel, *Wertung und Wirkung des Thukydideischen Geschichtswerks in der griechisch-römischen Literatur* (Diss. München, 1935), 27 ff.

[45] *De or.* II. 56.

[46] *Ad Att.* VII. 1. 6; X. 8. 7. The sole reference in all his letters to Pericles is in late January of 49—"at idem Pericles non fecit . . . cum praeter moenia nihil teneret" (VII. 11. 3).

[47] *Brutus* 284.

[48] For different types of Atticists, A. D. Leeman, *Rev.ét.lat.* XXXIII (1955), 200 ff.; for the origins and development of the doctrine, A. Dihle *Hermes* LXXXV (1957), 170 ff.

later age a catalogue of the great orators next in rank after Cicero registers Calvus, Pollio, Caesar, Caelius, and Brutus.[49]

In the *Brutus* Cicero sets out the annals of Roman eloquence in the form of a dialogue with Brutus and Atticus. The characters are strictly relevant—Brutus because of his decided opinions, Atticus for his devotion to history and chronology. The *Brutus* is a lengthy chronicle of names, interspersed with comment and criticism. The author gratefully acknowledges what he owes to his friend's erudition.

The work reveals traces of exacerbation. A failure in politics and lacking credit, Cicero had only his oratory left—and that was now under attack. The controversy went back some years (Calvus died in 54 or soon after), but there was probably a fresh cause of annoyance. Advocates of the plain style were now appealing not only to Lysias but to Thucydides.

Cicero comes out with a firm statement. Paramount for history, let it be conceded, Thucydides is no good for oratory. There are many speeches in his writings, it is true, but Cicero would never think of imitating them. Thucydides belongs to an early stage in the development of prose. Had he come later, his manner would have ripened and mellowed, he would be "maturior et mitior." [50]

The irritant name recurs in the *Orator* later in the year (dedicated to Brutus). Cicero now uses stronger language. The sectaries of Thucydides, he says, are an upstart and ignorant lot. The Athenian historian wrote about "res gestae," about war and battles—and he wrote "graviter et probe." Nothing of that can be taken over into public and forensic use. Still less the speeches —many of them are obscure or barely intelligible. No orator among the Greeks ever owed anything to Thucydides. As for his Roman fanciers, they are totally incompetent. They do not imitate the Thucydidean "gravitas" of language and thought. They claim to be "germani Thucydidae" if they utter "mutila quaedam et hiantia." To do that, no need of a master or model.[51]

What, it will be asked, is the relevance of all this to Sallust? The answer is clear, even if not conclusive. Aversion from the

---

[49] Tacitus *Dial.* 25. 3, cf. Quintilian X. 1. 113 ff. (omitting Brutus).
[50] *Brutus* 287 f.
[51] *Orator* 30 ff.; cf. *De optimo genere oratorum* 15 f.

eloquence of Cicero may have developed early in Sallust; in the
fifties he may have admired oratory of another type, or frequented
its exponents, whatever their political colour. Further, it is a question how and when he became familiar with Thucydides.

When Sallust was acquiring an education, the range of Latin
prose authors was narrow and unremunerative. No philosophy
yet, no treatise on oratory unless perhaps the *Rhetorica ad
Herennium*.[52] There were annalists, it is true, but of scant value
for education. Cicero, so Atticus affirms in *De legibus*, was always
talking about Cato. His writings, however, do not reveal close and
loving study, and he came late to Cato.[53]

Greek authors, therefore, and the traces of some of them are to
be detected in Sallust: the orators, Isocrates, Plato, Xenophon.
But he had not gone wide or deep. Selected books—and selections
from them—are surmised.[54]

Thucydides is on a different footing. That author cannot have
figured in any programme. His style, which from beneficent
necessity has become familiar to students of classical Hellas, was
peculiar, difficult, and unattractive to the later Greeks, and to the
Romans.[55] It is described as archaic, poetical, abrupt, contorted.[56]

Thucydides comes into the "Atticist" controversy at a late stage,
so it appears, perhaps after 50. And, for Sallust, Thucydides may
have been a late and sudden discovery. Less perhaps from literary
polemics than as a result of civil war, disillusion, and the impulsion towards history.

Sallust found his model. How was he to render the effect in
Latin? A remote old-fashioned style was the necessary equivalent.
Hence Cato.

That is important. Most of those who went in for Attic elo-

---

[52] But that peculiar treatise, built up on the author's school memories, it
can be argued, might be as late as 50 B.C., cf. A. E. Douglas, *CQ*² X (1960),
65 ff.

[53] For his knowledge of the annalists, H. Rambaud, *Cicéron et l'histoire
romaine* (1953), 25 ff.

[54] P. Perrochat, *Les modèles grecs de Salluste* (1949), 84; W. Avenarius,
Rendiconti dell' Istituto lombardo LXXXIX–XC (1956), 343 ff.; *Symb.Osl.*
XXIII (1957), 86. See further p. 244.

[55] E. Norden, *Die antike Kunstprosa* I (1898), 100.

[56] Dionysius, *De Thuc.* 24.

quence were purists. They shunned words out of the ordinary, "inaudita verba," as is exemplified for all time in a pronouncement of Julius Caesar.[57] A manner hostile to rhythm and adornment did not have to admit archaisms. Asinius Pollio, it stands on record, condemned Sallust's predilections.[58]

Pollio was judged old-fashioned in his orations, "durus et siccus." [59] Critics could not fail to advert on the unusual order of words and the broken rhythms.[60] Some orators of the Attic tendency admitted abnormal or obsolete words, it is true.[61] But, when one of them turned to history, nothing suggests that he would choose an archaic vocabulary—and enhance it, especially if he were writing about contemporary transactions (that bitter theme deserved a bare and prosaic rendering). Even if Pollio in his *Historiae* imitated Thucydides, there is no sign that he took that course, or aberration.[62] Sallust's procedure was deliberate. Nobody failed to see it.

Cato comes into the controversy in the *Brutus* by accident, if not through irony. Cicero astutely turns the flank of his critics.[63] If they want a plain style and go back to Lysias, why not to an early Roman writer? There is Cato, whom no modern orator reads, whom nobody at all knows. Cicero is not content to praise the speeches of the Censor. He extols the *Origines* for style—"quem florem aut quod lumen eloquentiae non habent?" He deplores the fact that Cato finds no fanciers—"amatores huic desunt." That, he adds, was the fate centuries earlier of the Syracusan Philistus, and even of Thucydides.

---

[57] Gellius I. 10. 4.

[58] Suetonius, *De gramm.* 10.

[59] Tacitus, *Dial.* 21. 7.

[60] His "compositio," according to Seneca, was "salebrosa et exsiliens et ubi minime exspectes relictura" (*Epp.* 100. 7).

[61] Thus Caelius Rufus, according to Tacitus, *Dial.* 21. 4: "sordes autem illae verborum et hians compositio et inconditi sensus redolent antiquitatem." Cf. Quintilian I. 6. 42. And one can add the archaic words favoured by T. Annius Cimber (*pr.* 44), cf. "Virgil," *Catalepton* 2; Suetonius, *Divus Aug.* 86. 3.

[62] Thucydides' influence on Pollio is more easily assumed than proved, cf. E. Kornemann, *Philologus* LXIII (1904), 148 ff.

[63] *Brutus,* 65 f.

Cicero overplayed his hand. Later in the dialogue Atticus takes
him to task. It was a joke to match Cato with Lysias—"bella
ironia, si iocaremur." [64] As for discovering eloquence in the
Origines or comparing Cato with Thucydides and Philistus, how
could he expect Atticus and Brutus to swallow that?

The collocation of Cato and Thucydides is instructive, but not
enough to enforce the notion that Sallust, in search of a style, got
from the *Brutus* the hint to render the one by the other.

Cato gave him the old-fashioned manner. Other Roman annalists went in for word creation as well as archaic turns (there is
evidence in Sisenna).[65] Thucydides invented a style, and Sallust
himself is innovatory as well as archaic. Sallust exploits Thucydides
in two ways.[66] First, translation or adaptation of phrases. Second,
and much more important, to produce an equivalence of manner
and atmosphere. Because of the historical and personal situation,
he might discern a congeniality with Thucydides, which he was
impelled to enhance, deliberately. Thucydides knew war and government, he failed as a general, and he wrote in exile. The subject
of his history was the empire of the Athenians, and how it was
brought to ruin.

The tone will also be predictable: harsh and disillusioned. To
that, Sallust's personal history and vicissitudes lent asperity. Also
the melancholy fate of Rome and the Republic. If Sallust had
ever hoped for anything from the benevolent autocracy of the
Dictator, that was dispelled—and soon the prospect of more civil
wars and a worse despotism. Sallust is the historian of decline and
fall.

In the prologue of the first work Sallust announces that he will
take certain portions of Roman history, selectively, according to
their interest and value.[67] He does not need to specify the period
and type of "res gestae" he envisages. It soon becomes clear that
he is not going back to the remote past (antiquarian or romanti-

---

[64] ib. 293.

[65] P. 259.

[66] P. 245.

[67] *Cat.* 4. 2: "statui res gestas populi Romani carptim, ut quaeque memoria
digna videbantur, perscribere."

cised) for a subject to convey his own apologia and scarify his seniors or coevals.

By good fortune a kind of disquisition on the monograph happens to be extant. In the summer of 56 a certain L. Lucceius received a missive from Cicero, carefully stylised, and, in places, artful from informality.[68] Lucceius after his defeat at the consular elections in 60 (he had been in a pact with Caesar against Bibulus, the candidate of the Optimates) turned for consolation to history and had now nearly finished a work on the *Bellum Italicum* and the ensuing civil commotions. Cicero helpfully propounds a new subject, from the inception of Catilina's conspiracy to Cicero's return from exile.

Cicero adduces Greek precedents for the monograph. He explains that concentration on one person and a single theme will make all things more rich and splendid, "uberiora atque ornatiora." Furthermore, Lucceius can benefit from experience of affairs, so as to offer political diagnosis and appraisal—and, since he is wont to speak out freely, he can show up the perfidy and treachery to which Cicero was subjected. The ups and downs of fortune excite the reader, not a mere annalistic record. What is needed to grip him is a portrayal of some excellent man in his dramatic vicissitudes. Indeed, Cicero's fortunes are a kind of stage play, "quasi fabula." And finally, genre and subject are far from forbidding a favourable presentation.

Such was the monograph, in Cicero's conception: drama, colour, concentration, and a theme of high politics. Lucceius missed his opportunity. He promised, he received material—and he did nothing.[69]

For Sallust, a wide choice offered in the last sixty years of Rome's turbulent history. The Ten Years War was too large and complicated—a full-length narrative in Sisenna and Lucceius. But

---

[68] *Ad fam.* V. 12. For the interpretation, R. Reitzenstein, *Hellenistische Wundererzählungen* (1906), 84 ff.; A.–M. Guillemin, *Rev.ét.lat.* XVI (1938), 96 ff.; B. L. Ullman, *TAPA* LXXIII (1942), 44 ff. It has been claimed that the notions stated or presupposed in this letter are not restricted in their validity to monographs, cf. N. Zegers, *Wesen und Ursprung der tragischen Geschichtsschreibung* (Diss. Köln, 1959), 82.

[69] *Ad Att.* IV. 6. 4; 9. 2; 11. 2.

it might be practicable to manage the *Bellum Italicum* by selective treatment, for example, the performance of the Roman government when confronted by the challenge of "Itala virtus." Or again, the early actions of Pompeius from the private army levied in Picenum in 83 to the coup d'état of 70. Further, there was plenty to exploit in the episode of M. Aemilius Lepidus and his failed attempt to overthrow the Sullan order; the adventurous career of Q. Sertorius, a man from Sabine Nursia, appealed to Sallust, for more reasons than one; and a *Mithridates* would exhibit the interplay of foreign wars and domestic politics, with scope for picturesque digression on far countries.

Sallust elected for his first essay the Conspiracy of Catilina. Time in its course produces ironies, sometimes quick and multiple. Cicero solicited Lucceius to write a monograph (the subject was obvious, splendid and instructive); and Atticus opined that Cicero and Cicero's consulate would be literature at last in Roman annals. It was Sallust who took up the challenge, but not with Cicero as the central subject. As Cicero explained to Lucceius, the vicissitudes of some excellent personage are indicated. The *Bellum Catilinae* is built up around a villain.

Cicero in the *Brutus* deprecated imitation of Thucydides. He complained that Cato had been grossly neglected, and he drew attention to the fine style of the *Origines*. Sallust went to Cato and Thucydides for models, creating a style that would have been most distasteful to Cicero.

The poet Catullus hailed Cicero as "disertissime Romuli nepotum." [70] For Sallust, Cato is "Romani generis disertissimus." Not for rich and abundant eloquence, but for brevity and concentration. [71]

History was waiting for its master. Echoing Atticus in *De legibus*, the loyal Cornelius Nepos affirms that only Cicero could have achieved the task worthily, to equal the Greeks; and he is

---

[70] Catullus 49. 1.

[71] *Hist.* I. 4: "Romani generis disertissimus paucis absolvit." Perhaps "multa" should be inserted before "paucis," cf. the scholiast on Horace, *Sat.* I. 10. 9.

emboldened to ask whether history had not more cause than had the Republic to lament the death of Cicero.[72] Cicero was killed on December 6, 43 B.C. Not many months after that event, Sallust was at work.

---

[72] Nepos, fr. 3: "ex quo dubito interitu eius utrum res publica an historia magis doleat."

VI

THE BELLUM
CATILINAE

When the end of an epoch is marked by the decease of some famous man, the obsequies elicit a historical commentary from those who possess understanding, the "prudentes." The classic example is the funeral of Caesar Augustus, with evocation of the arguments for and against (the latter in preponderance).[1]

The debate on the ruler of Rome appealed to curiosity, paradox, or malice. It stirred no passions. An age had elapsed since the first usurpations of Caesar's heir, the Proscriptions, the Triumvirate. Who cared now, who could remember the Republic?

And indeed, when did the Republic end? Cato, having become himself a figure of remote history in the epic of Lucan, delivers a funeral oration on Pompeius Magnus. True liberty, he argues, had perished long before. Magnus was not a genuine champion. Now that Magnus has been removed, only one of the dynasts is left, and the fight for the Republic can go on.[2]

That cause was defeated at the Battle of Thapsus in the spring of 46, and Cato's suicide at Utica solemnised the end. The repercussion was swift and enormous. Who could refuse admiration to the model of Roman "virtus"?[3] And some had a bad conscience,

---

[1] Tacitus, *Ann.* I. 9 f.

[2] Lucan IX. 265 f.: "unum fortuna reliquit/iam tribus e dominis."

[3] The cult begins at once at Utica—"propter eius singularem integritatem et quod dissimillimus reliquorum ducum fuerat" (*Bell.Afr.* 88. 5). For the various writings about Cato, see E. Meyer, *Caesars Monarchie und das Principat des Pompejus*[3] (1922), 434 ff.; M. Gelzer, *Caesar der Politiker und Staatsmann*[6] (1960), 279 ff.

seduced all too soon by the clemency of the victor or rebuked and shamed long since by Cato's constancy, themselves inadequate. Cicero responded, promptly. He composed a eulogy of Cato, under encouragement (so he professed) from the nephew of Cato.[4] The *Cato* did not, however, come into circulation before the beginning of 45. Caesar conceived annoyance. His retort was an *Anticato*, which of necessity paid handsome compliments to the literary genius of Cicero.[5] But this great gentleman, who had ever been eager to advertise "dignitas," descended to petty rancour when he reviewed the life and character of Cato, using the devices of personal and political invective normal at Rome when the living were under attack in Senate or Forum. Caesar was angry. Cato had scored—his suicide prevented Caesar from exhibiting magnanimity, clemency, concord.

Cato was more potent dead than alive. After a time his nephew duly came out with a *Cato* which was not at all to Cicero's liking.[6] Brutus before the Civil War nourished a personal feud against Pompeius, who had killed his father long ago in the insurrection of Lepidus.[7] It was Cato whom he followed when the Civil War broke out, not Pompeius, as defender of "liberty and the laws." Brutus, however, abandoned that cause after the Battle of Pharsalia, receiving marks of favour from Caesar and the governorship of a province in 46.

Guilt and remorse soon turned him against his benefactor—also a deep resentment because of the memory of his mother's amours with Caesar. In 45 Brutus divorced his wife Claudia, to marry Porcia, Bibulus' widow, the daughter of Cato. Cassius did not need many extraneous arguments to win over Brutus.

The Ides of March produced a second theme of high debate and

---

[4] *Orator* 35: "testificor me a te rogatum et recusantem haec scribere esse ausum."

[5] Pliny, *NH* VII. 117: "omnium triumphorum laurea maior, quanto plus est ingenii Romani terminos in tantum promovisse quam imperii." For the *testimonia* on Caesar's *Anticato* see the edition of A. Klotz (Vol. III, Teubner, 1927), 190 ff.

[6] *Ad Att.* XII. 21. 1 (before publication). The astute Balbus depreciated the style—"Bruti *Catone* lecto se sibi visum disertum" (XIII 46. 2).

[7] Plutarch, *Brutus* 4; *Pompeius* 64.

controversy. Men looked back to the early life and career of the Dictator. They found abundant material for curiosity or malice, and sharp relevance to the issues of the moment.

The facts about Caesar confirmed or surpassed what men had read in books and knew as a standard theory—the inevitable evolution from the demagogue to the tyrant. Cicero's observations in *De officiis*, composed in the summer of 44, are highly instructive. He equates monarchs and "populares homines," because they give away what is not theirs.[8] Demagogues attack the rights of property when proposing agrarian laws or a scaling-down of debts. They subvert the very foundations of the "res publica," they deny both "concordia" and "aequitas." [9] Then, a little later, harping on the subject of "tabulae novae," Cicero refers to certain violent attempts made manifest during his consulate, "armis et castris," but fortunately crushed. He proceeds to associate Caesar with Catilina. Caesar had been baffled then, it is true; but, subsequently victorious in the civil wars, he kept to the same revolutionary policy, needlessly and wantonly, from a sheer "peccandi libido." No true statesman, so Cicero proclaims, will ever allow himself to treat the possessing class in this fashion.[10]

Against Caesar stood also various ancient charges (ostensibly precise, with names and dates and documentation), and all manner of revelations now at last safely disclosed.[11]

Cicero in the famous letter which he addressed to Pompeius Magnus in the last days of his consulate asserted that the conspiracy which he crushed had an earlier origin, two years previously.[12] The notion was attractive, and worth developing. If Catilina's designs could be pushed back to 66–65, why not the criminal ambitions of Caesar?

Cicero was saving up certain revelations of dire import. The historian Cassius Dio refers to a work of Cicero, *De consiliis suis*. It contained damaging evidence against both Crassus and Caesar.

---

[8] *De off.* II. 21.

[9] ib. 78.

[10] ib. 84. The charge is unjust and dishonest. For Caesar's policy about debts and property, see M. Gelzer, *Caesar*[6] (1960), 203.

[11] For the anti-Caesarian writings, H. Strasburger, *Caesars Eintritt in die Geschichte* (1938), 34 ff.

[12] *Pro Sulla* 67.

Cicero gave the manuscript under seal to his son, not to be published before his decease.[13]

Cicero began to compose his apologia in 59. It is clearly identical with the *Secret History* he tells Atticus about: it will be like Theopompus, only more savage.[14] Then no trace, and a long delay. After the Ides of March, Cicero is found polishing it up, but the pamphlet was not ready to be given to the world in November.[15]

Cicero had other preoccupations—the struggle against M. Antonius and the literary elaboration of an invective that was never spoken, the *Second Philippic*. Events were moving quickly— Caesar's heir with his private army and the march on Rome, the consul Antonius going northward against D. Brutus, the proconsul of Gallia Cisalpina. The damaging revelations were becoming ancient history indeed.

What can be known about *De consiliis?* It is named and cited by Asconius when annotating the electoral campaign of 64.[16] How and when was the text made public? Plutarch in his *Life of Crassus* has a particular relevant to this question. Cicero (he says) in something published after the deaths of Crassus and of Caesar accused them of complicity in Catilina's conspiracy.[17] That does not take one very far. Cicero's accusation may have been couched in the most general terms—as when, for example, he blames Pompeius for the outbreak of the Civil War.[18]

If Dio is to be trusted, Cicero did not himself publish *De consiliis suis*. Further, if his son carried out the parental wishes, it will have to be asked how and when he hoped to reach any reading public, himself proscribed at the same time as his father (in November, 43), and far away in the eastern lands with Brutus or with Cassius. Arguments based on *De consiliis* become very

---

[13] Dio XXXIX. 10. 2 f. (under the year 57).

[14] *Ad Att.* II. 6. 2.

[15] ib. XIV. 17. 6; XVI. 11. 3 f. For the evidence about this work, see H. Peter, *HRR* II (1906), 4; K. Büchner, *R-E* VII A, 1267 f.

[16] Asconius 74: "et hoc ipse Cicero in expositione consiliorum suorum significat."

[17] Plutarch, *Crassus* 13. K. Büchner identifies this writing as *De consiliis,* which he consequently assumes published by Cicero before his death (*R-E* VII A, 1267 f.).

[18] *Ad Att.* VIII. 3. 3; *Ad fam.* VI. 6. 5.

flimsy, and the traces of the thing are not easily detected. None the less, a theory has been constructed that commanded wide assent among the learned and enjoyed a long life. Sallust's monograph (it was postulated) is the direct response to Cicero, *De consiliis suis*: a loyal (and crafty) partisan wrote it, to controvert Cicero's allegations, to defend and rehabilitate the memory of the Dictator.[19] The most extreme formulation of that theory will have it that Octavianus and his friends, taking alarm, commissioned Sallust to refute *De consiliis* in the year 42.[20]

All kinds of misconceptions are here proliferating. Sallust may have chosen his subject before the treatise *De consiliis* came into circulation. There was abundant material to the discredit of Julius Caesar, long known, recently elaborated, or waiting to be dug up a century and a half later. One has only to glance at the "authorities" cited by the biographer Suetonius.[21]

Moreover, the subject and purpose of Sallust's first monograph is clearly much larger than a defence of Caesar. The author is preoccupied all through with decline and fall, with the end of an epoch in Roman history. As he proclaims, when justifying his choice, the Conspiracy of Catilina is a topic exemplary in importance, "sceleris atque periculi novitate" (4. 4). Sallust is right.

In selecting this theme among others available or attractive in the recent history of Rome, Sallust may, it is true, have been influenced by a motive of convenience—to tidy it up and be rid of it. An author in his first essay does not always disclose his ulterior ambitions. Professing an intention to compose monographs, Sallust may none the less already have conceived the hope or design of writing the history of his own times, if he acquired skill and practice, if life were vouchsafed. He betrays no sign or hint.

---

[19] E. Schwartz, *Hermes* XXXII (1897), 580. The view has found favour with writers of the most diverse tendencies. Thus W. Schur, *Sallust als Historiker* (1934), 181 f.; the anonymous writer in CAH IX (1932), 890; F. Lämmli, *Mus.Helv.* III (1946), 101; A. D. Leeman, *Rev.ét.lat.* XXXIII (1955), 208. For scepticism, however, see T. R. S. Broughton, *TAPA* LXVII (1936), 41 f; A. La Penna, *Stud.it.fil.class.* XXXI (1959), 31.

[20] A. Rosenberg, *Einleitung und Quellenkunde zur römischen Geschichte* (1921), 174 f.

[21] Suetonius, *Divus Iulius* 9, cf. p. 96.

Normal prudence might dissuade an announcement of that order and magnitude.

Where would a man think of making his inception? Various dates offered, of cardinal significance. Perhaps the first consulship of Pompeius and Crassus, perhaps the return of Pompeius from the East in 62. Better, however, the compact of the three dynasts in 60, Metellus and Afranius being consuls. It was superficial to assume that the Civil War began when Caesar crossed the Rubicon. Not the quarrel of Pompeius and Caesar but their original alliance, there lay the clue. Cato said so.[22]

Announcing his theme, the author leads off with a vivid portrayal of the central person (5. 1–8). How was he to go on after this point? Since it is his purpose to demonstrate that Catilina is a natural product of the Sullan order in the State, he might have chronicled the life and actions of Catilina in a straight line down to the consular elections in the summer of 64, or even to that second failure in 63 which produced a radical revolutionary.

The first item could have been revealing, for more reasons than one. Catilina, it was agreed, had military experience, tastes, and talent of a high order.[23] He can be discovered among the young officers on the staff of the consul Pompeius Strabo besieging rebel Asculum in 89.[24] Strabo, the parent of Magnus, was a sinister character, a disturbing and prophetic phenomenon. After crushing the Italian rebels he pressed his own ambitions ruthlessly, playing a double game and using the army in repeated attempts to extort a second consulship, until he was removed by a providential decease.

Such was the apprenticeship of L. Sergius Catilina. It was as a partisan of Sulla that he acquired notoriety—cruel murders and rapacity when Sulla captured Rome.[25] At some time early in the seventies he had service as a *legatus* abroad, under a proconsul in

---

[22] Plutarch, *Caesar* 13; *Pompeius* 47. Taken up by Pollio, the notion became classic, influencing Livy, Velleius and Lucan. Cf. *Rom.Rev.* (1939), 8.

[23] *Pro Caelio* 12: "vigebant etiam studia rei militaris."

[24] *CIL* I². 709 = *ILS* 8888. The third name from the bottom stands as "L. Sergi L. f. Tro." Cf. the remarks of C. Cichorius, *Römische Studien* (1922), 172 ff.

[25] P. 84.

one of the many wars.[26] In 73 he was implicated in the case of
the Vestal Virgins, put on trial and acquitted.[27] And, a relevant
detail, the eminent consular Lutatius Catulus testified in his
favour.[28]

Catilina held the praetorship in 68 and governed Africa as his
province. On complaints, and a prosecution announced, he was
debarred from standing for the consulate in 66.[29] Something might
have been said about the elections of that year (P. Cornelius Sulla
and P. Autronius Paetus unseated for bribery), the various disturbances of public order and the rumours of worse violence.[30]
Catilina's trial for *repetundae* came on in 65. Many consulars
spoke in his defence.[31] He was acquitted (through bribery it was
said), but too late to stand for 64.[32] For 63 he stood in concert
with C. Antonius, but the Optimates took alarm, and a safe man,
M. Tullius Cicero, came in first; on the second round, C. Antonius narrowly defeated Catilina. Then another prosecution, for
murder committed in the days of Sulla, but once again an
acquittal.[33] In 63, however, the second failure, conclusive: L. Licinius Murena and D. Junius Silanus were elected.

Sallust chose a different procedure. The character sketch of
Catilina, symptomatic of all that was evil at Rome, the "corrupti
civitatis mores," introduces a long excursus on the history of the
Populus Romanus from the beginning.[34] It goes on to trace the

---

[26] *Hist.* I. 46: "magnis operibus perfectis obsidium cepit per L. Catilinam
legatum." An allusion to the capture of Praeneste has generally been assumed
(cf. Maurenbrecher ad loc.). Against, C. Cichorius (o.c. 173), who conjectures
that Catilina was in the province of Cilicia with P. Servilius Vatia (*cos.* 79).

[27] Asconius 82. For the date, *In Cat.* III. 9.

[28] Orosius VI. 3. 1, cf. Catilina in the letter to Catulus, "egregia tua fides,
re cognita" (35. 1).

[29] *Cat.* 18. 3, to be corrected by Asconius 79 f., cf. p. 100.

[30] P. 88.

[31] *Pro Sulla* 81.

[32] Asconius 76.

[33] ib. 81.

[34] The sketch ends with "incitabant praeterea corrupti civitatis mores
quos pessuma ac diversa inter se mala, luxuria atque avaritia vexabant"
(5. 8); and, after the digression, Sallust reverts with "in tanta tamque corrupta civitate Catilina" (14. 1).

decline of public morality subsequent to the last war against the
Carthaginians, with especial incrimination of Sulla, proconsul and
Dictator (6–13). The author then reverts to Catilina (14–16); he
produces a meeting of Catilina's associates in the summer of
64 (17), and an oration from their leader (20), but inserts in
between a short digression on previous subversive plotting (18–
19). The conspiracy proceeds and takes more definite shape after
the elections in 63 (21–24). Then, after a brief portrayal of a
lady called Sempronia (25), the conspiracy moves to a climax,
in its parallel and alternating aspects (at Rome and in Etruria),
down to Catilina's arrival at the camp of his partisan C. Manlius
(26 to 36. 3).

At this point the narrative is broken by an excursus on the
distressing conditions of Roman political life (36. 4 to 39. 4). The
story resumes with sundry activities of the conspirators left behind at Rome (Lentulus, Cethegus and the others), their intrigue
with the envoys of a Gallic tribe, their arrest, and the transactions
in the Senate (39. 6 to 50). Then follow the speeches of Caesar
and of Cato (51–53), with for epilogue a brief digression which
compares the two statesmen (53. 2 to 54). The conspirators are
executed (55). Then Etruria (56–57), a speech of Catilina before
battle (58–59), the desperate battle and the end (60–61).

The structure is complicated. The author has refused to write
a biography or reproduce a portion of Roman annals, from 66 to
63. Disdaining the easy way, he wrecks the narrative order and he
brings in digressions.

As in phrase and sentence, so in the whole composition of the
monograph: Sallust is rapid and abrupt, operating by contrasts.
The psychology of the writer might be invoked—a lack of ease
and harmony in his character. That could only be a partial explanation. The writer is wilful and impatient, not chaotic. He
knows what he is trying to do, he dominates the subject.[35]

Some hold that the *Bellum Catilinae* is built up like a tragedy.[36]
The notion would do no harm if it is not pushed to extremes in
the search for models. Enough to assume that the writer has a

---

[35] K. Latte, *Neue Wege zur Antike* II. 4 (1935), 47.
[36] R. Ullmann, *Rev.phil.* XLII (1918), 5 ff.

conscious purpose and has produced an intelligible structure.[37]

Sallust breaks and varies the action by digressions and orations. As for the digressions, two are of minor significance in the
design, namely the note on an earlier conspiracy in 66–65 (18 f.)
and the character sketch of Sempronia (25). The others stand in
close relation to the author's main preoccupations—Rome, public
morality, and true statesmanship. The first is concerned with the
past, but comes down to Sulla (6–13). The second, interpolated at
the climax of the narrative, analyses political behaviour in the
period after Sulla (36. 4 to 39. 4): it occupies the precise centre
of the monograph. That is important. The third, asserting the
paucity of great men in that epoch, proclaims the "virtus" of two
and two only: Caesar and Cato (53. 2 to 54).

Digressions and speeches lend variety. More than that, these
devices enable a historian, breaking loose from time and space,
to develop themes close to his heart. Hence the most valuable
of clues to his idiosyncrasy.

There are four orations: two from Catilina, one each from
Caesar and Cato. Here the author illustrates his favourite ideas,
linked to the digressions. That is shown directly, as in Cato's oration, in praise of the honour and majesty of the Roman past, and
denouncing the conduct of the aristocracy in his own day. Also
indirectly, and almost in parody: Catilina in preface to the harangue inciting the conspirators makes appeal to their "virtus" and
"fides," and in both speeches he arraigns the "potentia paucorum."

A monograph is limited in scope, and sometimes bound up with
the vicissitudes of one person, according to a known theory of
historiography. Sallust circumvents that theory. The subject is
the *Bellum Catilinae*, and Catilina is allowed two orations. But
the work rises to its culmination with Caesar and Cato. Together
they engross one fifth of the monograph. The book ends, to be
sure, with Catilina and the battle near Pistoria—a sombre anticlimax of desperation and futility, a fierce and fraudulent oration,
a useless and murderous battle.

---

[37] Much discussion has gone to the structure. See K. Latte, o.c. 30 ff.;
K. Vretska, *Hermes* LXXII (1937), 202 ff.; K. Bauhofer, *Die Komposition
der Historien Sallusts* (Diss. München, 1935), 45 ff.; K. Büchner, *Hermes*, Einzelschriften 9 (1953), 98 ff.; W. Steidle, *Historia*, Einzelschriften 3 (1958), 1 ff.

A monograph, demanding concentration, entailed omissions. The villain is lavishly delineated, but some of his earlier actions, which could have been exploited with telling effect, are left out.[38] About his adherents, next to nothing beyond their names. The surprise is the digression about Sempronia, who has no part in the action—her house is used on one occasion, that is all (40. 5). That item cannot fail to arouse curiosity or disquiet.[39]

Something is said about the boastful and incautious Q. Curius and his mistress Fulvia (who transmitted information to Cicero);[40] and the impetuous violence of Cethegus is on show.[41] One might, however, have expected to find one or two of the other leading Catilinarians sharply and severely described. Decayed *nobiles* were vulnerable to unfriendly presentation, as stupid or frivolous. In this company were both "stolidi" and "vani" (for these are the standard terms).[42] Sallust could have invented some deleterious label for L. Cassius Longinus, an unpromising candidate for the consulate of 63: he was a torpid fat man.[43] Or better, that scion of the patrician Cornelii, P. Lentulus Sura (consul in 71, but expelled from the Senate the year after), who is the ostensible head of the conspiracy next to Catilina. Sallust duly reports that Lentulus Sura was buoyed up by the oracle promising power at Rome to three Cornelii in sequence (47. 2). Something also could perhaps have been added to the detriment of this Lentulus, as is suggested by what Cicero says about his performance as an orator: slow to think and slow in speech, but he had a presence.[44]

The author's rigour and refusal of detail is apparent in respect of Caesar and Cato. The fact that Caesar won the office of

---

38 P. 85.

39 P. 133.

40 23. 1 ff.; 26. 3; 28. 2.

41 43. 4: "natura ferox vehemens, manu promptus erat, maximum bonum in celeritate putabat."

42 *Hist.* IV. 1 (on a Cornelius Lentulus), cf. p. 209.

43 Asconius 73: "Cassius quamvis stolidus tum magis quam improbus videretur." Cicero castigates "L. Cassi adipes" (*In Cat.* III. 16).

44 *Brutus* 235: "P. Lentulus, cuius et excogitandi et loquendi tarditatem tegebat formae dignitas, corporis motus plenus et artis et venustatis, vocis et suavitas et magnitudo." Cicero had derided "P. Lentuli somnum" (*In Cat.* III. 16).

pontifex maximus in 63 after bitter contest with leaders of the
Optimates only emerges in explanation of something else—the
rancour of Lutatius Catulus (49. 2). Again, when the Senate held
debate on the punishment of the conspirators, Caesar was praetor-
designate, Cato being tribune-designate. All that Sallust says, when
comparing the two, is that they were on a level for birth, age, and
eloquence (54. 1). An extreme simplification. To say nothing else,
five years divided them (relevant at this stage in a man's career).
Sallust is looking at them from a distant perspective, as characters
of history, and suppressing certain facts and dates that a reader
might know or could find elsewhere, if curious.

Many omissions, therefore, in any event. Not all of them, it
might seem, to be covered by the exigencies of brevity and artistic
composition. Curiosity might ask who was backing L. Sergius
Catilina and C. Antonius at the elections in 64.[45] And further,
at what precise point did that support for Catilina lapse? Who
was behind Catilina up to the elections in the next year? More
things than one are obscure about that contest and its background. Junius Silanus and Licinius Murena won. Not that Sallust
says so. He is only interested in the defeat of Catilina (26. 5).
Apart from Catilina, only one defeated candidate is anywhere on
record, Ser. Sulpicius Rufus. Since each was a patrician, both could
not be elected. Who was supporting whom? Sallust gives no hint.[46]

Balance and variety, selection and omission, the *Bellum Catilinae* is carefully combined. What material did Sallust employ?

---

[45] Asconius had the answer—"coierant enim ambo ut Ciceronem consulatu
deicerent, adiutoribus usi firmissimis M. Crasso et C. Caesare" (74). Going
on to elucidate a passage from *In toga candida* about the nocturnal visit of
Catilina and Antonius to the house "cuiusdam hominis nobilis et valde in
hoc largitionis quaestu noti," he says that either Caesar or Crassus is alluded
to; and, for their hostility to Cicero's candidature, he refers to what Cicero
said in *De consiliis suis*.

[46] Cato had been strong for Silanus, the husband of his half-sister Servilia;
and, along with the disappointed Sulpicius Rufus, he prosecuted Murena for
ambitus in November. As concerns Caesar, Silanus' wife was notoriously his
inamorata. And Caesar may have supported Sulpicius Rufus, the next hint
of whose consular prospects emerges precisely when Caesar is consul (*Ad Att.*
II. 5. 2). Though supporting Catilina in 64 (Asconius 74), Caesar may have
decided, before the elections of 63, that Catilina was compromising, dangerous, and not likely to win.

When Sallust was writing, an age seemed to have elapsed. In fact, only two decades. Sallust several times puts on record rumour or speculation current at the time—that is, items he is not prepared to vouch for.[47] He had known many of the leading figures, and he can quote from memory an assertion of Crassus (48. 9). Moreover, despite many casualties in the upper order (who was still extant of the consulars of 63?), there were survivors worth consulting. Too late to question P. Sulla, with whom Sallust had been in close contact in 47—[48] he perished at the end of the following year, and the first news (assassination or the results of overeating) made Cicero deliriously happy.[49] But Messalla Rufus (cos. 53), a friend of P. Sulla, lived on.[50] L. Calpurnius Bestia, tribune of the plebs in 62, after a long eclipse turns up in the camp of Antonius before Mutina;[51] and a shabby spectre of the past, the consular C. Antonius, is discovered paradoxically as censor in 42.[52]

It would not be easy to discern where truth lay in the alleged "prehistory" of the conspiracy in 66–65 (later events and manifold misrepresentations cast their shadow backwards), but the evidence for 63 was abundant, some of it precise and accurate. The author can present documents.

He inserts a letter from the insurgent leader Manlius to Q. Marcius Rex, urging the plea of men in distress, the "miseri" ground down by usurers and the injustice of Roman magistrates (33). But this does not purport to be authentic, for Sallust describes the missive as "mandata huiusce modi." The letter which Catilina after leaving Rome sent to his friend Lutatius Catulus is another matter. Sallust furnishes a copy, an "exemplum" (34. 3). Content and language are revealing (35). Appealing to the "fides" of Catulus, Catilina protests that he has been wronged, insulted

---

[47] 14. 7: "scio fuisse nonnullos, qui ita existumarent"; 17. 7: "fuere item ea tempestate qui crederent"; 19. 4: "sunt qui ita dicant"; 22. 1: "fuere ea tempestate qui dicerent"; 48. 7: "erant eo tempore qui existumarent."

[48] P. 37.

[49] Ad fam. XV. 17. 2.

[50] As P. Sulla and Messalla (Rufus) are together in 47 (Ad Att. XI. 22. 2), the latter is probably the M. Messalla of Pro Sulla 20, rather than Messalla Niger (cos. 61), whom Münzer prefers (R-E VIII A, 164).

[51] Phil. XI. 11; 13. 12. See p. 132.

[52] CIL I², p. 64; ILS 6204. See p. 131.

and thwarted in his "dignitas." He has taken an open stand as
champion of the unfortunate, not because of any debts of his
own, but because honour has been conferred on the unworthy
"quod non dignos homines honore honestatos videbam"; he refers again to the "dignitas" that is still left to him; and he ends
by entrusting his wife, Aurelia Orestilla, to the "fides" of his
friend Catulus.[53]

Here speaks the authentic Catilina, the aristocrat who in altercation with the consul Cicero spoke with contempt of the "in-
quilinus civis urbis Romae," proudly styling himself a patrician
who, like his ancestors, had conferred many "beneficia" on the
plebs of Rome (31. 7). It may be added that Sallust in his account
of the battle has Catilina push into the thick of it, "memor generis
atque pristinae suae dignitatis" (60. 7).

A second document is reproduced, again prefaced with the
word "exemplum" (44. 4). It is the brief message from Lentulus
that Volturcius was to take to Catilina early in December.[54] But,
a puzzle. Cicero quotes the document, to the same effect but not
quite in the same words.[55] Which version, if either, is verbally
correct? An answer can be given: Cicero's text.[56] Sallust improves
on the original by modifying two colloquial expressions and by
making two sentences more sharp and concrete.[57]

When Volturcius, the envoys of the Allobroges and the five
conspirators were brought before the Senate on December 3,

---

[53] The letter is remote from the style and language of Sallust. It has an
involved sentence, and a very clumsy expression—"satisfactionem ex nulla
conscientia de culpa proponere decrevi." The phrase "honore honestatos" is
Plautine (Captivi 247; 356). Sallust happens not to use "honesto"—or "satis-
factio," "commendatio," and "commendo." Further, the formula of farewell,
"haveto," is solemn and archaic: never in Cicero's letters.

[54] 44. 5: "qui sim ex eo quem ad te misi cognosces. fac cogites in quanta
calamitate sis et memineris te virum esse. consideres quid tuae rationes
postulent. auxilium petas ab omnibus, etiam ab infumis."

[55] In Cat. III. 12: "quis sim scies ex eo quem ad te misi. cura ut vir sis
et cogita quem in locum sis progressus. vide ecquid tibi iam sit necesse et
cura ut omnium tibi auxilia adiungas, etiam infimorum."

[56] G. Boissier had no doubts, La conjuration de Catilina (1905), 201. For
the detailed proof, see K. Latte, o.c. 19 f.

[57] The phrase "scire ex" is colloquial, and "cura ut" belongs to epistolary
style.

Cicero insisted that the depositions and avowals should be taken down in writing: for that task he selected four men of rank and repute, of speed and accuracy.[58] The consul will also have wanted a full recording of what happened at the two ensuing sessions. Cato's speech (so Plutarch states) was the only one of all his orations to be preserved.[59]

Sallust (it might be supposed) had access to versions of the speeches delivered by Caesar and by Cato on December 5. How closely he would wish to follow what was actually said is another matter.[60] About Caesar's oration, something can be recovered (not much) from Cicero's *Fourth Catilinarian*. For example, it appears likely that Caesar used the phrase "mansuetudo et misericordia," which is taken up by Cato and which recurs in the historian's comparison of the two men (52. 11 and 27; 54. 2). However, Cato's speech cannot have been quite so polite to Caesar as Sallust represents it. Cato (another source alleges) exclaimed that Caesar was lucky not to be on trial himself for treason.[61]

A historian would not neglect the *Cato* of Brutus. But the main sources of Sallust were probably the writings of Cicero.[62] A variety of compositions, prose or verse, Greek or Latin, extolled these memorable transactions.[63] Among them was the Greek memoir on his consulate which he sent to Posidonius, and which (so that artful man replied), so far from inspiring him to write on this theme, was a deterrent.[64] And the *De consiliis* with its alarming revelations will be borne in mind—or perhaps not.

---

[58] *Pro Sulla* 42.

[59] Plutarch, *Cato* 23, cf. *Cicero* 21.

[60] For the argument and tone of these orations, see p. 111; for the style, p. 266.

[61] Plutarch, *Cato* 23; *Caesar* 8; *Cicero* 21. Further, Cato praised Cicero and attacked Junius Silanus (*Cato* 23). For Plutarch's sources, cf. R. Wirtz, *Beiträge zur catilinarischen Verschwörung* (Diss. Bonn, 1910), 41 ff. He puts emphasis on Tiro's biography of Cicero. Plutarch's source knew *De consulatu* (*Caesar* 8) and *De consiliis* (*Crassus* 13), cf. E. Schwartz, *Hermes* XXXII (1897), 592; 599. Schwartz opted for Fenestella (ib. 602).

[62] R. Wirtz argued that Sallust derives almost entirely from Cicero (o.c. 25 ff.). That is an exaggeration.

[63] For Cicero's various writings and their subsequent traces, see H. Peter, *HRR* II (1906), IV ff.; 3 f.; K. Büchner, *R-E* VII A, 1267 ff.

[64] *Ad Att.* II. 1. 1 f.

The oration *In toga candida,* delivered in the Senate a few days before the elections in 64, carried much personal abuse, concentrated on Cicero's most dangerous competitors, Catilina and Antonius. The fragments, with Asconius' commentary, are of exceptional interest. Then the four orations *In Catilinam* which, along with eight other speeches of the year 63, Cicero subsequently worked up for publication in the summer of 60.[65] To those will be added the defence of L. Licinius Murena, the consul designate, at the end of November, and the *Pro Sulla* of the next year.

There were traps and hazards in using evidence of this kind. Revising the orations, Cicero from oversight or complacency was tempted to exaggerate his own foreknowledge. For example, in the *First Catilinarian* he claims to have predicted in the Senate the exact day on which Manlius was to raise the standard of revolt at Faesulae;[66] further, he alludes to the route that will take Catilina to the north (the Via Aurelia, but only as far as Forum Aurelii).[67] Doubts might be conceived. Furthermore, and in general, the time at which Cicero was writing—the politics of the day influenced his presentation of certain themes and persons.[68]

It is a melancholy truth that, the more abundant the sources of information, the greater are the chances of error. That is evident, for example, if one tries to sort out certain transactions in the best documented year of all Roman history, the twelve months subsequent to the Ides of March. Too much, therefore, to expect that Sallust's first essay would be free from mistakes. His technique of composition is partly responsible. Some of his links and sutures might display inadequacies. Abbreviation has its dangers. Further, the Roman system of dating was cumbrous and inartistic. For the events of 63, Sallust eschews indications of chronology: one date only by the day of the month, that of Manlius' rising

---

[65] ib. II. 1. 3.

[66] *In Cat.* I. 7.

[67] ib. I. 24: "quamquam quid ego te invitem, a quo iam sciam esse praemissos qui tibi ad Forum Aurelium praestolarentur armati?"

[68] Thus the polite treatment of Caesar (*In Cat.* IV. 9 ff.), whose prospects for the consulate were so favourable; and there is a clear hint of Clodius (ib. 20). For the later rewriting, R. Wirtz, o.c. 20 ff.; and, for the *Fourth Catilinarian,* the passages adduced by H. Fuchs, *Hermes* LXXXVII (1959), 464 ff.

in Etruria on October 27 (30. 1), but no other day or month in
the whole year is registered. The author could, however, without
precise dates, have furnished some indications about intervals of
time in the last three months of the year.

Errors can be discovered by checking Sallust with Cicero, with
Asconius, or with himself. Further, historical probability comes
in, or surmise about reasons for misconception or confusion. It
was for a long time the fashion to detect and assume deliberate
falsifications. A cool and juster estimate will suggest that a number of mistakes are due, not to deceit, but to plain inadvertence or
lapse of memory. A catalogue can be drawn up.[69]

There are, however, two large matters in which the credit and
honesty of the historian are under attack.

First, the inception of the conspiracy. It is put in 64, about the
beginning of June, shortly before the consular elections (17. 1).
Catilina summons at his house a meeting of his adherents, fifteen
of them certified by name (eleven senators, four men of equestrian
rank); and further, a large number of partisans from good families
in the towns of Italy. Sympathisers and secret supporters are also
noted. Catilina delivers a violent harangue, denouncing the
"potentia paucorum" (20. 2 ff). A minority is in possession of all
honour and resources—"omnis gratia potentia honos divitiae
apud illos." Catilina conjures up riches, mansions, art collections, in the monopoly of the few; and he makes appeal to the
energy and appetites of his friends, impoverished or labouring
under the burden of debt.

Drastic action is contemplated. In response to enquiry about the
strategy and the prizes of victory—"quae condicio belli foret,
quae praemia armis peterent"—Catilina announces a programme.
There will be *tabulae novae,* a proscription of the wealthy, and
offices and priesthoods as reward for the conspirators (21. 1 f).

The language and the methods (observe the mention of "bel-

---

[69] For a full list of errors or inadequacies, and a defence of some of
them, see O. Seel, *Sallust von den Briefen ad Caesarem zur Coniuratio
Catilinae* (1930), 49 ff. It will not be necessary to add that the classic study is
that of C. John long ago, *Jahrbücher für cl. Phil.,* Supp. VIII (1876), 703 ff.

lum" and "arma") are anachronistic if situated before the elections in 64. That is clear.[70] So long as he has a chance of being elected consul, a Roman politician does not descend to the inferior and desperate resort of revolution. Two defeats were necessary to produce the authentic conspiracy, which was to be a coup d'état at Rome combined with an insurrection in Italy.

On Sallust's showing, Catilina's appeal in 64 goes out to impoverished persons of the better sort. Only later does he turn to the poor and the dispossessed—the "causa miserorum" is explicitly mentioned in his letter to Catulus (35. 3). When did that change occur? In 64 he could count on reputable and powerful support, as Sallust himself indicates, referring to ambitious *nobiles* in the background.[71] He came close to success. The next chance was the election in 63. Catilina reckoned with help and connivance from the consul C. Antonius. That was promptly baffled by Cicero, who arranged that his colleague should have the profitable province of Macedonia. Shortly before the polls, it appears, Catilina, seeing his hopes fade, became angry and intemperate. Cato in the Senate threatened him with prosecution, provoking a violent retort.[72] Then there was a well-authenticated report of a meeting at Catilina's house, where he addressed his followers in outrageous language, spoke of the needs of the "miseri," and proclaimed himself the "dux et signifer calamitosorum." [73] The matter was brought to the notice of the Senate. Catilina, challenged by the consul, came out with a bold and menacing pronouncement. The State, he said, was not one body but two: one body weak and

---

[70] C. John, o.c. 763 ff. For an attempt to defend Sallust's procedure, see W. Steidle, *Historia,* Einzelschriften 3 (1958), 91 f.

[71] 17. 5: "erant praeterea complures paulo occultius consili huiusce participes nobiles, quos magis dominationis spes hortabatur quam inopia aut alia necessitudo." The author then mentions suspicions about the eventual role of Crassus.

[72] *Pro Murena* 51: "si quod esset in suas fortunas incendium excitatum, id se non aqua sed ruina restincturum." This item is transferred by Sallust and used as the climax of the altercation with Cicero on November 8— "quoniam quidem circumventus, inquit, ab inimicis praeceps agor incendium meum ruina restinguam" (31. 9).

[73] ib. 50. This "contio domestica" was also exploited by Sallust—for a meeting of conspirators and a speech in the summer of 64, though Sallust does not there make Catilina assert the cause of the "miseri."

with a weak head, the other strong but lacking a head. Catilina
would provide that head.[74] In consequence the Senate decided
to postpone the elections (though not for long).[75]

Sallust's presentation is therefore highly vulnerable. He can, it
is true, be partly exculpated. He does not in fact bring out
Catilina as a champion of the lower classes in the summer of 64.
The inducements then held out are not for them. None the less,
his Catilina expounds to the partisans a programme more than
electoral, contemplating "bellum" and "arma."

Sallust's antedating lures him into other anachronisms. The
woman Fulvia, the mistress of Q. Curius, one of the conspirators,
is already talking, hence sinister rumours which (the historian
asserts) are largely responsible for the election of Cicero in 64
(23. 4 f.). Again, between that point and before the elections in
63, Catilina sends money and weapons to various strategic points
in Italy, notably to Manlius at Faesulae (24. 2).

Sallust antedated the revolutionary designs of Catilina. Why
should he have made this assumption? One reason is artistic and
simplificatory—to demonstrate the coherent evolution of Catilina
as a product of the whole post-Sullan environment. In the author's
conception it was not enough that an electoral defeat should create
the criminal revolutionary. Something else has been suspected—
the intention, ingenuous or clumsy, to indicate that, since Catilina
was already an advocate of spoliation and violence in 64, no suspicion of complicity ought to adhere to Caesar (of which more
later).

The other charge of grave import concerns the order and interrelation of events in October and November of 63. On the lowest
count, inaccuracy has been assumed or conceded. At the worst, a
wilful distortion.

To assess the charge, it is necessary to have certain facts and
dates established beyond dispute. Catilina, defeated at the elections in July, resolved on revolution. His partisan C. Manlius
went to work in northern Etruria; he enlisted the rustic plebs,
brigands (who were numerous in the region), and discontented
veterans from the military colonies of Sulla (28. 4). On receipt of

---

[74] ib. 51.
[75] cf. M. Gelzer, *R-E* VII A, 874.

intelligence, Cicero made report to the Senate, and a decree was passed authorising the consuls to take full precautions expedient for order and security—the *senatus consultum ultimum,* as it is sometimes designated (29. 2). The date can be certified, October 21.[76] On October 27 Manlius started the insurrection (30. 1). That was announced in the Senate by L. Saenius, who had a letter from Faesulae (about November 2, allowing for time and distance). On this report, the Senate adopted military measures (30. 3 ff.). Precise instructions were given to two proconsuls (Q. Marcius Rex and Q. Metellus Creticus), who were waiting outside the gates of Rome for delayed triumphs, also to two of the praetors.

Meanwhile, Catilina was active in Rome. A meeting of the conspirators was convened at the house of M. Porcius Laeca on the evening of November 6.[77] They made several plans, among them the decision that two men (C. Cornelius and L. Vargunteius) should try to assassinate the consul early the next morning.[78] Cicero, forewarned, took precautions, and the two men were refused entry to his house. Another night passed. On November 8, Cicero denounced Catilina before the Senate (the *First Catilinarian*), and Catilina left Rome.[79] The next day, Cicero ad-

---

[76] *In Cat.* I. 4, cf. Asconius 5.

[77] The date is certain—"ad M. Laecam nocte ea quae consecuta est posterum diem Nonarum Novembrium" (*Pro Sulla* 52). Some scholars have incautiously taken this to be November 5, not November 6. Thus M. Gelzer, *R-E* IIA, 1706; VI A 877. He has been followed by W. Steidle, o.c. 93.

[78] The deed was to occur the morning after, "prima luce" (*Pro Sulla* 52). Compare, if necessary, *In Cat.* 1. 9: "fuisti igitur apud Laecam illa nocte, Catilina" with, after a few lines, "illa ipsa nocte paulo ante lucem." That is, the morning of November 7. None the less, some scholars put the attempt on November 8. Thus J. Carcopino, *Histoire romaine* II (1936), 642; A. La Penna, *Stud.it.fil.class.* XXXI (1959), 20.

[79] Cicero refers to two nights—"quid proxima, quid superiore nocte egeris" (*In Cat.* I. 1). That is, November 6 and 7. The night of the meeting at Laeca's house is described as "noctem illam superiorem" and "priore nocte" (ib. I. 9). It follows that the *First Catilinarian* was delivered on November 8. This is the chronology as established by C. John, o.c. 782 ff.; *Philologus* XLVI (1888), 650 ff.; and, for that matter, the essential is stated and argued in the unpretentious edition of A. M. Cook (1884), XXIII f. The case has been powerfully restated by T. Rice Holmes, *The Roman Republic* I (1923), 461 ff. None the less, some remain recalcitrant. M. Gelzer puts the meeting at

dressed the People (the *Second Catilinarian*). When the news came that Catilina had joined Manlius, they were declared public enemies (about November 17). In the last days of the month, Cicero defended L. Licinius Murena, consul-designate, under prosecution for electoral bribery. In the course of the night of December 2 to 3, the envoys of the Allobroges and Volturcius, carrying missives to Catilina, were apprehended at the Pons Mulvius. The next day, Cicero reported to the Senate the treason of Lentulus and three other conspirators, with documentary evidence, and spoke before the People (the *Third Catilinarian*). There was discussion in the Senate on December 4. The vital debate ensued on December 5. The consul introduced it. The consul-designate D. Junius Silanus, the first to be asked for his "sententia," proposed that the conspirators be put to death.

The order of events as set forth by Sallust must now be scrutinised. Recording Catilina's preparations at Rome, he proceeds to the meeting at the house of Porcius Laeca and the frustrated attempt to assassinate the consul (27. 3 to 28. 3). After that, the author turns to the armed insurrection—"interea Manlius in Etruria" (28. 4). He notes Cicero's reaction to reports about Manlius, registers the *senatus consultum ultimum,* the actual outbreak announced in the Senate by L. Saenius, the measures of military security, and concludes by describing the alarm that reigned at Rome (29. 1 to 31. 3). Then he reverts to Catilina—"at Catilinae crudelis animus" (31. 4). After mentioning an abortive attempt of L. Aemilius Paullus to prosecute Catilina "de vi publica," he comes to the oration of Cicero in the Senate, Catilina's retort, and Catilina's departure (31. 4 to 32. 1).

The charge against Sallust's accuracy—and Sallust's honesty—is as follows. Sallust in his arrangement of these transactions puts the Senate's decree (October 21) subsequent to the failed assassination (November 7). What is the reason? Some suppose negligence.[80] It would have to be criminal negligence. Therefore de-

---

Laeca's house on the night of November 5, the attempted assassination on the morning of November 7 (*R-E* VII A, 877): the former date runs counter to the repeated testimony of Cicero (cited in n. 78). And Gelzer has the oration on November 7.

[80] O. Seel, o.c. 62.

liberate choice. If so, why? It has been asserted that the author is trying to play down the importance of Manlius' activities in order to keep Catilina and Rome at the centre of the picture.[81] That is not at all convincing. The theory that has commanded widest assent assumes that Sallust is eager at any cost to malign Cicero: he is trying to show that Cicero's personal fears (consequent on the attempt of November 7) caused him to ask for the *senatus consultum ultimum*.[82]

Sallust's language, be it observed, gives no support to this notion about Sallust's purpose. The theory can be exploded. The true explanation was to hand, if one looked with proper care at the historian's method of composition. He is dealing with two separate series of events: the conspiracy at Rome, Manlius in Etruria. He carries the first as far as the failed assassination (28. 3). He then turns to the second—"interea Manlius" (28. 4). Then, after the Senate's decree, the military measures and the alarm at Rome, he goes back to Catilina—"at Catilinae crudelis animus" (31. 4), continuing the theme as far as the altercation in the Senate and Catilina's departure.

That is to say, so far from linking to the *senatus consultum* any fears of Cicero for his personal safety, Sallust disjoins them, clearly and emphatically: the two items belong to separate sections of narrative.[83] The historian might have done better to dispose differently those sections—but that is another matter.

---

[81] W. A. Baehrens, *Neue Wege zur Antike* IV (1926), 43. For various other and not convincing explanations, see W. Schur, *Sallust als Historiker* (1934), 190; K. Vretska, *Hermes* LXXII (1937), 207; L. O. Sangiacomo, *Sallustio* (1954), 118 f.

[82] E. Schwartz, o.c. 577.

[83] It was the signal merit of W. Steidle to establish this plain fact (o.c. 93 f.): unfortunately not accepted by K. Büchner, *Sallust* (1960), 294, cf. 425. The unskilful modern paragraphing of Sallust's text has contributed to the misunderstanding. If 27.1 is added to the preceding chapter, a new theme begins at 27.2: "interea Romae multa simul moliri." It ends at 28.3. Then should begin a new chapter, at 28. 4: "interea Manlius in Etruria." That section of the narrative ends at 31. 3. Then a new chapter at 31. 4: "at Catilinae crudelis animus."

For parallel, it may be noted that the paragraphing in Tacitus, impeccable for the beginning of the *Historiae*, is several times astray in *Ann.* I. 1–15. To take one instance: the last sentence of I. 10 should be added to the be-

Sallust is right. Further, the appearance of C. Cornelius and L. Vargunteius at Cicero's front door on the morning of November 7 was not the main reason for Cicero's convoking the Senate on November 8. Nor would it have been wise for him to assert that it was. Would the consul command instant credence? Senators knew that Cicero was prone to exaggerate his personal danger, and they recalled his wearing of a breastplate at the elections.[84]

Cicero's design and purpose is patent. If certain statements of Cicero can be trusted, the conspirators at the house of Laeca fixed the day on which Catilina was to leave Rome;[85] further, he was only waiting until the consul should have been assassinated.[86] The intended departure may have been postponed by a day. Cicero in the *First Catilinarian* exhorted Catilina to go, and he went. The consul was able to engross the credit for bringing the enemy out into the open, the glory of expelling him from Rome. "Abiit evasit excessit erupit." [87]

The historian is cleared. There was no deception. How difficult it is to combine in one narration contemporaneous events in different theatres without a lavish use of dates and sign posts is not always apparent to the erudite arbiters of praise and blame who eschew the writing of narrative history.

Sallust exhibits merit in his treatment of certain particulars that happen not to be mentioned in the writings of Cicero as extant. For example, a precious detail, L. Saenius who read out in the Senate a letter from Faesulae reporting what had occurred on October 27 (30. 1). Sallust may have felt doubts about Cicero's assertion that he both knew the date in advance and told the Senate so. Further, Sallust mentions Q. Fabius Sanga, the patron of the Allobroges: Cicero in the *Third Catilinarian* omits both his name and his role. The historian's fuller account reveals what the orator has glossed over.

---

ginning of the next chapter, for with it the scene changes from the Campus Martius to the Senate—"ceterum sepultura more perfecta templum et caelestes religiones decernuntur."

[84] *Pro Murena* 52.
[85] *Pro Sulla* 52.
[86] *In Cat.* I. 9.
[87] ib II. 1.

Sallust explains how the Allobroges were brought into touch with Cicero by Q. Fabius Sanga; they were induced to feign acceptance of Lentulus' propositions, and further to demand signed undertakings from the conspirators (41. 5; 44. 1). The Allobroges knew what was afoot. Was Volturcius innocent, a solitary dupe in the caravan which the two praetors stopped at the Pons Mulvius? The account of Sallust permits one to wonder. The Gauls gave in at once; Volturcius, it is true, drew his sword and called on the others to resist, but in the end, in fear and diffidence, he surrendered to the praetors, "velut hostibus" (45. 4). Questioned in the Senate, he at first pretended ignorance and innocence until the promise of immunity persuaded him to tell all he knew (47. 1).

Volturcius bore a message from Lentulus that sealed the doom of the conspirators: it urged Catilina to raise the slaves—"auxilium . . . etiam ab infumis" (44. 5). Now Catilina, as Sallust states explicitly at a later stage, refused to have slaves in his army (56. 5). It was not enough to prove by signed documents that Lentulus and his associates were in treasonable negotiation with a Gallic tribe. The odium of a *bellum servile* was fastened on them.[88] The message carried by Volturcius was providential for Cicero.[89]

It was expedient to terrify the possessing classes. Volturcius, it appears, also provided revelations about the plan of the conspirators in Rome—they were going to set fire to the city in twelve places (43. 2). That alarmed the urban plebs. They had previously been strong for Catilina (48. 1, cf. 37. 1).[90]

---

[88] Note how careful Caesar is to impugn his adversaries on that charge (*BC* I. 24. 2; 34. 2; 56. 3; 57. 3).

[89] That is to say, the counterplot may have been well laid, with Volturcius a good actor.

[90] The loyalty to the Roman government of "tenuissimi," of freedmen and shopkeepers, is fervently asserted by Cicero (*In Cat.* IV. 16 f).

VII

THE CREDULITY
OF SALLUST

In the prologue Sallust proclaims
that history is not at all easy—"arduom videtur res gestas scribere" (3. 2). In the first place, style and execution have to correspond with the theme—"facta dictis exaequanda." Next, when a
writer permits himself to allocate praise and blame, he is likely
to be misconstrued, the blame being put down to malignity,
whereas the praise fails to win credence because men hate to admit
excellence beyond their reach.[1]

A little further on, concluding his personal apologia, Sallust
affirms that he has no cause to write in a partisan spirit.[2] Ought
he not to have said something more—how hard it is to ascertain
the bare facts? That prime impediment was also neglected by
Cicero. Apart from style, honesty seems to be all that is needed.
As Cicero says in *De oratore*, the writer must tell the truth, and
the whole truth; he must not be swayed by favour or animosity.[3]

Sallust underestimated the difficulty of his new vocation. The
subject was recent history, with a plethora of evidence. Therein
lay the danger. It may be added that later writers in antiquity
(and modern critics) have not always been exempt from error and

---

[1] Exemplary sentiments, and enunciated long since, cf. Thucydides II.
35. 2; Isocrates, *Pan.* 13.

[2] 4. 2: "eo magis quod mihi a spe metu partibus rei publicae animus liber
erat."

[3] *De oratore* II. 62: "nam quis nescit primam esse historiae legem ne quid
falsi dicere audeat; deinde ne quid veri non audeat; ne quae suspicio
gratiae sit in scribendo; ne quae simultatis?"

confusion. A number of mistakes can be detected in Sallust's account. There is something worse, credulity.

Sallust used speeches of Cicero. Orators in forensic and electoral contests had a marvellous licence of abuse and defamation. The Romans worshipped *libertas,* enjoyed invective and revelled in scurrility. Contemporaries had their fun and recreation. Posterity is sometimes deceived; and, overawed by the renown of the great orator (and forgetting what a name he had for wit and humour), posterity admits with docile assent the wildest allegations. Sallust, however, ought to have been on his guard. He knew what manner of charges, scandalous or comic, were raked up against Clodius, Vatinius, Gabinius, Piso; and he had recently been reading the classic of political defamation, the artful and eloquent *Second Philippic,* immortal and deplorable.

The oration *In toga candida* retailed a variety of allegations about the behaviour of Catilina. First, deeds of blood when Sulla captured Rome. It was Catilina who, when M. Marius Gratidianus was butchered and mutilated, cut off the head and carried it through the streets of Rome from the Janiculum to the Temple of Apollo.[4] Also three other murders (Cicero furnished the names).[5] Next, he alluded to the affair of the Vestal Virgins (in 73), but only in a covert way. He could not exploit the theme fully, for Fabia, accused of adultery with Catilina, was acquitted —and she was a half-sister of Cicero's wife.[6] Finally, among Catilina's many acts of adultery was one that led to incest in the sequel. Catilina married the daughter of his mistress—his own child. The same charge was brought up in a speech by L. Lucceius, so Asconius reports. The commentator, who takes manifest pride in his erudite researches, with an especial delight in the identification of persons, is here at a loss. He confesses that so far he has not been able to ascertain the names of the women in question.[7]

---

[4] Asconius 80, cf. 75; 78.

[5] ib 75: "Q. Caecilium, M. Volumnium, L. Tanusium."

[6] ib. 82, cf. Orosius VI. 3. 1. Asconius praises the orator's decent reticence —"ita et suis pepercit et nihilo levius inimico summi opprobrii turpitudinem obiecit."

[7] ib. 82: "hoc Lucceius quoque Catilinae obiecit in orationibus quas in eum scripsit. nomina harum mulierum nondum inveni."

Asconius despaired too soon. The allusion points to Catilina's last (perhaps third) wife, the beautiful Aurelia Orestilla, whom the historian condemned in a curt phrase.[8] The previous wife earns an anonymous reference in Cicero's *First Catilinarian*; the villain, having recently got her out of the way, piled one crime on another (i.e., the murder of his son).[9]

It will be suitable to round off the catalogue of enormities with items from two other writers. The *Commentariolum Petitionis* (assigned to Q. Cicero, but highly dubious)[10] alleges that at the time of the Sullan proscriptions Catilina destroyed his brother-in-law, a harmless Roman knight called Q. Caecilius.[11] Plutarch, however, states that Catilina killed his own brother and had his name put on the lists posthumously; further, that Catilina was guilty of incest with his daughter.[12]

Turning to Sallust on these topics, one experiences surprise if not disappointment. No word of the murders perpetrated by Sulla's henchman. That item ought to have been attractive to the author. Especially M. Marius Gratidianus, a prominent politician —nephew of C. Marius, and also the first cousin of Cicero's father.[13] Furthermore, if an inference from a fragment of Sallust's own *Historiae* be allowed validity, Catilina's wife (i.e., his first

---

[8] 15. 2: "postremo captus amore Aureliae Orestillae, quoius praeter formam nihil umquam bonus laudavit." Clearly a daughter of the inconspicuous Cn. Aufidius Orestes (*cos.* 71), who was by birth an Aurelius Orestes, of consular descent. No conjecture can reach to her allegedly adulterous mother.

[9] *In Cat.* I. 14: "nuper cum morte superioris uxoris novis nuptiis locum vacuefecisses, nonne etiam alio incredibili scelere hoc scelus cumulavisti? quod ego praetermitto et facile patior sileri."

[10] Against authenticity compare the powerful arguments of M. I. Henderson, *JRS* XL (1950), 8 ff.; R. G. Nisbet, ib. LI (1961), 84 ff.

[11] *Comm.Pet.* 9: "Q. Caecilium, sororis suae virum, equitem Romanum, nullarum partium." On this suspect item, cf. M. I. Henderson, o.c. 10. Cicero's speech, according to Asconius (75), registered a Q. Caecilius, but with no hint of any relationship to Catilina.

[12] Plutarch, *Sulla* 32; *Cicero* 10. The brother lacks attestation; and note that incest with a daughter is here alleged, not marriage, as Cicero and Lucceius said (Asconius 82).

[13] F. Münzer, *R-E* XIV, 1825 ff. The parent, M. Gratidius of Arpinum, married Marius' sister; and a sister of Gratidius was the wife of Cicero's grandfather. Asconius was aware of a close kinship (75).

wife) was a Gratidia, a sister of M. Marius Gratidianus.[14] An important consequence follows. Catilina, like a number of other *nobiles,* was a renegade from the party of Marius and Cinna. Perhaps Sallust's information was defective at this stage in his researches—or his curiosity not yet aroused.

Instead, one finds it registered that this scoundrel seduced a "virgo nobilis," and also a Vestal Virgin (15. 1). The identity of the former would baffle any Asconius. As for the latter, she is Fabia, who was pronounced guiltless. Not very convincing examples of the "multa nefanda stupra."

Next, wife and family. To win Aurelia Orestilla, who did not want to be bothered with a stepson in the home, Catilina killed his own son. Sallust supports the item with the words "pro certo creditur" (15. 2). His source may be Cicero, as some suppose on a resemblance of phraseology.[15] Nothing is said by Sallust about the alleged fate of the previous wife.

The historian exploits this crime for a venture into psychology, dramatic effect, extravagant language and an illicit linking of events. Guilt and remorse dwelt with Catilina, night and day. He showed all the symptoms in his eyes, countenance, and gait. He was impelled to push on with his violent and revolutionary designs.[16]

The literary device enables the historian himself to come quickly to the formation of the plot. After describing in general terms the adherents of Catilina and the political situation, he produces an assembly at Catilina's house (with the fifteen names) shortly before the elections in 64 (17). But, before Catilina delivers his harangue, there is interpolated a digression about a previous conspiracy that formed in 66—"sed antea item coniuravere pauci contra rem publicam" (18 f.).

---

[14] *Hist.* I. 45: "et liberis eius avunculus erat," cf. the *Scholia Bernensia* on Lucan II. 173: "hunc Marium Gratidianum, uxoris suae fratrem." It can be taken that Catilina promptly discarded her.

[15] *In Cat.* I. 14. The resemblance is not close.

[16] 15. 4 f.: "namque animus inpurus, dis hominibusque infestus, neque vigiliis neque quietibus sedari poterat: ita conscientia mentem excitam vastabat. igitur colos ei exsanguis, foedi oculi, citus modo modo tardus incessus: prorsus in facie voltuque vecordia inerat."

That "conspiracy" is a peculiar fabrication, with variant versions and interchangeable names. It will be expedient to disentangle the original facts (they are few) and briefly trace the proliferations of rumour, allegation, and fable that confronted Sallust.

The whole context of 67 and 66 demands attention.[17] The leaders of the Optimates offered bitter resistance to Gabinius' bill that created the command for Pompeius against the Pirates. They had a strong champion in one of the consuls, C. Piso, also several tribunes at their call. The bill was passed amid scenes of disorder. Gabinius on one occasion threatened to depose Piso. Then, violence growing as the time of the polls drew near, the Senate instructed the consuls to use a bodyguard for their protection.[18] Among the competitors was a declared adherent of Pompeius, namely M. Lollius Palicanus, who had played a notable role in negotiations in 71. The consul Piso stood firm: he refused to admit the candidature of Palicanus. M'. Lepidus was elected, a good oligarch, with the colourless L. Volcacius Tullus for colleague.

Pompeius absent, the spirits of the Optimates revived. They could now hope to regain control of affairs.[19] Also, take vengeance on pestilential tribunes.

Gabinius escaped harm by going away to serve as legate under Pompeius. But C. Cornelius, who had been active with legislation to curb the illicit influence of the "pauci," was vulnerable. However, his friends organised gangs, they frightened off the prosecutors, the case was dropped. Later, on renewed charges in 65, five of the "principes civitatis" came forward to testify against Cornelius.[20]

Manilius was in for trouble, the author of the bill transferring

---

[17] The principal evidence derives from Plutarch, *Pompeius* 25 ff.; Dio XXXVI. 30; 36 ff.; Asconius, *In Cornelianam*.

[18] Dio XXXVI. 39. 1.

[19] As Sallust says, "plebis opes inminutae, paucorum potentia crevit" (39. 1).

[20] Asconius 53: "dixerunt in eum infesti testimonia principes civitatis qui plurimum in senatu poterant: Q. Hortensius, Q. Catulus, Q. Metellus Pius, M. Lucullus, M'. Lepidus."

Lucullus' command to Pompeius. Scarcely had his office expired in
December of 66 than he had to face an indictment—which, how-
ever, was deferred through an artifice of the praetor Cicero.[21]
Anger and discord accumulated.

Other items are relevant. Earlier in the year another enemy of
the Optimates had been prosecuted and condemned for *repetundae*, Licinius Macer (*tr. pl.* 73, *pr.* 68);[22] also, it can be suggested,
a certain L. Vargunteius for *ambitus*.[23]

As for the consular elections, one candidate, L. Sergius Catilina,
returning from the governorship of Africa, was blocked. That was
done by the consul L. Volcacius Tullus, after a consultation with
senior statesmen.[24] P. Cornelius Sulla and P. Autronius Paetus
won the election; but their defeated rivals, L. Manlius Torquatus
and L. Aurelius Cotta, put in an indictment for bribery. After two
attempts to break up the court with bands of gladiators and slaves,
Autronius and Sulla were condemned.[25] Torquatus and Cotta
were then elected. A fine collection of malcontents could have
mustered at the end of this exciting year. In the first place, Autronius and Sulla. Then Vargunteius—and Catilina, over whom hung
a prosecution for *repetundae*.

Some sort of demonstration was planned for January 1 against
the new consuls. The Senate voted them a bodyguard, nothing
happened, and no enquiry (a tribune intervened with his veto).[26]
Not long after, one of the quaestors, Cn. Calpurnius Piso, was
selected by decree of the Senate to be governor of Hispania
Citerior.[27] Piso was an enemy of Pompeius Magnus. That anomalous appointment caused talk and speculation. It was natural

---

[21] Dio XXXVI. 44. 1 f. Cicero as praetor set the trial for the last day of
the year, and, on protests at his conduct, promised to defend Manilius in
due course later on. When Manilius was prosecuted in 65 for *maiestas*, there
were disturbances (Asconius 58). Some scholars have incautiously transferred
that rioting to the last day of 66, thus E. G. Hardy, *JRS* VII (1917), 159 f.

[22] P. 47.

[23] Vargunteius' condemnation (*Pro Sulla* 6) can conveniently be assigned to
66.

[24] Asconius 79 f.

[25] *Pro Sulla* 15.

[26] Dio XXXVI. 44. 4 f.

[27] For his title, "quaestor pro praetore," cf. CIL I². 749 = *ILS* 875.

to assume (and probably true) that the job was managed by M. Crassus.[28] None the less, a small pretext could have been adduced for sending a quaestor. Few of the praetors of 66 seem to have wanted a province.[29] Piso was assassinated by natives in Spain.

That is all that can with safety be affirmed. Next, the growth of the legend. Cicero in the speech *In toga candida* (summer, 64) says that he will pass over Catilina's plot, in concert with Piso (to mention nobody else), the plot to massacre the Optimates. "Praetereo nefarium illum conatum tuum." [30] Why be so indulgent towards the rival he is seeking to damage? This engaging type of insinuation does not lack parallel. In the invective against P. Vatinius, Cicero generously withholds the full disclosure of that person's murky past: it is no concern of Cicero if the young Vatinius robbed his neighbours, burgled houses, and beat his mother.[31]

The speech carried a second reference to Cn. Piso. He is alluded to as the "stiletto in Spain." [32] Piso being now dead, there was free scope for the posthumous discovery of nefarious activities.

In the *First Catilinarian,* Cicero comes out with a plain bold assertion: on the last day of December, Catilina stood armed in the Comitium, he had gathered a band to murder the consuls and the "principes civitatis." [33] And the *Pro Murena* has a reference to the plot of Catilina and Cn. Piso to massacre the Senate.[34]

Most instructive is the speech *Pro Sulla,* and on various counts. The Catilinarians Autronius, Vargunteius, and others having been tried and condemned, P. Sulla seemed vulnerable from his past career, if nothing else. Young Manlius Torquatus set on him, the son of the consul of 65. Cicero undertook the defence, for an enormous fee.[35] The task called for unusual skill and equivocation.

---

[28] Thus Sallust (19. 1).

[29] Five of the eight praetors of 66 can be securely established (Broughton, *MRR* II, 151 f.). Cicero and C. Antonius did not govern provinces; and there is no evidence about the others.

[30] Asconius 82.

[31] *In Vatinium* 11.

[32] Asconius 83.

[33] *In Cat.* I. 15.

[34] *Pro Murena* 81.

[35] Gellius XII. 12. 2 ff.

His oration is so mendacious all through, it has been affirmed, that one must believe the opposite of what Cicero asserts.[36] The pronouncement is hasty and unjust. Cicero was much more crafty than that.

The advocate had much to explain away, including statements and conduct of his own. Early in the speech he alludes vaguely to the "former conspiracy," professing ignorance: he was not at the heart of affairs, he had not been initiated into governmental counsels.[37] That is a strange statement to come from one of the praetors of 66, the most alert and active of them all. At a later stage Cicero runs into trouble because, as the prosecutor pointed out, Cicero had linked the two conspiracies in his letter to Pompeius Magnus.[38] The advocate must therefore exert himself to disculpate P. Sulla. He essays two devices. First, all the blame on the violent Autronius for the two riots when he and Sulla stood trial in 66; the virtuous Sulla sought no help but "suus pudor ac dignitas." [39] Second, he drags in Catilina.

The orator designates Catilina, Cn. Piso, Autronius, and Vargunteius as the culprits; and he implies that Catilina and Autronius were to have taken the place of the murdered consuls.[40] But, having removed P. Sulla and substituted Catilina, he comes onto slippery ground. The consul Manlius Torquatus had testified for Catilina at the trial for *repetundae* in 65.[41] Cicero somehow manages to play down that fact (which ought to have disproved Catilina's participation in a plot to murder Torquatus). The consul Torquatus supported Catilina because he was a friend; and, according to Cicero, he said that he had heard something or other about a conspiracy, but refused credence.[42]

Sulla was acquitted. No complicity therefore in either con-

---

[36] E. Meyer, *Caesars Monarchie und das Principat des Pompejus*[3] (1922), 21.

[37] *Pro Sulla* 11: "quod nondum penitus in re publica versabar, quod nondum ad propositum mihi finem honoris perveneram."

[38] ib. 67.

[39] ib. 15, cf. 71 (the detestable character of Autronius).

[40] ib. 67 f.

[41] ib. 81.

[42] ib. 81: "se audisse aliquid, non credidisse."

spiracy. Cicero's version is accepted by Sallust. He may have been influenced by a prepossession in favour of P. Sulla, whom he had known.[43]

A neglected aspect of the two electoral contests in 66 will repay scrutiny. Catilina, P. Sulla and Manlius Torquatus were patricians. Only one of them could be elected. Catilina would have to make his bid in concert with a plebeian candidate, Autronius or somebody else. The consul Volcacius Tullus, debarring Catilina, promoted the chances of either Torquatus or P. Sulla. Perhaps he was for Sulla, who with Autronius secured election. As for Catilina, out of the running himself, he now had the choice of supporting either of the two patricians. Nothing shows that he was for Sulla. If he helped Torquatus now and at the second contest, all is clear. Torquatus in the next year exhibits gratitude and amity. It is not likely that Catilina went with Sulla and Autronius in a plot (or demonstration) against Torquatus and Cotta. Catilina can be disjoined from Sulla—but not in the way Cicero argued.

Sallust's account registers the mishap of Autronius and Sulla, but omits Sulla from the "conspiracy." Instead, it is the plot devised by Catilina (who has the prime role), along with Autronius and Piso (18). The consuls killed, Catilina and Autronius were to seize the *fasces* and send Piso to take charge of both Spanish provinces. News got out, however, and they postponed action until February 5 (when, along with the consuls, many senators were to be killed). But Catilina gave the signal too soon, and nothing happened. Subsequently Cn. Piso went out to govern Hispania Citerior (19.1). That was due to the exertions of Crassus, for Piso was a bitter enemy of Pompeius; and the Senate concurred, for various reasons.[44]

The question arises, why did Sallust take seriously the story in this version or in any version? It is a tissue of improbabilities. None the less, it was believed and perpetuated. Livy, it appears, kept Sulla in the plot, conflating two versions. The *Periocha* of

---

[43] P. 71.

[44] 19. 2: "neque tamen senatus provinciam invitus dederat, quippe foedum hominem a re publica procul esse volebat, simul quia boni complures praesidium in eo putabant et iam tum potentia Pompei formidulosa erat."

Book CI has a reference to the conspiracy of Autronius and Sulla (without the names).[45] It is not likely that Livy pushed criticism and scepticism so far as to disallow Catilina and Piso. Cassius Dio (who may be supposed to follow the Livian tradition) has the plot of Autronius and Sulla, who were joined by the other two.[46]

It is perhaps superfluous to add that if there were anything to deserve the name of a plot against the consuls of 65, it is Autronius and Sulla who had a grievance. Catilina, however, was a friend of Torquatus. If Catilina stood in the Comitium with a dagger, it was perhaps to defend rather than assassinate Torquatus. As for Cn. Piso, anything could be said about him in the aftermath.

It is Suetonius who supplies, so it seems, the clue to Sallust's procedure. Caesar, he says, was suspected of planning a coup d'état along with Crassus, Autronius and Sulla.[47] After killing a number of senators on January 1, Crassus would seize the dictatorship, with Caesar as his *magister equitum,* while Sulla and Autronius would get their consulship back. Suetonius cites a farrago of "authorities" (on whom more later); and reasons are adduced for the failure of the attempt—Crassus did not turn up on the appointed day (from fear, or because he thought better of it), and therefore Caesar did not give the agreed signal. The biographer also registers a subversive movement in northern Italy, arranged by Caesar in concert with Cn. Piso, to take effect after Piso was installed in Spain.[48]

In this version, Catilina gets left out. That is significant.[49] Once

---

[45] Livy, *Per.* CI: "coniuratio eorum qui in petitione consulatus ambitus damnati erant, facta de interficiendis consulibus obpressa est."

[46] Dio XXXVI. 44. 3 ff. E. Schwartz stated an extreme view: Dio's narrative of this period down to the death of Caesar, and probably further, derives solely from Livy, "aus Livius und nur aus Livius" (*Hermes* XXXII [1897], 583). Most implausible. For Dio's methods and merits see the overfavourable estimate of E. Meyer, o.c. 610 f.

[47] Suetonius, *Divus Iulius* 9.

[48] ib. 9. 3: "pactumque ut simul foris ille, ipse Romae ad res novas consurgerent, per Ambranos et Transpadanos; destitutum utriusque consilium morte Pisonis."

[49] These allegations against Caesar failed to get incorporated in the standard tradition. They were discovered in forgotten historians—and Suetonius does not seem aware that he is narrating a version of the "First Conspiracy of Catilina." Cf. M. I. Henderson, o.c. 13 f.

again interchangeable names, as in Cicero's defence of P. Sulla. This time Sulla is kept—and there is much more of names and details. The mention of Crassus and Caesar makes many things clear. In the campaign of 64 they had been running Catilina against Cicero. That is stated by Asconius in his commentary on *In toga candida*, with a reference to *De consiliis suis*.[50] Further Sallust, describing the meeting of conspirators in 64, reports a belief that Crassus would emerge and take charge if they succeeded: his motive was hostility to Pompeius.[51] Attempts were made to get both of them implicated in 63, and the allegations were not forgotten. If one conspiracy, why not both? Cicero in *De consiliis* asserted that Crassus had been behind the murder plot of Catilina and Cn. Piso.[52] As for Caesar, no mention here. But the imputation can be traced back as far as 59: Suetonius cites in evidence the edicts of the consul Calpurnius Bibulus and the orations of Scribonius Curio.[53]

Sallust was aware of those charges and the like. If he disbelieved them, three ways offered.

First, Sallust might have thrown doubt on the alleged plot to murder the consuls of 65, by whomsoever engineered, or he might have discarded the story altogether. It needed no great acuity to discern vulnerable aspects or interested motives: for example, P. Sulla disculpated in order to bring in Catilina. But Sallust, following Cicero (that is the irony), credits a "first conspiracy" with Catilina as the prime mover.

Second, Sallust might have admitted and proclaimed that Catilina did not become a dangerous revolutionary before his failure in 63. He would be free to demonstrate that no reproach attached if a man was a secret ally of Catilina previously—or an open champion. Eminent consulars had spoken for Catilina when he was on trial in 65 and in 64.[54] Cicero himself had once thought

---

50 Asconius 74.
51 17. 7: "fuere item ea tempestate qui crederent M. Licinium Crassum non ignarum eius consili fuisse: quia Cn. Pompeius, invisus ipsi, magnum exercitum ductabat, quoiusvis opes voluisse contra illius potentiam crescere."
52 Asconius 74.
53 Suetonius, *Divus Iulius* 9. 2.
54 *Pro Sulla* 81 ff.

of being his advocate in 65, as a letter happens to reveal.[55] (Sallust will not have known that item.) Moreover, both Crassus and Caesar were behind Catilina's candidature in the summer of 64. But Sallust has committed himself to the notion that the great conspiracy took shape precisely at that time.

Sallust was forced into the third path. He had allowed himself to believe that Catilina was the predestined villain and criminal, the corrupt product of a corrupt system, hounded on by crime and a bad conscience. Lending credence to a story about a murder plot, and further admitting the Ciceronian version of that story, Sallust thought that it sufficed to clear Caesar if he disregarded the allegation against Caesar.

The purpose of Sallust can be divined—at least so it seems. But, it might be asked, has he not distorted history by suppressing valuable information about Crassus as well as about Caesar? It will be expedient to cast a passing glance at the ostensible conspirators and their peculiar behaviour.

They had a precise plan, to murder the consuls. The plan was extensible—it could include as victims the consulars and a great mass of other senators. And, a further advantage, it admitted postponement. However, those desperadoes put up a miserable performance. They show their hand, nothing happens, nobody is incommoded, and Manlius Torquatus bears no malice.

How explain the paradox? Many scholars of gravity and repute believe in the existence of a conspiracy.[56] They inadvertently betray the case by the weakness of their explanations. Catilina, it is said, "was observed to be making overt preparations for some kind of foul play." And further, "the rashness of the conspirators in inviting detection was matched by their luck in escaping punishment." [57]

If authentic, the comportment of the conspirators might be

---

[55] *Ad Att.* I. 2. 1: "hoc tempore Catilinam competitorem nostrum defendere cogitamus." Fenestella thought that he did so (Asconius 76): perhaps deceived by a pastiche.

[56] The names are chronicled by H. Frisch, *Class. et Med.* IX (1947), 21 ff. See below, n. 86.

[57] Thus M. Cary in *CAH* IX (1932), 476 f.

put down to an essay in intimidation rather than violence and murder intended; and, if they could induce a consul to seek protection or don a breastplate under his toga, they would show him no true "consul populi Romani." For the rest, when an alleged scheme fails of action because somebody gave the signal too soon or somebody else neglected to turn up, there are grounds for scepticism or ridicule. Cicero in one of his orations had an easy game when mocking a story about men who emerged too soon from ambush in a bath house.[58]

Careless and incompetent, these conspirators. No matter. They were only tools and agents. Behind them stood power and resolution—Crassus, with Caesar for ally. Hence the theory, based on Suetonius (of all people), that Crassus and Caesar plotted a genuine and complete coup d'état. The theory derives from allegations made by enemies of Caesar. By paradox, it has been eagerly embraced by those who admire and enhance him, being commended by weighty authority and persuasive to many in the sequel. It will be salutary to put on brief record the "plot of Crassus," as it has been expounded in the extremest form, which combines the various rumours and allegations (though certain items are patently alternative and interchangeable), and comes close to romantic fiction in the guise of scholarly reconstruction.[59]

About December 5 of the year 66 Crassus convoked a meeting at his house. Autronius and Sulla were there, likewise Catilina and Piso. Also (one notes with some surprise) Caesar, the praetor C. Antonius—and even P. Sittius of Nuceria (one misses L. Vargunteius). The action planned for January 1 fell through and was put off to February 5. In the meantime, Cn. Piso had managed to get himself sent to Spain, and be killed there. In consequence of which, Caesar, who was free from the rancour and illusions of Crassus, Caesar who disliked bloodshed and now became conscious of the fact that the consul Cotta was a near kinsman, sud-

---

[58] *Pro Caelio* 64: "quos quidem tu quam ob rem temere prosiluisse dicas atque ante tempus non reperio."

[59] J. Carcopino, *Histoire romaine* II (1936), 610 ff. Compare the verdict of H. Frisch, o.c. 35: "the fairy tale . . . which . . . became a main point in modern historiography, reaching its climax in Carcopino's novel."

denly decided to wreck the whole affair. He deliberately refrained from lifting up his toga, the agreed sign for the massacre.

No words need be wasted on the miraculous celerity with which Piso's journey was consummated, his opportune decease (while leading an army in the back country) reported at Rome. It will be enough to point out that the assembly at the house of Crassus is a complete fabrication. Asconius is cited. But Asconius is here commenting on a reference in Cicero to the electoral campaign in 64: the candidates Catilina and Antonius were at the house of a certain *nobilis* who was a master in the technique of distributing bribes (either Crassus or Caesar, so the commentator opines).[60]

In this reconstruction, credulity and error have been seconded by fantasy. It will be observed that only Suetonius (of extant writers) incriminates Caesar. He names several authorities. That is impressive, on a surface view. The authorities need to be scrutinised.[61]

Nothing is known about M. Actorius Naso.[62] Tanusius Geminus was a historian, an elusive figure. One thing is clear: he was hostile to Caesar.[63] Suetonius also cites the edicts of Bibulus and the orations of Scribonius Curio. Startling erudition, but deceptive. The biographer probably got those items from the forgotten historian he had dragged up, namely Tanusius Geminus. Bibulus and Curio are contemporary. Of what value and validity? Nobody would worry much about what the consul Calpurnius Bibulus asseverated, even in an edict. Bibulus was a baffled and an angry man: Caesar in the *Bellum Civile* alludes to his "iracundia." [64] The testimony of Scribonius Curio is an even worse case. Not everybody has observed that the eminent consular had a hopeless memory and was pathologically inaccurate. Entertaining instances

---

[60] Asconius 74.

[61] H. Strasburger, *Caesars Eintritt in die Geschichte* (1938), 107 f., cf. 26.

[62] Except that he is the Naso who reported Caesar's amours with Eunoe, the wife of a Mauretanian prince (Suetonius, *Divus Iulius* 52. 1).

[63] For Tanusius, cf. F. Münzer, *R-E* IV A, 2231 ff. Other items in Suetonius where Curio and Bibulus are cited can be claimed for Tanusius (49. 1 f.; 50. 1; 52. 3). It is worth noting that the learned Asconius ignored him. W. A. Baehrens regarded the testimony of Tanusius as "äusserst zuverlässig" (*Neue Wege zur Antike* IV [1926], 55): how could he tell?

[64] Caesar, *BC* III. 8. 3; 16. 3.

are vouched for by Cicero.[65] Curio in 59 delivered violent speeches against Caesar. In the version he worked up for publication, he inadvertently stated that he had never entered the Senate during Caesar's consulship; and he brought in a reference to Caesar's conduct in Gaul.

Bibulus and old Curio can be discarded without loss or repining. The remaining "authority" is Cicero in a letter to Axius: Caesar planned a "regnum" when he was aedile and established it as consul. The term "regnum" is sinister and conventional. Suetonius, while eager to advertise the range and depth of his scholarly researches, betrays his failure to understand the political language of the Roman Republic.[66]

Such is the evidence that has been taken up and embraced, incautiously or with avidity. The plot of Crassus and Caesar entailed or enlisted the notion that these men were the leaders of the "Popular Party." Their aim was to get control of the State, not only against the Optimates but as enemies of Pompeius.[67]

Crassus (it is supposed) was seeking to establish a base of armed power against Pompeius. Hence, to be sure, the sending of Cn. Piso to Hispania Citerior in the year 65. But Crassus in the sequel seems to lose all interest in the Spains. Again, Crassus proposes to enroll the communities of Transpadane Italy on the list of citizens, but is thwarted by the other censor, Lutatius Catulus.[68]

---

[65] *Brutus* 218 f.

[66] H. Strasburger, o.c. 108; W. Allen, *TAPA* LXXXIV (1953), 227 ff.

[67] For this "traditional" notion, cf. E. G. Hardy, *JRS* VII (1917) 155; J. Carcopino, *Histoire romaine* II (1936), 663: "les chefs du parti populaire." And, in its extreme form, A. Rosenberg, *Einleitung und Quellenkunde zur römischen Geschichte* (1921), 175: "tatsächlich war Catilina in den Jahren 66–63 nur ein Gehilfe der Popularpartei und ihrer Führer Caesar-Crassus im Kampf gegen die Optimaten und Pompeius." It is further suspicious and revealing when scholars have the order "Caesar and Crassus," e.g. L. Pareti, *La congiura di Catilina* (1934), 200: "quando Cesare e Crasso concepirono il colpo di stato." E. G. Hardy uses that order several times and (in reference to 63) adds "that Caesar was already looked to by the populares as their real head seems clear" (*Some Problems in Roman History* [1924], 99). It is fallacious to put Caesar on a level with Crassus (consul and censor) before 59—or even later. And it is no help to speak, as does Hardy, of Crassus' "comparative indifference to politics" (*JRS* VII [1917], 155).

[68] Dio XXXVII. 9. 3 (the only evidence).

Crassus, it is suggested, had his eye on the military potential of
that region.[69] Then he tries to have Egypt annexed—which is
prevented by Catulus.[70] In another version of this episode, it is
alleged that Caesar, using tribunes, attempted to get himself a
special command in Egypt: that was blocked by the "factio
optimatium." [71]

So far, failure on the foreign front. And no luck at home.
Crassus and Caesar help Catilina, but Cicero gets elected. Cicero
on the first day of his consulship brought to defeat the grandiose
agrarian law of Servilius Rullus. Cicero affirms that the tribune
is only an agent, the real authors are in the background (one is
perhaps meant to surmise Crassus and Caesar).[72] Cicero further
argues that the bill is really an attack on Pompeius Magnus.[73]

That notion was attractive—and superficial. Doubts may be
conceived on examination of some of Caesar's known activities in
this year. Caesar prosecutes the consular C. Piso for extortion and
the execution of a Transpadane.[74] C. Piso, the consul of 67,
was a bitter enemy of Pompeius. When C. Rabirius was put on
trial for murder on an archaic form of procedure, the hand of
Caesar can plausibly be discerned. But proceedings were cut short
by a device of the praetor Metellus Celer.[75] This man had been
serving as a legate of Pompeius in the East; and the tribune T.

---

[69] M. Cary in *CAH* IX (1932), 481: "presumably, therefore, the main
object of Crassus' manifesto was to secure the military support of the Trans-
padanes, as Carbo in the civil war against Sulla had won that of the Samnites."

[70] *De lege agraria* II. 44; Plutarch, *Crassus* 13.

[71] Suetonius, *Divus Iulius* 11. This is accepted by M. Gelzer, *Caesar*[6] (1960),
36. For due scepticism, H. Strasburger, o.c. 112 ff.

[72] *De lege agraria* II. 20. For a catalogue of modern opinions, see
A. Afzelius, *Class. et Med.* III (1940), 222 f. Hardy even makes Caesar the
sole originator (*Some Problems in Roman History* [1924], 68 ff.). Against,
H. Strasburger, o.c. 114 ff. However, the insistence on a *lex curiata* for the
election of the agrarian commissioners (ib. 26) may reflect the antiquarian
expertise of Caesar.

[73] ib. 49: "dum patefacio vobis quas isti penitus abstrusas insidias se
posuisse arbitrantur contra Cn. Pompei dignitatem."

[74] Hence his rancour against Caesar (49. 2). Cicero defended Piso (*Pro
Flacco* 98).

[75] Dio XXXVII. 27. 3.

Labienus who prosecuted Rabirius was a firm partisan of Pompeius, it can be argued.[76] Collusion is the answer.

On the face of things, a run of disappointments all along the line, ever since the "first conspiracy." Curiosity asks whether the authors of some of the projects ever hoped, or intended, those projects to succeed. Demonstrations had been made, appetites whetted—and the Optimates harried and annoyed. The Transpadani could be kept waiting for their enfranchisement (they had to wait a long time); and the bill of Rullus might be saved up or brought out in different dress when the People's general needed lands for his veterans.[77]

Crassus did not forfeit influence in these years, and the star of Caesar rose steadily.[78] His curule aedileship is significant of success —holders of that magistracy seldom fail to reach the consulate. When praetor-designate he won the office of *pontifex maximus*, defeating Lutatius Catulus. And, in the historic debate on the Catilinarian conspirators Caesar took a bold line. He had made many enemies, it was dangerous—and it was worth it.

In the first days of his praetorship, Caesar is found acting in concert with Metellus Nepos, sent back by Pompeius to be tribune and protect his interests.[79] The Imperator himself would soon be returning. Where would he look for support and allies?

To revert to Sallust. He goes out of his way to narrate, with names and details, a plot to assassinate the consuls L. Manlius Torquatus and L. Aurelius Cotta. It would have been expedient to assess the evidence and probabilities. Presenting as he does the "first conspiracy," the author runs into various kinds of trouble.

The skill of Sallust in structural composition is generally praised.[80] This digression, however, is not well placed. It comes

---

[76] cf. the arguments adduced in *JRS* XXVIII (1938), 113 ff.

[77] That is to say, it crops up again in the *Lex Flavia* of 60 (*Ad Att.* I. 18. 6) and in the legislation of 59.

[78] For this conception, cf. H. Strasburger, o.c. 126 ff.; R. Syme, *JRS* XXVIII (1938), 116 f.; ib. XXXIV (1944), 97 f., reviewing M. Gelzer, *Caesar*[3] (1941).

[79] Suetonius, *Divus Iulius* 16. 1.

[80] Fronto p. 114 N = II. 48 (Haines): "historiam quoque scripsere, Sallustius structe, Pictor incondite," etc.

between the assembly of the conspirators in 64 (17) and the oration they were to hear from their leader (20). Perhaps it was an afterthought. In epilogue on the list of conspirators, Sallust mentioned secret sympathisers and named M. Licinius Crassus: among his motives was hostility to Pompeius (17. 7). That theme, it might be supposed, evoked Crassus in relation to Cn. Piso, a decided enemy of Pompeius: Piso who was sent to Spain through the exertions of Crassus (19. 1), and who was there assassinated by natives, faithful clients of Pompeius, so some held (19. 5). Hence, to explain and elucidate Piso, the author was drawn to expound the "first conspiracy." Piso played an important part therein, at least according to statements made by Cicero in 64 and in 63.[81]

If that is so, the digression forfeits most of the significance with which it has been invested. It ceases to be a clue to the general intention of the author or to the particular purpose of shielding Caesar by a studious omission of his name. Instead, the digression arose from a need of annotation, and it has no structural function either—on the contrary, it disturbs.

In any event, this passage, it can be argued, would have had a better lodgment before the assembly of conspirators (17. 1 ff.). For various reasons. One is historical continuity. Another is the abundance of personal names in the digression. Some of them occur in the assembly (and subsequently), but others not. Also, choosing to notice these transactions in a compressed form, the author renders himself liable to errors—and he makes a double error. Catilina's abortive candidature in 66 is put after the unseating of Autronius and Sulla, and Sallust assumes that Catilina was already under prosecution for extortion (18. 3).[82]

Further, two items germane to this affair crop up in Catilina's oration—one more slip, if not two. Encouraging his partisans, Catilina points to support abroad—Cn. Piso in Spain, P. Sittius in Mauretania with an army (21.3). Now Piso was dead before the summer of 64.[83] Sittius might have been in Mauretania more than once between 66 and 64, but not at the head of armed forces. He

---

[81] Asconius 74; 82; *Pro Murena* 81.

[82] According to Asconius, however (79 f.), Catilina was blocked by the consul L. Volcacius Tullus before the election of Autronius and Sulla. The order of events was established by C. John, *Rh. Mus.* XXXI (1876), 401 ff.

[83] Asconius 83.

was a Campanian banker who had lent a large sum of money to the Mauretanian king.[84] His exploits as a condottiere came twenty years later, in the Civil War, and were familiar indeed to Sallust. The truth about his earlier activities is not easy to disentangle. The prosecutor of P. Sulla alleged that Sulla had despatched Sittius to Hispania Ulterior to stir up trouble there in the interest of Catilina.[85] But, says Cicero, Sittius went to Spain before there was any suspicion of Catilina's conspiracy, he went in 64, it was for a necessary purpose, namely the debt owed by the King of Mauretania; further, Sittius had already been in those regions several years earlier. What then emerges? Only the chance that P. Sittius in fact visited Mauretania as well as Hispania Ulterior in 64 (those regions lay close together)—and that is not enough to vindicate wholly the accuracy of Sallust.

To conclude: Sallust comes out of this sorry affair not at all well. He believed (and with good cause) that the charges against Caesar were flimsy and fraudulent. But, for one reason or another, he took the "first conspiracy" seriously, and his authority has exercised a pernicious influence in the sequel.

If harsh words are in place, it is a little late in the day to condemn Sallust. Equity will not omit those scholars who, even if they reject the complicity of Caesar, have none the less accepted allegations about other characters, selecting or combining according to their fancy.[86] The whole edifice is ramshackle. It ought to have been demolished long ago.[87]

---

[84] For the life and actions of P. Sittius of Nuceria, see F. Münzer, *R-E* III A, 409 ff.

[85] *Pro Sulla* 56.

[86] H. Frisch, *Class. et Med.* IX (1947), 21 ff. He chronicles, beginning with Mommsen, the names of C. John, Meyer, Rosenberg, Gelzer, and Carcopino. Add that Rice Holmes admits Catilina and even allows Crassus, and probably Caesar, to give countenance to the intended coup d'état (*The Roman Republic* I [1923], 235, cf. 449). Note that Gelzer, while toning down his earlier account (*Caesar*³ [1941], 49) and now exculpating Caesar, none the less accepts a conspiracy of Sulla, Autronius, and Catilina (ed. 6, 34). A. La Penna, however, assumes that Caesar was probably in it: one of his reasons is the fact that P. Sulla was (later) a partisan of Caesar (*Stud.it.fil.class.* XXXI [1959], 35).

[87] The procedure of J. L. Strachan-Davidson was exemplary (and rarely

The deleterious consequences of the story have been many and various. One of them is the failure to keep the absent Pompeius in mind from 66 to 63—the neglect to look for links between Pompeius and the persons or activities of tribunes, consuls, and conspirators.[88]

---

imitated)—"the evidence is so inconclusive, and the story, as told, contains so many contradictions and improbabilities, that I prefer to pass it over as wholly or almost wholly apocryphal" (*Cicero and the Fall of the Roman Republic* [1894], 91). For a brief essay at demolition, see *JRS* XXXIV (1944), 96 f., in review of Gelzer, *Caesar*³ (1941); for the full exposure, H. Frisch, o.c. 10 ff.

[88] cf. E. Badian, discussing A. Gabinius and the Catilinarian P. Gabinius Capito (*Philologus* CIII [1959], 87 ff.). Alluding to the importance of the subject, he states that it invites further investigation.

A neglected link is to hand. (C.) Memmius, Pompeius' quaestor killed in Spain, was the husband of Pompeius' sister (Orosius V. 23. 12). Pompeia married P. Sulla not long after, as may be inferred from the existence of Sulla's stepson Memmius, with P. Sulla in 54 (*Ad Q. fratrem* III. 3. 2). Cf. F. Münzer, *R-E* XV, 616. This item (P. Sulla as brother-in-law of Magnus) may help to elucidate the elections in 66—and various other matters.

On Pompeius in relation to events at Rome in 63 and 62, see now C. Meier, *Athenaeum* XL (1962), 103 ff.

VIII

CAESAR AND CATO

After naming the conspirators mustered at the house of Catilina in 64, the historian alludes to secret allies and goes on to chronicle a belief then current: Crassus knew what was afoot, and he might exploit the enterprise for personal domination if it succeeded (17. 7). On this item follows the digression about the previous subversive movement at Rome and the sending of Cn. Piso to Spain (18 f.). That whole passage, it can be conjectured, was evoked by the mention of Crassus— and designed by the author as annotation on Crassus.[1]

Finally, the conspiracy itself. When the informer L. Tarquinius was questioned in the Senate on December 4, he uttered the name of Crassus (48. 4). His testimony was explicit—a message from Crassus to Catilina urging him not to lose heart. Some thought the revelation incredible, others believed it true (yet not expedient to be acted on), but a large number of senators, being bound by secret ties to Crassus, cried out in protest, and a decree of the Senate duly pronounced the fellow a perjurer. The historian subjoins comment. Some divined a device of Autronius, to imperil Crassus and thus induce him to protect the conspirators.[2] Others, however, held that Tarquinius had been put up by Cicero—and that was Crassus' own version.[3]

---

[1] For this thesis, cf. p. 100.

[2] 48. 7: "quo facilius appellato Crasso reliquos illius potentia tegeret." If Autronius had previously been an adherent of Crassus, that would be highly relevant to events in 66.

[3] 48. 9: "ipsum Crassum ego postea praedicantem audivi tantam illam contumeliam sibi ab Cicerone impositam." Possibly, as some conjecture, dur-

Crassus in resentment refused to attend the Senate on the following day. Whatever Crassus later proclaimed in public or told
Sallust, it is most unlikely that the consul would have wished to
antagonise Crassus at this critical stage. Moreover, it was Crassus
who, along with other senators, had previously given secret warning to Cicero about Catilina (before October 21). That was affirmed by Cicero in De consulatu suo.[4] He may have contradicted
himself later in De consiliis suis.

And now, Caesar. He crops up for the first time incidentally,
as one of the five senators (Crassus among them) to whose domestic custody the conspirators were entrusted after their arrest
(47. 4). Then, after the failed attempt to incriminate Crassus,
it is stated that Lutatius Catulus and C. Piso made strenuous
efforts to induce Cicero to bring out evidence against Caesar, but
in vain (49. 1). Whatever authority Sallust had for this transaction,
the names were plausible, and he specifies the personal motives
for the enmity of the two consulars. Further, baffled by Cicero's
refusal to play their game, they went about stirring up ill-feeling
against Caesar, with the result that some Roman knights, standing on armed guard before the House, threatened Caesar when
he came out (49. 4).

The incident of the Roman knights, it will be noted, probably
falls after Caesar's oration and role in the debate of December 5.[5]
In disposing his material, Sallust is perhaps guilty of modest
artifice.

Sallust goes to great pains in selection and omission, in grouping
and emphasis. He has chosen his own way of showing what he
thought of attempts to implicate Caesar (and subsequent allegations). It is subtle and indirect. How far does his disdain to give
a straight answer touch and impair his credit as a historian?

Sallust's honesty cannot be called into question—for he is not
trying to suggest anything he believed false. Hence it has been
conceded that Sallust in this instance is a partisan writer—and

---

ing that notorious altercation in the Senate in 55 when Crassus used the
word "exul" (Dio XXXIX. 60. 1, cf. Ad fam. I. 9. 20). Better, in private
conversation, cf. K. Büchner, Sallust (1960), 34 f.

[4] Plutarch, Crassus 13, cf. Cicero 15; Dio XXXVII. 31. 1.

[5] Suetonius, Divus Iulius 14. 2; Plutarch, Caesar 8.

claimed that he is a good one.[6] The reader is left with the persuasion that Caesar cannot have been involved.

A grave charge, however, subsists. Sallust's convictions about Caesar may have induced him to antedate the revolutionary designs of Catilina—and also have influenced his presentation of the "first conspiracy." But that is far from certain.[7]

Sallust's defence of Caesar does not exhaust the count. What is his attitude towards Cicero? At first sight it might seem that he has done less than justice to the consul. Much worse has been discovered—systematic defamation. Not only distortion or omission in large things but covert malice in small things.

That assumption, once made, was defended with authority and prevailed for a long time.[8] It can now be regarded as obsolete. The main charges collapse on inspection.[9] First, the placing of the *senatus consultum ultimum*. The historian, it was suggested, was trying to make out that Cicero got the decree passed because of his personal fears. That notion, as has been demonstrated above, is baseless, the product of an inept failure to understand the historian's technique of narration.[10]

Second, no oration from Cicero. What of that? It should have been asked, how was the author to proceed? To render in his own style one of the classic performances of the master of Roman eloquence was awkward, invidious, superfluous. The Catilinarian

---

[6] Thus, following Mommsen, H. M. Last, *Mélanges Marouzeau* (1948), 368.

[7] For Sallust's technique and purpose in the placing of the "first conspiracy" (18 f.), see p. 100.

[8] E. Schwartz, *Hermes* XXXII (1897) , 575 ff. Accepted and commended by G. Funaioli, *R-E* I A, 1922 f. The doctrine still finds supporters, e.g., F. Lämmli, *Mus.Helv.* III (1946), 112; M. L. W. Laistner, *The Greater Roman Historians* (1947), 56; E. Löfstedt, *Roman Literary Portraits* (1958), 100 f.

[9] J. Tolkiehn, *Phil.Woch.* XLV (1925), 1404 f.; W. A. Baehrens, *Neue Wege zur Antike* IV (1926), 38 ff.; O. Seel, *Sallust von den Briefen ad Caesarem zur Coniuratio Catilinae* (1930), 63 ff.; W. Schur, *Sallust als Historiker* (1934), 183 ff. And, recently, W. Steidle, Historia, Einzelschriften 3 (1958), 15 f.; 93 f.; A. La Penna, *Stud.it.fil.class.* XXXI (1959), 18 ff. It is a melancholy fact that the truth, the "bescheidene Wahrheit," was there all the time, in Drumann-Groebe, *Geschichte Roms* V² (1919), 463 ff.

[10] P. 80.

orations had been published. Roman historians follow a sensible
practice, as is exemplified by Livy when he refuses to reproduce
the famous speech of Cato the Censor on the Rhodians.[11] Sallust
accords praise to the *First Catilinarian*. He describes the speech
as "luculentam atque utilem rei publicae" (31. 6). Sallust thereby
rebuts the notion that Cicero's action was unwise or detrimental
if it caused Catilina to leave the city and join the insurgents in
Etruria. Is the praise faint and grudging? No—it is not Sallust's
habit to indulge in laudatory superlatives or adorn an obvious
truth. As for the *Fourth Catilinarian*, the historian gives no sign.
Rightly: it was anything but a decisive contribution to the debate
of December 5.[12]

Certain trivial items can be at once dismissed. Sallust refers to
Cicero as "optumus consul" (43. 1). Now Cicero, so it happens
to be known (from a letter to Atticus), conceived great annoyance
because Brutus in his *Cato* called him "optimus consul": could
any enemy, he exclaims, have been more flat and neutral in
comment? [13] Second, Cicero was immensely proud of having "ascertained" so many facts about the conspiracy—"comperi omnia." [14]
The verb was gleefully taken up by enemies such as C. Antonius
and P. Clodius.[15] Sallust uses the word when stating that Cicero
had no precise information at a certain juncture (29. 1). The statement is plain and harmless. Indeed, "comperio" happens to be
one of Sallust's favourite verbs (at least sixteen times in his various works). Finally, Catilina in the harangue to the conspirators
appears to parody the exordium of the *First Catilinarian*—"quo
usque tandem?" (20. 9). If that is malice, it is not very noxious.

Other features in the portrayal of Cicero will be worth ex-
amining. Describing the measures of precaution taken against
Catilina, Sallust observes that Cicero was not all deficient in craft

---

[11] Livy XLV. 25. 1: "non inseram simulacrum viri copiosi quae dixerit
referendo: ipsius oratio scripta exstat, *Originum* quinto libro inclusa."

[12] G. Boissier, *Cicéron et ses amis* (1870), 48; *La conjuration de Catilina*
(1905), 236 ff. Moreover, what survives is a composite product, cf. H. Fuchs,
Hermes LXXXVII (1959), 464 ff.

[13] *Ad Att.* XII. 21. 1.

[14] *In Cat.* I. 10.

[15] *Ad Att.* I. 14. 5; *Ad fam.* V. 5. 2.

or guile—"neque illi tamen ad cavendum dolus aut astutiae deerant" (26.2). The facts confirm—Cicero's use of spies, the pact with his colleague C. Antonius, the friends and clients secretly enlisted for personal protection.[16] Then, it is stated, Cicero is embarrassed, "ancipiti malo permotus," because of the situation at Rome and in Etruria, and consequently makes report to the Senate, whereupon the *senatus consultum ultimum* is passed (29. 1). That is fair comment.

The consul had the decree behind him, and a few days later news arrived about the insurrection in Etruria. But what was he to do about the conspirators at Rome? Some blame him for weakness.[17] That is perverse. Cicero had to wait on opportunity or proofs that carried conviction. The scene at his front-door (on the morning of November 7)—or rather, perhaps, intelligence that Catilina was in fact proposing to leave Rome—gave Cicero his chance. Hence the *First Catilinarian*. Sallust attributes motives to the consul, fear of Catilina or anger—"sive praesentiam eius timens sive ira commotus" (31. 6). That again is not an unfair appraisal. As the facts demonstrate, which Sallust sets forth, the timing was masterly. Cicero could not compel Catilina to leave Rome. To be sure, if Cicero said nothing, Catilina would have departed (according to plan, one presumes). But it was necessary that Catilina should be denounced and unmasked.[18] The historian approves what was done.

There remained Catilina's associates in Rome. Their folly and Cicero's craft brought them into the net. When Volturcius and the Allobrogic envoys were captured, with the documents, what was the next step? Exultation possessed Cicero, and anxiety—"at illum ingens cura atque laetitia simul occupavere" (46. 2). The historian puts the anxiety first. He is right, and he expounds the

---

[16] To be sure "astutiae" is not a nice word, as G. Jachmann points out: a friend might have used "vigilantia" or "providentia" (*Misc.Ac.Berol.* [1950], 254). None the less, if the word is not praise, it is not disapprobation either, cf. A. La Penna, o.c. 20. It is perhaps worth noting that Sallust has "providentia" only once (*Jug.* 7. 5), "vigilantia" never.

[17] J. Carcopino, *Histoire romaine* II (1936), 640.

[18] G. Boissier, *La conjuration de Catilina* (1905), 179 ff.

reason. Cicero none the less came to a decision. Not in fact without taking advice, but Sallust does not bother to add that anyone
helped to overcome his hesitations.[19] The conspirators (Lentulus
and four others) were arrested and brought before the Senate.

The State was manifestly in danger. Furthermore, attempts
were on foot to rescue the conspirators, but the consul took the
proper steps. That is an important fact, and highly relevant to
the debate ensuing on December 5. Sallust does not omit that fact
(50. 1 ff.).[20]

The consul introduced the debate, asking the consul-designate,
D. Junius Silanus, for his *sententia*. After that he fades from the
narrative until the time comes for him to carry out the vote of
the Senate. Caesar and Cato dominate the scene. Apart from
their orations, the historian evinces scant interest in the proceedings. Indeed, he operates in a most peculiar fashion.[21]

Silanus the consul-designate pronounced for the extreme penalty. There is subjoined an awkward footnote to the effect that he
subsequently changed his mind and acceded to the proposal of
Ti. Claudius Nero, who argued for deferring decision (50. 4).
Next, Caesar spoke when his turn came. No mention of the fact
that all the consulars present (they were fourteen in number)
concurred in Silanus' motion.[22] Again, after the oration of Caesar
and before that of Cato, all that is said is vague as well as brief—
"alius alii varie adsentiebantur" (52. 1). The motion of Ti.
Claudius Nero (a senator of praetorian rank), which was a modification of Caesar's proposal, apparently belongs here.[23] Moreover,

---

[19] At least he had the advice of his brother and of P. Nigidius Figulus
(Plutarch, *Cicero* 20).

[20] For the danger of a rescue, cf. also 52. 4; 14 f. Cicero later scouted the
notion in dishonest eloquence (*In Cat.* IV. 17).

[21] In spite of, or rather because of, the abundance of evidence, it is not
easy to sort out the order of certain motions and interventions in the debate,
or establish their precise tenor. For a lucid statement of the problem, T. Rice
Holmes, *The Roman Republic* I (1923), 467 ff.

[22] Fourteen ex-consuls. The list in *Ad. Att.* XII. 21. 1 omits Crassus and
Hortensius but includes Gellius Poplicola and Manlius Torquatus. In *Phil.*
II. 12 f., however, the omissions and inclusions are reversed.

[23] In Appian, the only other source to mention Ti. Nero, his amendment
is placed before Caesar's speech (*BC* II. 5. 19). Wrongly. But the proposal in

some missing facts—one of the consulars spoke against Caesar, namely Lutatius Catulus,[24] and the consul-designate explained, perhaps in a quibble, that he had not really meant the death penalty;[25] and the consul intervened in the debate. Sallust does not bother about those details. He is preoccupied with Caesar and with Cato. He probably wrote the orations first and then supplied the context of the debate. His procedure betrays itself. Observe the clumsy if not superfluous reference to Ti. Claudius Nero (50. 4).

Caesar's arguments, firm, subtle, and insidious, had shaken the consul-designate and enforced the assent of everybody (except one consular) until the round got as far as the tribunes-designate. At that point Cato's strong speech changed everything. The fact could never be gainsaid. Cicero proclaims it in 56, praising Cato who was "dux, auctor, actor illarum rerum." [26] A decade later Cicero was angry when Brutus in the *Cato* made it all too plain.[27]

As for Sallust, omitting so many particulars of the debate, he could not be expected to bring in a reference to the *Fourth Catilinarian*. Cicero's intervention (it is clear, and it is generally admitted) was cautious and ambiguous, as was proper in a presiding magistrate. It led to nothing. The oration which he published in 60 reflects subsequent events and attitudes.[28]

When Cicero produced the evidence about Lentulus and the others and initiated the debate, his task was completed, his duty done. On Sallust's presentation, the consul comes out very well. Mastering the irresolution in his own character, and evading the manifold traps in his path, Cicero adopted crafty measures against secret enemies and came to firm decisions at the right time.[29] The events in Etruria helped. When Catilina joined Manlius, both

---

Appian, enjoining delay until Catilina is defeated and more is ascertained, is more enlightening than Sallust's brief interpolation—"de ea re praesidiis additis referundum censuerat" (50. 4).

[24] Plutarch, *Cicero* 21; *Caesar* 8.

[25] Plutarch, *Cato* 22.

[26] *Pro Sestio* 61.

[27] *Ad Att.* XII. 21. 1.

[28] P. 74.

[29] J. L. Strachan-Davidson, *Cicero and the Fall of the Roman Republic* (1894), 157: "not a single false step."

could be proclaimed public enemies. Further, by documentary evidence Lentulus and his allies were not only linked to the insurgents in Etruria but involved in treasonable negotiations with a Gallic tribe.

That was perfect, and it was not all. Cicero did his best to saddle the Senate with the responsibility for the execution of the conspirators. That was right, and reasonable.[30] Cicero took a great risk, and he deserved to come off unscathed in the aftermath and secure protection. That prospect was wrecked by political vicissitudes, the envy of the Optimates, and his own exuberant vanity. His management of the crisis of 63 deserved full and frank praise.[31] Cicero overdid the self-laudation—"non sine causa sed sine fine."[32] Men of the time grew tired and annoyed.[33]

Cicero's version was abundantly proclaimed to the world, and, through the glory of his oratory and his subsequent fate, it incurred little danger of being depreciated by posterity. The danger, Sallust saw, was all the other way. Sallust is a highly antisuggestible author. He redresses the balance by producing a *Bellum Catilinae* of which Cicero is not the inevitable and central figure. And, it can be said, Sallust earns some justification, such has been the prevalence of blind Cicero worship, the easy and congenial habit of writing the Roman history of that age very much as a biography of Cicero.

Sallust's procedure is very far from a denigration of Cicero. On the contrary. Some will incline to believe that Sallust, writing when the Triumvirs ruled at Rome, is quietly and firmly putting forward a defence of Cicero.[34]

---

[30] As Cicero claims (e.g., *In Pisonem* 14). For the legal issue, see the lucid exposition of Strachan-Davidson, o.c. 151 ff.; Rice Holmes, o.c. 278 ff. According to M. Cary it was "a comparative trifle" (*CAH* IX [1932], 504).

[31] It is significant and entertaining that Carcopino, relating "les erreurs d'une carrière manquée," is able to glide over the Catilinarian affair in a few lines (*Les secrets de la correspondance de Cicéron* I [1947], 317 f.).

[32] Seneca, *De brevitate vitae* 5. 1.

[33] Plutarch, *Cicero* 24. He had not failed to equate himself with Romulus —"profecto, quoniam illum qui hanc urbem condidit ad deos immortalis benivolentia famaque sustulimus, esse apud vos posterosque vestros in honore debebit is qui eandem hanc urbem conditam amplificatamque servavit" (*In Cat.* III. 2).

[34] G. Boissier, o.c. 18; T. R. S. Broughton, *TAPA* LXVII (1936), 34 ff.

Opinion has therefore moved a long way in reverse. But not without aberrations. One scholar who argues that Sallust is objective none the less denies that he is genuinely and honestly objective—Sallust displays equity towards Cicero, but only in order the more cunningly to disguise his purpose of demolishing *De consiliis* and exculpating Caesar from any complicity with Catilina.[35]

Once again is manifested the obsessional belief that Sallust writes as, and because he is, a partisan. The true explanation of Sallust's equity towards the memory of Cicero may be totally different, and honourable. Is it too much to suppose that Sallust, with the lapse of time, was capable of subduing a personal antipathy and contemplating Cicero in historical perspective? Sallust appears to have made that effort.[36] Even of oblique malice there is scarcely a trace, unless it be in "quo usque tandem?"

Antipathy there had been. Why not? Sallust now transmutes personal hostility into emulation in the field of letters, wilfully creating a style and manner that defies and denies everything that is "Ciceronian." [37]

On Sallust's showing, the consul acquits himself nobly and deserves well of the Republic. But he has to yield prominence at once to Caesar and to Cato.

Caesar's oration is couched in a strain of quiet reasonableness (51). He deprecates decisions taken under the sway of emotion, especially fear, anger, and rancour; he puts emphasis on the laws which forbade the execution of citizens without trial; and he adduces the peril of creating precedents for quasi-legal acts of arbitrary violence. For these reasons the speaker proposed that the conspirators, their property confiscated, should be held in strict custody in certain towns of Italy.[38]

---

[35] W. A. Baehrens, o.c. 46.

[36] G. Boissier, o.c. 14: "en somme, cet ouvrage d'un ennemi lui est plus favorable que ne le seraient toutes les flatteries et tous les mensonges qu'il mendiait des poètes et des historiens de sa connaissance."

[37] G. Boissier, o.c. 17; *Journal des Savants* 1903, 66.

[38] 51. 43. That is to say, until it was safe and expedient to bring them before a court of law. That particular may have been made more explicit in the

Cato argued for a sharp and energetic decision (52). He arraigned the aristocracy, with bitter words—enslaved to birth and to great possessions, no care for the Commonwealth, no thought for the honour of an imperial people. As for the appeal to legality, he brushed it aside as dangerous sophistry: the conspirators had plainly put themselves in the position of public enemies.

The situation and the speeches exhibit a number of surprises. Cato in his political creed held rigorously by the laws and the constitution; he refused to allow any plea of exception; and he was against extending the sphere of governmental authority. On December 5, it is Caesar who is the champion of legality, whatever be his design or motives.[39] Again, Cato adhered to a philosophical doctrine. He could even be described as a "perfectissimus Stoicus."[40] That was no mere matter of private belief or conduct. In orations before the Senate Cato was wont to import themes of high argument, and he succeeded in making acceptable and convincing the most arid of abstract doctrines.[41] But it is Caesar who has recourse to the teachings of a school—that of Epicurus, which denied any life beyond the grave.[42]

The paradox was not lost on Sallust. He enhances it. Caesar, arguing for tolerance and clemency, invokes the example of "maiores nostri," and adduces the wise and magnanimous conduct of the Romans towards the Rhodians (51. 5). The reader would call to mind the oration of Cato's ancestor.[43] That is a subtle and deadly device.

The Censor was generally fierce and uncompromising. Not so

---

amendment of Ti. Nero, cf. Appian, *BC* II. 5. 19. Cicero alleged that Caesar's motion entailed imprisonment for life—"vincula vero, et ea sempiterna" (*In Cat.* IV. 7, cf. 10).

[39] Caesar's proposal has been variously estimated, from "a practical piece of advice" (E. G. Hardy, *Some Problems in Roman History* [1924], 40) to "this impudent motion" (W. E. Heitland, *The Roman Republic* III [1909], 105).

[40] *Brutus* 118.

[41] *Paradoxa* I, *praef.* 1: "animadverti, Brute, saepe Catonem, avunculum tuum, cum in senatu diceret, locos graves ex philosophia tractare abhorrentes ab hoc usu forensi et publico."

[42] 51. 20; 52. 13; cf. *In Cat.* IV. 7.

[43] Large sections are preserved in Gellius VI. 3, whence H. Peter, *HRR* I² (1914), fr. 95.

on that occasion.[44] In his exordium the orator argued for moderation and for delay before a decision about the Rhodians. He was
careful to remind his audience of the "superbia et ferocia" that
tends to accrue from success. Adversity, he said, is a more useful
instructor.[45]

Caesar argues in a similar strain. Hate or excessive zeal is
deleterious—and anger above all. If small men surrender to
anger, few know or care. It is otherwise with persons of rank
and authority—"in maxuma fortuna minuma licentia est" (51. 13).
What in an individual passes for "iracundia," that in a government is "superbia atque crudelitas" (51. 14). Furthermore, wind-
ing up his discourse, Caesar deprecates innovation and extols
the "virtus et sapientia" of the Roman tradition, as any Cato
might have done.[46]

After Cato's speech and the Senate's decree the historian turns
aside to digress on the past greatness of Rome (53. 2 ff.). It was
due, he concludes, to the superior excellence of a few men only
—and there was a notable dearth of them at many epochs once
the decline had set in. To his own recollection, two men stood
out, "ingenti virtute, divorsis moribus" (53. 6). The author will
not neglect the occasion to illustrate and enforce that judgment.

It is a foible common in any age to deplore the lack of talent
and energy. Politicians only become statesmen when they die.
Sallust is perhaps a victim of convention or delusion. His verdict
is "haut sane quisquam Romae virtute magnus fuit." That at
once excludes the man who had "Magnus" for *cognomen*. What
of the other consulars, the men whose function it is to guide and
direct the policy of the Roman State?

Cicero in the *Pro Sulla* comes out with a glowing and enthusi-
astic testimony to the consulars—did any age witness their equal
for "gravitas," for "constantia," for devotion to the Common-

---

[44] Livy XLV. 25. 1: "qui asper ingenio tum lenem mitemque senatorem
egit."

[45] Gellius VI. 3. 14: "adversae res edomant et docent quid opus siet facto."
Further, Cato ridicules anger—"idne irascimini, si quis superbior est quam
nos?" (ib. 50).

[46] 51. 37: "maiores nostri, patres conscripti," etc.

wealth?[47] It may be salutary to observe in passing that a number of those incomparable statesmen had testified in favour of Catilina in 65 and in 64. However that may be, the facts of the great debate stand in refutation. Fourteen consulars. They were cowed and dismayed by the speech of Caesar. It took young Cato to bring them back to courage, dignity, and resolution.

The "principes" are in eclipse. Two men, their juniors, exemplify "virtus" and acquire an "auctoritas" that was normally confined to ex-consuls.

"Virtus" each had, but they were antithetic in behaviour, so Sallust explains in brief delineation (54). Caesar was splendid and lavish, clement and forgiving; but Cato, austere and inflexible, gave no favours. Men praised the one for "facilitas," the other for "constantia." Caesar spared no exertion in the strenuous pursuit of high ambitions, but Cato's efforts were spent in a different battle, for honesty and integrity. His goal was the reality of virtue not the appearance ("esse quam videri"); and the less he sought glory, the more surely it accrued.

The comparison demands attentive scrutiny. The men are not portrayed exactly as they would have been seen in 63. For example, Cato proclaims in his oration "saepe numero, patres conscripti," whereas he had only been a senator for two years. That can pass. But Caesar is praised for his "facilitas." It is doubtful whether that amiable feature was much in evidence in the sixties, for example during the altercations with Catulus.[48] Moreover, what came out soon after in Caesar's consulship was an arrogant imperious temper, notably in his attitude towards certain of the "principes," such as Lucullus.[49] Nobody would guess that the Caesar of Sallust's character sketch would end by composing an angry and malicious *Anti-Cato*.

Again, Caesar's generosity, his forgiveness of enemies, his ready succour for the unfortunate. It stands on record that he bore no malice towards poets who had lampooned him (there are anec-

---

[47] *Pro Sulla* 82.

[48] Velleius II. 43. 3.

[49] Suetonius, *Divus Iulius* 20. 4. When consul Caesar exclaimed "invitis et gementibus adversariis adeptum quae concupisset, proinde ex eo insultaturum omnium capitibus" (ib. 22. 2).

dotes); he was eager to gather clients and partisans anywhere; and Sallust, for example, had cause for personal gratitude. But it will be recalled that Caesar had neither the occasion nor the means for such conspicuous liberality and help until he acquired the gold of Gaul and the full stature of a party leader.

However, the anachronistic colouring does not much concern the crucial question. What is the author trying to convey, where does his preference lie?

Caesar, some opine, is depicted as the great statesman, while Cato by contrast is a mere doctrinaire.[50] That is false, doubly so.[51] Men of the time allude to Cato's pursuit of abstract ideals with deep reverence—or with impatience and derision. Both aspects are reflected by Cicero, according to his mood or the occasion.[52] Sallust might have expatiated on Cato's addiction to doctrines; he might have censured this un-Roman aberration. He does nothing of the kind. The Cato of the oration discards theory, neglects precedent and overrides legality. The State is in peril, that is all that matters. Cato is a practical statesman—and effective.

Perhaps he was a little too effective (as on later occasions). Was it not the part of prudence to defer the decision? On the other hand, two considerations can be urged. First, there was some danger of an attempt to rescue the conspirators (50. 1 ff.). Second, the news of their execution in fact weakened Catilina's army (57. 1).

Cato after his death became a kind of lay saint. Tradition exalts Cato—and belittles him. It was not principle and courage alone that gave Cato a claim to leadership at Rome. Through ties of kinship and matrimonial alliances (Ahenobarbus married his sister, Bibulus his daughter), Cato was at the centre of a powerful group in the *nobilitas*.[53] He had a policy, albeit negative in the main, pursued with obstinacy and not unimpaired by conceit.

---

50 O. Seel, o.c. 43 ff.; W. Schur, o.c. 200; E. Löfstedt, o.c. 98.

51 V. Pöschl, *Grundwerte römischer Staatsgesinnung in den Geschichtswerken des Sallust* (1940), 11; A. La Penna, *Stud.it.fil.class.* XXXI (1959), 148.

52 *Ad Att.* II. 1. 8: "dicit enim tamquam in Platonis πολιτείᾳ non tamquam in Romuli faece sententiam." On the other side, *Pro Sestio* 61.

53 *Rom.Rev.* (1939), 21; 44. For Cato's political importance see also A. Afzelius, *Class. et Med.* IV (1941), 100 ff.

Cato's ancestor had broken Scipio Africanus, and Cato fought against the predominance of one man in the State. He proclaimed that "extraordinaria imperia" would be the ruin of the Republic, and he was right.[54] When, after long and bitter hostility, he came to terms with Pompeius Magnus, his aim can be divined. Not to accept Pompeius but to ensnare him, to weaken the dynast by the destruction of his ally, the proconsul of Gaul.

To revert to the comparison in Sallust. Cato is not only portrayed with reverence and sympathy. The author intends him to have the advantage, if only because the episode concludes with Cato and Cato's glory.[55] And there is something else. The ideals expounded by Cato in the oration correspond closely with those of the historian as discoverable in prologue and digressions.[56] As for those ideals, Sallust intends to call up the Censor in the portrayal of his descendant.[57] Further, he may have drawn on some of the orations, such as that denouncing Ser. Sulpicius Galba, an aristocratic governor in Spain, and defending the honour of the imperial Republic: it was incorporated in the *Origines*.[58]

That Cato should earn from Sallust a favouring presentation has not failed to cause surprise.[59] How explain the apparent anomaly? One scholar has a desperate remedy—Sallust, disguising his own political convictions, exalts Cato for the greater glory of the man with whom Cato is matched.[60]

Once again, the phantom of the party pamphleteer. It will be expedient to look a little more closely at what Sallust says about Caesar. Certain expressions may be revealing. Sallust is acutely

---

[54] *Pro Sestio* 60.

[55] H. Drexler, *Neue Jahrbücher* IV (1928), 390 ff.; E. Skard, *Symb.Osl.* IX (1930), 93; F. Egermann, *Wiener S-B* 214. 3 (1932), 20; F. Lämmli, *Mus.Helv.* III (1946), 94 ff.; D. C. Earl, *The Political Thought of Sallust* (1961), 111.

[56] E. Skard, o.c. 94; V. Pöschl, o.c. 10 f.

[57] D. C. Earl (o.c. 100 f.), citing Plutarch, *Cato Maior* 10 to illustrate 54. 5: "non divitiis cum divite neque factione cum factioso," etc.

[58] Gellius XIII. 25. 15.

[59] H. M. Last, o.c. 365; E. Löfstedt, o.c. 97.

[60] R. Wirtz, *Beiträge zur catilinarischen Verschwörung* (Diss. Bonn, 1910), 40.

aware of how treacherous is political and ethical terminology. Words are employed in a partisan sense or convertible into an opposite meaning. That was one of the lessons which Sallust, emulating Thucydides, was eager to inculcate.[61] Was he totally unaware that some of his own statements about Caesar were equivocal or vulnerable?

On an unfavourable interpretation, Caesar's "facilitas" would emerge as complaisance or connivance. And, if a politician is said to make his way "dando, sublevando, ignoscundo," others might employ less friendly terms to designate his conduct: where does liberality end and bribery begin? As Cato points out in his speech, words are now perverted—it is called "liberalitas" when you give away what belongs to other people (52. 11).[62] Further, Caesar was help and succour to men in trouble, "miseris perfugium." From that it is a short step to the "patrocinium malorum" as practised by M. Crassus (48. 8).

Caesar, says Sallust, was yearning for a great command, an army and a war in which his "virtus" might discover scope for action and glory. That is not in itself a mark of disapprobation. Ambition was praiseworthy in a Roman. Or, if ever to be questioned, it was the nearest thing to positive excellence, as the historian observes in his diagnosis of the Roman past—"quod tamen vitium propius virtutem erat" (11. 1). But there is no hint from Sallust that Caesar in his aspirations for war and conquest was moved by any thought for the Commonwealth.

The portrayal of Caesar is pervaded by doubts and ambiguity. Likewise, it can be conjectured, Sallust's own sentiments.[63]

Caesar was impelled by ambition, and he went on until no competitor was left among the living (but the prestige of Cato for

---

[61] P. 255.

[62] 52, 11 f.: "iam pridem equidem nos vera vocabula rerum amisimus: quia bona aliena largiri liberalitas, malarum rerum audacia fortitudo vocatur. sint sane, quoniam ita se mores habent, liberales ex sociorum fortunis, sint misericordes in furibus aerari."

[63] G. Boissier, o.c. 12: "il ne paraît pas, quand on lit Salluste, qu'il eût conservé pour son ancien chef une affection sans mélange." This modest statement can be set against all the asseverations (no need to chronicle them) that Sallust was a devoted Caesarian.

rebuke and posthumous rivalry). Forced by Pompeius and the Optimates to have recourse to arms, Caesar asserted above all things a personal plea, the protection of his "dignitas." That is the excuse published more than once in the *Bellum Civile*.[64] Contemporaries noted it, not all with approbation. Cicero has a pained comment on Caesar's invasion of Italy—"atque haec ait omnia facere se dignitatis causa!" [65] Sallust's use of the word is instructive. It is applied to Cato, not to Caesar (54. 2). Caesar himself, addressing the Senate, has "vostra dignitas" (51. 7). For the rest, Cato refers ironically to the "dignitas Lentuli" (52. 32); and Catilina in the letter to Lutatius Catulus twice appeals to his own "dignitas" (35. 1; 3), of which, says the historian, he was not unmindful at the end (60. 7).

Caesar and Catilina, descendants both of the ancient patriciate, asserted the claims of birth and rank, with strenuous efforts to refurbish the "dignitas" of their line. The Julii had been rising again in powerful momentum—Caesar's aunt married to Marius, and his uncle consul in 91. Caesar, with many advantages, none the less needed energy, daring and a cool head. And he was lucky. In contrast, Catilina. The Sergii (no consul for more than three centuries) found their chance with Sulla, himself of a decayed patrician family, and with Sulla's oligarchy. The "victoria nobilium" was stained with blood, Catilina had been guilty of atrocities, he was a desperate character driven by failure into armed revolution.

Insistence on "dignitas" to the limit came close to "superbia"; and the arrogance of a Roman noble often issued in anger and inhumanity. Caesar deprecated that kind of behaviour. So did Marcus Brutus. In a letter to Cicero, Brutus quietly pointed out that it is more urgent to prevent civil wars than to vent "iracundia" on the defeated.[66] As for Caesar, a remarkable pronounce-

---

[64] Caesar, *BC* I. 9. 2, etc. Cf. *Rom.Rev.* (1939), 48.

[65] *Ad Att.* VII. 11. 1.

[66] *Ad M. Brutum* I. 2a. 2: "scribis enim acrius prohibenda bella civilia esse quam in superatos iracundiam exercendam. vehementer a te, Brute, dissentio nec clementiae tuae concedo, sed salutaris severitas vincit inanem speciem clementiae."

ment is on casual record—"the remembrance of cruelty is poor equipment for old age." [67]

Caesar at the outbreak of the Civil War announced a new way of winning: it was generosity and compassion.[68] During hostilities and after, he was at great pains to advertise his clemency. It did him less good than he fancied.[69] "Clementia" is the virtue of a despot, not of a citizen and an aristocrat. What right had Caesar to exercise pardon? His enemies resented the assertion of power and magnanimity, or denied it utterly: the son of Domitius Ahenobarbus refused to be pardoned.

Cicero in several orations celebrated the mercy of the Dictator, lavishly—not always perhaps in entire innocence, but insidiously overdoing.[70] The word "clementia" acquired an invidious connotation. Caesar himself is careful not to use it in the books on the Civil War; and Sallust eschews "clementia" altogether in the monograph. Elsewhere he admits only the appeal to "clementia populi Romani." [71] Speaking of Caesar, he has "mansuetudo et misericordia" (54. 2). And that phrase had been duly taken up by Cato in his oration, and subjected to unfriendly scrutiny (52. 11 and 27).

Caesar won the war, but the victor had no policy for peace.[72] Men looked for a regeneration of the Roman State, and were disappointed. Caesar took plenary powers, he even became "dictator perpetuo" in February of 44. Whatever his ultimate designs, his

---

[67] Ammianus XXIX. 2. 18: "ut dictator Caesar aiebat, miserum esse instrumentum senectuti recordationem crudelitatis." Not among the fragments listed by A. Klotz (Teubner, Vol. III, 1927).

[68] *Ad Att.* IX. 7c. 1.

[69] *Rom.Rev.* (1939), 51; *Tacitus* (1958), 414.

[70] *Pro Ligario* 6: "o clementiam admirabilem atque omnium laude praedicatione litteris monumentisque decorandam!"

[71] He has only "clementia populi Romani" (*Jug.* 33. 4) and "clementia et probitas vestra, Quirites" (*Hist.* I. 55. 1). As for "clemens," only "is rumor clemens erat" (*Jug.* 22. 1).

[72] H. Strasburger, *Hist.Zeitschr.* CLXXV (1953), 225 ff.; J. H. Collins, *Historia* IV (1955), 445 ff.; J. P. V. D. Balsdon, ib. VII (1958), 80 ff. But, against the extreme negation of Caesar's statesmanship, cf. the protest of M. Gelzer, *Hist.Zeitschr.* CLXXVIII (1954), 449 ff.

position had become monarchic. There is no sign that the author of the *Bellum Catilinae* was an advocate of monarchy.[73]

Caesar was assassinated by honourable men, Cato's nephew in the forefront. Caesar before the end confessed the vanity of ambition—he had lived long enough, whether his life be reckoned in terms of years or of glory.[74] Caesar for all his genius was baffled. The disillusion of Caesar, and the tragedy, was felt and shared by the historian. Sallust knew something about ambition.

Both Caesar and Cato exhibit "virtus." Cicero in the *Pro Sestio* produced an eloquent panegyric of Cato, in the *Second Philippic* a guarded appraisement of Caesar.[75] It was a temptation to combine the two themes and neatly bring to a climax that double and contemporary debate on the illustrious dead which had been provoked by Utica and the Ides of March.

Caesar and Cato were divergent in conduct, principles, and allegiance. Their qualities could be regarded as complementary no less than antithetic. In alliance the two had what was needed to save the Republic. That may be what the historian is gently suggesting. Fate or chance determined otherwise. Caesar pursued personal ambition, ruthlessly, but Cato went with the Optimates (he knew they were no good); and, in the end, he accepted Pompeius, the old enemy of the oligarchy.

---

[73] E. Skard, o.c. 70 ff.

[74] *Pro Marcello* 25: "satis diu vel naturae vixi vel gloriae." Adopted by Cicero for himself, *Phil.* I. 38; *Ad fam.* X. 1. 1. Observe also Servius Tullius in his oration (Dion. Hal. IV. 11), and Camillus, "cum vitae satis tum gloriae esse" (Livy VI. 23. 7).

[75] *Pro Sestio* 60 f.; *Phil.* II. 116.

IX

SALLUST'S PURPOSE

An attempt can now be made to ask what the historian was trying to convey. On one count, Sallust, it has been thought, betrays himself. He is anxious to defend the memory of Caesar. Overanxious, for the allegations were trivial, dishonest, or grotesque. But Caesar's repute is not his main concern; and, in the contrasted appraisal, it is not Caesar but Cato who commands the author's unequivocal approbation.

The leaders of the Caesarian party would not have liked the eulogy of Cato. It called up Marcus Brutus, who inherited the cause which Cato had glorified and strengthened by his suicide. That was alarming and scandalous if the monograph was written in the year when the armies clashed at Philippi, when the Republic went down, "cum fracta Virtus." [1]

Nor would the authors of the Proscriptions wish to be reminded of the consul whose actions saved the Commonwealth from treason and armed rebellion.[2] Cicero suffered blame, hazard, and exile because he had carried out a sentence of death, decreed by the Senate. The Triumvirs, seizing absolute power, inaugurated a systematic massacre by an abominable parody of legal form and sanction.

Yet it is not through Cato or Cicero that Sallust makes the most

---

[1] Horace, *Odes* II. 7. 11. Observe that Cato could be styled "homo Virtuti simillimus" (Velleius II. 35. 2).

[2] Sallust's treatment is indeed a defence of Cicero, cf. T. R. S. Broughton, *TAPA* LXVII (1936), 34 ff. To attack Cicero would now be safe, easy, and profitable, cf. Quintilian XII. 10. 13 (referring to "adulatores etiam praesentis potentiae").

insidious stab at the Triumvirs. He exploits Caesar against the
heirs of Caesar. The oration deprecates anger, rancour, and bloodshed, the plea is for good sense, and calm restraint. The speaker
adverts on Sulla and Sulla's proscriptions (51. 32 ff.). Some of the
first actions after victory, he concedes, earned approval, such as
the killing of Junius Damasippus, and some others—this man, a
partisan of Marius, was the author of murders when that cause
was collapsing. But the thing went on to generalised massacre and
spoliation. Nothing of the kind, the speaker continues, is to be
apprehended at the present juncture, or from a consul like Cicero
(51. 35). But anything can happen. In some other season, with another consul (especially if he has an army at his call), action may
be taken on some false assumption. If that consul has a precedent,
and, supported by a decree of the Senate, draws the sword, where
will it end? "Potest alio tempore, alio consule, quoi item exercitus
in manu sit, falso aliquid pro vero credi" (51. 36).

The speaker refers, it is true, to a consul who might be acting
under authorisation from the Senate. But Sallust slips in a parenthesis—a consul with an army. That is not the customary adjunct
to a consul in this period. Is there not a hint of Octavianus, insidious and sinister? A hint, but not quite a precise reference.
Caesar's heir marched with his army on Rome in August of the
year 43 and extorted the consulate. After which, the pact concluded near Bononia with Antonius and Lepidus, the youthful
consul returned in their company to institute Triumvirate and
Proscriptions, by the *Lex Titia* of November 27.[3]

The despotism of the Triumvirs, it was said, made Caesar's
rule by contrast appear an age of gold.[4] The time of Sulla had
come again—murder, proscription, the expropriation of the better

---

[3] It is not only the parenthesis about a consul with an army that looks
significant. There is also the next phrase, "falso aliquid pro vero credi."
Octavianus, to justify his change of front, adduced various excuses, cf.
Suetonius, *Divus Aug.* 12: "causam optimatium sine cunctatione deseruit, ad
praetextum mutatae voluntatis dicta factaque quorumdam calumniatus, quasi
alii se puerum, alii ornandum tollendumque iactassent ne aut sibi aut
veteranis par gratia referretur." Cicero, to be sure, denied that he had said
"laudandum adulescentem, ornandum, tollendum," as was reported by a
certain Segulius Labeo (*Ad fam.* XI. 20. 1, cf. 21. 1).

[4] Dio XLVII. 15. 4.

sort in the towns of Italy, and colonies of veterans who in the sequel might be expected to behave like Sulla's men.

Sallust, eschewing the word "clementia" (for good reasons), puts emphasis on the "mansuetudo et misericordia" of Caesar. Caesar showed humanity and good sense. But that Caesar, who coolly dismissed beliefs in any form of life after death, was himself consecrated by the Triumvirs on the first day of January, 42. "Divus Julius" became an instrument in their detestable policy.

Praising Caesar, Sallust is ostensibly loyal to the party of Caesar. But when he matches Cato with Caesar, he strikes a deadly blow against the Triumvirs. Let it be granted that he idealises. There are worse things, such as subservience to power.

It has been suggested that Sallust exalted Cato at the cost of his credit as a historical authority.[5] The historian needs no timid or anxious apology. Rather firm praise. The world was now at the mercy of lesser men, and some very nasty.[6]

For Marcus Antonius, something could be said in extenuation. This consul had been attacked on two flanks, by ostensible champions of the Republic and by the young adventurer with his private army levied in the colonies of veterans. But no plea availed to excuse the pretentious and flimsy Lepidus (pedigree, not principle or capacity), and nothing for Caesar's heir, who recalled the earliest actions of Sulla's partisan, the young Pompeius, and his murderous deeds—"adulescentulus carnifex."[7]

Sallust's portrayal of Caesar is ambiguous, insidious even. There is no equivocation in his view of Sulla, but a self-avowing obsession.

---

[5] M. L. W. Laistner, The Greater Roman Historians (1947), 57. And it is also fallacious to suggest that "in the eulogy of Cato we may perhaps also see the initial stage of the process by which in a generation or two he became an almost legendary figure, an actual example of the Stoic sage." The process had already begun—and would have gone on without Sallust.

[6] The notion that Sallust wrote under direct commission from Octavianus was put out by A. Rosenberg, Einleitung und Quellenkunde zur römischen Geschichte (1921), 174 f. And, according to G. Jachmann, Octavianus would find the monograph satisfactory, "so dürfte denn Oktavian alles in allem Grund genug gehabt haben mit dem Buch nach Inhalt und Tendenz zufrieden zu sein" (Misc.Ac.Berol. 1950, 255).

[7] Thus was Pompeius styled by a man in 55 (Valerius Maximus VI. 2. 8).

Catilina is linked to Sulla by various devices or assumptions. More than that, the author transfers to his picture of Catilina (it has been supposed) the image and features of Sulla already dominant in his mind.[8] Whatever be thought of that notion, Sallust can be convicted of a flagrant exaggeration. The example of Sulla, he suggests, inspired Catilina with a lust to seize power at Rome (5. 6).[9]

Sulla was a name of abomination, damned forever.[10] Even the *nobiles*, to whom he gave dominance and enrichment, were inhibited from defending his memory. And the municipal aristocracy (many of them on the side of Marius) refused to condone, even if they had not been despoiled. Cicero urges a double charge in *De officiis* (in the summer of 44).[11] First, the honour and credit of the imperial people. Before Sulla, Rome's dominion over the nations was moderate and acceptable. It was a kind of trusteeship—"patrocinium orbis terrae." Sulla changed that, with naked imperialism as the consequence. Second, his proscriptions. Seizing and putting up for sale the property of men of substance and repute ("boni viri et locupletes"), the Dictator proclaimed that it was loot and booty, it belonged to him as the prize of victory.[12] Cicero, it is true, here deviates into a dishonest attack on Caesar. He evokes P. Sulla, the kinsman of the Dictator, who became Caesar's partisan and a double profiteer after an interval of thirty-six years.[13]

In another work Cicero mobilises moral indignation against Sulla. The Dictator was an evil preceptor. He taught and inculcated three "vitia pestifera," namely "luxuria, avaritia, crude-

---

[8] L. Alheit, *Neue Jahrbücher* XLIII (1919), 34 f.

[9] 5. 6: "hunc post dominationem L. Sullae lubido maxuma invaserat rei publicae capiundae."

[10] Seneca, *Ad Marciam* 12. 6: "deorum quorum illud crimen erat Sulla tam felix"; Pliny, *NH* VII. 137: "cum nemo Sullam non oderit."

[11] *De off.* II. 27 ff.

[12] ib. 27: "praedam se suam vendere." Cf. *In Verrem* III. 81.

[13] ib. 29: "quam [*sc.* hastam] P. Sulla cum vibrasset dictatore propinquo suo, idem sexto tricensimo anno post a sceleratiore hasta non recessit." For another view, *Pro Sulla* 72: "at vero in illa gravi L. Sullae turbulentaque victoria quis P. Sulla mitior, quis misericordior inventus est?"

litas." [14] In this matter, as in others, Sallust could have appealed to Cicero—and it is a pity that Cicero himself refrained from drawing the parallel between Sulla and Catilina. Cicero had close ties with the faction of Marius; while Sallust's town and family may have been penalised by Sulla's victory.

To be against Sulla demands no excuse or apology. Sulla's domination, however, was not a transient phenomenon. He stood as champion of the "causa nobilium," and he restored the government of the Optimates.[15]

Sallust by various devices marshals a consistent indictment against the *nobilitas*. Catilina he introduces as "nobili genere natus" (5. 1). Catilina's friend and ally Cn. Piso is characterised as "adulescens nobilis, summa audacia, egens, factiosus" (18. 4). Also, Catilina has support from ambitious young *nobiles* (17. 6). Other persons in that company or on its fringes are similarly designated. Thus Fulvia, the mistress of Q. Curius, is "mulier nobilis" (23. 3), and Sempronia is presented as a lady of rank (25. 2). Young men who were going to assassinate their parents are described as "ex nobilitate maxuma pars" (43. 2). And Cato in his oration declared a plain fact—"coniuravere nobilissumi cives" (52. 24).

Cato presents the historian with a marvellous opportunity, which he seized with alacrity. The ancestor, a man of vigour and integrity, scourged the *nobiles* of his day for vice, inertia, incompetence. Sallust exploits him for style—but also as a precedent and a weapon, with a double edge. His descendant was a leader of the Optimates, lending strength sorely needed, and a greater prestige after his death. It is Cato in his oration who presents the case against the oligarchy, torpid, corrupt, and unpatriotic.

The assault is contrived by the historian with diabolical skill.[16] He uses Cato to suggest and evoke his ancestor. He might have known or guessed that Cato the Censor was not in truth an enemy of the Roman aristocracy but a recent arrival who wished

---

14 *De finibus* III. 75.

15 *Pro Sex. Roscio Amerino* 135; 138; 142.

16 Compare the technique of Tacitus, using a speech of an aristocratic emperor that denounces the sloth of *nobiles* (*Ann.* II. 38).

to purge it of distempers and rebuild its predominance.[17] No
Roman could conceive a better form of government than the
supremacy of an oligarchy.

Sallust is intent to demonstrate that the heirs of a great tradition had betrayed their trust. Hence the repetition of "nobilis"
and "nobilitas." But it is with melancholy rather than derision
that he pronounces the verdict on Lentulus Sura, strangled by
the public executioner—"ita ille patricius ex gente clarissuma
Corneliorum . . . dignum moribus factisque suis exitum vitae
invenit" (55. 6).

Sallust is against the *nobilitas*. But he is not wholeheartedly
on the side of its enemies. The excursus which is central in the
economy of the monograph conveys the author's reflections on
what happened after the assault on Sulla's order in 70—and discloses a kind of subversive equity (36. 4 to 39. 4). After that year,
young men of spirit and ambition were able to exploit the exorbitant power of the tribunate, they harried the Senate and stirred
up the plebs. Sallust pronounces a crushing verdict. They were
equally culpable, those politicians who claimed to assert the
rights of the People and those who stood by the authority of the
Senate. A specious pretext, only "honesta nomina" (38. 3). What
the politicians wanted was personal power.[18]

Sallust, who himself held the tribunate not so long after in a
year of turbulence, deserves to be reckoned among the "homines
adulescentes . . . quibus aetas animusque ferox erat" (38. 1). Is
the author inadvertent when employing that language—or is he
not rather allowing himself, in retrospect, the privilege and
luxury of an ironical censure on his own conduct in 52? In the
prologue Sallust confesses that he fell a prey to political ambition.
He was not as bad as the others, yet none the less enslaved and
possessed by the same "honoris cupido" (3. 5).

Sallust is careful to insert his personal apologia. Renouncing
politics, he purges and transmutes his desire for action and fame.

---

[17] D. Kienast, *Cato der Zensor* (1954), 31 ff.; 91 ff.

[18] 38. 3: "post illa tempora quicumque rem publicam agitavere, honestis
nominibus, alii sicuti populi iura defenderent, pars quo senatus auctoritas
maxuma foret, bonum publicum simulantes pro sua quisque potentia
certabant."

When he writes history, it is not to defend a leader or a party. And, for all that Sallust believed and proclaimed about the utility of his new vocation, his prime motive is the passion to excel as a writer—"égoïste et artiste de génie." [19]

The choice of subject derived from a variety of reasons, convergent and (it should seem) not mysterious. The time of composition is relevant, could it be established. Different questions wait on an answer.

First, when and why did Sallust decide to give up the career of honours? Immediately after the Ides of March, and for that reason, so many suppose. That opinion, however, carries with it assumptions that may be very far from Sallust's true sentiments. A man who deplored the deed and refused to share the easy illusions which some people kept for a few months may still not have despaired entirely until the autumn of the year when a private army was levied against a consul, when a new civil war began. On the other hand, Sallust's retirement might belong more than a year earlier, in the sequel of his governorship of Africa.[20]

Second, Sallust's resolve to devote his leisure to the writing of history. When was it taken? Perhaps not long after the assassination of Caesar. But the Ides of March may not be the cause. Rather perhaps the turn of events late in 44.

Third, the subject. A theory widely held will have it that Sallust wrote with the precise design of refuting allegations against Caesar brought up in Cicero, *De consiliis suis*. As has been indicated above, many things must remain obscure about that elusive document.[21] It may not have seen the light of day before 42 (if then) or have exercised any influence. Nor was it by any means the sole source of aspersions against Caesar. Too much has been made of the document. And Sallust's purpose goes far beyond a mere defence of Caesar. Too much of that motive also.

Fourth, the date of inception. How soon may Sallust be sup-

---

[19] H. Taine, *Essai sur Tite-Live* (1856), 327.

[20] That is a common assumption. Thus E. E. Sikes in *CAH* IX (1932), 767, or M. L. W. Laistner, o.c. 48—however, erroneously making Sallust's proconsulate end in 46. That page exhibits other errors of fact.

[21] P. 63.

posed to begin writing? Opinions diverge. One scholar suggests
that Sallust went to work before the assassination of Caesar, and
may have published the *Bellum Catilinae* not long after Cicero's
Second Philippic, while Cicero was still alive.[22] That notion is
supported by a corollary or refinement: that Sallust may have
finished his second monograph before the establishment of the
Triumvirate.[23] These dates are not easy to accept or approve. It
might be argued (it is true) that no detail or comment in Sallust's
presentation of Cicero demands the assumption that Cicero was
dead. A different consideration is valid, that of artistic propriety.
Would Sallust be likely to select for historical treatment a theme
in which one of the leading characters was a living person?

Finally, the date of completion. Early in 42, it has been proposed.[24] That might be a little too early—and, again, would pre-
suppose a beginning before the death of Cicero (December 6, 43).

Attempts to arrive at some sort of plausible dating adduce the
contemporaneous situation. They also appeal to change and development in the opinions of the author. The prologue of the
second monograph discloses a writer much more confident in the
value of his task and vocation. Also, a more sombre view of
political life at Rome. That view is assumed to derive from the
impact of Triumvirate and Proscriptions. Hence a lapse of time
to be allowed for, putting the *Bellum Catilinae*, at least in its
inception, before the institution of the Triumvirate.

The conclusion is not compelling. The *Bellum Catilinae* may
have been begun in 42, and not completed before 41.[25] The mono-

---

[22] L. Wohleb, *Phil.Woch.* 1928, 1242 ff. Completion before the death of
Cicero was also assumed by O. Gebhardt, *Sallust als politischer Publizist
während des Bürgerkrieges* (Diss. Halle, 1920), 20. According to the fiat of
K. Büchner, "der Jugurtha muss also 44/3 enstanden sein" (*Sallust* [1960],
109). If that were so, when did Sallust write the previous monograph?

[23] L. Wohleb, o.c. 1244. To state his arguments is enough: Sallust could
not have expressed his detestation of politics (*Jug.* 3. 1) after Octavianus became Triumvir, or his strong views about civil war and massacre (42. 4)
after the Proscriptions.

[24] H. M. Last, *Mélanges Marouzeau* (1948), 360: "I suspect that it was in
fact finished, at the latest, soon after the beginning of 42 B.C."

[25] G. Boissier, *La conjuration de Catilina* (1905), 10. Though unverifiable,
this is better than the wide margin of the cautious Funaioli—"wohl etwa
zwischen den J. 43/42 und 41/40" (*R-E* I A, 1921).

graph does not, it is true, make sharp and severe comment on present conditions, as does the prologue of the *Bellum Jugurthinum*. That only shows that the author is not as bold as he subsequently became. His technique is different—he eschews direct criticism. But sundry features can and should be interpreted as a veiled attack on the rulers of Rome (notably the treatment of Caesar and of Cato). Why not the year of Philippi?

There is a topic which has not been adequately explored in scholarly investigations hitherto (and is sometimes left out of the reckoning), namely the repercussion of contemporary events and persons.[26] Indications of value might be discovered in Sallust's selection of minor or subsidiary characters. It was clearly not desirable to have too many of them in a monograph. Indeed, a rule has been divined and promulgated authoritatively. Sallust, it is alleged, never brings on a character for single and solitary mention: the person must recur in the narration.[27] This rule evaporates on a reading of the text—a dozen exceptions.[28]

The bare mention of certain names might be significant, especially if isolated. A name may be unavoidable, for documentation. Too many items of that kind disperse the interest—and may suggest clues that lead nowhere. Sallust is an economical writer.

First of all, therefore, two items, that add nothing—and even impede the exposition.

L. Aemilius Paullus started an indictment against Catilina un-

---

[26] That line of enquiry has been unduly neglected, according to V. Pöschl, *Grundwerte römischer Staatsgesinnung in den Geschichtswerken des Sallust* (1940), 83.

[27] E. Schwartz, *Hermes* XXXII (1897), 563: "er hat es sich zum strengen Gesetz gemacht, keine Person nur einmal zu erwähnen." Pursuant to the law, Schwartz identified the knight M. Fulvius Nobilior, one of the original conspirators (17. 4), with "Fulvius, senatoris filius" (39. 5), although the latter is classed with "extra coniurationem complures." Either he or his father had the praenomen "Aulus" (Valerius Maximus V. 8. 5; Dio XXXVII. 36. 4).

[28] P. Sulla Ser. f. and M. Fulvius Nobilior (17. 3 f.); P. Sulla (18. 2); P. Sittius (21. 3); Septimius and C. Iulius (27. 1); Q. Metellus Creticus (30. 2); L. Paullus (31. 4); Fulvius (39. 5); C. Murena (42. 3); P. Furius (50. 4); Ti. Nero (ib.). And some others.

der the provisions of the *Lex Plautia,* the author states (i.e., *de vi publica*). Was this before or after the incident at Cicero's front door on the morning of November 7? The date is not registered (the author has a vague pluperfect tense), and Paullus' initiative was cancelled by what happened in the Senate on November 8.[29] The name and the abortive prosecution could have been dispensed with. And, in fact, Paullus is absent alike from the Catilinarian orations of Cicero and from the main line of tradition as represented by other historians.[30]

But Paullus is a character of subsequent notoriety and no good fame. Consul in 50, he changed course, being purchased by Caesar; and he managed to keep out of the armed conflict. He was put on the proscription lists by the Triumvirs, one of them his own brother. Like a number of other *nobiles,* this Aemilius benefited from pedigree and protection. He was allowed to make his escape, and he took up his residence in a city on the coast of Ionia, unmolested in the sequel.[31]

Similarly, the historian interpolates a reference to the motion of Ti. Claudius Nero into the debate of December 5, without stating clearly how and when it came up (50. 4). It was not very important (a modification of Caesar's proposal), and only one other source happens to mention it—a source which derives ultimately from Sallust.[32] Nothing stands on later record about this man. His son, however, emerged into sudden and unexpected notoriety—at another session of the Roman senate, comparable in renown to that of December 5, 63.

The young Ti. Nero (like certain other members of the old patriciate) had been a partisan of Caesar. Quaestor in 48 and commanding the fleet at Alexandria, he had for reward a priesthood and was charged with the establishment of military colonies in Gallia Narbonensis. At the debate of March 17, 44, however, he forswore the memory of his leader and benefactor: he came out

---

[29] Dio states that Cicero prepared an indictment against Catilina, *de vi* (XXXVII. 31. 3). That may be identical, hence clearly previous to November 7.

[30] Paullus' action is once alluded to (*In Vat.* 25, cf. *Schol.Bob.* p. 120 H.).

[31] Appian, *BC* IV. 37. 155.

[32] ib. II. 5. 19.

with a proposal of public honours for the tyrannicides.[33] Praetor
in 42, Ti. Claudius Nero refused to lay down office; he opposed
Octavianus in the aftermath of Philippi, took the side of the consul L. Antonius, and played a part in the War of Perusia.[34]

Time in its course throws up many paradoxes. Some obvious to
the vulgar, others most acute and entertaining to a member of
the governing order in any age. It was a scandal, but no paradox,
that characters from the Catilinarian past came on the stage of
history again, restored and refurbished by Caesar or, later, by the
Triumvirs.

C. Antonius, the equivocal consul of 63, was prosecuted and
condemned in 59. He went away and lived comfortably for long
years on a Greek island, where he exercised a kind of despotism.[35]
His nephew made no effort to induce Caesar to bring him back to
public life, for which dereliction of family piety he is hypo-
critically rebuked by Cicero.[36] But C. Antonius came back. This
drab and discredited character held the office of censor in 42 (only
accidental evidence reveals it).[37] A surprise that he was still alive.
His historical role in 63 had been subordinate and inglorious, but
he had to be mentioned in the *Bellum Catilinae*. Sallust's presentation allows nothing in his favour.[38] But Sallust in this instance
was neither inadvertent nor overbold. Marcus Antonius, who
paraded "magnitudo animi," would not have minded.

A historian could not omit Cicero's colleague in the consulate,
whether his treatment was apologetic or insinuating the worst.
But there was no necessity to obtrude L. Calpurnius Bestia,
tribune of the plebs in 62.[39] What is Sallust's motive?

---

[33] Suetonius, *Tib*. 4. 1 (the sole source for this fact).

[34] ib. 4. 2; Velleius II. 75.

[35] Strabo X, p. 455.

[36] *Phil*. II. 56; 98 f.

[37] *CIL* I², p. 64; *ILS* 6204.

[38] 21. 3; 26. 1 and 4. He could not take command in the field at Pistoria
because of gout (59. 4).

[39] The identity of the tribune and the man defended by Cicero in 56 was
long doubted or denied (F. Münzer, *R-E* III, 1367; M. Gelzer, ib. VI A, 935).
But everything speaks for it, cf. the arguments of R. G. Austin in his edition
of *Pro Caelio* (ed. 3, 1960), 154 ff. Identity is conceded by Broughton in *MRR*,
Supp. (1960). Useful consequences follow.

Bestia, entering on his tribunate on December 10, 63, joined
action with his colleague Metellus Nepos, harried Cicero in the
last days of his consulship and raised protest against the execution
of Roman citizens.[40] A few years elapse, and Cicero is advocate
for the defence when Bestia is on trial for *ambitus* (he had stood
for the praetorship in 57). Despite Cicero's eloquence, exerted
more than once, Bestia succumbed.[41] Then a long silence—no
word of Bestia among those brought back to station and office
by Caesar. But Bestia emerges as a partisan of Antonius in the
War of Mutina. Cicero in the *Philippics* refers to his past defence
of Bestia and asserts that Bestia, though a failed praetor, is advertising a claim to the consulship.[42] The name of this man was
indeed evocative of past history. It is mentioned opprobriously
(in relation to Cicero) by Brutus in a letter of June, 43.[43]

Peculiar, and not a little disturbing, is the procedure of Sallust.
He takes care to register L. Calpurnius Bestia among the fifteen
original conspirators at the general assembly in 64 (17. 3). Further, he assigns him a precise role for revolutionary action in
December, 63 (after Catilina had left Rome). The tribune, Sallust
alleges, was to deliver a harangue attacking Cicero (43. 1). That
was the signal. The night after there would be an armed rising
(the city fired in twelve places, Cethegus attacking Cicero's house,
and so on).[44] This is the plan which, according to Cicero, was to
have been put into execution at the *Saturnalia* (on December

---

[40] Plutarch, *Cicero* 23. This is the only source to name Bestia: elsewhere
Nepos is more prominent. Cicero alludes opprobriously to a tribune who de-
plored the fate of the conspirators (*Pro Sulla* 31, cf. *Pro Sestio* 11): the *Schol.
Bob.* correctly divine Bestia (p. 5 and p. 85 H).

[41] *Ad. Q. fratrem* II. 3. 6; *Pro Caelio* 7; *Phil.* XI. 11; XIII. 26.

[42] *Phil.* XI. 11; XIII. 26.

[43] Brutus was angry because Cicero, apparently, had referred to Servilius
Casca as an assassin, just the language Bestia had used about Cicero. That
charge falls back on Cicero—"quod et pluris occidit uno seque prius oportet
fateatur sicarium quam obiciat Cascae quod obicit, et imitatur in Casca Bes-
tiam" (*Ad M. Brutum* I. 17. 1). For "imitatur" read "imitetur" (D. R. Shackleton Bailey).

[44] cf. Appian, *BC* II. 3. 12. Apart from Sallust, the only source to register
the proposed harangue of Bestia—which is clearly a retrojection of the notorious speeches against Cicero, in fact delivered after December 10 (Plutarch,
Cicero 23).

17).[45] Sallust, retailing the unverifiable at a distance of twenty years, cannot be acquitted of malice against Bestia. Perhaps that person was no longer among the living, having perished in the War of Mutina.[46]

Similarly P. Sittius. Whether or no Sittius was in fact in Mauretania in 64, as an ally of Catilina, it is clear that Sallust would hardly have put him into Catilina's speech to the conspirators (21. 3), if it had not been for his subsequent vicissitudes. Sittius, incriminated in 62 (the prosecutor of P. Sulla made play with his name), somehow evaded condemnation. He remained a vulnerable and unpopular character, to succumb finally (so it appears) in 57 on a charge of manipulating the grain market.[47] P. Sittius is not again heard of for a decade. Then the adventurer is discovered at the head of a small private army. Along with Bocchus, the ruler of Mauretania, he invades Numidia in 46 and renders signal services to Caesar in the African campaign—when Sallust must have come across him.[48] Installed by Caesar as ruler of a kind of principality at Cirta, Sittius was killed by a Numidian chieftain soon after the Ides of March. Which gave acute pleasure to some people.[49]

Lastly, and on a different footing, there is Sempronia, the wife of the consular, D. Junius Brutus. She benefits from a full-length portrayal, although she takes no part in the action (25). What is this lady doing in the pages of Sallust?

The historian has next to nothing to report between the consular elections in 64 and those in 63. He is reduced, for example, to inserting military preparations of Catilina in Etruria and elsewhere (24. 2)—which is anachronistic. Sempronia is welcome to fill space, lend variety, and exhibit a female counterpart to Cati-

---

[45] *In Cat.* III. 10, cf. Plutarch, *Cicero* 18.

[46] The emergence of Bestia in 43 would have another point of interest. It recalled famous and classical contests of oratory in 56. Not only Bestia attacked by Caelius Rufus and defended by Cicero, but Rufus prosecuted by Sempronius Atratinus (*Pro Caelio* 1): this youth, later consul suffect in 34, was the son of Bestia (*ILS* 9461).

[47] *Ad fam.* V. 17. 2, as elucidated by J. Heurgon, *Latomus* IX (1950), 369 ff.

[48] For his operations in Numidia and their reward, see S. Gsell, *Histoire ancienne de l'Afrique du Nord* VIII (1930), 80 f.; 137 f.; 157 f.

[49] *Ad Att.* XV. 17. 1: "Arabioni de Sittio nihil irascor."

lina. Sempronia is a type and model of crime and depravity in the Roman aristocracy.

So far so good. The explanation is adequate and convincing. But curiosity still asks, why Sempronia? An answer has been given that seemed attractive and won wide acceptance. Sempronia was the mother of Decimus Brutus, one of the assassins. Decimus for his flagrant ingratitude incurred the especial dislike of the Caesarians. A bitter word of M. Antonius is on record.[50] Sallust is therefore wishing to put the reader in mind of D. Brutus, not in a friendly way.[51]

A doubt arises. It is not at all clear that Sallust was hostile to Decimus. Indeed, he says of Sempronia that she was happy in her husband and children—"satis fortunata" (25. 2). That is high praise, coming from Sallust.

Furthermore, there is a chance that Decimus was not her son but only her stepson.[52] He bears a second cognomen, "Albinus." That item proclaims a link with the patrician Postumii and suggests that he had been adopted by one of them (the last of his line).[53] Such adoptions generally indicate kinship somewhere. Decimus was born about 81. His mother might have been a Postumia (i.e., an earlier wife of the consul of 77).

Whether or no Sempronia was the mother of Decimus, another path of enquiry lies open. What was her parentage?[54] Sallust had in fact known another Sempronia. This is "Sempronia, Tuditani filia," the wife of Fulvius Bambalio and mother of Fulvia. The killing of P. Clodius brought both ladies into notoriety. They

---

[50] Phil. XIII. 25: "ut venefica haec liberetur obsidione."

[51] E. Schwartz, o.c. 570. The notion was widely taken up. Observe, e.g., F. Münzer, Römische Adelsparteien und Adelsfamilien (1920), 272; K. Latte, Neue Wege zur Antike II. 4 (1935), 31; R. Syme, Tacitus (1958), 567.

[52] As briefly suggested in Proc.Am.Philosophical Soc. CIV (1960), 326 f.

[53] F. Münzer, R-E Supp. V, 369 f. On coins he is styled "Albinus Bruti f." (BMC, R.Rep. I, 507 ff.). For that form of name cf. "Scipio Lepidi filius" (Orosius V. 22. 17). The son of Ser. Sulpicius Rufus and a Postumia is described as a "consobrinus" of Decimus (Ad fam. XI. 7. 1). On the hypothesis here indicated he would be a cousin by blood, not merely by adoption.

[54] Münzer suggested that Sempronia was nothing less than a daughter of C. Gracchus (o.c. 273; R-E II A, 1446). That conjecture has not found much favour.

testified at the prosecution of Milo, with lamentation, and with great effect.[55] Fulvia, married in turn to Clodius, to Curio, and to Antonius, was a bold and vigorous woman. Her character and her pedigree figure prominently in the polemical invectives of Antonius' enemies. And she was to play a notable role in the disturbances of 41, which ended in the War of Perusia.

That is to say, the Sempronia of Sallust, who had committed many deeds of "virilis audacia," might be a sister of "Sempronia, Tuditani filia." Hence the aunt of Fulvia.

Sempronii and Fulvii were great houses of the plebeian nobilitas now in eclipse. The Fulvii show no consul ever again after the fate of the consular ally of C. Sempronius Gracchus. Fulvia, virile and ambitious, did all that a woman could to retrieve the prestige of her family.[56]

It may be noted in passing that the Fulvia who rendered services to Cicero in espionage was a "mulier nobilis" (23. 3). Further, among the conspirators is registered a Roman knight with historic nomenclature, recalling consuls and conquerors— M. Fulvius Nobilior (17. 3). There is no indication about what happened to him. Fulvia the spy may still have been alive in 52. But that could only be conjecture, and most insecure. Some have thought to discover her in one of the two ladies of birth who were the prime exhibits at the scandalous banquet offered in honour of the consul Metellus Scipio and the tribunes of that year.[57] However, without that item, it is clear that Sallust, when

---

55 Asconius 35: "ultimae testimonium dixerunt Sempronia, Tuditani filia, socrus P. Clodi, et uxor Fulvia, et fletu suo magnopere eos qui assistebant commoverunt."

56 For the conventional view, cf. Velleius II. 74. 3: "nihil muliebre praeter corpus gerens." For a defence of this maligned lady, F. Münzer, R-E VII, 283 f.; R. Syme, Rom. Rev. (1939), 208.

57 Valerius Maximus IX. 1. 8: "lupanari enim domi suae instituto Muniam et Flaviam, cum a patre tum a viro utramque inclitam, et nobilem puerum Saturninum, in eo prostituit." That is the text of C. Kempf (Teubner, 1888), with support of the best mss. Earlier editors preferred to read "Muciam et Fulviam," and F. Münzer in fact identified this Fulvia with the spy (R-E VII, 281). To have a Fulvia was tempting, to be sure, and no suitable Flavia seemed available. Also a Mucia, probably because of Mucia, the third wife of Pompeius, who was no model of conduct. Pompeius divorced her in 62. She mar-

writing the *Bellum Catilinae,* was able to indulge in personal reminiscence, from time to time.

To conclude. What is the value of the monograph? If Sallust had lived to write nothing else, it was an epoch-making achievement in the literature of the Latins, creating a new style and manner. Examined as history, it exhibits manifold defects, and harsh things can be said.

Cicero and Cicero's influence magnified Catilina unduly, as other writers in antiquity were aware.[58] Sallust took over and developed Cicero's conception. That is his prime delinquency. Further, when he elected to become a historian, he underestimated the plain and elementary difficulty of the task. A slow composer, a careful contriver—yet hasty and inaccurate.

None the less, the *Bellum Catilinae* is a precious document. Sallust may fatigue with repetitive harping on the "corrupti civitatis mores." Yet he had a just cause. There was something radically wrong with a state if a man like Catilina could get so far with impunity, protected by consulars high in public repute, if armed insurrection could break out in Italy. The social diagnosis of Sallust reveals the dominance of wealth—and its corollary, the evil appetites of impoverished aristocrats. It shows how, behind the façade of laws and constitution, there operated "amicitia" and "factio" (its other name), how the traditional devices of the *nobilitas* were now enhanced and perverted, from the contest for office, honour, and glory into conspiracy against the Commonwealth.

Further, the condition of Italy. For Varro and the friends of Varro, the land was one great garden, tilled and beautiful. It could also be described as a wilderness, "solitudo Italiae." [59] Great

---

ried M. Aemilius Scaurus (*pr.* 56), who is not heard of after his condemnation and exile (? in 53). Otherwise, for the name "Munius," observe "M. Munius M. f. Lem." on the *SC de agro Pergameno* in 129, claimed as a senator by Broughton (*MRR* II, 493) and early instances in the Sabine country, viz. *CIL* I². 632 = *ILS* 3410 (Reate) ; 1875 (Amiternum). Rather, perhaps, conjecture a Mummia.

[58] Dio XXXVII. 42. 1.
[59] *Ad Att.* I. 19. 4.

estates of the rich, and gangs of slaves, but scant livelihood for the rustic poor. Many of them migrated to the provinces in this period, it can be conjectured, notably to Africa.[60]

Catilina's army was heterogeneous. Not only the discontented veterans from Sullan colonies, but "homines tenues," and also brigands (the vicinity of Faesulae had an abundance of them).[61] The disorders were widespread. In the first place Etruria, but also Cisalpine Gaul, Picenum, Bruttium, Apulia.[62] Two of the praetors of 62 were instructed by the Senate to put down disturbances among the Paeligni and in Bruttium;[63] and when C. Octavius went out to his province of Macedonia in 60, he met and destroyed near Thurii a band of slaves, remnants from the days of Spartacus and of Catilina.[64]

The new Sullan age of which Sallust witnessed the red dawn ended by producing a partial alleviation. The labourers and "latrones" of Italy, conscripted for the vast armies of the Caesarian leaders, found steady employment through long years (it was not fighting all the time) and were established in numerous colonies in Italy and throughout the world, all the way from Spain to Pontus, Pisidia and Syria.

---

[60] That notion is contested by W. E. Heitland, *JRS* VIII (1918), 34 ff. But the study of rare names in Africa lends support. Thus "Aufustius," "Farsuleius," "Fidiculanius," "Furfanius" (cf. *Historia* IV [1955], 56).

[61] 28. 4. Only a quarter of Catilina's army had proper weapons (56. 3). Cicero, classifying the supporters of Catilina, briefly registers, after the ruined Sullan veterans, "non nullos agrestis homines tenuis atque egentis," alleging that they have been incited by the veterans (*In Cat.* II. 20).

[62] 27. 1; 42. 1; *Pro Sulla* 53.

[63] Orosius VI. 6. 7.

[64] Suetonius, *Divus Aug.* 3. 1. The enemies of Caesar were not wholly without a pretext when arranging that the consuls to be elected in 60 should have the "silvae callesque" (*Divus Iulius* 19. 1). Observe, in relation to Catilina's prospects (if he evaded the army of C. Antonius), "Italiae callis et pastorum stabula" (*Pro Sestio* 12). Scholars have sometimes taken an overoptimistic view of the condition of Italy. Thus, in epilogue on the Conspiracy, M. Cary in *CAH* IX (1932), 502: "Italy finally settled down and forgot the disorders of the Social and Civil Wars."

X

THE BELLUM
JUGURTHINUM:
WARFARE

The next historical study stands
in close relation to its predecessor. Catilina, the Roman patrician
and revolutionary, is ostensibly the central character in the monograph that bears his name. Ostensibly—for that work is designed
to carry a damaging diagnosis of the whole post-Sullan order,
with sharp relevance to the present, to the return of civil war,
proscription, despotism. In like manner, the second monograph
appears to be built up around the character and vicissitudes of
one person, the Numidian prince—energy and criminal ambition,
ending miserably. Indeed, the person of Jugurtha is enhanced by
the author. Once again, however, the appearance proves deceptive. The *Bellum Jugurthinum* is not just a biography. It is the
narration of a foreign war that impinges on the internal politics
of Rome, with dire and distant repercussions. In fact, prefatory to
the *Bellum Italicum*, the civil war of Marius and Sulla, the dictatorship of Sulla. The author makes that clear.

First of all a prologue, asserting a claim for the writing of history in default of political action. After which, Sallust proceeds
to announce his theme, explaining how and why it mattered.
"I propose to narrate the war which the Roman people waged
against Jugurtha, the king of the Numidians. First, because it was
a great war, fiercely fought and hazardous. Next, because it
brought the first effective challenge to the arrogant rule of the
nobilitas" (5. 1). That statement, it will be observed, does not

138

exhaust the significance of the Numidian War. The author goes on to develop the second aspect, with emphasis on the passions evoked and the strife that ensued—the outcome was "bellum atque vastitas Italiae." [1]

The Numidian War arose from the relations between the Roman government and a native dynasty. The connection rested on clientship rather than treaty, and it was complicated by personal ties between the dynasty and certain families in the Roman governing class.[2]

Scipio Africanus acquired Masinissa as an ally. The link was reinforced and perpetuated when Scipio Aemilianus, regulating the affairs of Africa after Masinissa died (during the third war against Carthage), appointed his son Micipsa to hold rule over the greater portion of Numidia. Micipsa duly sent troops to Spain, to help Aemilianus at the siege of Numantia. They were led by a certain Jugurtha, the son of Mastanabal (an illegitimate son of Masinissa). Jugurtha won distinction at Numantia, and useful friends. Aemilianus strongly commended Jugurtha to Micipsa, who adopted him and put him on a level with his own sons, Adherbal and Hiempsal. After Micipsa died (probably in 118), the princes came quickly to open dissension. Hiempsal was assassinated; Adherbal, defeated in the field, fled to Rome and made complaint about Jugurtha. The Senate, after some discussion, sent out a commission of ten, who were instructed to divide the kingdom of Numidia between Jugurtha and Adherbal (117 or 116). However, hostility flared up again, and Jugurtha, winning the mastery in the open country, besieged Adherbal at Cirta. A Roman commission arrived to mediate, and a second, to no avail. Cirta fell, and Adherbal was killed (in 112).

That was not all. A number of Roman and Italian traders were massacred at Cirta. Hence indignation at Rome, which was exploited by one of the tribunes designate for the next year (111),

---

[1] *Jug.* 5. 2: "quae contentio divina et humana cuncta permiscuit eoque vecordiae processit ut studiis civilibus bellum atque vastitas Italiae finem faceret."

[2] cf. E. Badian, *Foreign Clientelae (264–70 B.C.)*, (1958), 192 ff.; D. Timpe, *Hermes* XC (1962), 334 ff.

namely C. Memmius, a powerful speaker and a pertinacious enemy of the governing oligarchy (27. 2). As a result, the Senate was compelled to announce vigorous measures: an expedition to Numidia, which fell to L. Calpurnius Bestia (*cos.* 111), and the enrolment of an army for that purpose (27. 4 f.).

From this point may be reckoned the inception of the Numidian War, not terminated until Jugurtha was captured in 105. The operations exhibit three phases, clear and distinct. The first is marked by hesitancies, by compromise, and by criminal incompetence. The consul Calpurnius Bestia invades Numidia, displays the Roman arms—and concludes an armistice with Jugurtha. The peace is disowned and warfare resumes, conducted by Sp. Postumius Albinus, the consul of 110, but in a fashion far from vigorous; when Albinus departs to hold the elections, his brother Aulus, left in charge, indulges in a rash foray and involves the army in a capitulation. In the second phase Q. Caecilius Metellus (*cos.* 109) wages energetic warfare, but with no decision, for after two campaigns Jugurtha is still at large, and he has induced Bocchus, the ruler of Mauretania, to intervene on his side. The third phase (from 107 to 105) brings victory under the generalship of the *novus homo* C. Marius, consul in 107.

In outline, the economy of the monograph is prescribed by the three phases of the Numidian War. But Sallust defines his theme as political also, and the two strands are tightly and artfully interwoven from the outset. Various devices indicate pause, transition, or high point; while digressions and speeches are inserted with notable effect. Thus the Numidian history down to the division of the kingdom between Jugurtha and Adherbal (5–16) leads naturally to a disquisition on the geography and peoples of Africa (17–19). The narration resumes, down to the fall of Cirta (20–26). Upon which, action decided and the consul Calpurnius Bestia to have charge of operations (27. 4 f.), the Numidian War begins.[3] And, soon after the first and deplorable stage of the war (Calpurnius Bestia and the Postumii Albini), comes a new turn,

---

[3] Some scholars, discussing the structure of the monograph, prefer to put the inception of the Numidian War after the excursus on Africa, to make it begin with the aggression of Jugurtha against Adherbal (20 ff.). It does not matter much.

emphasised by a historical excursus on Roman political life (41 f.) —central in significance, though not, like the comparable passage in the *Bellum Catilinae*, placed at the precise centre of the monograph.

The *Bellum Jugurthinum*, it will be repeated, expounds two contests, the one waged against Jugurtha, the other against the *nobilitas*. The second deploys in three significant episodes. First, following on the fall of Cirta, the intervention of C. Memmius, at that time tribune-designate (27. 2), reinforced a little later by the oration he delivers after the terms of peace arranged by Calpurnius Bestia (31). Second, the bill of the tribune C. Mamilius Limetanus in 109, setting up a court of enquiry to investigate various kinds of corrupt practices in relation to Numidian affairs (40): this introduces the excursus on party politics (41 f.). Third, the candidature of Marius in 108, and his success at the elections (73. 4–7). To enhance that success, the author gratuitously produces a lengthy harangue in which the new consul speaks for merit against birth and pedigree (85).

Sallust is a careful contriver. He wrote "structe," that is the verdict pronounced by one of the ancient critics of literature.[4] The devices which Sallust employed in building up this monograph will repay inspection. Scholarly investigation has not been remiss. On the contrary. It brings up subtle discussions, detailed analysis, elaborate subdivisions and correspondences—and not a little disagreement.[5] In proportion to the space engrossed and the

----

[4] Fronto p. 114 N = II, 48 (Haines).

[5] K. Latte, *Neue Wege zur Antike* II. 4 (1935), 33 ff.; K. Büchner, *Hermes*, Einzelschriften 9 (1953); K. Vretska, *Wiener S-B* CXXIX. 4 (1955); A. D. Leeman, *Med.der Kon.Ned.Ak. van Wetenschappen* XX. 8 (1957), 200 ff. For criticism of the moralistic point of view of Büchner and Vretska, see Leeman, o.c. 230. And further on Büchner, G. W. Williams, *JRS* XLIV (1954), 158 f.; E. Paratore, *Maia* VII (1955), 69 ff.; A. La Penna, *Ann.della Scuola Normale Superiore di Pisa* XXVIII (1959), 53 ff. For a protest against those who elaborately divide the monograph into "Szenen und Akten," see H. Drexler, *Gnomon* XXXIII (1961), 573.

W. Steidle argues that Sallust was firmly guided all through by his historical theme, *Historia*, Einzelschriften 3 (1958), 33 ff. For comments on Steidle, see G. W. Williams, *Gnomon* XXXII (1960), 509 ff.; A. La Penna, o.c. 54 f. And D. C. Earl will now be consulted with profit, *The Political Thought of Sallust* (1961), 60 ff.

effort, it is a temptation to ask how much clear profit accrues, especially if the accuracy and integrity of the historian are neglected or postponed.

The *Bellum Jugurthinum* presents a variety of problems. Since warfare is the large portion, the first question goes to the accuracy of the narrator—time, place, and the relation of events. Years registered without fail by the names of consuls could have provided firm guidance, or a strict alternation of summers and winters (that might have appealed to a writer zealous to emulate Thucydides). But Sallust eschews the annalistic schema. He is found defective on chronology, and harsh censure fastens on his procedure. Years and intervals of time, it is affirmed, have no meaning for Sallust.

His shortcomings are not everywhere flagrant or even detrimental. The operations belonging to the first phase can be sorted out—except that there appears to be one mistake in the indication of time. Aulus, the brother of the consul Sp. Postumius Albinus, set out on his ill-starred expedition in the winter season (i.e., the winter 110–109), precisely "mense Januario" (37. 3). But, after his capitulation, the author registers Metellus and his colleague as the "consules designati" for the year 109 (43. 1). That is to say, the year 109 had not begun, and there is a patent contradiction. Sallust has been inadvertent. It is an irony that this unique indication of a precise date (not another in the whole narration of the warfare) should be either erroneous itself or prove error in another item.

Yet it is not at all clear how far Sallust is in error. He states that tribunes blocked the elections for the whole year.[6] And he has a later reference to the delay.[7] Therefore a perceptible interval may have occurred after January 1 before the consuls of 109 took office.[8]

---

[6] 37. 2 f.: "quae dissensio totius anni comitia impediebat. ea mora in spem adductus Aulus . . . milites mense Ianuario ex hibernis in expeditionem evocat."

[7] 44. 3: "aestivorum tempus comitiorum mora inminuerat" (in reference to Metellus' first activities in Africa).

[8] Therefore the only inadequacy of Sallust would be his describing Metellus and Silanus as "consules designati" (43. 1), for they would surely have

The chronological perplexity that emerges in relation to the expedition of A. Postumius Albinus does not, so it happens, have a bearing on any topic of serious debate, military or political. But the campaigns of Metellus and of Marius (from 109 to 105) are attended by sundry problems. Winter quarters at the end of Metellus' first campaign are registered (61. 2), but not for the second, before he was superseded by Marius, the consul of 107. That omission need not in fact provoke any difficulties. The real crux emerges in Marius' operations—no sign of a break between 107 and 106.

In consequence, much (and too much) discussion has been devoted to the dating of the campaigns of Metellus and Marius. Thanks to which (or, it might be said, in spite of which, for scholarly research is sometimes found to ignore or override plain indications in the text of Sallust), a more or less satisfactory framework can be reconstructed.[9]

First, the campaigns of Q. Caecilius Metellus. Consul in 109, Metellus could not take the field at once. And, when he landed in Africa, he had to knock the army into proper shape—the troops were in poor condition after the command of the two Postumii. Invading Numidia, the consul occupied Vaga (47. 1 f.). Proceeding southwestwards, he soon had to fight a great battle, which after

---

entered office as soon as elected. That is the explanation of S. Gsell, *Histoire ancienne de l'Afrique du Nord* VII (1930), 174 f. A. H. J. Greenidge proposed to take "consules designati" as nontechnical—"appointed consuls" (*A History of Rome* I [1904], 380).

For a long and laborious study of this point, see H. Chantraine, *Untersuchungen zur römischen Geschichte am Ende des 2. Jahrhunderts v. Chr.* (1959), 50–62. Following H. Wirz (*Festschr. Zürich* [1887], 8 ff.) and others, he proposes to expunge "mense Ianuario" as an interpolation. That done, he can date the expedition of A. Postumius to November of the year 110. Similarly, but without indication of a problem, H. M. Last, in *CAH* IX (1932), 121: "probably in the autumn."

[9] The chronology for Metellus (109 and 108) and for Marius (107–105) here adopted depends on a study of the text. In essentials it is the same (that can be counted fortunate) as that of M. Holroyd, *JRS* XVIII (1928), 20; S. Gsell, *Histoire ancienne de l'Afrique du Nord* VII (1930), 178 ff.; H. M. Last in *CAH* IX (1932), 122 ff.; J. Carcopino, *Histoire romaine* (1935), 305 ff. The case has been restated by K. Vretska, *Gymnasium* LX (1953), 339 ff. Also by H. Chantraine, o.c. 62, after a long and complicated doxology (32–50).

grievous hazards ended to the advantage of the Romans (48–53). The site was close to the river Muthul, a tributary of the Bagradas, so it appears (not that the Bagradas is named anywhere by Sallust); in any case, not far to the north of Sicca, which city then came over to the Romans (56. 3).[10] After the battle, Metellus went on into the richest part of Numidia, capturing and burning many towns. The final episode of the campaign was a vain attempt to capture Zama and a fierce battle in the vicinity (56–60). Then Metellus retreated, taking up winter quarters in the Roman province of Africa (61. 2).[11] The Senate prorogued his command (62. 10). These operations, there is no doubt, can be circumscribed to a small area in the northeast of Numidia.

The winter saw the loss and recapture of Vaga (66 f.).[12] Then followed Metellus' intrigue with Bomilcar, a native chieftain. After that, Metellus took the field again (73. 1). There was a battle in which Jugurtha was defeated. Jugurtha thereupon retired into the steppe and took refuge at Thala (where much of his treasure was deposited), described as "oppidum magnum atque opulentum," and situated fifty miles distant from the nearest river (75. 1 f.). Metellus marched to Thala and captured the town; but Jugurtha slipped away and fled into the country of the Gaetulians. After a time he induced Bocchus, the King of Mauretania, to intervene and give help. The two kings appeared in force near Cirta, which had come into Roman possession (81. 2), it is not said how or when. Negotiations followed and warfare lapsed.[13]

Metellus meanwhile had received information from Rome not

---

[10] The Muthul has generally been identified as the Oued Mellag, cf. S. Gsell, o.c. 190. If that were not correct (and other rivers have been proposed) it signifies little for the interpretation of Sallust.

[11] Probably at Tisidium: Metellus summoned Jugurtha to come there (62. 8).

[12] The winter season is stated (68. 2). The conspirators at Vaga fixed a day —"in diem tertium constituunt, quod is festus celebratusque per omnem Africam ludum et lasciviam magis quam formidinem ostentabat" (66. 2). By a notable conjecture J. Carcopino divined "in diem Cererum," that is, December 13 (*Rev.hist.* CLVIII [1928], 1 ff. = *Aspects mystiques de la Rome païenne* [1941], 13 ff.).

[13] 83. 3: "eo modo saepe ab utroque missis remissisque nuntiis tempus procedere, et ex Metelli voluntate bellum intactum trahi."

only that Marius had been elected consul, but that Numidia had been assigned to him (82. 2). So far the operations of 108. If Sallust is to be given credit, it is clear that no decisive activities of Metellus in the field can be dated subsequently and put in 107, before the arrival of the new consul.[14]

To sum up. Sallust indicated the end of Metellus' first campaign by winter quarters (61. 2). No statement about the second. Yet there is a clue that should not be missed. It is the digression about Lepcis (78 f.), ostensibly justified by the arrival of envoys from that city to treat with the Roman general (77. 1). Digressions are inserted for a variety of reasons by the more artful type of historian. Not merely elucidation (an excursus of this length and character was not required) but for variety, to register a pause, or to manage a transition. This digression is placed after the capture of Thala, and Thala should belong to the autumn of 108.[15] No warlike actions of Metellus are subsequently noted, only negotiations with Bocchus, conducted in the vicinity of Cirta (82 f.) The passage about Lepcis therefore marks and represents the winter of 108 to 107.

Next, Marius in 107. After preliminary operations, he was able to defeat Jugurtha in a battle near Cirta (88. 3). He then took a number of towns and castles (the region is not specified). After which, Marius conceived and planned a long march, to surpass Metellus' exploit at Thala and to spread terror of the Roman

---

[14] Mommsen's theory, putting the two campaigns of Metellus not in 109 and 108 but in 108 and 107, tends to recur, with unhappy results. And, a further complication, the rediscovery of D. E. Bosselaar, *Quomodo Sallustius historiam belli Jugurthini conscripserit* (Diss. Utrecht, 1915). Bosselaar argued for three campaigns of Metellus: the first ended in 109 after the Battle at the Muthul, the winter camp in 61. 2 is that of 108–107, and the capture of Thala belongs to 107.

A. La Penna, in his acute study of the War as history, discovered signal merits in the neglected Bosselaar (o.c. 47). For chronology he is content with a brief reference to Bosselaar and to Büchner (243). Now Büchner follows Bosselaar, but not with adequate clarity (o.c. 69; 92). An independent scrutiny of the chronology ought to have suggested grave doubts. The author who needed to be revived was M. Holroyd (*JRS* XVIII [1928], 1 ff.)—as W. Steidle with proper candour confesses (o.c. 80).

[15] M. Holroyd put the capture of Thala in the spring of 108 (o.c. 19), because of the rain (75. 9). That could fit autumn no less.

arms. His goal was Capsa, far away in a snake-infested desert (in fact, about a hundred and thirty miles south of Sicca); and he set out from the neighbourhood of Lares (Lorbeus, between Sicca and Zama). A river was crossed, the Tanais (unidentifiable);[16] and, achieving a complete surprise, Marius captured Capsa and destroyed it (89–91).

The expedition to Capsa belongs late in the summer—Sallust is explicit (90. 1). That is to say, the summer of 107. He goes on to record the capture of a number of places (no names). Then he announces a new enterprise of Marius (92. 4); and, suddenly, the army is discovered attacking a castle of Jugurtha on a precipitous rock not far from the river Muluccha. That river is described as the limit dividing the realms of Jugurtha and of Bocchus the Mauretanian (92. 5). Now the Muluccha (Moulouya) lies far in the west, beyond Oran: it enters the sea at a point only thirty miles short of Melilla (in Spanish Morocco).[17] Hence a double perplexity. No name or sign to show how Marius reached this remote region, and no winter quarters recorded—that is, between 107 and 106. Perhaps the campaigning went on without a sensible break—as has happened in other African wars.

By a stroke of luck, the castle near the Muluccha was captured, and with it treasures of Jugurtha. The next scene reveals Marius in retreat. He had to fight two battles towards the end of his march, the second near Cirta (101. 1); he reached Cirta, the goal of his march (102. 1); and the army went into winter quarters (103. 1).[18] To the following winter and spring therefore belong the negotiations with Bocchus, as a result of which he was persuaded to surrender his ally, largely through the diplomatic address of Sulla, the quaestor of Marius. The year 105 is indicated by a vague reference, "per idem tempus" (114. 1), to a defeat of the Romans in Gaul (that is, the Battle of Arausio, fought on October 6, 105).

[16] Unless the Tanais be the Oued el Derb, as Gsell (o.c. 233), following Tissot.

[17] For the problem of the Muluccha, see p. 147.

[18] 100. 1: "dein Marius, uti coeperat, in hiberna it"; 102. 1: "consul haud dubie iam victor pervenit in oppidum Cirtam, quo initio profectus intenderat"; 103. 1: "exercitu in hibernaculis composito." If the "Livian tradition" is correct, Cirta had been lost to the Romans during Marius' absence (Orosius V. 15. 10; Dio XXVI. 89. 5a).

The monograph ends by chronicling the Numidian triumph which Marius celebrated on the first day of his second consulship; and in that season, says Sallust, all the hopes and resources of Rome were concentrated on the person of Marius (114. 4).

An intelligible chronology of the years 109 to 105 can thus be established. So far so good. Other problems subsist. Sallust's treatment of the campaigns is uneven and capricious. Some episodes are worked up and rendered at length, such as the Battle at the Muthul, certain transactions at Vaga, or Marius' march to Capsa. Other operations, however, are left vague and nameless. That phenomenon is partly to be explained by the nature of the sources, not everywhere detailed and abundant. More important, perhaps, the author's technique of selection and emphasis.

Again, not only vagueness but serious omissions. Metellus in his first year operated in a restricted area of northeastern Numidia, which can be roughly defined as the triangle Vaga-Sicca-Zama. At the end of his second year, the Roman general is discovered holding Cirta (81. 2). It is a position of conspicuous strength, in a wholly different region, and not easy of access: Cirta lies about a hundred and fifty miles to the west of Sicca. How did Metellus get there? A long and arduous march has been suppressed, whether from the region of Sicca or from Thala.

Nor is there any place name or indication of the route followed by Marius between his capture of Capsa and his appearance at the castle near the river Muluccha. Sallust describes the latter enterprise as comparable to the former, but not quite so arduous (92. 4). Which is peculiar, given the distance to be traversed. The Muluccha, which is described here (92. 5) and in two other places (19. 7; 110. 8) as the boundary between Numidia and the kingdom of Bocchus, is five hundred miles in a straight line to the west of Cirta. Such an expedition deserves signal renown in the military annals of any age. Sallust's report and his comment ought to evoke surprise—and some conceive a grave suspicion that the historian is the victim of error or confusion, deceived by another river of the same (or similar) name, or by a later boundary.[19] Bocchus as the reward of his treachery received a tract of western

---

[19] Thus E. Cat, *Essai sur la province de Maurétanie Césarienne* (1891), 32.

Numidia;[20] and subsequently two Mauretanian kingdoms emerge, separated by the river Muluccha.[21] At the time of Caesar's campaign in Africa, eastern Mauretania was ruled by a second Bocchus, who, along with P. Sittius, invaded Numidia and captured Cirta.[22] It would be worth knowing where the eastern border of Mauretania ran in this period; and there is a chance that, in one instance out of three (92. 5), Sallust's Muluccha is not the Moulouya in the far west.[23]

Cirta (in relation to Metellus) and the expedition of Marius to the river Muluccha are the items most damaging to the credit of Sallust as a narrator of warfare. But there are a number of other inadequacies about time and place. Various explanations avail— and some to palliate. First of all, the author had recourse to heterogeneous sources. Hence the danger of inserting episodes out of their proper chronological order. For example, the arrival of the quaestor Sulla in the camp of Marius (he had been left behind in Italy to muster auxiliary cavalry) is put at the time when Marius was besieging the castle near the Muluccha (95. 1)—perhaps too late, and the cavalry was needed before that.[24] Second, two sets of actions, Rome and Numidia, with the delicate problem of registering their precise interrelation. Third, the geography of North Africa. It is hostile to readily apprehended demarcations, there is a lack of clear points of reference. In any event, Roman historians evince a reluctance to inflict on their readers a plethora of strange names. Sallust is economical—he specifies only three rivers and seven towns in the zone of Numidia covered by the marches and battles of Metellus and Marius.[25]

---

[20] S. Gsell, o.c. 264.

[21] Pliny, NH V. 19. It was also the boundary of the Roman provinces Caesariensis and Tingitana. There are many perplexities in the geographical writers. For a succinct statement about some of the problems touching the Muluccha, see S. Weinstock, R-E XIV, 2365 f.

[22] Bell.Afr. 25. 2.

[23] A. Piganiol, La conquête romaine³ (1940), 274: "mais nous n'oserions pas dire avec Salluste qu'il vint jusqu'a la Muluccha (Moulouia)."

[24] Some suggest that the placing of Sulla's arrival is a deliberate device of the author. Thus K. Büchner, o.c. 58 f.

[25] Three rivers: Muthul, Tanais, Muluccha. Seven places: Vaga, Sicca, Zama, Cirta, Thala, Capsa, Lares.

Fourth, the general technique of the writer: strict concentration on what he deems essential to his theme, ruthless excision of peripheral detail or annotation that might have been helpful to slow understandings. For Sallust, the ultimate fate of Jugurtha is irrelevant, likewise the territorial dispositions made at the end in Numidia.

The behaviour of the historian being so conscious and wilful (omission, abbreviation, or the artistic arrangement of events), the suspicion has been entertained that he misleads of set purpose.

Relating the early life of Jugurtha, Sallust assigns a decisive moment to his experiences in the camp of Scipio at Numantia: he asserts that Jugurtha's Roman friends incited his ambitions and revealed the maxim that anything could be got at Rome for money (8. 1). Is this an invention of Sallust? It may well be that Sallust was not the first writer to establish the nexus—one of the Roman annalists had been at Numantia, Sempronius Asellio.[26] Further, Sallust puts Jugurtha's adoption by Micipsa in immediate sequel to his sojourn at Numantia (9. 3). That is perhaps careless rather than artifice. It emerges a little later that Jugurtha was not adopted until three years before Micipsa's decease (11. 6).

Another instance is instructive. Sallust omitted to indicate a winter intervening between the operations of 107 and 106. The omission is deliberate, it has been supposed—to magnify Marius by implying that manifold exploits were achieved by him in one season only.[27]

That notion can be firmly repulsed. Lack of thought is the better explanation. Those who are at pains to censure Sallust are themselves not always above reproach. Thus a theory once promulgated, that the campaigns of Metellus should be assigned, not to 109 and 108 but to 108 and 107, has been uncritically perpetuated.[28] Or again, one scholar puts the river Muluccha almost three hundred kilometres from Capsa, another more than two hundred

---

[26] Gellius II. 13. 3. Asellio as a source has plausibly been invoked by W. Steidle, o.c. 52. The censorious Rutilius Rufus (p. 155) should not be neglected.

[27] W. A. Baehrens, Neue Wege zur Antike IV (1926), 81: "mit bewusster Fälschung."

[28] P. 145, with n. 14. On this perverse chronology, see also M. Holroyd, who notes various "omissions and misrepresentations," not only in Mommsen, but also in Pelham's criticism of Mommsen (JRS XVIII [1928], 19).

miles from Cirta.[29] The prime exhibit is an abbreviated account
where the expedition to Capsa occurs in a winter (that of 107–
106), followed by the march to the Muluccha; and Marius is
credited with a siege of Cirta in that same winter, the town
capitulating in the spring of 106.[30]

However, it is not necessary to exculpate Sallust in this indirect
fashion. Narrating transactions of warfare, Sallust was not proposing to furnish full particulars about the size of armies, precise
intervals of time, or exact itineraries. That was the function of
commentarii. Historians are selective, dramatic, impressionistic.
A later writer duly and deliberately reproduces the Sallustian
manner when he recounts the campaigns of Agricola in Scotland
or the operations waged against Tacfarinas by four proconsuls of
Africa.

Sallust offers a picture of African warfare, valid in any age.
Vivid phrases call up the desert, the scrub, the broken country, the
elusive enemies, thirst and fatigue, treachery and murder. In this
matter, the merits of Sallust are patent and acknowledged.[31] It
remains to ask whether he has brought out properly the specific
character of this war—cause, duration, and conclusion.

Sallust, it can be argued, has the correct diagnosis, which is presupposed all through the narrative, though not summarised anywhere in a single and memorable phrase. Once the Roman legions
had been engaged in the field and had suffered a discomfiture,
there could be no compromise, no place for Jugurtha as a chastened
and repentant vassal. The Numidian himself was willing enough
—but he soon came to understand that Rome would not condone
the affront to the "dignitas" of the imperial Republic, or abate its
resentment and rancour. Other enemies of Rome learned the same
lesson.[32]

---

[29] Respectively, W. A. Baehrens, o.c. 80; D. E. Bosselaar, o.c. 87. Neither
scholar gives any indication that he takes the Muluccha to be a different river
from the river which according to Sallust was the boundary of Bocchus' kingdom.

[30] A. Piganiol, o.c. 274. Cirta, it is true, had been lost to the Romans (Orosius V. 15. 10; Dio XXVI. 89. 5a).

[31] S. Gsell, o.c. 129; 132; G. Boissier, L'Afrique romaine⁴ (1909), 21 f.

[32] In a much discussed matter, the Roman decision to make war on Philip
V in 200, not everybody has seen the motive force of resentment and the assertion of "dignitas imperii."

Hence the Roman generals devoted their efforts not so much to the conquest of territory as to the pursuit of an individual.[33] Jugurtha eluded sieges and escaped after battles. Treachery was the next resort, to ensnare Jugurtha or to murder him. Indeed, Metellus began with such an attempt, tampering with envoys of Jugurtha before he took the field (46. 4); he tried again after the occupation of Vaga (47. 4); and he later made an elaborate plot with Bomilcar, which was detected and suppressed (70–72).

That being so, a further question permits of an answer: to whom should go the credit of winning the Numidian War? The tradition of the Optimates exalted Metellus, asserting that he had broken the back of Jugurtha's resistance when for reasons of domestic politics he was superseded by Marius, most unjustly.[34] That conception lost none of its plausibility when a similar situation recurred forty years after, with the allegation that Pompeius annexed a glory that of right belonged to Lucullus, the general of the aristocracy in the war against Mithridates.

Sallust's account redresses the balance, without depreciation of Metellus. Though Metellus had won victories in the field, Jugurtha was still at large in the empty land; he had acquired an ally, and no end was in sight. Marius, however, spread his operations much more widely, harrying Jugurtha and leaving him no place of refuge. Jugurtha was driven to depend on Bocchus entirely; and Bocchus, being made to realise the strength and tenacity of the Roman strategy, proved accessible to intimidation and cajolery. The agent was the quaestor Sulla, to whom Jugurtha was handed over, but the credit goes to Marius.[35]

Sallust knew warfare. He also knew Numidia, having been left in charge of the new province which Caesar established. A rare advantage for a historian. His work might be expected to benefit, visibly and notably.

---

[33] That is the thesis convincingly expounded by M. Holroyd, o.c. 1 ff.

[34] That conception was transmitted by Livy, cf. *Per.* LXV: "Q. Caecilius Metellus cos. duobus proeliis Iugurtham fudit totamque Numidiam vastavit"; Velleius II. 11. 2: "bellique paene patrati a Metello qui bis Iugurtham acie fuderat." Also Florus I. 36. 11 ff.; Eutropius IV. 27. 2 f.

[35] M. Holroyd, o.c. 18.

As governor, Sallust took up residence, it is presumed, at Zama, which had been the capital of Juba.[36] Hence his statement that Zama lies on the plain and is not a strong place by nature will be accorded value (57. 1). But it is not certain that he had visited Thala—at least his description (75. 2) seems not to fit the place of that name forty miles northeast of Theveste, and many are disposed to deny identity, looking for Sallust's Thala somewhere else.[37] As for Cirta, strange misconceptions emerge. Cirta, on its first mention, is defined as situated not far from the sea (21. 2). Next, Jugurtha when besieging Adherbal surrounds Cirta with a rampart and a ditch (23. 1).[38] That is impossible: Cirta is a promontory, girt with precipitous ravines on all sides, except for a narrow isthmus. Sallust, it is clear, had never seen Cirta—and, in fact, Cirta was not included in his province.[39] Caesar had given it to the Campanian condottiere P. Sittius, to rule there like a native vassal.

Roman historians do not always choose to proclaim, or even to disclose, geographical information which they undoubtedly possessed. Literary tradition and written sources tend to be on show rather than personal experience. Sallust appropriately inserts a digression on Africa. It is of extreme brevity, as he is careful to state and to repeat—"quam paucissumis" (17. 2; 7). Nothing in what he relates conveys any suggestion of autopsy. After pointed and succinct phrases describing the land and its inhabitants, the author passes quickly to origins and antiquities. Greek erudition and fancies betray their usual devastating effects. One learns that miscellaneous remnants from the western expedition of Hercules came to Africa; Medes, Persians, and Armenians mixed with the indigenous Libyans and Gaetulians; and the term "Maurus" has an etymology, for it derives by corruption from "Medus." Those

---

[36] Zama, i.e., Zama Regia, cf. S. Gsell, o.c. 197.

[37] S. Gsell, o.c. 208 f. See, however, the firm arguments of C. Courtois, *Recueil . . . Constantine* LXIX (1955–1956), 55 ff.

[38] The same statement occurs in Diodorus XXXIV. 31.

[39] S. Gsell, o.c. 125; 128. The notion has been argued that the Cirta of Sallust is really Sicca (R. Charlier, *L'ant.class.* XIX [1950], 289 ff.). That notion is not likely to find many fanciers.

quaint speculations are introduced with appeal to Punic books, attributed to King Hiempsal: they had been translated for Sallust's use (17. 7). It is fair to add, however, that Sallust covers himself by disclaiming responsibility for the opinions he reports.[40]

Books by Hiempsal, it will be added, even if written in Punic, would probably owe more to Greek science than to authentic and native tradition. Sallust may also have drawn on Posidonius, whose trace is so often sought or surmised in ethnographical disquisitions.[41] In fact, the forms of several geographical names in Sallust's excursus betray a Greek original.[42] Furthermore, two errors in Sallust have their parallel in Strabo the geographer, who is presumed to derive from Posidonius. Sallust is careless about the position of the Arae Philaenorum (the old boundary between the dominions of Carthage and Cyrene);[43] and he advances the peculiar opinion that the more fertile parts of Numidia are those adjacent to Mauretania.[44]

The name of the illustrious Greek historian who elected to continue Polybius brings on the general question of Sallust's sources.[45] Here obscurity prevails. Posidonius wrote from the point of view of the Roman governing class; and something of Posidonius' account of those transactions can be divined in Plutarch's *Life of Marius,* and in Diodorus: for example, certain imputations to the discredit of Marius.[46] Sallust's preference may have gone rather to Latin writers (some of them sources of Posi-

---

[40] 17. 7: "ceterum fides eius rei penes auctores erit."

[41] S. Gsell, o.c. 127 f. For doubts about the Posidonian origin of the excursus on Africa see K. Trüdinger, *Studien zur Geschichte der griechisch-römischen Ethnographie* (Diss. Basel, 1918), 127 ff.

[42] Thus 19. 3: "Cyrene est, colonia Theraeon."

[43] 19. 3, cf. Strabo III, p. 171.

[44] 16. 5, cf. Strabo XVII, p. 831.

[45] cf. the lucid and balanced account of Gsell, o.c. 126 ff.

[46] Notably as concerns the affair at Vaga and the execution of Turpilius (Plutarch, *Marius* 8). On Plutarch see A. Passerini, *Athenaeum* XXII (1934), 17 ff.; K. v. Fritz, *TAPA* LXXIV (1943), 166 f. For the *Historiae* of Posidonius, K. Reinhardt, *R-E* XXII, 630 ff. Much use of Posidonius (perhaps overmuch) is postulated by W. Schur, *Sallust als Politiker* (1934), 163 ff.

donius). The name of Sempronius Asellio can be invoked, who in
his prologue proclaimed and set for himself an austere purpose:
not mere annalistic recording but historical diagnosis. Asellio,
military tribune under Scipio Aemilianus at Numantia, lived long
enough to carry his narrative at least as far as 91.[47] The period was
also covered by Valerius Antias and Claudius Quadrigarius.[48]

The type and quality of Valerius Antias does not baffle conjecture. It appears that Livy kept on using Antias though he had
become aware at an earlier stage of his barefaced inventions.
Orosius, drawing on Livy, reports two battles which Marius fought
against the combined forces of Jugurtha and Bocchus.[49] They
resemble nothing in Sallust, and present various characteristics
of romantic fiction. In the first battle, near Cirta, the enemy had
sixty thousand cavalry; in the second, a total force of ninety thousand. Both armies were wiped out. The second battle is vividly
narrated: the Romans, brought to extremities, were providentially
saved by a storm of rain. Livy, it will further be observed, did not
refrain from citing Antias for the Roman casualties at Arausio:
eighty thousand soldiers killed, and forty thousand camp followers.[50] Sallust eschews any estimate of numbers in the Jugurthine
War, even on the Roman side. Sallust, it is a fair conjecture, will
not have put any higher value on Valerius Antias than did Cicero,
who by silence denies him a place among the recent historians.[51]

Some of Sallust's requirements were met, though imperfectly,
by the contemporary memoirs of Roman politicians. Autobiography preceded biography at Rome—it arose, like history, from
Roman public life. The great Aemilius Scaurus (cos. 115), one of
the principal managers of policy for nearly thirty years, wrote an
account of his life (he had plenty to explain away). Cicero in his
Brutus alludes to those books as something of a treasure—"sane

---

[47] For the fragments of Asellio, see H. Peter, HRR I² (1914), 179 ff.

[48] But not by Sisenna. The strange idea that Sisenna was "eine Haupt-
quelle" stands on record in Schanz-Hosius, Gesch. der r. Literatur I⁴ (1927),
367. His name is also canvassed, superfluously, by Lenschau, R-E X, 6.

[49] Orosius V. 15. 10 ff.

[50] ib. 16. 3.

[51] P. 47.

utiles quos nemo legit."[52] In this matter as in others, Sallust may have taken a hint from the *Brutus*, a recent publication.

The memoirs of Rutilius Rufus also had a strongly apologetic flavour, as the fragments reveal.[53] Rutilius, a coeval of Scaurus and a bitter rival at the elections for 115 (reciprocal charges of *ambitus*), did not reach the consulate until a decade had elapsed. And, many years later, succumbing to a malicious prosecution in 92, Rutilius went into exile in Asia, ostentatious in seeking approbation from the Greeks he was alleged to have treated badly and finding solace in talk and writing. The name of Rutilius stands for conscious rectitude and philosophical studies.[54] It will not be forgotten that he was interested in the science of warfare, and had seen service in the field (beginning, like so many others who come into the story of Jugurtha, at Numantia).[55]

Finally, the autobiography of Sulla the Dictator, which he dedicated to his friend Lucullus.[56] This curious document, cynical at times in its bold mendacity, set a high standard for persons and a whole class not disposed to self-dispraisement.[57] Sallust used it, as is manifest in the full account of the surrender of Jugurtha, and as can also be assumed for the two battles west of Cirta. Similarly, as showing Rutilius Rufus the source, will be observed the excellent narration of the Battle of the Muthul—Rutilius was there as a legate under Metellus (50. 1).

There is no trace of any memoirs written by Metellus himself. Men of the time held this nobleman in high esteem, and the

---

[52] *Brutus* 112. For the scanty fragments, *HRR* I², 185. See further E. Pais, *Dalle guerre puniche a Cesare Augusto* I (1918), 137 ff.; P. Fraccaro, *Rend.-Ac.Lincei*⁵ XX (1911) 169 ff. = *Opuscula* II (1957), 125 ff.

[53] *HRR* I², 189 f.; *FGrH* 815. Cf. F. Münzer, *R-E* IA, 1277 ff.; G. L. Hendrickson, *CP* XXVIII (1933), 153 ff.

[54] Velleius II. 13. 2: "virum non saeculi sui sed omnis aevi optimum."

[55] Appian, *Ib*. 88. Apart from Marius, C. Memmius (*tr. pl.* 111) was also there (Frontinus, *Strat*. IV. 1. 1). And perhaps others, such as Scaurus (cf. *De viris illustribus* 72. 3: "primo in Hispania corniculum meruit").

[56] Plutarch, *Lucullus* 1.

[57] For the fragments and traces, *HRR* I², 195 ff. For the *Autobiography* as a source of Sallust, G. Vitelli, *Stud.it.fil.cl*. VI (1898), 353 ff.; I. Calabi, *Mem. Acc. Lincei*⁸ III. 5 (1950), 247 ff.

historians treated him handsomely. According to Sallust, a splendid welcome acclaimed Metellus from all classes at Rome when he came back from Africa in 107 (88. 1). Sallust omits his triumph —deliberately, but not from malice. He also omits the fact that a tribune intervened to block that triumph, which was only celebrated in the next year.

Three quotations have been preserved from orations delivered by Metellus in those transactions.[58] Hence the chance that other political speeches of the period were extant and accessible to Sallust. For example, Cicero as a boy knew and studied the peroration of C. Sulpicius Galba, one of the guilty men indicted by the *quaestio Mamiliana* in 109.[59]

The harangue of C. Memmius, tribune of the plebs in 111, is a highlight and a significant moment in the *Bellum Jugurthinum*. Cicero in the *Brutus* referred to Memmius, but only as a forensic advocate and in terms of no great approbation.[60] The tradition survived, however, if nothing more, that Memmius was a powerful public speaker. To Sallust, the eloquence of Memmius is "clara pollensque"; and he affirms that he will therefore reproduce one of the numerous orations of Memmius (30. 4). Sallust's language seems to imply that he has in mind a precise and recorded oration. But one might well wonder whether his effort, introduced by "huiusce modi verbis," is based upon an original document. No less than the other speeches in the monograph, this is free composition by Sallust.

Sallust, himself a tribune and an orator, did not lack interest in past practitioners and enemies of the oligarchy; and of some he had known the descendants, such as Memmius' grandson, the praetor of 58, consular candidate in 54. Sallust dashes off a tribunician harangue in fine style, with obvious delight and relish. But there is no reason to believe that he had given anxious study to original documents of any kind. His portrayal of the political scene at the time of the Jugurthine War is mainly and patently his own invention.

---

[58] H. Malcovati, *ORF*[2] (1955), 211 ff.

[59] *Brutus* 127.

[60] ib. 136: "tum etiam C. L. Memmii fuerunt oratores mediocres, accusatores acres atque acerbi."

XI

THE BELLUM JUGURTHINUM: POLITICS

In spite of many things either inadequate or peculiar, the military operations as narrated in the *Bellum Jugurthinum* do not appear to have been distorted by prejudice against persons or by party animus. What Metellus achieved in warfare is set forth in full detail and favourably; Marius is prominent on show, but not magnified unduly; nor is the alert diplomacy of Sulla in any way depreciated.

The other aspect has to be considered. The war and the generals are caught up in a tight nexus with the politics of the capital. Since the author defines the theme as not warfare only but a challenge to the "superbia" of the aristocracy, his choice of language declares a decided point of view—and perhaps bias from the outset, general and pervasive.

That bias will be looked for in the treatment of individuals. Also in the diagnosis of Roman political life and in the underlying presuppositions about the *nobilitas*.[1]

First, the generals. Calpurnius Bestia, the consul of 111, was impugned for the treaty he made with Jugurtha. It comes as some-

---

[1] It was long the fashion to assume not only bias but deliberate and systematic distortion in the portrayal of events and persons. Thus, in an extreme form, C. Lauckner, *Die künstlerischen und politischen Ziele der Monographie Sallusts über den Jugurthinischen Krieg* (Diss. Leipzig, 1911). And K. v. Fritz admitted too much to the detriment of Sallust (*TAPA* LXXIV [1943], 134 ff.). For a corrective, see K. Vretska, *Wiener S-B* CCXXIX. 4 (1955). That scholar has a clear and fresh approach to Sallust's treatment of Metellus, Marius, and Sulla. For an acute analysis of the long controversy about the purpose and value of the monograph, see A. La Penna, *Ann. della Scuola Normale Superiore di Pisa* XXVIII (1959), 45 ff.

thing of a surprise that Sallust should concede him signal merits.
Bestia had energy, a keen intelligence and skill in warfare. But
the good qualities of Bestia were hampered by his greed for profit
—"avaritia praepediebat" (28. 5). He chose as legates men of
birth who would be likely to cover up his delinquencies;[2] and,
after opening hostilities vigorously, he slackened off in hope of
gain when Jugurtha's envoys appeared.[3] Finally, his venality was
a bad example to the Roman officers (32.2). The next commander,
the consul Sp. Postumius Albinus, is described as eager to take
the field—"avidus belli gerundi" (35. 3). That is not in itself any
kind of stricture. But Albinus allowed operations to drag. That
was guile (some thought), not sloth (36. 3). The damaging charge
is that Albinus failed to repair discipline among the troops after
his brother's incompetent and catastrophic behaviour (39. 5); and
Sallust paints a sombre picture of conditions at the camp when
Metellus arrived—a whole army allowed to rot and decay (44).

The war takes a new turn and aspect with the coming of
Metellus. That aristocrat on his first presentation is introduced
as a man of energy, of unimpeachable repute (43. 1); and, in contrast to his predecessors in Numidia, he was impervious to money
and profit (43. 5). The measures he took to bring the army into
fighting shape are described in full detail, with earnest approbation. The historian puts in a weighty verdict—"magnum et
sapientem virum fuisse comperior" (45. 1). Sallust by habit is
grudging of praise. Nobody else in his pages earns the epithet
"sapiens." A writer in a later age, likewise not prone to enthusiasm, adopts and transfers this Sallustian phrase to denote
the highest commendation he can award to a Roman nobleman.[4]

Again, when Metellus has won his hard-fought battle beside
the river Muthul, the historian relates with unaffected pleasure
the joy and relief at Rome. General and army had comported
themselves as Roman tradition, the "mos maiorum," enjoined;
and the fame of Metellus was resplendent (55. 1 f.). But Metellus

---

[2] 28. 4: "legat sibi homines nobilis factiosos, quorum auctoritate quae deli-
quisset munita fore sperabat."

[3] 29. 1: "animus aeger avaritia facile conversus est."

[4] Tacitus, *Ann.* IV. 20. 2: "hunc ego Lepidum temporibus illis gravem et
sapientem virum fuisse comperior."

falls from grace. He conceives annoyance when his legate Marius
wishes to go to Rome to stand for the consulate. Beginning with
friendly counsel, as it were, Metellus goes on to dissuade and ends
with insult: Marius can wait until Metellus' own son becomes
eligible. Metellus, so the historian explains, though he had
"virtus" and "gloria" and whatever else is good, in abundance,
was dominated by disdain and arrogance, as were all the *nobiles*
—"commune nobilitatis malum" (64. 1). Later, when Marius has
not only been elected but acquires by decree of the People the
Numidian command, Metellus is exacerbated and confounded—
weeping and bitter words (82. 2 f.). His "superbia" again and the
personal affront, the honour won by Marius being worse than
supersession (so Sallust affirms). Yet in the end, Sallust will not
omit to set on record the magnificent reception that awaited
Metellus on his return, all ill-feeling having abated—"plebi patri-
busque . . . iuxta carus" (88. 1).

On this showing, it can hardly be maintained that Sallust is
unfair towards Metellus.[5] But Marius is matched against Metellus.
Sallust is not only a subtle writer but a man with a political past.
Has he not exalted and embellished the People's general?

The question of Sallust's political allegiance crops up once again
at this juncture, to mislead. Caesar by his family had a link with
Marius and his party, which he reinforced by marrying Cornelia,
the daughter of Cinna; his early political actions in contest with
the Optimates did not fail to exploit the defeated cause; and that
cause benefited from a sudden revival when Pompeius, turning
against Caesar, entered into coalition with the oligarchy. The
Civil War took the shape of an earlier struggle, and many families
of old Marian allegiance, Roman or municipal, came back with
Caesar. All of which is known and conceded. What consequences
then follow?

Marius has the large part in the *Bellum Jugurthinum*. Some
therefore claim him as its radiant and martial hero.[6] For others,

---

[5] cf. K. Vretska, o.c. 94 ff. C. Lauckner had suggested that Sallust spoke
well of Metellus only and precisely to demonstrate that Marius was superior
to the best general the aristocracy could produce (o.c., 7 ff.).

[6] E. Bolaffi, *Sallustio* (1949), 68: "balza fuori la figura simpatica di un giovane soldato," etc.

the general is nothing less than the living embodiment of the
ethical qualities most precious to Sallust.[7] Indeed, and further,
Sallust wrote the monograph, it is assumed, with a precise intent
—to glorify the patron of the cause for which the *Populares*
stood.[8]

These notions have been put forward with sublime confidence
as though the truth were plain and manifest. On a cool appraisal,
Sallust's presentation will be found to convey doubts and ambiguity, suggesting a different view, closer to the complexities of
human character and behaviour as seen by a historian.

First, Marius as a legate under Metellus. He shares in the first
expedition, to Vaga; he is present at the Battle of the Muthul,
but with no action recorded; he defends the town of Sicca; he
plays a valiant part at Zama, which the Romans failed to capture.
It does not appear that Marius is accorded undue prominence.

Then chance takes a hand and ambition is sharpened, with a
dramatic turn of events. When Marius was making sacrifice at
Utica, a soothsayer announced what destiny portended, "magna
atque mirabilia." To achieve which, Marius had only to go on
boldly, relying on the gods (63. 1). Marius, it is stated, was already
in the grip of an ardent desire for the consulship, an "ingens
cupido." And Marius already had everything that was needed,
save birth alone. The historian subjoins some remarks about the
origin of Marius, his training and career, his prestige earned in
warfare. Hence the military tribunate, hence one magistracy after
another.[9] Each time men deemed him deserving of something
better. But so far he had not been bold enough to go for the
consulate (63. 6). That was the close preserve of the *nobilitas*.[10]

According to Sallust, the course of Marius ran swift and even.
That is erroneous, totally. Is the historian trying to deceive the
reader? That does not have to be believed. The reasons are plain

---

[7] J. Pajk, "Sallust als Ethiker I" (*Progr.Wien,* 1892), 19: "Marius ist das
Tugendideal des Sallust."

[8] H. M. Last in *CAH* IX (1932), 137.

[9] 63. 4 f.: "ergo, ubi primum tribunatum militarem a populo petit, pleris-
que faciem eius ignorantibus, factis notus per omnis tribus declaratur. deinde
ab eo magistratu alium post alium sibi peperit."

[10] 63. 7, cf. *Cat.* 23. 6 (in relation to Cicero's candidature).

enough—he did not know, and he made a hasty assumption. On the experience of his own time, Sallust assumed that military talent in an energetic *novus homo* would bring him as far as the praetorship, easily (though not further, to be sure, unless by the especial help and favour of a faction or a leader). Sallust omitted to investigate the earlier career of Marius, all for brevity and not wishing to overburden the narration.[11]

Research would have brought up some salutary facts and startling disclosures.[12] Marius was born about 158 B.C.; he saw service under Scipio Aemilianus at Numantia; and he held the tribunate of the plebs in 119, which is his first office on detailed record. A bill which the tribune proposed (to restrict one of the ways of peacefully intimidating voters) incurred the disapprobation of the Senate and led to conflict with the consuls, one of them a Metellus.[13] Marius tried for both aedileships (the curule and the plebeian), and failed.[14] And, running for the praetorship in 116, he came in last and had to face a prosecution for bribery.[15] His subsequent governorship of a province, Hispania Ulterior, was not attended with conspicuous fame.[16]

There is something else. Curiosity might ask whether this municipal man might not properly be regarded as a client of the great house of the Caecilii Metelli.[17] Further, as relevant to the social advancement of a parvenu, the matrimonial tie he contracted about the year 112. He married a Julia, whose family was not merely noble but belonged to the ancient patriciate—though far from opulent or influential in this age. In the event, Marius was to contribute more to the Julii than he received.

---

[11] Yet he can insist on Marius' election to the military tribunate, an item that no other source transmits.

[12] For the early career of Marius, see Weynand, *R-E* Supp. VI, 1369 ff.; A. Passerini, *Athenaeum* XXII (1934), 10 ff.; H. Chantraine, *Untersuchungen zur römischen Geschichte am Ende des 2. Jahrhunderts v. Chr.* (1959), 63 ff.; Broughton, *MRR,* Supp. (1960), 40; E. Badian, *Historia* XI (1962), 214 ff.

[13] *De legibus* III. 38, cf. Plutarch, *Marius* 4. On this matter, cf. E. Badian, *JRS* XLVI (1956), 94.

[14] *Pro Plancio* 51.

[15] Valerius Maximus VI. 9. 14; Plutarch, *Marius* 5.

[16] Plutarch, *Marius* 6. The sole evidence.

[17] E. Badian, *Foreign Clientelae (264–70* B.C.*), (1958), 194 f.

However that may be, the historian, eschewing prolegomena, comes quickly to the quarrel between legate and general. Rebuffed, Marius surrenders to desire and resentment, the most pernicious of counsellors (64. 5). To further his ambition, he left nothing undone or unsaid. He tried to win the troops by deliberately allowing loose discipline. And he made approach to traders at Utica, boastfully and with odious language—he could finish off the war with half the forces (he asserted), whereas Metellus was prolonging hostilities from pride and vanity. Furthermore, he solicited a certain Numidian prince, Gauda (a grandson of Masinissa), whom Metellus held in scant honour (with reason, it appears), promising him the kingdom in the event of victory. Finally, a number of Roman knights (officers in the army and businessmen), tired of the war and inflamed by the intrigues of Marius, wrote letters to Rome of predictable tenor and secured wide credence for their complaints. And the political atmosphere already favoured the election of a *novus homo,* the nobles having been routed by the *quaestio Mamiliana* (65. 5).

The narrative now reverts to Numidian affairs for a long stretch, into which is interpolated a short account of the election (73), which takes up the effect of the missives from Africa. Party spirit (Sallust adds) counted for more than the merits of Metellus or Marius.[18] Furthermore, turbulent magistrates (that is tribunes of the plebs) stirred up the populace. Artisans and the rural plebs in great numbers dropped their work and glorified Marius. Of the candidate himself, no act or attitude is registered.

After his election, Marius pressed his advantage—"multus atque ferox instare." He assailed the aristocracy with vaunting and invective (84. 1). Then, but not until troops and supply have been voted, the historian produces a violent and lengthy harangue before the People (85).

So far, therefore, the great *novus homo,* for all his military merit, is depicted as a crafty intriguer, a blatant demagogue. Marius in Africa undermined the reputation of his commander. That type of behaviour is elsewhere stigmatised by the historian as "prava ambitio" (96. 3). This is the man who in his oration

---

[18] 73. 4: "ceterum in utroque magis studia partium quam bona aut mala sua moderata."

alleges that virtuous conduct has become his second nature (85. 9).

Next, and notable, the preparing of the expeditionary force. The consul violated the "mos maiorum," for he enlisted a large number of men lacking the property qualification. The historian renders his motives in the form of anonymous comment (86. 3). Some adduced the shortage of suitable recruits. Others, however, put Marius' action down to political ambition. Which note is enlarged upon. Marius had enjoyed the support and favour of the poor. That class has no substance or attachment, but profit the only incentive—"omnia cum pretio honesta." If a man seeks "potentia," he looks to the lowest of the low—"egentissimus quisque opportunissimus."

These are strong words (except in orations, Sallust tends to shun the superlative). Nor is everything for praise in the narration of the campaigns. The luck of Marius is emphasised (92. 2); and his march to the River Muluccha was an act of rashness which only chance corrected (94.7). Finally and above all, since to Sallust "virtus" is the supreme value, it will be observed that he concedes "virtus" to Metellus, but never, speaking in his own person, to Marius. It is the tribunes of the plebs who extol and exaggerate his "virtus" (73. 5); and the soldiers are allowed to celebrate the "virtus" of their general, whether he wholly deserved it or not (92. 2).

Sallust has evaded any temptation to convert the People's general into a hero or a model of behaviour. In rendering this ambiguous character he skilfully mixes the good and the bad. And he is right. Cicero offers a pertinent contrast.[19] He fails to present a complete and credible portrait of his fellow townsman. In the public speeches (with two exceptions only) all is praise for courage, constancy and integrity.[20] It can even be asserted that, though Marius had many enemies, nobody ever brought up his humble origin against him.[21] The letters and the philosophical works disclose a different point of view. For example, the author can allude to Marius with deep distaste as a master of craft and

---

[19] K. Vretska, o.c. 126 f. For Cicero's views about Marius (a long story) see T. F. Carney, *Wiener Studien* LXXIII (1960), 83 ff.

[20] The only exceptions come late, viz. *Phil.* VIII. 7; XI. 1.

[21] *Pro Sulla* 23.

cunning. The "divinus vir" of the *Pro Sestio* becomes "omnium perfidiosissimus." [22]

Sallust's portrayal of Marius speaks for his judgment and his independence.[23] The prepossession thus nascent in the author's favour is disturbed and impaired by what he says about Aemilius Scaurus.

That person is brought on at an early stage (in 117 or 116, when Adherbal, expelled from his kingdom, has come to Rome to beg for help and restitution). He gets a sharp characterisation —a nobleman energetic and a master of intrigue, avid of power, honour, and riches but crafty in dissembling his vices (15. 4).[24] On this occasion, observing that the bribery practised by the agents of Jugurtha was open and flagrant, Scaurus took alarm and curbed his normal impulses. Scaurus is next named among the envoys sent to Jugurtha during the siege of Cirta; and the prince (it is stated) feared Scaurus more than anybody else (25. 10). Then he is chosen as legate by the consul Calpurnius Bestia, along with other "homines nobiles factiosi" (28. 4); carried away by the prospect of vast profit, he becomes the associate and counsellor of Bestia (29. 2); and Jugurtha, gaining confidence because of Scaurus, agrees to a secret pact with Scaurus and Bestia (29. 5).

The transaction becoming known at Rome, opinion was divided. The "potentia" of Scaurus was likely to prevail and prevent the right course of action, but the tribune Memmius was not deterred (30. 3). Further, according to Sallust, Scaurus was among those whom Memmius incriminated for taking bribes (32. 1). After this, Scaurus fades out, to be mentioned once again, and only once. When a court of enquiry was established by the bill of the tribune C. Mamilius Limetanus in 109, to investigate the various malpractices in relation to Jugurtha, Scaurus managed to get himself appointed as one of the three members (40. 4).

Sallust's account is patently vulnerable. On the large issue, it is enough to point out that bribery does not have to be invoked

---

[22] *Pro Sestio* 50, contrasted with *De natura deorum* III. 80.

[23] K. Vretska, o.c. 129.

[24] 15. 4: "Aemilius Scaurus, homo nobilis inpiger factiosus, avidus potentiae honoris divitiarum, ceterum vitia sua callide occultans."

to explain why Scaurus and the consul made an arrangement with Jugurtha, securing his submission and arresting hostilities. And the author shows animus, unmistakably, by one of his devices. He goes out of his way to introduce Scaurus at an early stage, when describing transactions in which this ostensibly corrupt character was not involved, in which he does nothing at all (15. 4).

Sallust portrays Scaurus as a typical *nobilis*, and history reckons him as a steady adherent of the Metelli.[25] Scaurus rose to prominence in the epoch when the influence of that family was predominant (six consulates in fifteen years). He acceded to the *fasces* in 115 as colleague of a Metellus, he became *princeps senatus*, and he was later (about 101) to marry a daughter of Delmaticus. *Princeps senatus* from 115, he was elected censor in 109. But Scaurus began in poverty and obscurity. To make his way, he had to struggle like any *novus homo*. Though his stock was illustrious and patrician, the family had been out of high office for many generations, and had even lapsed from the senatorial order.[26] His consulate was not won easily—Rutilius Rufus for rival (who had powerful support), and a prosecution for bribing the electorate. Nor was his policy when a consular statesman unambiguous through the long years of his paradoxical survival. Alliance with the *Equites* might be surmised, on some occasions. That there should be a dual tradition about this alert and artful performer need occasion no surprise.

Scaurus may have advocated a policy unimpeachable: the close union of the propertied classes. In other words, a "concordia ordinum." For Cicero, Scaurus is the paramount statesman and master of civic wisdom, never named except for praise—and perhaps quietly annexed as a precursor of himself. That would be enough to excite the attention of Sallust.[27] His suspicions would further be sharpened by inspection of the politician's autobiography.

---

25 For the career and policy of Scaurus, see M. Bloch, *Univ. de Paris, Bibliothèque de la Faculté des Lettres* XXV (1909), 1 ff.; P. Fraccaro, *Rend.Ac. Lincei*[5] XX (1911), 169 ff. = *Opuscula* II (1957), 125 ff.

26 Asconius 24.

27 It has further been suggested that Sallust's disapproval of Cicero's political opportunism sharpened his portrayal of Scaurus (A. R. Hands, *JRS* XLIX [1959], 56 ff.).

Again, the name and memory of Aemilius Scaurus was attached in more ways than one to the cause and family of Sallust's enemies. Caecilia Metella, the widow of old Scaurus, passed in matrimony to Sulla. She had borne two children to Scaurus. The daughter married Pompeius (his second wife) but died not long after; the son is the praetor of 56, consular candidate in 54. When this man married Mucia (a lady of lax conduct whom Pompeius divorced on his return from the East) he became the stepfather of the sons of Magnus. He was already the half-brother of Faustus and Fausta.

The Numidian War has a political significance (the author is explicit at the outset). It is the challenge to the rule of the aristocracy—"quia tunc primum superbiae nobilitatis obviam itum est" (5. 1). In later passages the nobles are designated as "pauci," the "pauci potentes," or the "factio." They exercise "potentia," their behaviour is overbearing, luxurious, and corrupt. Hence gross mismanagement of Rome's imperial heritage. That is the historian's axiom.

As has been indicated, the attack on the oligarchy develops in three episodes—Memmius, the *quaestio Mamiliana*, Marius. The author binds those episodes together by various devices of echo or repetition. Thus on each occasion it is emphasized, by a turn of phrase almost identical, that the *nobilitas* took a hard blow.[28]

Memmius on his first presentation is styled hostile to the "potentia nobilitatis" (27. 2). On the second, the phrase recurs (30. 3). And Memmius in the exordium of his speech proclaims that he is impelled "obviam ire factionis potentiae" (31. 4)— which carries a clear reference backwards to the author's definition of his theme. The speech itself appeals to the dignity and majesty of the Roman People, "imperatores omnium gentium" (31. 20, cf. 11), with repeated incitements to the assertion of "libertas." The tribune alludes to the ancient secessions of the plebs, to the cruel repression of the Gracchan movement; and he raises angry protest against the monopoly of office, power and profit exploited by

---

[28] 32. 5: "perculsa omni nobilitate"; 65. 5; "nobilitate fusa per legem Mamiliam"; 73. 7: "ita perculsa nobilitate post multas tempestates novo homini consulatus mandatur."

"homines sceleratissimi . . . nocentissimi et idem superbissimi" (31. 12).

The harangue is a spirited piece of work, a stirring call to violent action, it might seem. It fits what the author has said (and other evidence supports) about the personality and the eloquence of the tribune. Yet it will have to be asked how well the speech fits the situation and the policy advocated by Memmius—which was merely to persuade the People to send to Africa a man of integrity, with the duty of bringing Jugurtha under safe conduct to give testimony at Rome. This item exhibits less of the historian, more of the literary artist and contriver.

Next, the bill of the tribune Mamilius. The terms of the *quaestio* are set forth. The author eagerly adds the appointment of Scaurus, and, noting the excesses of party spirit, passes to a digression on Roman politics (41 f.). Something is lacking. To reinforce the argument, and to express a personal satisfaction, ought not the writer to have furnished the names of the guilty men on whom condign punishment was visited? A senatorial historian will not easily miss the occasion to document public disgrace by registering a sequence of illustrious names.[29]

The *quaestio* produced a historic massacre of birth and station. Four men of consular rank succumbed, also one holder of a priesthood, the patrician C. Sulpicius Galba: it was noted that his catastrophe lacked precedent.[30] Calpurnius Bestia and Sp. Postumius Albinus now paid the penalty for what they had done (or not done) in Numidia. The third victim, C. Porcius Cato (*cos.* 114), had held a command in Macedonia, where he suffered defeat in the field: his other shortcomings are not attested. As for the fourth, he is none other than L. Opimius, of hated memory, the consul of 121. Sallust, when mentioning Opimius previously (he was leader of the commission which divided Numidia between

---

[29] Compare the technique of Tacitus, who, after cataloguing seven names, proceeds "quorum auctoritates adulationesque rettuli ut sciretur vetus id in re publica malum" (*Ann.* II. 32. 2).

[30] *Brutus* 127 f. Bestia, prosecuted by Memmius, was able to invoke the testimony of Scaurus in his favour (*De oratore* II. 283). It is to be presumed that the brother of Sp. Postumius Albinus also succumbed.

Jugurtha and Adherbal), did not omit what he did earlier, suppressing C. Gracchus and M. Fulvius Flaccus, and cruelly punishing their adherents among the Roman plebs.[31] It is strange that Sallust now neglects this signal act of justice and revenge.[32]

With Marius, the attack on the oligarchy moves to a climax, with a harangue which is a social as well as a political indictment. Marius not only arraigns the *nobiles* as a caste, but parades "novitas mea" against them. He uses direct vituperation, also irony and sarcasm (features not elsewhere much in evidence in Sallust). The tone is harsh and crude.[33] Archaic expressions reflect the ostensible plain man; and some suppose that the speaker's lack of metropolitan refinement is also brought out by colloquial phraseology or an inelegant construction here and there.[34] If the personality that emerges is vaunting and self-righteous, it will be recalled that the *novus homo*, speaking before the People, had to push his claims loudly. He had no ancestors, and nobody else was going to proclaim his merits. In that matter Cato set a high standard.[35] This is patently a Catonian speech.[36]

The oration, designed less to illustrate a situation or policy than to portray a character, is skilfully constructed. The speaker begins with language of reason and moderation. He alludes to the difficulties of his position—others have birth, ancestral prestige, family ties, and numerous clients to support or shield them, whereas the *novus homo* must rely on his own qualities of "virtus et innocentia." Passing to the War, he indicts aristocratic

---

[31] 16. 2: "L. Opimius, homo clarus et tum in senatu potens quia consul C. Graccho et M. Fulvio Flacco interfectis acerrume victoriam nobilitatis in plebem exercuerat."

[32] The mere name of Opimius could also have served as a link between the mention of the Gracchi in the oration of Memmius (31. 7) and in the excursus (42. 1).

[33] Derivation from Cynic and Stoic diatribes has been surmised by E. Skard, *Symb.Osl.* XXI (1941), 98 ff. But that is not a very helpful notion, cf. K. Büchner, *Sallust* (1960), 409.

[34] H. Schnorr v. Carolsfeld, *Über die Reden und Briefe bei Sallust* (Leipzig, 1888), 52 ff.

[35] Livy XXXIV. 15. 9: "haud sane detrectator laudum suarum."

[36] V. Pöschl, *Grundwerte römischer Staatsgesinnung in den Geschichtswerken des Sallust* (1940), 48 ff.; E. Skard, *Symb.Osl.*, Supp. XV (1956), 92 ff.

generals for ignorance—some of them have had to learn the military art from foreign text books. Also incompetence in the field. Birth is invoked as a prerogative, but nobles would do well to mark how and when nobility was first conferred—"ex virtute nobilitas coepit" (85. 17). Marius, it is true, can exhibit no family portraits, no consulates or triumphs of his forebears, but he has scars won in war, and the decorations. The ancestors of the *nobiles* bequeathed a glorious heritage, but one thing they could not transmit, "virtus." Aristocrats deride Marius because he is a stranger to the refinements of life, they call him grubby and uncivilised—and their own conduct proves them idle voluptuaries, pernicious to the Commonwealth.

The orator ends on a note of confidence about affairs in Numidia. The Roman People by its actions has now abolished "avaritia, imperitia atque superbia." Energy and valour will do the rest. No parent prays that his sons will live for ever, nobody has achieved immortality through sloth, and words cannot engender courage.

According to Sallust, the consul spoke in order to stimulate recruiting—and at the same time to indulge his habit of harrying the aristocracy (84. 5).[37] The second motive almost extinguishes the first. The oration frequently takes up various themes earlier in evidence (as in the speech of Memmius), to reinforce them. Metellus is not named. But Metellus had been labelled as arrogant (64. 1; 82. 3), and the oration brings in the word "superbia" no fewer than five times, besides denouncing the "homines superbissimi."

Sallust betrays—or rather avows—strong feelings against the *nobilitas.* Their enemies (it will pertinently be observed) do not always come off very well. Thus the circumstances of Marius' election and the role of tribunes, characterised as "seditiosi" (73.

---

[37] The oration is Sallust's own, but goes back in some particulars to things said, or rather allegedly said, by Marius. Compare the parallels in Plutarch, *Marius* 9, adduced by A. Passerini, o.c. 20 ff. Marius is there represented as deliberately appealing to the lower classes, with invective against the failed generals of the aristocracy, Bestia and Albinus. But it may be too much to claim that Sallust reproduces "substantially the trend of Marius' actual words on the occasion" (T. F. Carney, *Symb.Osl.* XXXV [1959], 69).

5). Moreover, the author passes severe censure on the agitation which produced the bill of Mamilius—not care for the Commonwealth but detestation of the *nobiles*. The *quaestio* (he says) was conducted in a deplorable and unruly fashion—"aspere violenterque ex rumore et lubidine plebis" (40. 5). All too often in the past the nobility had been evilly elated by success, and now it was the turn of the plebs.[38]

At this point the author seizes the opportunity to digress on party and the spirit of party (41 f.)—an excursus which, like that in the previous monograph, is of central importance in the economy of the work. This time he goes back to the destruction of Carthage. Before that turn in history, concord prevailed among the Romans—fear of the foreign enemy imposed a curb. But peace and good times proved detrimental and disastrous. Released from all constraint, nobility and people followed their contrary propensities, the Commonwealth was torn asunder and split in two.

The *nobiles*, having monopoly of office and the sources of imperial profit, exploited their advantages avidly and pitilessly. The class which provided soldiers was ground down by continuous military service and lost its farms to greedy and powerful neighbours. Two men there were, however, nobles themselves, who put genuine glory before power and oppression, the Gracchi. They tried to protect the plebs and expose the crimes of the oligarchy. But the *nobilitas* were able to thwart and defeat the Gracchi. In the licence of victory they killed and exiled many—but could achieve no security for themselves. When each side is out to win at any cost and wreak a cruel vengeance on the vanquished, that is what has brought great states down in ruin many times (42. 4).[39]

Such is the author's conclusion, solemnly enhanced by the archaic "pessum dedit." It is a general maxim not without relevance to recent and murderous transactions, and to the time of writing.

---

[38] 40. 5: "uti saepe nobilitatem, sic ea tempestate plebem ex secundis rebus insolentia ceperat."

[39] 42. 4: "igitur ea victoria nobilitas ex lubidine sua usa multos mortalis ferro aut fuga exstinxit plusque in reliquom sibi timoris quam potentiae addidit. quae res plerumque magnas civitatis pessum dedit, dum alteri alteros vincere quovis modo et victos acerbius ulcisci volunt."

The digression is linked to one of the three stages by which the attack on the *nobiles* develops. It raises a question surpassing mere bias. Is Sallust clear and satisfactory in his diagnosis of the forces that determined the political life of the Roman Republic in this epoch? His categories, affirmations and presuppositions are such as to excite grave doubts.[40]

Sallust operates with "patres" and "plebs" (or, less often, "populus") as units not only contrasted but opposed and hostile. Also, "nobilitas" and "plebs." The reality, however, was complex, transcending classes and orders and defying utterly the resources of traditional terminology; and Roman society was built up on a vast nexus of personal relationships which can be summed up in the word "clientela."

The governing class itself, though easily defined, was not homogeneous. Even when the Senate, as before Sulla's ordinances, numbered only three hundred, not all of its members were *nobiles,* that is, descendants of the consular families. Nor did the *nobilitas* present a united front. A great family might dominate the scene with its many alliances, like the Scipiones, and give its name to an epoch. But there were always rival groups. And the contest for office, honour, and glory led to scission or new combinations. History, legend, and biography focus attention on the persons of the two Gracchi. A truer intuition might divine a split in the Scipionic group, the young Tiberius Gracchus being dissident, hostile to his cousin Scipio Aemilianus—and captured by the Claudian faction. No history of the two tribunes is any good if it neglects the influence behind them of certain eminent *nobiles;*[41] and something of a party-grouping can be surmised on various criteria, such as, for example, the political eclipse of a number of senatorial families in the sequel.[42]

The Scipiones had not been able to maintain any prominence after the decease of Aemilianus. They were superseded by the Metelli, whose direction of imperial affairs can be presumed at

---

[40] P. 17.

[41] F. Münzer, *Römische Adelsparteien und Adelsfamilien* (1920), 257 ff.

[42] That is one of several indirect lines of approach in Roman history that has not yet been explored.

the time of the Numidian War. Curiosity would ask about their rivals in the *nobilitas*, about the senatorial adherents Marius could count upon already, or was soon to acquire.[43]

Various factors conspired in his favour. The *quaestio Mamiliana* was not the only cause or symptom of exacerbation. Scaurus managed to get elected censor; and, on the decease of his colleague, he refused to resign office, until the tribunes threatened to throw him into prison.[44] Further, one of the consuls designated for 108 succumbed to prosecution, a certain Hortensius, whose son was to become a notable champion of the Optimates.[45] And when, the Numidian War progressing slowly under Metellus, there supervened a disaster in Gaul (M. Silanus defeated by the Cimbri), enemies of the dominant group no doubt saw a fair pretext for anger and recrimination.[46]

The Metelli at this juncture, to keep out the odious Marius, needed two strong candidates, or failing that, one to curb him. No names are on record anywhere—or for that matter, any ally or partner of Marius.[47] Concentrating all his effects on Marius, Sallust allows no hint of an important fact: the identity of the man whom the elections brought in as his colleague. It was no other than L. Cassius Longinus who when praetor had been sent at the instance of the tribune Memmius to bring Jugurtha to Rome. Registering that transaction, the historian paid a high compliment to

---

[43] For the importance of this topic, cf. *Rom.Rev.* (1939), 86; for Marius' allies and adherents later, in 100, see E. Badian, *Foreign Clientelae* (1958), 200 f.

[44] Plutarch, *Quaest.Rom.* 50. The *Fasti Capitolini* annotate the name of Aemilius Scaurus with "coact(us) abd(icavit)" (*Inscr. It.* XIII. 1. 54).

[45] The *Fasti Capitolini* have "[da]mn(atus) est," with the note that he was replaced by (M. Aurelius) Scaurus (*Inscr. It.* XIII. 1. 54). The *Chronographer of the Year 354* supplies the name of Hortensius. Cf. Broughton, *MRR* I, 541 f. He is generally assumed to be L. Hortensius, the parent of the consul of 69—but might have been an uncle.

[46] Despite "M. Iunius Silanus cos." (Livy, *Per.* LXV), his defeat can belong to 108, not 109.

[47] No conjecture can help. It would be needful to know about the successful men, the praetors of 111 and 110 now returning from provincial commands. Only one of them stands attested, viz. L. Cassius Longinus, consul in 107 with Marius.

his integrity.[48] The Cassii, a family of recent emergence in the plebeian *nobilitas* (their first consul in 171), acquired through Ravilla (*cos.* 127) the renown of stern impartial justice. There was something else. Ravilla when tribune of the plebs in 137 introduced the secret ballot. That was not to the liking of oligarchs or good conservatives.[49] It is pertinent to observe that another Cassius Longinus, tribune in 104, carried laws designed to abate the "potentia nobilitatis."[50]

Sallust puts emphasis on the eager popular support accruing to Marius. He was elected "cupientissuma plebe" (84. 1). Given the way in which the electoral body was organised, no consul could be produced in defiance of the holders of property and wealth. Sallust, it is true, refers to the effect of the letters sent from Africa by "equites Romani" (65. 4). More should have been said about this order of men. The nobles, to be sure, embody the "dignitas" or "superbia" of the governing order; but they could not take all the profits of empire, or all the blame for wide estates and the expropriation of the peasant soldier. Not nobles, perhaps, but "boni viri et locupletes" have the larger portion.

When C. Gracchus transferred the courts of law from the Senate to the Knights, he split the possessing class, producing conflicts of interest and dire consequences in political life. Sallust does not mention equestrian juries. Elsewhere in the monograph "equites Romani" occur only once. Sallust in the digression states that they were employed by the *nobilitas* to thwart the Gracchi (41. 2). A serious omission has been detected, if nothing worse.

Sallust's portrayal is therefore both schematic and defective. One is further impelled to scrutinise his whole conception of the Numidian War. He appears to assume from the outset that this

---

[48] 32. 5: "privatim praeterea fidem suam interponit, quam ille non minoris quam publicam ducebat: talis ea tempestate fama de Cassio erat."

[49] *De legibus* III. 35: "secuta biennio post Cassia est de populi iudiciis a nobili homine lata, L. Cassio, sed, pace familiae dixerim, dissidente a bonis atque omnis rumusculos populari ratione aucupante." But Cassius was not really a "popularis" (*Ac. Prior.* II. 13).

[50] Asconius 69. His colleague Cn. Domitius Ahenobarbus prosecuted both Scaurus and M. Silanus (ib. 18; 71).

was a necessary war which the *nobilitas* first tried to evade and then mismanaged culpably, corrupt at home and calamitous abroad —at least until the *quaestio Mamiliana* shook them and Metellus retrieved Rome's honour in the field.

Various questions arise.[51] Some of them admit an answer, but a long way short of entire confidence. First, the degree of Rome's responsibility for Numidia, and the right of Rome to intervene when there was discord and conflict in the dynasty. It can hardly be denied that, whatever its origin, the relation was one of clientship.[52] Good sense was against meddling—but a direct appeal from a prince could not be disregarded.[53] On the other hand, who was to challenge the result if the imperial Republic decided that, without infringing its interests, it could condone crime in a vassal?[54]

Second, the expedience of war against Jugurtha. Rome, it is argued, had to face a grave emergency on the northern frontiers, provoked by the migrations of the Cimbri and Teutones.[55] Their impact was first felt in the Danubian basin, driving the Scordisci southwards against Macedonia. That province already had troubles of its own, from the Dardanians and the Thracians: wars, defeats, and triumphs of proconsuls are on record for a decade or more. When the Cimbri themselves turned westward, a Roman consul crossed the Julian Alps, met them near Noreia and suffered a catastrophic disaster. That was in 113. The Cimbri now disappear from view for several years. An interval elapsed before the Romans

---

[51] Severe strictures on Sallust's whole conception of the Numidian War (as concerned both the historical situation and the policy of the Roman government) were passed by G. De Sanctis, *Problemi di storia antica* (1932), 187 ff.; K. v. Fritz, *TAPA* LXXIV (1943), 134 ff. The historian has been defended on several points by W. Steidle, *Historia*, Einzelschriften 3 (1958), 37 ff. See also comments by A. La Penna, *Ann.della Scuola Normale Superiore di Pisa* XXVIII (1959), 63 ff.

[52] E. Badian, o.c. 154 ff.

[53] W. Steidle has argued that intervention was both right and expedient (o.c. 40 ff.).

[54] Rome was the sole arbiter of what "amicitia" entailed. For sinister maxims about vassal states compare Tacitus, *Ann.* XII. 48. 1: "paucis decus publicum curae, plures tuta disserunt: omne scelus externum cum laetitia habendum, semina etiam odiorum iacienda."

[55] G. de Sanctis, o.c. 193 f.

became fully aware of the danger—and, before the Battle of
Arausio in 105, they cannot have fancied that Italy itself was
menaced.[56]

If the Cimbri be left out of the reckoning, strong reasons dis-
suaded a war in Africa. Nobody had the right to expect it to be
short, easy and advantageous. Therefore, even after the fall of
Cirta, when a number of Roman and Italian traders were massacred, with anger aroused and a show of force imperative, prudence dictated measures such as were taken by the consul Bestia
with the approval of a senior statesman.[57] The arrangement was
vulnerable to criticism, and party spirit took a hand. The war
went on, but Sp. Albinus apparently did not wish to push things
to an extremity. His brother's folly abolished all hopes of an accommodation: Jugurtha had to be killed or captured.

Third, the imputations of bribery, gladly taken up by Sallust,
and generalized: "Romae omnia venalia," as Jugurtha learned
already at Numantia.[58] It was no new thing that foreign princes
should be generous of gifts to their Roman patrons. Partisan
enemies of the nobilitas exaggerated. The Jugurthine scandal,
however, seems to have gone beyond what was normal and admitted, affecting the interests as well as the honour of the Roman
government.[59] On the other hand, the quaestio went too far, as
Sallust concedes.

Fourth, the forces at work to promote intervention in Numidia.
One should ask who was behind Memmius. Tribunes at Rome are
less often initiators of policy than agents of powerful groups or
interests in the background. Suspicion fastens on commerce and
finance.[60] The Knights, it is held, saw profit from contracts for
transport and supply in a war; and they might hope to exploit the
natural resources of Numidia if after victory the land was con-

---

[56] However the danger from the North is too much discounted by W.
Steidle, o.c. 43 f.

[57] G. de Sanctis, o.c. 206; K. v. Fritz, o.c. 164.

[58] 8. 1. This is taken up again by "omnia Romae venalia" (20. 1), to foreshadow the exclamation of Jugurtha, "urbem venalem et mature perituram
si emptorem invenerit" (35. 10).

[59] And the corruption was well rooted in the story, not an invention of
Sallust, cf. A. La Penna, o.c. 63.

[60] G. de Sanctis, o.c. 199; 207.

verted into a Roman province. Furthermore, the election of Marius is not easy to explain without keen support from this class. The theory is seductive—and in danger of being overplayed. The influence that the financial interests could exercise at this time defies estimate. In the event, the long and arduous war brought no accession of Roman territory. Numidia was not annexed. The western portion fell to Bocchus the Mauretanian as his recompense, and Gauda was installed in the east. The traditional policy of the Roman Senate prevailed.

Finally, whose the credit for victory? The answer emerges from Sallust's account. As has been shown, Marius followed in its main lines the strategy devised by Metellus—or rather, imposed on him. Marius surpassed Metellus, creating by his generalship the conditions in which Roman diplomacy could achieve its ends through native treachery.[61]

The subject of the monograph, as conceived and announced by the author, belongs to a chain of events that will end in "bellum atque vastitas Italiae." He brings on the two protagonists of the conflict. Marius is depicted in various episodes, not at all to general advantage. And there is inserted the sinister foreshadowing that at the last Marius came to grief—"postea ambitione praeceps datus est" (63. 6).

Sallust takes leave of Marius at the point and season when Rome looked to him for salvation (114. 4). The monograph ends abruptly. There was melancholy and irony if the reader gave a thought to how the great general was to fare in later years: victory over the northern invaders, but eclipse thereafter, rancorous ambition and the seventh consulship achieved in war and murder. Marius had saved the Republic, only to subvert it by all manner of craft and violence. That is the verdict of Livy.[62]

---

[61] As explained by M. Holroyd, *JRS* XVIII (1928), 1 ff.

[62] Livy, *Per.* LXXX: "adeo quam rem p. armatus servavit eam primo togatus omni genere fraudis, postremo armis hostiliter evertit." Also, deriving from Livy, Velleius II. 11. 1 and Dio XXVI. 89. 2, who enlarges on his craft and perfidy. Cicero can style Marius "callidissimus" (*Ad Att.* X. 8. 7) and "perfidiosissimus" (*De natura deorum* III. 80). For the tragedy of Marius' career see the notable conclusions of E. Badian, *Historia* VI (1957), 342 f.

As for Sulla, on his arrival as quaestor of Marius, the author introduces him with a character sketch (95): a *nobilis* of a decayed patrician house, a man of parts, of education and taste; he was devoted to the pursuit of pleasure, but more to glory; luxurious but active and capable; eloquent, insinuating, deep, and crafty. Until his victory in the Civil War, Sallust adds, he enjoyed and deserved the greatest good fortune. But, for what came in the sequel, one could only express utter repugnance.

Sallust's portrayal of Sulla need occasion no surprise, and it does not support imputations of an especial bias.[63] Let there be recalled what Cicero was capable of saying about the Dictator.[64] And Livy is relevant. Sulla, he affirms, won a glorious victory, but went on to defile that victory by cruelty the like of which was in no man.[65] Cicero and Livy reflect the sentiments of the better sort in the towns of Italy.

Inserting brief observations on Sulla, Sallust goes out of his way to explain what he is doing. Of the historians who wrote about Sulla, the best and the most accurate was Sisenna; but Sisenna had been too favourable. Sallust, however, is impelled to portray Sulla's character at this point for he has no intention of narrating the history of Sulla—"neque enim alio loco de Sullae rebus dicturi sumus" (95. 2).

That is a clear statement—and perhaps a valuable clue. How should it be interpreted? Some take the sentence to mean that Sallust at this time had no thought of writing any full-length history. On the contrary, Sallust appears to disclose a project that will not involve discussion of Sulla at all. That is to say, from monographs, which had cleared the ground, he was moving forward to a narration of his own time. But Sallust proved unable to shake off the obsession and break loose from Sulla. When he launched his *Historiae*, it was a work that had not a little to say about Sulla's character and actions.

---

[63] K. Vretska, o.c. 129 ff.; W. Steidle, 83 ff.

[64] P. 124.

[65] Livy, *Per.* LXXXVIII: "reciperataque re p. pulcherrimam victoriam crudelitate quanta in nullo hominum fuit inquinavit."

XII

THE HISTORIAE

Sallust decided to begin at 78 B.C., the year of M. Aemilius Lepidus and Q. Lutatius Catulus. Before death cut him short, he got as far as the twelfth year thereafter. Of the *Historiae* there survive four orations and two letters, excerpted from the main work and transmitted in a separate edition along with the speeches from the monographs. Also about five hundred fragments, preserved by various channels and hazards. Sallust exercised a strong and divergent appeal in the later age— not the chronicle of events in history, but moralising or the unusual style which captured the professional attention of grammarians and scholiasts. One valuable extract happens to carry a large portion of the historian's prologue; but most of the fragments, brief and scrappy, are grammatical citations of idiom and oddities. In supplement may be noted several important pieces from a manuscript—and two small bits of papyrus.[1]

That is not all. Sallust's presentation of those dozen years dominated subsequent writers. His trace can be detected in their arrangement of events, in the emphasis and in the colouring. Plutarch in his *Lives* of Sertorius and Lucullus is of prime value. Whether or no the biographer went to the Latin original (and he

---

[1] B. Maurenbrecher, *C. Sallusti Crispi Reliquiae:* I. *Prolegomena* (1891); II. *Fragmenta* (1893). A. Kurfess (ed. 3, Teubner, 1957) prints the orations and letters, the various fragments deriving from the Orleans Codex, and also the two pieces of papyrus published by C. H. Roberts as *P. Rylands* III (1938), 473. See also V. Paladini, *C. Sallusti Crispi. Orationes et epistulae de historiarum libris excerptae* (1956).

might have been drawn to that effort by the noble and congenial figure of Sertorius) is a question. Most assume that he did.[2] If a doubt arises, that need not matter much. On the lowest count, a Greek source of Plutarch made abundant use of Sallust. As confrontation with a number of fragments makes clear, that writer gave a fairly close rendering of the Latin. And errors of translation can even be surmised.[3]

In these diverse ways, the lost masterpiece becomes palpable— content, architecture, and tone. Moreover, since the grammarians frequently cite the books by their numbers, erudition can combine with imagination to reconstruct both the outline and the detail of sundry notable transactions. That scholars should be found divergent is no proof that the method is vain and delusive.[4]

Nor is conjecture wholly idle in another matter. The motives behind a historian's choice of subject and point of departure invite curiosity, legitimate and not to be evaded. Digressing to depict Sulla's personality and habits in the *Bellum Jugurthinum,* Sallust came out with a firm pronouncement: he will not have any future occasion to relate the history of Sulla (95. 2). But the *Historiae,* it seems, had a lot to say about Sulla. That is the impression which at least one writer formed in late antiquity.[5]

---

[2] H. Peter, *Die Quellen Plutarchs in den Biographieen der Römer* (1865), 61; 106; B. Maurenbrecher, *Prol.* (1891), 27 ff.; 48. Sallust is named twice in the *Lucullus* (11; 33), not at all in the *Sertorius*. Scholars incline to recognise in the *Lucullus* a blend of Sallust, Livy, and Strabo. For the *Sertorius,* see p. 203.

[3] Thus the verb δολοφονεῖν, which damns a man as traitor and assassin (*Sertorius* 7), probably derives from a misunderstood phrase describing a military ruse in the passage of the Pyrenees, cf. *Historia* IV (1955), 58 f.

[4] Maurenbrecher's arrangement was seldom questioned, but a number of modifications were proposed by K. Bauhofer, *Die Komposition der Historien Sallusts.* Diss. München, 1935. Not always to advantage. For the structure of the *Historiae* see further W. Schur, *Sallust als Historiker* (1934), 214 ff.; K. Büchner, *Sallust* (1960), 256 ff. And, for the overlap in 75–74 between Books II and III, see the acute and convincing exposition of H. Bloch, *Didascaliae* (1961), 61 ff.

[5] Augustine, *De civ. Dei* II. 22. This testimony was emphasised by F. Klingner, *Hermes* LXIII (1928), 180.

And, as inspection of the fragments will demonstrate, not only
Sulla's character but Sulla's actions.[6]

After a prologue discussing history, politics, and human nature,
Sallust inserted a resumptive narration, covering the previous
fifty years (I. 19–53). It carried much matter, to judge by some of
the items preserved about the *Bellum Italicum*, the civil war and
the proscriptions. For example, military operations in detail and
the vicissitudes of Marian generals. And even the gruesome fate
of Marius Gratidianus.[7] Furthermore, when the action opens in
78, it leads off with a long oration from the consul Aemilius
Lepidus, arraigning Sulla and all his works (I. 55).

Taken in isolation, the speech would induce an incautious
reader to fancy that the Dictator was still enjoying the plenitude
of his authority. In fact, Sulla was in retirement. His abdication,
though productive of anecdote or fable, does not happen to be
registered in the ancient sources with any approach to precision
of dating. Hence a problem. Some will have it that Sulla did not
resign until the summer of 79, after the consular elections.[8] Too
late, that is clear. It will be plausible to assume that Sulla, consul
in 80 with Metellus Pius and gliding gently towards legality and
the Republic, ceased to be dictator when he laid down the consulship on the last day of December.[9] A year passed, the year of the
consuls Ap. Claudius Pulcher and P. Servilius Vatia. Then Sulla
died, in March or April of 78.

The obsequies were celebrated in pomp and magnificence not
seen before.[10] The procession began in Campania, augmented all
the way by the veterans from their several colonies, who took up

---

[6] Sulla's character is alluded to in I. 58–61. Bauhofer even suggested that
there was a kind of excursus on Sulla (o.c. 117).

[7] I. 44 f., cf. p. 84.

[8] The thesis argued by J. Carcopino, *Sylla ou la monarchie manquée* (1931),
207 f. It may suffice in passing to knock down one of the three props of the
edifice. It is asserted, with discussion of Gellius (XV. 28. 3), that the speech
Pro Sex. Roscio Amerino belongs to 79, not 80. Carcopino betrays no sign
that he is arguing against the testimony of Asconius (ib. 4).

[9] As assumed, for example, by E. Gabba, commenting on Appian *BC* I.
103. 480 (in his edition, 1958). E. Badian, however, suggests that Sulla's dictatorship may have lapsed at the end of 81 (*Historia* XI [1962], 230).

[10] Appian, *BC* I. 105. 493 ff. Sisenna may have used the funeral for the conclusion of his *Historiae*.

their positions, each bearing his arms. When the corpse, borne on a golden bier with royal adornment, entered the city, Senate and magistrates duly mustered for welcome; and the knights joined the cortège. A great wailing went up from the concourse: some in grief for the Dictator, but others fearing the troops and fearing Sulla no less than when he was alive, as they reflected on his deeds.

Senators carried the bier on their shoulders to the Campus Martius, the knights and the soldiers marched round the pyre. The luck of Sulla Felix held to the end. Rain was expected that day but the sky cleared and the elements were propitious to his incineration.[11]

The occasion was a challenge to historical talent. Tacitus when taking leave of Caesar Augustus eschewed the pageantry. Sallust might have dwelt upon it, for derision and indignation. There was a funeral oration, delivered by the best speaker of the time.[12] But Sallust, like Tacitus, knew better than to produce a laudation. He might, it is true, have hit upon a deadly substitute—informed comment from men of understanding, praise being the smaller portion. Instead, he passed judgment in his own person, as four fragments attest, with censure of Sulla for his sexual behaviour (adultery as well as debauchery).[13]

An important conclusion follows. Sallust modified his design, taking an earlier point of inception which entailed lavish treatment of Sulla. The phenomenon is not anomalous that a historian will discover the need to go further back—and he is lucky to become aware of it before being caught and involved in a major work. Sallust's first ideas may have gone to the year of Metellus and Afranius. An obvious convenience, since he had got the conspiracy of Catilina out of the way, and it was a date heavy with history. Cato, and others beside Cato, saw the civil war of Pompeius and Caesar as originating not in the breach between the dynasts but in the fatal compact of the year 60.[14]

---

[11] Plutarch, *Sulla* 38.

[12] Appian, *BC* I. 106. 500. Presumably the senior consular L. Marcius Philippus (*cos.* 91).

[13] I. 58–61. There are no names in evidence for Sulla's adulteries.

[14] P. 65.

However that may be, it was a good choice to begin with 78. Sulla's abdication or Sulla's funeral, that was where another historian may have terminated—Cornelius Sisenna, favourable to Sulla and the *nobiles*. Sallust takes up the story with an assault on Sulla's system which moves quickly from words and invective to dissension and warfare. The theme lay at the heart of his preoccupations, sharply relevant to Rome's recent past and terrifying present: how long can concord and the Republic stand when a ruler disappears, how soon will civil strife return, with despotism once again?

Opening with his consular date, Sallust embarks on a prologue (I. 1–18). It begins with comment on historians and concludes with a disquisition on the forces determining the course of Roman history. Sallust named Cato the Censor with praise for style and conciseness.[15] But only for those qualities—Cato in a very long life made many false statements to the detriment of good men.[16] By contrast, Fannius (who wrote about the Gracchi) was fair-minded.[17] There was an allusion, it appears, to Sisenna.[18] And the author had something to say about himself, in decent brevity: his allegiance in a civil war had not estranged him from the truth.[19]

In his diagnosis of Roman history, Sallust affirms that concord stood firm at Rome between the second and third wars against the Carthaginians.[20] But not previously: he is careful to add a corrective, alluding to the long struggle between plebeians and patricians. Stability was disrupted after the "metus Punicus" vanished. In the years of peace arose "discordia et avaritia atque ambitio," with dissension in their train and civil wars at the end. Powerful individuals sought domination under the specious pretext of defending either Senate or People; the denominations of good citizen or bad bore no relation to any service to the Com-

---

[15] I. 4: "Romani generis disertissimus paucis absolvit."

[16] I. 5: "in quis longissimo aevo plura de bonis falsa in deterius composuit."

[17] cf. Victorinus, *Ad Cic. rhet.* p. 570, cited by Maurenbrecher under I. 4.

[18] I. 2: "recens scriptum."

[19] I. 6: "neque me diversa pars in civilibus armis movit a vero."

[20] I. 11 (most of it from Augustine, *De civ. Dei* II. 18). As confirming "non amor iustitiae sed stante Carthagine metus pacis infidae fuit" add Velleius I. 12. 6: "infida pax," as observed by W. Clausen, *AJP* LXVIII (1947), 301.

monwealth, all being equally corrupt, but the men who had
wealth and power benefited from the better name because they
stood for the existing order.[21]

After those remarks, the author turns to his historical summary,
beginning with the Gracchan sedition, which was described as the
first shedding of blood at Rome (I. 17). Next, the narration of the
year 78, which quickly brings on the consul M. Aemilius Lepidus.

In depicting the acts and policy of this person, there was (and
there is) a danger of running into trouble. His hostility to Sulla
tends to be antedated in the light of what occurred subsequently.
Lepidus, it is assumed, was a renegade from the Marian party—
not that any actions attest his allegiance.[22] So were others among
the illustrious, whom birth or protection kept from harm. Sulla
stood for the "causa nobilium." Restoring the rule of the oligarchy, he needed noble names to adorn the *Fasti* and conduct
the government—and especially members of the primeval aristocracy, if he could find them. They were not numerous. A
patrician himself, of a family long relegated to obscurity, Sulla
was eager to revive the order. No surprise therefore to find a
scion of the Aemilii in the first consular pair elected after Sulla's
abdication.

It was an easy and winning plea at Rome to extol the "bene
facta gentis Aemiliae." [23] For Lepidus spoke the fame of his grandfather: twice consul, censor, further *pontifex maximus* and *princeps senatus* through long years.[24] Since then, the family had
declined. The parent escapes all record, he is only Quintus, an
item in genealogy. Lepidus himself in the years of tribulation
was able to avoid mention for good or evil. Few aristocrats can
have been with Sulla during the eastern campaigns; but some
raised armies in the provinces for the "causa nobilium" or fought

---

[21] I. 12.

[22] Only Appian affirms it (*BC* I. 105. 491). An Appuleia is on record, wife
of a M. Lepidus "nobilissimae stirpis" (Pliny, *NH* VII. 122; 186), hence, it is
generally assumed, a daughter of L. Appuleius Saturninus (*tr. pl.* 103). Date
and identity are far from certain. But there was a "Scipio Lepidi filius" (Orosius V. 22. 17), i.e., an Aemilius Lepidus adopted by L. Scipio Asiagenus (*cos.*
83), hence perhaps a clue to alliances in the time of Cinna's domination.

[23] I. 77. 6 (the speech of Marcius Philippus).

[24] *Phil.* XIII. 15 (Cicero in reference to the consul of 46).

in the reconquest of Italy. Lepidus, according to a fragment of
Sallust, lacked experience with the armies.[25] Like others against
whom no reproach stands, later leaders of the Optimates such as
Lutatius Catulus and Q. Hortensius, he abode quietly in Rome
under the domination of Cinna—until the better cause was seen
to prevail. An Aemilius as consul, that fitted Sulla's design for
his renovated and traditional Republic.[26]

The election of Lepidus is the subject of a peculiar anecdote
which earns general credence and is reproduced without misgiv-
ings in standard history. Pompeius, the story runs, supported
Lepidus in defiance of Sulla and got him into the consulate ahead
of Lutatius Catulus. Sulla expressed annoyance. Catulus, he said,
was the most excellent of men, Lepidus the most pernicious. But
Sulla did nothing. He merely reinforced his rebuke by uttering
grim and pertinent forebodings.[27]

The circumstances of this election ought to have been a challenge to curiosity. How many candidates were there in fact? None
other is named, no loyal partisan of Sulla put up to keep out the
deleterious Lepidus. Eager but safe men were to hand.[28] One must
ask what the government was doing, if it wanted Lepidus to be
defeated. However, the transgression of Pompeius, so far as revealed by the anecdote, seems modest. Merely that he caused

---

[25] I. 78: "numeroque praestans, privos ipse militiae." To be sure, Lepidus
can be discovered as the tenth name in the consilium of Pompeius Strabo at
Asculum, "[M. Aem]ili Q. f. Pal." (*CIL* I². 709 = *ILS* 8888), cf. C. Cichorius,
Römische Studien (1922), 147. The Lepidus who captured Norba in 82
(Appian *BC* I. 94. 439) was probably Mamercus (*cos.* 77), cf. E. Badian, *JRS*
LII (1962), 53.

[26] cf. *Tacitus* (1958), 569.

[27] Plutarch, *Sulla* 34; *Pompeius* 15 f. Observe the words ἀπεθέσπισε and
τὰ μαντεύματα. The sole source for the story.

[28] Notably the next consuls. Lepidus upbraids the "praeclara Brutorum
atque Aemiliorum et Lutatiorum proles" (I. 55. 3). D. Junius Brutus exhibits no signs of youth and success. Mam. Lepidus Livianus was probably a
brother of M. Livius Drusus (*tr. pl.* 91), cf. F. Münzer, *Römische Adelsparteien und Adelsfamilien* (1920), 312. Somebody put in a special plea for him
—"Curionem quaesit, uti adulescentior et a populi suffragiis integer aetati
concederet Mamerci" (I. 86). That incident will belong to the contest for the
consulate of 77. Mamercus had certainly failed previously (cf. *De off.* II. 58),
perhaps in 79: if so, competing with M. Lepidus, for both were patrician.

Catulus to miss the first place at the polls (which carried precedence and the tenure of the twelve *fasces* for the first month of the year).[29]

Stories that exemplify the prescience of Sulla may well excite distrust. Not only concerning Lepidus—Sulla was also able to warn the Optimates against the young Julius Caesar, who was destined (he said) to destroy their party.[30] Or again, his prophecy uttered when abdicating, that no man at Rome ever after would resign the supreme power.[31]

That is not the worst. It staggers belief that any candidate could stand and succeed in 79 against the will of Sulla.[32] No longer dictator, it is true. But, so long as he lived, the prestige of victory abode with him, the terror of his name, and the power of the veterans in their garrison-colonies.

Nor would that consul have been free to attack Sulla and his acts.[33] Sallust produces a harangue of Lepidus in his first days of office (I. 55). It is a violent and personal invective, denouncing Sulla as a tyrant who thinks any means good enough for retaining his domination.[34] All the authority and attributes of the Commonwealth, the orator affirms, are in Sulla's control.[35] The speech ends with a stirring appeal: the Roman people is incited to follow the consul and recapture its liberty.

Prologue, historical summary, and speech: the architecture is impeccable, and it earned its proper compliment, being emulated by Tacitus in Book I of his *Historiae*. But the speech is a protest,

---

[29] Monthly rotation of the fasces is attested by Suetonius, *Divus Iulius* 20. 1.

[30] Suetonius, *Divus Iulius* 1. 3: "quandoque optimatium partibus, quas secum simul defendissent, exitio futurum; nam Caesari multos Marios inesse."

[31] Appian, *BC* I. 104. 486.

[32] That, however, is generally believed, cf. H. M. Last, *CAH* IX (1932), 314: "he stood as a candidate for the consulship . . . as an open enemy of the dictator."

[33] J. Franke, *Jahrbücher für cl. Phil.* XXXIX (1893), 49; J. Neunheuser, *M. Aemilius Lepidus* (Diss. Münster, 1902), 25.

[34] I. 55. 7: "nisi forte speratis taedium iam aut pudorem tyrannidis Sullae esse et eum per scelus occupata periculosius dimissurum. at ille eo processit ut nihil gloriosum nisi tutum et omnia retinendae dominationis honesta aestimet."

[35] ib. 13: "leges iudicia aerarium provinciae reges penes unum, denique necis civium et vitae licentia."

not a programme. The nearest the consul comes to a tangible proposal is flimsy and derisory—he is ready to surrender what he got from the Proscriptions.[36] The oration led to no immediate action. Nor could it have. Lepidus' policy of revolution needs time to develop, aided by chance or pressure of events—in the first place, the decease of Sulla.

The oration, it follows, cannot stand as a piece of authentic history. The author, after the long prolegomena, must come to grips with his subject and produce action—or the semblance of action. Refusing to begin with the obsequies of Sulla, he brings on Lepidus, prematurely. He has surrendered to artistry, and worse. His bold and wilful contrivance is not merely designed to illustrate the situation created by Sulla at Rome and throughout Italy. It enables him to indulge his propensities and produce a long denunciation of Sulla, in a sharp and vivid form, going beyond what the factual digression had permitted.[37]

Lepidus and his colleague, already at enmity for various reasons, separated with angry words after the funeral of Sulla.[38] In the course of the year, a rising was reported in northern Etruria, at Faesulae, where the evicted made an attack on the veteran colonists (I. 65 ff.). The consuls were dispatched to compose the disturbance. When Catulus returned to Rome, Lepidus stayed behind in Etruria, playing a double game. He mustered partisans from the disaffected throughout the Etrurian country and announced a subversive programme, which included the restoration of the tribunes' rights. The next year opened without consuls, for Lepidus had refused to come back and hold the elections. Moreover, his position grew menacing, for he had control of Cisalpine Gaul. That region had been allocated as province either to Lepidus or to his firm ally M. Junius Brutus.[39] A party in the

---

[36] ib. 18.
[37] cf. *Tacitus* (1958), 144. Not all recent apologists of Sallust have brought out the flagrant anachronism of his procedure.
[38] Appian, *BC* I. 107. 501.
[39] Appian states that Lepidus' province was Gallia Transalpina (*BC* I. 107. 502). It would be needful to know whether M. Brutus was proconsul in Cisalpina or merely legate of Lepidus. Perhaps it is the best solution that Cisal-

Senate was for acceding to the rebel's demands. At this juncture the senior consular, L. Marcius Philippus, delivers a powerful oration (I. 77). The Senate takes courage, and the ultimate decree is passed.

Lutatius Catulus received authority as proconsul, and a command was given to Pompeius, a young man who had military glory but no official status. The counter-measures succeeded. Catulus defeated Lepidus in battle outside the gates of Rome and compelled him to retreat. After a second discomfiture near Cosa on the coast of Etruria Lepidus fled to Sardinia.

Though Lepidus had been driven from Italy, the government was vexed by an emergency no less grave, according to one of the fragments (I. 84). That is Sallust's way of making the transition to another subject—Spain and Sertorius. At this point he had to go back several years. Sallust alluded to Sertorius' attainments and earlier career (I. 87–92). Then his governorship in Spain —Sertorius had been sent out by the Marian faction in 82. Expelled in 81 by a general of Sulla, Sertorius wandered from place to place, and, after adventures in Mauretania, invaded Hispania Ulterior in 80, on invitation from the Lusitanians. Metellus Pius was sent against Sertorius. He could make no headway, and other Roman commanders suffered defeats. Sertorius spread his activities far and wide, winning numerous allies among the tribes of the interior. Before the end of 77, a large part of the peninsula had broken loose from the Roman government. Here the author takes leave of Sertorius.

So far, in outline, the structure of Book I. On first inspection, the subject of the work (as far as it went) might be described as the struggle against the Sullan oligarchy. Book I leads on the first rebels—Lepidus (a miserable failure) and Sertorius (a better man, but in vain). The fight is kept going by a sequence of tribunes, not of much account, but it culminates in an alliance between tribunes and generals, with the compact of Pompeius and Crassus (in 70), when Sulla's ordinances are subverted; and three years later the bill of the tribune Gabinius, defying the Optimates,

---

pina and Transalpina together were the provincia of Lepidus, cf. E. Badian, *Foreign Clientelae* (1958), 275.

creates for Pompeius the extraordinary command against the Pirates.

In Book I Sallust put two large and dramatic episodes, permitting concentration on the persons of Lepidus and Sertorius. The episode of Lepidus produces two orations; and the vicissitudes of Sertorius down to the year 80, no less than what followed, were related in lavish detail (I. 84–103). For the rest, two large figures offered, Pompeius and Lucullus. Sallust's first essays gave him skill in arranging material, and he was free to omit many things, or curtail drastically. That was a beneficial apprenticeship.[40] But Sallust now had to organise a complicated sequence of events, year by year. He was writing the annals of Rome—"res populi Romani . . . militiae et domi gestas" (I. 1). It will be observed how wilfully Sallust wrecks and inverts the consecrated phrase "domi militiaeque." And in fact, the greater portion of his narration is warfare.

The Roman government faced urgent problems in its imperial dominion all the way from west to east. Spain the most pressing, but Illyricum, the Balkan lands, and the south of Asia Minor were in disturbance: the author could have enounced emphatically the theme of four foreign wars in 78.[41] Before Sulla's death the consuls of the previous year had departed from Rome, Ap. Claudius Pulcher for Macedonia, P. Servilius Vatia for Cilicia. The former fell sick at Tarentum, and returned to Rome.[42] However, Book I contained some record of operations in both regions (I. 127–134). Geography imposed a double task on Servilius—not only to clear the coast of piracy but to subdue the fierce tribes in the mountain hinterland, in Pisidia and Isauria. His command was prolonged, and he did not return for his triumph until 74.

---

[40] K. Bauhofer (o.c. 74 ff.) exploited this notion in an extreme fashion. Arguing that Sallust concentrated dramatically on individuals, he suggested (against Maurenbrecher) that Sertorius provided an effective climax at the ends of Books II and IV; and further, that a character sketch of Mithridates introduced Book III. For criticism, cf. K. Büchner, o.c. 257; 261 ff. And, especially, H. Bloch, *Didascaliae* (1961), 70 f.

[41] If so, that notion was taken up by Livy, as appears from Orosius V. 23. 1; Eutropius VI. 1. 1. (cf. *Harvard Studies* LXIV [1959], 33).

[42] I. 127. He is mentioned as *interrex* in the speech of Philippus (I. 77. 22).

The annalistic framework entailed certain drawbacks—large themes cut into small sections and the interest dispersed over miscellaneous items. Historians sometimes make complaint. If they know their business, they have devices to exploit or evade the rigid annual record. It may be expedient to go back some way and recapitulate, as Sallust had to do with Sertorius. But exact chronology has its advantages, as that author may have discovered after he completed his *Bellum Jugurthinum*. It appears indeed that the *Historiae* narrated most events under the precise year of their occurrence.

That did not preclude artistic contriving. To make a book terminate with a year's end might be of obvious benefit. Roman imperial annals in the hand of a master can show that technique, with the added refinement of significant items saved up for a conclusion of powerful effect, notably the deaths of famous men.[43] In Sallust, however, ends of books and ends of years seem never quite to coincide. Which is strange at first sight—this author could easily have managed it. He decided against. Instead, he chooses to end with a person or an episode set in strong and deliberate emphasis. The traditional unit was the consular year. Sallust substitutes a combination of smaller units and larger—episodes and books (the latter, after Book I, each cover the equivalent of three years). As for chronology, he could exploit a double advantage for clarity and emphasis. He had the consuls' entry on office—and various devices to indicate intervals. The letter of Pompeius marks the winter of 75–74, and that of Mithridates 69–68 (II. 98; IV. 69).

Book I concludes with Sertorius at the peak of his power.[44] Book II continues with events of 77—Lepidus, an ignominious anticlimax, perishing in Sardinia, and Pompeius sent to Spain. It carried the Spanish War as far as the letter of Pompeius to the Senate in the winter of 75 (II. 98); and it contained operations in other lands—P. Servilius in Cilicia, Ap. Claudius Pulcher and C. Scribonius Curio in Macedonia. But it also impinged briefly

---

[43] Tacitus, *Ann.* II. 88 (Arminius, with reflections on fame and history); III. 76 (Junia, Cassius' widow and Brutus' sister, evoking the Liberators).

[44] Not that Sertorius himself need be supposed the very last item.

on the year 74: the receipt of Pompeius' letter leads at once to measures taken by the new consuls.[45] Early in Book III occurred the dispatch of the praetor M. Antonius with a special command over the Mediterranean coastlands (III. 2–4). A great conflict in the East now develops and proceeds, including the first victories of Lucullus over Mithridates. Warfare in Spain was narrated, down to the tragic end of Sertorius. Further, the war against the rebellious slaves in Italy, which began in 73—the defeat of the consul Lentulus Clodianus in 72 was registered in this book (III. 106), but not the campaign of Crassus, which falls in the autumn. The climax or end of this book cannot be determined.[46] Book IV opens still in 72, for it has a law of the consul Clodianus (IV. 1). The greater part of it was taken up with the exploits of Lucullus in his operations against Mithridates and Tigranes. He won a great victory over the Armenian monarch at Tigranocerta in 69. In the next year he invaded inner Armenia, fought a battle at the river Arsanias, but had to retreat with the onset of winter. If the book ended with Lucullus' capture of Nisibis in Mesopotamia, that point marked the last of his successes. Book V is manifestly incomplete, to judge by the latest items that can be dated. It began with a sudden reversal when Mithridates recovered Pontus; and it went as far as the debate about the *Lex Gabinia,* early in 67 (V. 19–24). There is no fragment that can with certainty be assigned to Pompeius' campaign against the Pirates (or, for that matter, to the Cretan operations of Q. Metellus, the consul of 69).[47]

It would not have exceeded the constructive talent of a writer like Sallust to bring a history to a suitable termination almost

---

[45] II. 98 (D). See H. Bloch, o.c. 61 ff.

[46] K. Bauhofer (o.c. 26) proposed the death of Sertorius as an emphatic ending for Book III. But that event perhaps belongs, not in 72 but in 73, so it can be contended, cf. W. H. Bennett, *Historia* X (1961), 459 ff.

[47] The total of fragments cited with book numbers by grammarians, declining steadily after Book I, drops to only eleven for Book V. That is not a criterion, however, for the relative bulk of Book V. Maurenbrecher (o.c. 196 f.) suggests that the campaign of Pompeius and his return to Rome (V. 25 f.) could have been mentioned. He detects an allusion to disturbances when the tribune C. Cornelius proposed a law (V. 27). It will be noted that none of these fragments is certified to Book V.

anywhere. The great command which Gabinius produced for Pompeius marked a significant turn in the history of the Republic.[48] But there is no sign that Sallust proposed to end here.[49] He was not composing a monograph about the rise of Pompeius Magnus. His design was larger, the term more remote, as is shown by the prologue and by the amplitude of the prefatory narrative in Book I.

How far did he intend to go? The rest of Book V and a sixth book would carry the narrative as far as 63 or 62, one might suppose. The death of Mithridates in 63, it has been argued, was the ideal term for Sallust's *Historiae*.[50] The notion is to be rejected. It implies an exorbitant magnification of a foreign monarch. Also of Pompeius, the victor in the Mithridatic War. Some Romans, such as Cato, opined that too much had been made of Mithridates.[51] Sallust is no friend to Magnus—and he was writing the annals of the Roman People.

Nothing forbids the hypothesis of a later date. Perhaps the momentous year of Metellus and Afranius. If so, would not the author have found himself in trouble, having related already the conspiracy of Catilina? A difficulty, but in no way insuperable. Later historians had to face like problems. Aufidius Bassus after his *Bellum Germanicum* (which probably covered the campaigns of Tiberius and Germanicus from A.D. 4 to 16) subsequently embarked on a full-length history.[52] Nor did the *Agricola* deter Cornelius Tacitus from writing the annals of Rome under the Flavian dynasty.

Sallust may have proposed to go further still and cover nearly

---

[48] Plutarch called it οὐ ναυαρχίαν, ἄντικρυς δὲ μοναρχίαν (*Pompeius* 25). There is perhaps a danger of exaggeration.

[49] W. Schur assumed that Sallust completed this book with the *Lex Manilia* (early in 66), and that such was his design—"die fünf vollendeten Bücher bilden eine abgeschlossene Einheit und behandeln ein gestelltes Thema erschöpfend" (o.c. 222, cf. 214).

[50] K. Bauhofer, o.c. 109 ff. L. O. Sangiacomo puts the term in 64, since the Catilinarian conspiracy began in that year (*Sallustio* [1954], 219, cf. 225). That is not convincing either.

[51] *Pro Murena* 31: "bellum illud omne Mithridaticum cum mulierculis esse gestum."

[52] cf. *Tacitus* (1958), 697.

thirty years. The prologue of the *Bellum Jugurthinum* shows decision and great confidence. To set 51 or 50 as his goal (the breach between Pompeius and Caesar) and a history in twelve books may not have surpassed his belief in his own powers, the style having been created, and the theme irresistible in appeal. A passage in the prologue happens to register a date emphatically, by consuls. It is 51, the widest extension of Rome's empire now achieved by the subjugation of Gaul.[53]

Sallust's theme is not merely the attack on the post-Sullan system. It is the whole interval of precarious peace between the two ages of civil war—he was familiar with the notion of "infida pax." Or better, the decline and fall of the Republic, with Pompeius Magnus the principal agent, one of Sulla's men to begin with, then through long years the enemy of the oligarchs, to become at the end their false friend, and calamitous, bringing them to ruin, their delusion matched with his own jealous ambition.[54]

In Sallust's narration political issues at Rome interlocked with warfare abroad, first through Sertorius and then through Mithridates (the latter variously recalling Jugurtha). Apart from that, the wars had ever been the principal concern of Roman annals, which began (or were thought to have begun) as a bare chronicle of events. For history to become an art, it was necessary to adorn, elaborate, and diversify the narration—and Sallust went far beyond his latest predecessors in style and colouring. Further, he exploited certain devices of composition, in order to import variety, facilitate a transition, bring out a personality, or summarize a situation. These devices not only illustrate the talents and technique of a writer—some of them may furnish a clue to his innermost preoccupations, since he operates from free choice.

First, the digression. Sallust now refrains from inserting dis-

---

[53] I. 11: "res Romana plurimum imperio valuit Servio Sulpicio et Marco Marcello consulibus omni Gallia cis Rhenum atque inter mare nostrum et Oceanum, nisi qua paludibus invia fuit, perdomita."

[54] cf. *Rom.Rev.* (1939), 248; *Tacitus* (1958), 134. M. Bonnet even suggested that it was Sallust's design to go as far as 40 B.C. (*Rev.ét.anc.* II [1900], 117 ff.). Despite the appeal of contemporary history to an emulator of Thucydides, there is the danger to be considered. Also the unity of the theme.

quisitions on Roman politics. The monographs exhausted that
theme, and he did not need to say very much in the prologue of
the *Historiae*. Nor is there any sign that he went in for erudite
annotation on the legal and religious institutions of the Roman
People.[55] That material had recently been studied with care and
affection, not always alien to its political bearing and exploitation. The fashion was spreading fast when Sallust wrote. Anti-
quarianism had a strong and normal appeal for authors enamoured of the Roman past, and scholarship was infected with romantic notions, coloured by distaste for the deplorable present.[56]
But Sallust, despite the studious archaism of his manner, had no
care for these things.

Instead, a different type of erudition, for variety, instruction,
and delight. Sallust had recourse to descriptions of far countries
and peoples, not eschewing fable and the picturesque. The first
instance is noteworthy. When Sertorius in his wanderings passed
through the strait of Gades he fell in with certain mariners newly
returned from a voyage to the Isles of the Blest in the western
ocean. They told him about the delectable spot, and he conceived
a desire to sail away into the West, and live at ease, escaping from
tyranny and the interminable wars.[57] But the Cilician pirates who
had been conveying him would have nothing of these aspirations,
so Sertorius and his allies parted company.

Sertorius now went to Mauretania, there to lend a hand in
local warfare. He fought against the prince Ascalis, and captured
Tingi. Then, so the report runs, he excavated the tumulus that
covered the bones of the giant Antaeus.[58] Here was scope for
erudition about the wanderings of Hercules, such as a man might

---

[55] He might have noted the proposal of Scribonius Curio when consul to
have the Sibylline Books brought from Erythrae (Lactantius, *Inst.Div.* I. 6.
14, from Fenestella): Curio was influenced by ritual, cf. III. 50: "Curio re-
ligione Volcanaliorum diem ibidem moratus."

[56] P. 233.

[57] I. 100 f., cf. Plutarch, *Sertorius* 8.

[58] Plutarch, *Sertorius* 9. According to Strabo, this item was reported by
Γαβίνιος ὁ τῶν 'Ρωμαίων συγγραφεύς (XVIII, p. 829). The name has been corrected to Τανούσιος (B. Niese, followed by many), or even to Σαλλούστιος
(F. Buecheler). On this problem, F. Münzer, discussing Tanusius, is inconclusive (*R-E* IV A 2232).

have found in the books of Hiempsal the Numidian.[59] Further, Sallust may have said something about the strange and sapient behaviour of the elephant.[60]

Next, early in Book II, the actions of Lepidus in Sardinia furnished an excuse to describe that island, its products and its peoples. The author further expatiated on ancient migrations and the origins of towns.[61]

There is no trace of any comprehensive excursus on Spain. But Sallust might discover from time to time items worth brief description, such as the mines in the south, the tunny fisheries, or the habits of the remoter tribes. And there was Hercules' renowned temple at Gades, with the statue of Alexander the Macedonian. Legend and anecdote knows of Caesar's visit, when he was quaestor. Pompeius may have been there before him.[62] A fragment of the *Historiae* mentions Magnus in relation to Alexander: from early youth he was in the habit of imitating his actions.[63] That fragment is generally taken to allude to the magniloquent memorial of victory which Pompeius set up beside a pass in the Pyrenees, when returning to Italy in 71.[64] The fact that it is cited as coming from Book III supports a doubt.[65]

Sallust's most memorable and lengthy performance was the description of the Black Sea, inserted in Book III somewhere in the course of Lucullus' operations against Mithridates in 73 (III. 61–80). It was known, admired, and copied by writers ever after, verse as well as prose.[66] The author started off with Hellespont,

---

[59] *Jug.* 17. 7.

[60] Strabo, proceeding, says that the same historian produced fables about elephants. Not all of Plutarch, *Sertorius* 9 can derive from Sallust, for Plutarch towards the end of the chapter has a reference to Juba.

[61] II. 1–12 (with the traces of this excursus in later writers, Maurenbrecher, 60 ff.). Also *P. Rylands* 473. 2.

[62] As suggested by J. Gagé, *Rev.ét.anc.* XLII (1940), 425 ff.

[63] III. 88: "sed Pompeius a prima adulescentia sermone fautorum similem fore se credens Alexandro regi, facta consultaque eius quidem aemulus erat."

[64] III. 89: "de victis Hispanis tropaea in Pyrenaei iugis constituit."

[65] Maurenbrecher assumes that Pompeius' last actions and departure from Spain were recorded in Book III. But Book IV has some events of 72—and Pompeius did not leave until 71, cf. M. Gelzer, *Pompeius*² (1959), 53.

[66] III. 61–80, cf. Maurenbrecher, 134 ff.

Propontis, and Bosporus, registering the sites of ancient renown in legend and history from Troy to Byzantium; and he did not omit the fish which contributed to the wealth of the latter city (III. 66). Passing through the Symplegades, he turned eastward to describe the coasts of Bithynia, Paphlagonia, and Pontus, and then by a wide sweep north came to the Chersonnesus, the Scythian shore, the Danube mouths, and his point of departure. What Sallust furnished, however, was not merely a coastal voyage, interlaced with mythological lore about Argonauts and Amazons. The excursus *De situ Ponti* carried ethnography. Remote peoples were portrayed in their habits as determined by environment.[67] To the nomads of the northern steppe the fancy of the ancients accorded a place of favour: they were models of the plain life and unsophisticated virtue. "Campestres melius Scythae," that is the strain that runs through most of the Greek and Latin authors; and their traits were sometimes transferred to other natives, to Gauls and Germans. How far Sallust respected the convention is a question.[68]

Such was the major and classic digression. It is to be regretted that Sallust in his narration did not reach Alexandria, the land of Egypt, the Jews, and the Arabs. However, operations against pirates brought in various islands and coasts—Sicily and southern Italy, Crete, the Cilician shore (and also the mountainous country behind Cilicia and Pamphylia).[69] There should have been some account of Sophene, Gordyene, and Mesopotamia, for Lucullus, crossing Euphrates and Tigris, took the Roman arms into regions not entered by any general hitherto (Tigranocerta captured, and Nisibis, and a winter spent in Gordyene, that curious and opulent territory). A fragment stigmatises the inhabitants of Mesopotamia as "libidinous beyond all bounds." [70]

A second device is the full-length character sketch. Historians

---

[67] III. 74: "namque omnium ferocissimi ad hoc tempus Achaei atque Tauri sunt, quod, quantum ego conicio, locorum egestate rapto vivere coacti."

[68] There is only III. 76: "Scythae nomades tenent, quibus plaustra sedes sunt."

[69] Italy and the Sicilian Strait, brought into the narration of the war against the Slaves, produces a large crop of fragments (IV. 23–29).

[70] IV. 78: "Mesopotameni homines effrenatae libidinis sunt in utroque sexu." Sallust also noticed the fragrant amomum of Gordyene (72), and the naphtha (61).

frequently and suitably would put it in the form of an obituary notice. Sallust (so it was observed in antiquity) by contrast to other writers of classic rank was somewhat sparing of this practice. [71] Despite the attractiveness of concluding a year or a book with the decease of some great man, Sallust preferred to render his characters in a different and superior fashion, through actions and through orations. Not but what he is eager to label a character, on his earliest or significant entrance, with some brief and pointed phrase, generally for detriment. Thus the praetor M. Antonius early in Book III: "a spendthrift born, and ever refusing to care until he had to." [72]

Finally, and above all, the speeches.[73] Book I exhibits Philippus balancing Lepidus, the senior statesman against the revolutionary consul. Book II has a consul, C. Aurelius Cotta (*cos.* 75), Book III a tribune, C. Licinius Macer (*tr. pl.* 73). And there are two letters, in II and in IV respectively. The epistle of Pompeius marks the end of one stage in the war against Sertorius. That of Mithridates, soliciting the aid of the Parthian monarch, conveys a denunciation of Roman imperialism: it comes in an appropriate place, after the great victory of Lucullus at Tigranocerta.

That total does not represent an excessive indulgence in the practice of historical speeches, at least by some standards. A question arises: apart from those six items (which were excerpted), did the *Historiae* contain any others?

Standing in high prominence in the narrative, Sertorius and Lucullus clamoured for orations, it might seem.[74] Not all his-

---

[71] Seneca, *Suas.* VI. 21: "hoc semel aut iterum a Thucydide factum, item in paucissimis personis usurpatum a Sallustio."

[72] III. 3: "perdendae pecuniae genitus et vacuus a curis nisi instantibus."

[73] On the speeches in the *Historiae* see H. Schnorr von Carolsfeld, *Über die Reden und Briefe bei Sallust* (Leipzig, 1888), 57 ff.; R. Ullmann, *La technique des discours dans Salluste, Tite-Live et Tacite* (Oslo, 1927), 24 ff.; K. Büchner, o.c. 204 ff. Büchner insists on irony in the speeches and in their setting (162; 221; 234). But one cannot go the whole way with him in all his postulates (238 ff.)—the speeches, he argues, always belong to important occasions and are devised for some practical purpose. Nor is it easy to agree that "hinter allen Reden und Briefen stehen historische Reden und Briefe" (241). On the other hand, independence of formal rhetoric and artistic superiority to Livy is vindicated by Ullmann (o.c. 24 f.).

[74] Such are assumed by Carolsfeld, o.c. 11 f.

torians could have resisted the temptation of stirring rhetoric and martial "contiones." But Sallust is an economical writer, averse from rhetoric. The military achievements of Sertorius and of Lucullus stood uncontested. What would they have to talk about? Each may have been accorded brief statements in indirect discourse somewhere or other. Not indeed that any fragments can be adduced with confidence.

The debate about the *lex Gabinia* early in 67 is another matter. The consular Q. Lutatius Catulus was the head and front of the Optimates, and he spoke against the bill. One of his arguments was prudential—and hypocritical. It was dangerous, he urged, to risk everything on one individual. Pompeius was precious to Rome. What would happen if he perished?[75] That notion happens to be reflected in a fragment from Book V—but not in direct discourse.[76]

Gabinius, however, was worth an oration. The policy of the imperial Republic came under review, and the tribune was bringing in a momentous innovation. He had a clear line of argument: the vast command was necessary for the honour of the Roman People and the security of its imperial dominion, but not a danger to the rule of Senate and People, and not lacking a precedent (that of M. Antonius). And the speaker would hint (if nothing more) that no man but Pompeius was capable of dealing with the Pirates.

A speech by Gabinius in Sallust might have several functions. Not only to arraign the negligence of the Optimates and expound the arguments of a statesman, but also to serve as a pendant to Mithridates' attack on Roman imperial policy (greed, perfidy, and the planned sequence of aggression). It might also convey a foreshadowing of what was to happen in the next year when another tribune's bill consigned to Magnus the charge of the eastern war, superseding Lucullus. Book V needed such a speech. No other theme offered, unless it were the next command for Magnus. But Sallust was not proposing to rewrite the *Pro lege Manilia* of Cicero.

Two fragments are cited from Book V, each with a verb in the

---

[75] *De imp. Cn. Pompei* 59.
[76] V. 24: "nam si in Pompeio quid humani evenisset."

first person (V. 21 f.). One of them surely alludes to Magnus—the
orator urges a man not to be deterred by the prestige that has accrued to his name and fame.[77] The fragments therefore belong to
the oration of Gabinius.[78] The excerptor did not include that oration in his collection. It may have been missing from a text damaged at the end—or perhaps never completed, the author dying.

There are not many speeches in the *Historiae*. Sallust gave careful thought to their placing in the structure of the work, and to
their composition. He is intent on illustrating a personality as
well as a situation, more so indeed than most historians in antiquity. For that purpose he uses subtle variations of style to
convey an individual's fashion of eloquence; and he is alert to
make the speaker demolish himself by allegations contrary to facts
which are supplied in the narrative or obvious to men of understanding.

When a senator writes history, he knows how to render the
speech of a politician. Deceit and distortion are proper ingredients. Nor is plain mendacity out of place.[79] That is patent in
the letter of Pompeius to the Senate (II. 98); and Licinius Macer
addressing the People alleges that a consul has done to death an
innocuous tribune of the plebs.[80]

More instructive the harangue delivered by the consul Lepidus
(I. 55). It attacks Sulla, but it achieves a double demolition—not
only Sulla but the ostensible champion of liberty. Lepidus duly
makes appeal to ancestry and "dignitas." [81] He also parades the
purest of motives. If he acquired property in the Proscriptions,
it was through purchase and under intimidation from Sulla; but he
will sacrifice his investments in the name of justice.[82]

---

[77] V. 21: "speciem et celebritatem nominis intellego timentem."

[78] An oration of Gabinius is assumed by Carolsfeld (o.c. 13) and by Büchner
(o.c. 205 f.). Dio has an oration (XXXVI. 27 ff.), but that is no guidance. He
also produces speeches of Pompeius and of Catulus.

[79] cf. *Tacitus* (1958), 191 f.; 207; 453; 612 f.

[80] III. 48 .10: "dein C. Curio ad exitium usque insontis tribuni dominatus
est."

[81] I. 55. 26.

[82] ib. 18: "atque illa, quae tum formidine mercatus sum, pretio soluto,
iure dominis tamen restituo."

The speech was hollow, the outcome calamitous. About Lepidus as an orator, nothing stood on record. Cicero in the *Brutus* furnished a catalogue of Roman eloquence so exhaustive that his friend Atticus was moved to complain—he was going down to the dregs.[83] Most of the consulars of the previous forty years find entry and some amicable compliment, for example all five of the Cornelii Lentuli. That is too much. Not Lepidus, however. Cicero detested his son, consul in 46 (partisan of Caesar, and brother-in-law of Marcus Brutus).

History showed Lepidus vain, ambitious, and turbulent. The oration is violent and vaunting. Also (and significant of Sallust's art), abrupt and disjointed. Philippus by contrast exhibits the balance and measure of senatorial eloquence, copious and flowing, but with no loss of bite and vigour (I. 77). Philippus left no written memorials, but the man and his style were not forgotten. Sallust could have recourse to various verdicts of Cicero: Philippus was a highly educated man, and a wit, ready in attack (he generally spoke without preparation), and he was not afraid of anybody.[84]

Rallying the Senate against a rebel in arms, Philippus stands out, firm and resolute. That favourable impression could have been undermined by the author somewhere in the context. Philippus, consul in 91, was a survivor of an earlier age. Men might remember his variegated career and allegiances, his consummate craft and guile. In fact, the orator is made to supply statements damaging to himself, if anybody reflected. Philippus asks whether his audience has forgotten the crimes of Cinna, whose return to Rome extinguished the Senate's dignity and honour.[85] And, a little further on, he refers contemptuously to Cethegus and other traitors.[86] Now Philippus held the censorship under the domination of Cinna, and P. Cethegus was not the only turncoat of the age.

---

[83] *Brutus* 244.

[84] *De or.* II. 316; *Brutus* 173; 186.

[85] I. 77. 19: "obliti scelerum Cinnae, cuius in urbem reditu decus ordinis huius interiit."

[86] ib. 20: "agite ut libet, parate vobis Cethegi atque alia proditorum patrocinia."

Totally different in manner from Philippus was C. Aurelius
Cotta (cos. 75). According to Cicero, he had a weak voice. Denied
amplitude and splendour, he went in for a plain unadorned style,
and he was neat and intelligent.[87] The Sallustian oration conforms admirably (II. 47). The speaker makes gentle appeal to the
good will of his audience, with repeated recall of his age, his past
misfortunes and a long and disinterested career of service to the
Commonwealth.[88] That audience may have been deceived, but
not Sallust. Cotta had earned a place in the inner ring of the
oligarchy, "ex factione media" (III. 48. 8). He was a master of
intrigue. Sallust had put his readers on guard at the first introduction of this consul.[89]

Cotta spoke to deprecate ill-feeling and conciliate popular
favour, not to support or thwart any law. Nor is Licinius Macer's
intervention the cause or consequence of any important transaction. Macer, being a historian as well as a tribune, had an especial
interest for Sallust; and Sallust neatly makes him begin by affirm-
ing that he might easily discourse at length on past history and
secessions of the plebs (III. 48. 1). Macer delivers a violent attack
on the aristocracy—for which Sallust may have drawn on speeches
in Macer's historical work. As Sallust saw Macer, he was a genuine
and convinced champion of popular rights, not, like Lepidus, an
opportunist. And, unlike Lepidus, Macer conducts his attack
with order and logic. Cicero, who disparaged the man, paid handsome tribute to his skill in arrangement.[90]

The speeches in Sallust echo one another for resemblance or
contrast and contain allusions to past or future events. Thus
Macer mentions what happened to tribunes in 76 and in 74; and,
reassuring the plebs, he tells them that Pompeius will prefer to
take the first place in the State as their leader rather than share

[87] Brutus 202, cf. De or. II. 98: "acutissimum ac subtilissimum dicendi
genus"; III. 31: "elimatus alter ac subtilis."

[88] Already in 91 he went in for earnest appeals, cf. Appian BC I. 37. 167:
σεμνολογήσας δὲ ὑπὲρ ὧν ἐπεπολίτευτο.

[89] II. 42: "quorum Octavius languide et incuriose fuit, Cotta promptius
sed ambitione tum ingenita largitione cupiens gratiam singulorum."

[90] Brutus 238: "at in inveniendis componendisque rebus mira accuratio."
Though his skill, to be sure, was rather "veteratoria" than "oratoria."

dominion with the oligarchs; further, that he will be active to restore the tribunes' powers.[91]

To render Pompeius, Sallust could have produced an oration to the People outside the gates of Rome, on the invitation of the tribunes. The general was not a bad performer, at least when he spoke about himself.[92] There was an oration. It proclaimed a policy, and it is mentioned in one of the fragments.[93] For one reason or another (and that was a late season for Magnus to recapitulate his merits), Sallust opts for a dispatch to the Senate in the winter of 75–74, with imperious demands for troops and supplies (II. 98). The document discloses chill ambition, boasting, menace and mendacity. Pompeius alleges, for example, that in forty days he not only raised an army but chased Rome's enemies all the way from the Alps to Spain. And he boldly misrepresents the battle at the river Sucro—it was in fact not Pompeius but his legate Afranius who captured the hostile camp (only to lose it again), and Pompeius was rescued from utter defeat by the arrival of Metellus Pius. Nor has the author neglected the chance to indulge malice against Magnus: forty days is Pompeius' standard assertion about the time he needed to begin and end a campaign.[94]

Sallust intended that Pompeius Magnus should develop into the principal character. The preliminary survey was conceived in scope and detail adequate to set on record the earliest actions, namely the private army levied in Picenum and the reconquest of Sicily and Africa. And not without items to the discredit of the

---

[91] III. 48. 23: "mihi quidem satis spectatum est Pompeium, tantae gloriae adulescentem, malle principem volentibus vobis esse quam illis dominationis socium, auctoremque imprimis fore tribuniciae potestatis." K. J. Neumann here saw a hint of Octavianus, and precisely to the year 36 (*Hermes* XXXII [1897], 314). Not in any sense plausible.

[92] Quintilian XI. 1. 36: "sicut Pompeius abunde disertus rerum suarum narrator." The phrase has a Sallustian flavour.

[93] IV. 44, cf. 45. Pompeius announced that the tribunes would get their powers back. Further, "populatas vexatasque esse provincias, iudicia autem turpia ac flagitiosa fieri: ei rei se providere ac consulere velle" (*In Verrem* I. 45).

[94] Plutarch, *Pompeius* 12 (the reconquest of Africa); 26 (the clearing of the western seas).

ruthless young adventurer, for the killing of the Marian consular
Papirius Carbo found a mention (I. 52). No doubt also the fate
of the young Cn. Domitius Ahenobarbus in Africa.[95] The narrative proper contained exploits of Pompeius in 77. Conducting the
campaign against M. Brutus in the Cisalpina he besieged him at
Mutina—and had him killed after surrender, so it was alleged.[96]

Chronicling the dispatch of Pompeius to Spain in the same year,
Sallust furnished some resumptive remarks about his character
and achievements (II. 16–19).[97] The war took him down to 71 and
his return to Italy. Next, his consulate, with Crassus for colleague,
after a victory over the slaves on the way. The *Historiae* break off
when Pompeius receives the command against the Pirates, or soon
after. In contrast to Pompeius stood two figures—Sertorius, the
great adversary, and the rival Metellus Pius. A later rival to
glory in the field is Crassus, who had broken the back of the slave
rebellion.

Metellus and Lucullus were the best generals of the aristocracy,
but they proved unable to finish their wars. Metellus had been in
the peninsula since 79. Sallust, for various reasons (equity as well
as artistry) did not wish him to be overshadowed by the young
Pompeius; and he would be prepared to concede courage, integrity, and competence, as previously to his parent Numidicus.[98]
But not without reservations on other counts.

As for Lucullus, Sallust was at pains to emphasize his eager
ambition in the expedients of intrigue he adopted when he got
the command in 74—and when he tried to avoid supersession.[99]
The campaigns were narrated in full, with generous appreciation
for Lucullus' talents as a strategist and an organiser.[100] Nor may

---

[95] The version transmitted by Livy has Ahenobarbus killed in battle
(Orosius V. 21. 13). See, however, Valerius Maximus VI. 2. 8.

[96] Plutarch, *Pompeius* 16—which shows that there was something to be
covered up or explained away.

[97] Notably II. 17: "modestus ad alia omnia, nisi ad dominationem." To
Pompeius might perhaps be assigned II. 23: "multos tamen ab adulescentia
bonos insultaverat."

[98] I. 116: "sanctus alia et ingenio validus." Büchner, however, suggests that
this definition would apply better to Sertorius (o.c. 268).

[99] Plutarch, *Lucullus* 6; 33, cf. IV. 71.

[100] IV. 70: "imperii prolatandi percupidus habebatur, cetera egregius."

Sallust have omitted other particulars to his credit. Lucullus treated the subject populations gently and protected them from exploitation by Roman business men (whose bitter enmity he thereby incurred). A shining exception in this matter, Lucullus otherwise resembled all too closely the common run of aristocratic generals—avid for profit as well as glory, and he drove the troops too hard.[101] Resonant victories and long marches—but the enemy was able to take the field again at the end of 68. What had been gained in years of arduous warfare was lost in a moment.

Towards Lucullus, the historian is more or less equitable. The point of crucial debate and genuine perplexity is his presentation of Sertorius. The hero of the long war against the generals of the oligarchy captured his sympathies. Why not? The facts demonstrate his genius as a leader, a general and a diplomatist. And Sertorius was an enemy of Sulla, and a man from the Sabine country. Has not the author embellished the personality of Sertorius and magnified his importance—with dire repercussion in historical and ethical writing ever after?

Certain fragments speak warmly of Sertorius. For example, on his first introduction it is affirmed that the fame of his earlier exploits was obscured through prejudice.[102] Further, even in civil war Sertorius sought a reputation for fair dealing (I. 90); and his moderation won the affection and respect of natives in Spain (I. 94). But the fragments will not take one very far. Sallust is known, or rather divined, largely through Plutarch. It is premature and hazardous to equate the two writers.

Three questions have to be kept separate—Plutarch, the veracity of Sallust, the truth about Q. Sertorius.[103] Enquiry must con-

---

[101] V. 10 (from Plutarch, *Lucullus* 33, where Sallust is cited). Cf. Dio XXXVI. 16. 2.

[102] I. 88: "magna gloria tribunus militum in Hispania T. Didio imperante, magno usui bello Marsico paratu militum et armorum fuit, multaque tum ductu eius peracta primo per ignobilitatem, deinde per invidiam scriptorum incelebrata sunt."

[103] For the modern controversy about Sertorius see H. Berve, *Hermes* LXIV (1929), 199 ff.; M. Gelzer, *Phil.Woch.* 1932, 1129 ff.; P. Treves, *Athenaeum* X (1932), 127 ff.; V. Ehrenberg *Ost und West* (1935), 177 ff.; E. Gabba, *Athenaeum* XXXII (1954), 293 ff.; L. Wickert, *Rastloses Schaffen.* Festschrift F. Lammert (Stuttgart, 1954), 97 ff.

centrate on the Greek biographer. His account reflects other sources, not Sallust only, or even perhaps in preponderance. For example, what Plutarch relates concerning the early history of Sertorius patently does not derive from Sallust.[104] And the biography has a peculiar structure. After carrying the campaigns down to the end of 75, with Pompeius and Metellus going into winter quarters, the book takes a new and different course. It abandons annalistic history, to diverge into panegyric of Sertorius, with examples of his virtue, also emphatic and verbose apologia.[105] It gives no hint of what happened in 74 and 73—defeats and the dispersal of Spanish allies, bringing Sertorius to a desperate pass. One looks in vain for the sequence of events that encouraged Sertorius' officers to plot his removal and contrive the fatal banquet at Osca.

Something else is missing, the psychological penetration of Sallust. Would he not have been alert to mark the turn in Sertorius' fortunes and trace the tragic degeneration of an active and ambitious temperament (comparable to Jugurtha), impatient under defeat, exacerbated by desertion and driven to live under constant fear? [106]

That is not the only problem. Sertorius in the course of 75 had opened negotiations with Mithridates, and an alliance was concluded. The terms, which naturally became a subject of polemics for and against Sertorius, are not easy to establish. Sertorius was willing, it appears, to let Mithridates occupy the vassal kingdoms of Bithynia and Cappadocia. The hostile tradition, however, avers that he made further concessions, that he admitted Mithridates' claim to the Roman province of Asia.[107] Now Plutarch in the

---

[104] Plutarch, Sertorius 2–5 clearly cannot derive from I. 88 (quoted in n. 102), cf. Maurenbrecher, *Prol.* (1891), 28 f. Otherwise it has to be supposed that Sallust had previously narrated those transactions in detail. Thus W. Stahl, *De bello Sertoriano* (Diss. Erlangen, 1907), 5 ff.

[105] The annalistic and factual portion terminates with ch. 21, cf. H. Berve, o.c. 204 ff.; W. Schur, o.c. 231 ff.

[106] In *Sertorius* 10 is interpolated a remark about Sertorius' later conduct, with the suggestion that he was not clement by nature. Plutarch criticises that suggestion, and defends his hero. That defence is generally taken to represent Sallust, thus W. Stahl, o.c. 10; W. Schur, o.c. 235. Büchner argues that it is Plutarch's defence of Sertorius against Sallust's portrayal (o.c. 419).

[107] Appian, *Mithr.* 68. 288.

later part of his biography adduces it as an example of Sertorius' great soul and inflexible patriotism that he refused to make this surrender.[108]

Hence a double perplexity. Did Sertorius in fact agree to surrender a Roman province? Some scholars assume that he did, and can therefore demolish the notion of Sertorius as a noble patriot —and further, impair the credit of Sallust as a historian.[109] But the fact itself is in question.[110] Nor can there be certainty about the attitude of Sallust, for, as has been shown, Plutarch in his apologia does not appear to be reproducing Sallust.

Sallust's prepossession in favour of Sertorius has been shared and transmitted by illustrious names. And, outdoing even Plutarch, idealisation has been carried to extravagant lengths. One estimate exalts him as "one of the greatest men, if not the very greatest man that Rome had hitherto produced—a man who under more fortunate circumstances would perhaps have become the regenerator of his country." [111] Or again, it is asserted that Sertorius is the last statesman in the history of Rome who can be said to embody an ideal.[112]

Sallust has to bear a share of the responsibility for these aberrations. He went too far. But it can be assumed that Sallust's account was very different from an encomiastic biography.[113]

The portrayal of Sertorius brings up in an acute form the problem of Sallust's methods, his credit, his sources. Introducing Sertorius, he alludes to writers whose malevolence suppressed facts.[114] But that is in reference to early exploits of Sertorius,

---

[108] Plutarch, *Sertorius* 23 f.

[109] H. Berve, o.c. 204, cf. 211.

[110] M. Gelzer, o.c. 1129 ff.

[111] Thus, quoting Mommsen, R. Gardner in *CAH* IX (1932), 325. The exaggerated estimate of Sertorius is explicit in A. Schulten, *Sertorius* (1926). It is not certain that there was anything remarkable about the policy he adopted in Spain, cf. H. Berve, o.c. 226. And it can be argued that he was really a "hostis populi Romani" (Berve, o.c. 227).

[112] W. Schur, o.c. 222: "der letzte Ideenpolitiker der römischen Geschichte."

[113] cf. K. Büchner, o.c. 268; 418.

[114] II. 88, quoted in n. 102.

notably in the *Bellum Italicum*. Which Roman annalists had
dealt with the seventies, continuing the works of Sisenna and
Lucceius? It is a baffling question.

Touching the Spanish campaigns, certain later writers are dis-
crepant: not so much on facts as giving an interpretation contrary
to Sallust. It is therefore not safe to postulate a general tradition
divergent from his exposition.[115] Perhaps a single source, which
can be divined, namely Varro, used both by Sallust and by other
writers. He served under Pompeius in Spain, described his own
campaigns, and also composed three books *De Pompeio*.[116] A fragment of the *Historiae* shows Varro credulous about rumours.[117]

Varro can be traced in an interesting particular. Pompeius was
good-looking. He had an "os probum"—so Varro described it.[118]
Sallust took over the phrase, with a damaging appendage—"oris
probi, animo inverecundo" (II. 16). Further, there is the emulation of Alexander. According to Sallust, Pompeius was encouraged
by eager partisans, from his youth onwards.[119] Other friends or
clients of Pompeius may have celebrated his deeds in the peninsula. It happens to be recorded that the first freedman to write
history was a certain L. Voltacilius Pitholaus, the tutor of Pompeius.[120] And, when Sallust came to deal with eastern affairs, he
would encounter the lavish and encomiastic narration composed
by Pompeius Theophanes of Mytilene.

Lucullus, to whom Sulla dedicated his memoirs with the injunction to polish and improve, is not on record for having written
any of his own during the years of his luxurious retirement.[121]
But Lucullus did not lack commemoration in Greek and Latin

---

[115] cf. the arguments of P. Treves, *Athenaeum* X (1932), 127 ff.

[116] For these writings of Varro, see C. Cichorius, *Römische Studien* (1922),
193 ff.; H. Dahlmann, *R-E*, Supp. VI, 1248 ff.

[117] II. 69: "haec postquam Varro in maius more rumorum audiit." Not
that the phrase shows any bias against Varro.

[118] Pliny, *NH* VII. 53; XXXVII. 14. From Varro, cf. F. Münzer, *Beiträge
zur Quellenkritik der Naturgeschichte des Plinius* (1897), 283.

[119] III. 88, quoted in n. 63.

[120] Suetonius, *De rhet.* 3.

[121] When a young man he had written, in an amiable literary competition
with Hortensius and Sisenna, a history of the *Bellum Italicum* in Greek
(Plutarch, *Lucullus* 1). He added soloecisms, deliberately (*Ad Att.* I. 19. 10).

writers.[122] Among them was Archias, who wrote an epic poem.[123] And there might be called up the names of Greek writers about Mithridates, not that anything of value can emerge.[124]

Of political orations subsisting from the seventies, there seems hardly a trace. It was not a brilliant period. Cotta, so Cicero states, left nothing behind.[125] Sallust therefore fell back on tradition and his own imagination. For Macer he may have had recourse to tribunician harangues of old time in that person's historical work. He must have been acquainted with Macer's son, Licinius Calvus, a spirited orator. Again, family records may have divulged funeral laudations on ex-consuls who had fought wars and earned triumphs, such as Scribonius Curio and P. Servilius. Curio died in 53, Servilius only in 44, at the age of ninety.

Old men can bridge wide tracts of time. To elicit their recollections would be normal for a senatorial historian—and sometimes indispensable. In their own persons ex-consuls were history, and they could tell things never published in debate or consigned to any document. In default of consulars surviving to Sallust's season of writing, others could help. It was not so long ago. Given the paucity of historical narrations, Sallust must have drawn heavily on personal informants.[126] All in all, heterogeneous sources and some not veracious, he would require diligence and independence of judgment. If a writer likes names and facts, he cannot expect to avoid errors.[127]

Roman annals entail a plethora of names, from consuls, generals, and orators down to tribunes of the plebs and all the minor fauna of the political jungle. That is proper, and welcome. Yet fatigue and bewilderment may ensue unless the author is on guard. He must be able to hit off a character in brief and memorable fashion, he must manage the subtle arts of verbal echo and significant recurrence.

---

[122] *Ac. prior.* II. 4.

[123] *Pro Archia* 21. Perhaps one of Plutarch's sources.

[124] Th. Reinach, *Mithridate Eupator* (1890), 429 f.

[125] *Orator* 132.

[126] P. 224.

[127] Mistakes in the narration of Lucullus are registered by Th. Reinach, o.c. 424.

When Sulla assumed the dictatorship, there were hardly any ex-consuls among the living, and, for all his efforts to reinstate the *nobilitas*, it became difficult in the sequel to find suitable candidates. The consuls of the seventies are a poor lot. Who was there to stand for Sulla's system when the government had to face the coalition of tribunes and army commanders? Age and debility, conceit and arrogance, intrigue and venality—their failings are shown up by Sallust with relish and ridicule.

Sulla had married a Metella, and his most loyal ally was Metellus Pius, his wife's cousin. Sulla and Metellus, consuls in 80, advertise the alliance. And the consuls of 79 represent that faction— P. Servilius Vatia through his mother, Ap. Claudius Pulcher through his wife. Further, Lucullus was a first cousin of Metellus Pius.[128]

The pride of the Metelli degenerated into pomp and vanity. Sallust described a banquet in Spain where Metellus Pius wore an embroidered vestment. An image of Victory by a mechanical device deposited a wreath on his head, and incense was burned before the *imperator*. The repast was luxurious, fish and game being imported from distant regions. The spectacle was a disgrace to Rome. Disgust was voiced by "veteres et sancti viri" (II. 70).

Various consuls earn damaging notice or labels of dispraisal. Scribonius Curio (*cos.* 76) was highly eccentric in speech and deportment: somebody, perhaps the tribune Cn. Sicinius, called him by the name of a deranged actor, Burbuleius.[129] His colleague Cn. Octavius is a mild-mannered man, crippled in the feet (II. 26). Jokes were made about both of them.[130] The consuls of 75 receive a characterisation when they enter office: L. Octavius a tired man, not wanting to be bothered, C. Cotta more prompt, but crafty and ingratiating (II. 42).

---

[128] For the stemma of the Metelli see *Rom.Rev.* (1939), Table 1.

[129] II. 25: "quia corpore et lingua percitum et inquietem nomine histrionis vix sani Burbuleium appellabat."

[130] *Brutus* 217: "numquam," inquit, "Octavi, conlegae tuo gratiam referes: qui nisi se suo more iactavisset, hodie te istic muscae comedissent." The speaker is the tribune Cn. Sicinius. Curio lurched and wobbled when orating (ib. 216).

Next, Lentulus Clodianus and Gellius Poplicola, the consuls of 72. The patrician Lentulus takes a double knock. Aristocrats could be classified for contumely as either heavy-weights or light-weights—"stolidi" or "vani." Where did Lentulus belong? He defied the categories—"perincertum stolidior an vanior" (IV. 1).[131] Nor is it likely that old Poplicola got off lightly. Both consuls were routed by Spartacus. Two years later they held the censorship, on which occasion they expelled a number of persons from the Senate, among them two of subsequent notoriety in 63: the ex-consul Lentulus Sura and C. Antonius.

Sallust took a keen interest in censors. He could allude to senators struck off the rolls, some a disgrace to the high assembly, but others damned through an allegiance or a personal feud. The tribunate of the plebs also recalled his past career. There were good tribunes and bad. Licinius Macer is in a special case, and Sallust may also have credited Gabinius with sincerity and patriotism. Gabinius rose high (consul and proconsul of Syria) but his memory needed rehabilitation. He had run into a double misfortune—traduced by Cicero in public orations, discarded by Pompeius, his leader and patron. Gabinius, like others, turned to Caesar. Nor could Sallust easily have denied recognition (if he got so far) to the proposals of C. Cornelius, another tribune of 67: Cornelius tried to curb bribery and restrict various types of political jobbery practised by the Optimates.[132]

Other tribunes were sordid, disreputable, and widely detested. Sallust may have had some indulgence for Cn. Sicinius, who mocked the consuls Octavius and Curio.[133] But he had no reason to give a good report of agitators like L. Quinctius, who held the office in 74 and who, through intrigue and effrontery, made something of a career, ending as praetor.[134] As for M. Lollius Palicanus, who negotiated with Pompeius and Crassus towards the end

---

[131] The passage is fully discussed in Gellius XVIII. 4. See p. 300.

[132] V. 27, cf. Maurenbrecher 196 f., adducing Dio XXXVI. 39. 3.

[133] II. 25, cf. *Brutus* 217. Cicero calls him "homo impurus, sed admodum ridiculus" (216). He is mentioned in the oration of Macer (III. 48. 8)—and styled "insons" (ib. 10).

[134] Quinctius is lavishly described in *Pro Cluentio* 110 ff. He comes into the story of Lucullus, twice, when tribune and when praetor (Plutarch, *Lucullus* 5; 33), cf. III. 48. 11; IV. 71.

of 71, Sallust dismisses him as base-born and no speaker at all—
"humili loco Picens, loquax magis quam facundus" (IV. 43). In
67, Palicanus wanted to stand for the consulate, but was blocked
by the consul C. Piso.[135]

The intrigues and influence of certain minor characters in 74
enabled Sallust to expose the Sullan oligarchy in its secret work-
ings. At the beginning of the year an anomalous command was
established for the praetor M. Antonius. The artful Cotta, helped
by P. Cethegus, managed the job.[136] Cethegus, once a partisan of
Marius and declared a public enemy by the Senate, made his
peace with Sulla, to become a political force subsequently. In the
Senate he acquired the authority that normally attended on ex-
consuls, for he knew the "res publica" inside out, so it is asseverated.[137] And something is known about the detail of his
devious operations. When Lucullus wanted the Cilician command
he had to use Cethegus. Access to Cethegus he got through a lady
of elegant pretensions and dissolute life called Praecia. Sallust
duly noted that lady.[138] He had not forgotten his Sempronia.
But a proper care for the dignity of history may have excluded
from his pages the beautiful Flora, among whose lovers had been
the young Pompeius.[139]

The annals of the twelve years from the consulship of Lepidus
and Catulus conveyed sheer delight and diversion in all manner
of ways, relevant to personal experience or to the first monograph.
Lepidus in the oration is made to name for detriment Vettius the
Picentine and the scribe Cornelius, satellites of the Dictator (I.
55. 17). Sallust knew who they were. The former is the notorious
rogue who in 62 produced revelations about the Catilinarian conspiracy, and who later, after other revelations in 59, perished mys-

[135] Valerius Maximus III. 8. 3.

[136] Pseudo-Asconius p. 259 St.

[137] *Brutus* 178. For his importance, *Historia* IV (1955), 60; Broughton,
MRR, Supp. (1960).

[138] III. 18: "cultu corporis ornata egregio." Assigned by Maurenbrecher
to Praecia, on whom and Cethegus see Plutarch, *Lucullus* 5.

[139] Plutarch, *Pompeius* 2. This is the lady celebrated by Philodemus of
Gadara (*Anth.Pal.* V. 132. 7).

teriously in prison.[140] The latter, escaping notice for long years
was elected quaestor for 44, much to men's distaste.[141]

Lepidus also denounces a certain L. Fufidius in a phrase of
memorable grandeur—"honorum omnium dehonestamentum" (I.
55. 22). Fufidius is one of the centurions whom Sulla promoted to
senatorial rank. In one account he is the man who urged Sulla to
publish a proscription list.[142] Fufidius recurred later in the *Historiae*, being defeated by Sertorius at the river Baetis (I. 108).
Another adherent of Sulla who acquires an early entry is the
patrician L. Sergius Catilina (I. 45).

Cicero emerged later in the narrative. His prosecution of Verres
was no doubt registered, and assigned its proper context and
value. A historian, anticipating the posthumous fame of classic
oratory among the uncritical, would be alert to interpose facts for
corrective. Sallust notes that Verres when governor of Sicily
protected the coasts against pirates and slaves.[143]

Catilina, the reader would recall, was a close friend of the
eminent Lutatius Catulus, whom some praised for character and
integrity, the principal leader of the Optimates after the decease
of Philippus: Catulus defended him in the affair of the Vestal
Virgins in 73.[144] Now Catulus no doubt received credit for energy
in his campaign against Lepidus. And he was courageous in the
firm stand he took against the bill of Gabinius.[145] But the historian will not have forgotten Catulus' rancour against Caesar at
the time of the Catilinarian debate. Nor did he omit to record
how C. Piso, another of Caesar's enemies, when a candidate in 68,
bought off a prosecutor with an enormous bribe (IV. 81).

---

[140] Suetonius, *Divus Iulius* 17. For L. Vettius cf. H. Gundel in *R-E* VIII A,
1844 ff.

[141] *De off.* II. 29: "alter autem qui in illa dictatura scriba fuerat, in hac
fuit quaestor urbanus." He is to be identified as Q. Cornelius (Josephus,
Ant.Jud. XIV. 219).

[142] Orosius V. 21. 3: "auctore L. Fufidio primipilari."

[143] IV. 32: "C. Verres litora Italia propinqua firmavit." For a different
view of Verres' conduct, *In Verr.* V. 5. Note also that in the "vitiosis
magistratibus" of III. 46 there is probably a reference to Fonteius the proconsul of Gaul, whom Cicero defended in 69.

[144] Orosius VI. 3. 1.

[145] V. 23: "sane bonus ea tempestate contra pericula et ambitionem."

Looking back into the past, the historian came upon sundry items about the parents of his friends or enemies. He had an eye for the consuls Ap. Claudius Pulcher, P. Servilius Vatia, and C. Scribonius Curio. And it was an especial excitement to discover persons he had known, already prominent or emerging for the first time. In the *Bellum Catilinae* Sallust alluded to Crassus in ambiguous terms, and he reported words uttered by Crassus.[146] The *Historiae* enabled him to bring up particulars for dispraisal, for example Crassus' comportment as consul: when he opposed Pompeius, it was not from political judgment.[147] Vanities clashed. Pompeius tried to treat Crassus like a junior colleague, he expected admiration and deference.[148] Whereas a Licinius would look down on Pompeius as an upstart. The two consuls were soon at variance.[149] Later in the year it became expedient to advertise harmony by a public reconciliation.[150] A spectacle no doubt full of irony for the "prudentes."

For malice against Pompeius, the *Historiae* offered opportunity ever and again, gladly taken. The denigration looks like an obsession. There may be personal grounds. Pompeius had a bad name for duplicity or ingratitude. Perhaps Sallust had himself experienced that perfidy of Magnus in 52 or in 50—for it is not clear how early Sallust became an adherent of Caesar.

Caesar happens not to be named in what survives of the *Historiae*. There is a fragment which conveys his attitude towards the rule of Sulla, so it is generally held.[151] The note may refer to the time when Caesar served as military tribune under P. Servilius

---

146 P. 103.

147 IV. 51: "Crassus obtrectans potius collegae quam boni aut mali publici gnavos aestimator." The last two words are Maurenbrecher's proposal. But the original text (the grammarian Arusianus Messius) gives "gravis exactor," which is surely right, cf. W. Clausen, *AJP* LXVIII [1947], 297).

148 IV. 48: "collegam minorem et sui cultorem exspectans."

149 Plutarch, *Crassus* 12; *Pompeius* 22. In this place can perhaps go IV. 37: "dissidere inter se coepere neque in medium consultare." Maurenbrecher, adducing Plutarch *Crassus* 11, suggests an incident in Crassus' campaign against the slaves.

150 Plutarch, *Crassus* 12. Perhaps a scene on the last day of the year.

151 I. 57: "nam Sullae dominationem queri non audebat qua fuit offensus."

in Cilicia.[152] The author would not miss his prosecution (in 77) of Cn. Cornelius Dolabella, consul and proconsul of Macedonia. That was a notable action, whence fame accrued.[153]

Incidents in Caesar's early life tended to be magnified, or misconstrued—ignorance and legend as well as defamation. Sallust should have been on guard. In reaction, he may have decided to say very little about Caesar, before Caesar came to matter. However, he did not fail to register the young Clodius, who turns up at the camp of Lucullus (the husband of one of his sisters), turbulent and fomenting sedition.[154]

Sallust as he composed the *Historiae* was coming ever closer to persons and events familiar from his early manhood. He did not have to wait for the onset of old age before he meditated on chance and change. As another senatorial historian with solemnity avowed, the more a man reflects on things ancient or recent, the more is he impressed by the "ludibria rerum humanarum cunctis in negotiis." [155] What struck Sallust, writing under the Triumvirs about Sulla and the time after Sulla, was not merely the fortuitous resemblances, the ironies, the paradoxes, but the whole grim tragedy of Roman history enacted again before his eyes.[156] That experience underlies his writings all through—and comes out explicitly in the prologue of the *Bellum Jugurthinum*, conveyed in the form of personal testimony and bitter protest.

---

152 That is Maurenbrecher's proposal.

153 Velleius II. 43. 3; Tacitus, *Dial.* 34. 7; Suetonius, *Divus Iulius* 4. 1; 55. 1.

154 V. 11: "qui uxori eius frater erat"; 12: "ex insolentia avidus male faciendi."

155 Tacitus, *Ann.* III. 18. 4.

156 cf. *Rom.Rev.* (1939), 249.

XIII

THE TIME
OF WRITING

Sallust's second monograph opens with a bold and splendid negation—the word "falso." Men complain about their common lot, wrongly.[1] Life, they say, is a feeble thing, brief in duration, the sport of chance. They forget the spirit of man, which is "pollens potensque et clarus." Fortune does not confer its noble qualities, and fortune cannot take them away. People attribute their failings to circumstances. It is their own fault if, surrendering to sloth and the pleasures of the body, they discover that they have dissipated their lives. On the contrary, if the zeal that is spent in pursuit of the futile or noxious were devoted to good ends, men would be able to rise superior to chance and accident, and, mortal though their condition, would achieve an immortal renown.

Body and soul share the nature of man and divide his activities. Beauty of form and strength and wealth and the like fade and pass away, but the "egregia facinora" of the mind are eternal. None the less, through singular perversity, so many waste their lives through indulgence and idleness, while the mind goes to rot. Yet the pursuits are many and various whereby the mind can thrive and excel.

At this point the author turns aside for a powerful negatory comment. Public office (he affirms) is not one of those pursuits in this season, nor is any form of political activity to be recommended.

---

[1] *Jug.* 1. 1: "falso queritur de natura sua genus humanum."

Office confers neither credit nor even security now.² Any form of governance by force is a harsh and cruel thing; and all revolutions bring murder and exile in their train. To offer vain resistance is sheer insanity; and, on the other hand, who would sacrifice personal honour and freedom to serve despotism?

Reverting to his central theme, Sallust declares the most excellent of all intellectual pursuits. It is history. Many indeed have praised history—and he does not want to be extolling the activity he has chosen. But some there will be no doubt who censure Sallust's decision to abandon public life, denouncing his noble and valuable task as a mere excuse for idleness. These are the people whose most exacting occupation is to court the populace or give political dinner parties. Let them cast their minds back to the time when Sallust won office (and others could not); let them observe the sort of men that have entered the Senate subsequently. They will have to confess that Sallust made the right decision for the right reasons; that greater benefit will accrue to the Commonwealth from the fruits of Sallust's retirement than from the employments of anybody else.

Indeed, that argument is to be reinforced. A Fabius, a Scipio, and other famous men of old used to say that they were inspired to excellence and emulation when they contemplated the portraits of ancestors. It was not the mere images, but recollection of what the men had done, "memoria rerum gestarum." Who among all the *nobiles,* behaving as they do in these days, cares to vie with an ancestor in vigour and integrity? Wealth and extravagance, that is their only field of competition. Even *novi homines,* who in previous times got ahead of birth through "virtus" now make their way by craft or crime. But, no matter. Praetorships, consulates and the like have no intrinsic honour or credit. They rate according to the men that hold them.

In the prefatory remarks of the *Bellum Catilinae* Sallust was discreetly on the defensive, and he eschewed direct comment on affairs. Conscious and more confident, he now goes over to the at-

---

² 3. 1: "quoniam neque virtuti honos datur neque illi, quibus per fraudem is fuit, tuti aut eo magis honesti sunt."

tack. He asserts the positive value of his chosen vocation. And, combined with that assertion, there stands a double indictment, closely interwoven: against the present dispensation and against the *nobiles*.

The language is vigorous and aggressive. And sharp political comment, condemning the rule of violence—"vi quidem regere patriam aut parentes" (3. 2). Who, it might be asked, is alluded to in that phrase? Some suppose that the author has Caesar in mind, and the dictatorship of Caesar. A policy of disciplined reform appears to be indicated as a kind of extenuation—"quamquam et possis, et delicta corrigas." That might fit Caesar. But Caesar's despotism belonged now to the past, or rather was continued and reinforced by the Triumvirs, who patently reënacted dictatorship under another name. If the allusion does not exclude Caesar, it can be held to subsume him in the worse tyranny of the renovated Caesarian party. And, going on to mention "caedem fugas aliaque hostilia" (3. 3), the author intends to evoke the Proscriptions. Furthermore, the choice of the solemn phrase "patriam aut parentes," while generalising and hence innocuous, may at the same time convey a hint of protest against the fraudulent "pietas" advertised by the avengers of Caesar, who seized power with the ostensible purpose and title of "constituendae rei publicae."

The passage concludes with disdainful words. Sallust despises the forfeiture of honour in subservience to power.[3] A reference to Cicero has been detected.[4] In the summer of 43 Cicero incurred severe censure, from Brutus at least, because of his dealings with Octavianus. Cicero, so Brutus asserted, was accommodating himself to servitude, he was seeking a propitious master.[5] Cicero in fact was ready for any expedient as he clung desperately to his policy of using the young adventurer to save the Republic. The

---

[3] 3. 3: "nisi forte quem inhonesta et perniciosa lubido tenet potentiae paucorum decus atque libertatem suam gratificari."

[4] F. Lämmli, *Mus.Helv.* III (1946), 110. And, in the strictures on *novi homines* in 4. 7 f., A. Ernout strangely detects an allusion to Cicero (ed. Budé [1941], 24). On the contrary, Cicero belongs with those "qui antea per virtutem soliti erant nobilitatem antevenire."

[5] *Ad M. Brutum* I. 17.

consulate was vacant, Hirtius and Pansa having perished in the War of Mutina. Cicero had been hoping to secure a second consulship with Octavianus for colleague.[6]

The notion does not have to be entertained of a definite reference to any person. Sallust passes a general condemnation on the servants of power, abased through an "inhonesta et perniciosa lubido." The higher in rank, surely the greater disgrace. If it is anybody, Sallust has in mind therefore those aristocrats who lent their names to a dishonourable cause for profit and advancement. The scandalous paragons are Servilius Isauricus and Domitius Calvinus.

Servilius, praetor in 54 and at that time a staunch adherent of Cato, had later been won over by Caesar with the promise of a consulate (that of 48). Servilius did nothing to equal his parent, the proconsul of Cilicia, the author of his proud *cognomen*. Active in the Senate in 43, he clashed with Cicero more than once. Servilius' ambitions were high, his paths devious. One casual fact is significant: he managed to betroth his daughter to the heir of Caesar.[7] From the Triumvirs he got an abnormal distinction, a second consulate in 41.

Domitius Calvinus had been consul with Messalla Rufus in 53, a disturbed year which the historian had good cause to remember. Messalla was prosecuted and condemned in 51; and something may have happened to Calvinus, who lapses from record between his consulship and the year 48.[8] He came back with Caesar and fought in the wars. Signally defeated by the admirals of the Republic in 42, Domitius Calvinus became consul again in 40.

On any count, the prologue reflects Rome under the rule of the Triumvirs. A single item in the language of Roman politics marks the distance between the author's theme and the time of writing, and it links them both. In the age of the Metelli, it was

---

[6] Plutarch, *Cicero* 45 f.; Appian, *BC* III. 82. 337 ff.; Dio XLVI. 42. 2. Brutus heard a report that Cicero had been elected, *Ad M. Brutum* I. 4a. 4 (May 15).

[7] Suetonius, *Divus Aug.* 62. 1 (the only evidence).

[8] That Messalla Rufus was condemned is barely reported (*Ad fam.* VIII. 4.1). It is therefore not rash to conjecture a similar fate for Calvinus.

the "potentia nobilitatis" that the tribune Memmius attacked.[9] Through threat and hazard the oligarchy kept going for long years. The power of Pompeius was ominous, but the "pauci potentes" revived for a season when the People's general went away to the eastern lands, so it is stated in the first monograph;[10] and Catilina, both at the outset of his enterprise and at the end, arraigns the "pauci potentes."[11] History moves. In the prologue of the Bellum Jugurthinum "potentia paucorum" denotes three men, precisely (3. 4).

No tribune can now show up the holders of exorbitant power, and the consuls are their creatures. But no man who respects anything will serve them—and a historian, continuing the good cause, can take the despots on the flank, insidious when he praised Caesar and Cato, bolder the second time.

Not content with condemning both the Triumvirs and the nobiles, Sallust winds up his prologue with a sharp edge against the successful novi homines. Their path to "imperia et honores" leads through deceit or open violence (4. 7). The terms he uses, "furtim" and "per latrocinia" convey an antithesis, brought out by the verbal inconcinnity.[12] Two categories of upstart thus stand in contrast.

They are exemplified among the adherents of Octavianus, in splendid infamy. The one is Cornelius Balbus, that unobtrusive master of secret intrigue who emerges for a brief tenure of the consulate at the end of 40. The other is the base-born marshal Salvidienus Rufus, flaunting the titles of "imperator" and "consul designatus," though not a senator.

As the historian had earlier observed, the servants of despotism are not always "tuti" or "honesti" (3. 1). Salvidienus came to ruin, abruptly. In the autumn of 40 he made some false step, and a complaisant Senate ordered him to be executed for treason towards his leader.

---

[9] Jug. 27. 2; 30. 3. Cf., in his speech, "obviam ire factionis potentiae" (31. 4).

[10] Cat. 39. 1.

[11] Cat. 20. 7; 58. 12.

[12] In the phrase "furtim et per latrocinia" (4.7), sense and antithesis counsel a change from "et" to "aut." Cf. Philologus CVI (1962), 302.

Balbus and Salvidienus—a temptation no doubt to see a precise allusion and place the writing of the prologue at the end of 40. A preface is often the latest portion of a work to be composed, or at least revised. That date might be correct. Not, indeed, that the language of the historian has to be explained by any names or single episodes. None the less, it will be reasonable to assign the monograph to the period of the Perusine War and to its sequel in 40.[13]

In February of that year Perusia fell. Thus ended the attempt made by the brother of Antonius to subvert Octavianus, and a confused contest, most detrimental to the towns of Italy. Fire destroyed Perusia, and a massacre commemorated the city's name evilly for ever. Sentinum in Umbria was wiped out. Nursia in the recesses of the Sabine country made a capitulation. But the citizens of recalcitrant Nursia erected a monument to the dead who fought for freedom: Octavianus punished them with a heavy fine.[14]

A larger war now loomed, with Antonius returning from the eastern lands, and a prospect as grim as when Sulla came back to conquer Italy. Diplomacy intervened. The dynasts composed their differences at Brundisium, in the autumn of the year that bore the names of Domitius Calvinus and Asinius Pollio.

Sallust went on to write the *Historiae*. After Caesar and after Sulla, the events showed a marvellous resemblance as they de-

---

[13] A dating previous to November, 43, was argued by L. Wohleb, *Phil.Woch.* 1928, 1244: "jedenfalls . . . ist die Staatsverdrossenheit des Verfassers nicht mehr denkbar, nachdem Oktavian als Triumvir mit das Staatsruder führte." He seems to fancy that Sallust was a partisan of Octavian—as have others, e.g., H. J. Rose, *A History of Latin Literature* (1936), 218. K. Büchner follows Wohleb—"der Jugurtha muss also 44/43 enstanden sein" (*Sallust* (1960), 109). On the date of the first monograph see p. 128.

K. Vretska essays to date the prologue in the late autumn of 40, *Wiener S-B* CXXIX. 4 (1955), 22. Not all of his arguments are valid. He inadvertently assumes that the *Lex Titia* was renewed at the beginning of 39. Further, he sees a reference to Octavian and to Lepidus in the persons who acquire "honos" (i.e., the consulship) "per fraudem" (3. 1). But these people are clearly not the Triumvirs, but their creatures. The Triumvirs are alluded to lower down, under "potentia paucorum" (3. 4).

[14] Dio XLVIII. 13. 6. Wrongly dated in Suetonius, *Divus Aug.* 12.

veloped, even in details and personalities, with an exciting scope
for paradox, irony and malice.

The consul Aemilius Lepidus launched the attack on Sulla's
system with ostentation and loud talk of liberty. But there was
no strength or substance in Lepidus. His son won advancement
likewise through pedigree, Caesar no less than Sulla favouring
the old patriciate inordinately. Holding a province and an army
in 43, Lepidus deserted the cause of the Republic—and he used
noble and fraudulent language to cover his treachery. As men
of the time describe him, Lepidus was a "homo ventosissimus." [15]
Father and son, both flimsy and calamitous. The son was Triumvir: it pleased Sallust's irony to have the father denounce murder
and spoliation in crude and vigorous terms—"humanas hostias
vidistis." [16]

The insurrection of Lepidus in 77 involved the Cisalpina, his
ally M. Brutus being defeated by Pompeius. The new civil war
in the winter of 44 saw another Brutus besieged at Mutina, Decimus to parallel Marcus, the father of the tyrannicide.

There was a more general and ominous parallel of situation.
To counter the insurgent Lepidus, an old man intervened, Marcius Philippus, who arraigned the inertia of the senators. [17] They
were willing to negotiate with a rebel in arms, they spoke still of
peace and embassies. Philippus invoked the authority of the State,
and the ultimate decree was passed.

For his *oratio Philippi,* the historian had the best of models. [18]
In December of 43, twenty years from his consulship, Cicero
emerged, an isolated figure and damaged in reputation, but eager
to assert primacy among the "principes civitatis." Cicero advocated
a bold policy against Antonius. Eloquent and deceitful, he even
argued that Antonius had no legal claim to the Cisalpina. Cicero's
extreme proposal was to declare Antonius a public enemy. That
was blocked by the opposition of certain consulars, among them
the excellent L. Piso, and an embassy was sent out (early in Janu-

---

[15] *Ad fam.* XI. 9. 1 (D. Brutus).

[16] *Hist.* I. 55. 14.

[17] I. 77.

[18] Parallels in language and situation (but not all of them) were noticed
by C. Moravski, *Eos* XVII (1911), 135 ff.

ary). However, Cicero secured the rejection of Antonius' counter-proposals, and the ultimate decree was then passed.

There was another side to Cicero's policy—legal cover for the private army which a young adventurer had levied against a consul. That was achieved at the debate early in January, with a special command for Octavianus in the contemplated war, and further, rank as a senator with various privileges. Cicero argued the claims of youth, patriotism—and the emergency of the Republic.[19]

Old Philippus had occasion to urge that kind of plea, in 77. The Senate had given a command to Pompeius in the war against Lepidus, probably as legate under Lutatius Catulus. But Pompeius after his victories in the North had higher ambitions, and he re-frained from disbanding his army. Neither consul (and no ex-consul) showed alacrity to go to Spain and fight against Sertorius. The Senate voted that Pompeius be sent with *imperium*, though not a senator. It was Philippus who sponsored the proposal, with the witticism "pro consulibus." [20]

A minor paradox by the way: the son of Philippus (*cos.* 56) was the stepfather of Octavianus. Guileful like his father, he gave the young Caesar the benefit of his counsel in 44, but kept out of sight. Philippus lacked both the courage and the eloquence of his parent. It was Cicero who took the lead in the Senate. Philip-pus' only contribution was to propose a gilded equestrian statue in the Forum; and he was one of the three consular envoys who, according to Cicero, preferred peace to honour.[21]

Cicero, assuming the mantle of old Marcius Philippus, de-nounced embassies. Firm and confident, he argued for war to the death against the enemies of the Republic. He adduced the plea made for the young Pompeius in 77, but he knew better than to expatiate on the events of that year. A brief sentence only.[22] To evoke anything more would be detrimental. Lepidus, the son of the insurgent, had to be spared and conciliated.

At the beginning of January Cicero duly proposed extravagant

---

[19] *Phil.* V. 43 ff.

[20] XI. 18.

[21] VIII. 28, etc. That Philippus proposed the statue is attested only by *Ad M. Brutum* I. 15. 7.

[22] XI. 18.

honours for Lepidus, with praise of his wisdom, his patriotism, his love of liberty.[23] That was easy, and the irony congenial. The next time the orator needed all his guile. In March came a joint despatch from Lepidus and Plancus urging peace and an accommodation with Antonius. Cicero adopted a severe and lofty tone, with admonishment of Lepidus and an appeal to the memory of the illustrious ancestor, the *pontifex maximus*.[24] The next oration is devoted to celebrating the victory of the Republic at Mutina (*Philippics* XIV). On that delusive peak ends the collection so far as extant.

At the end of May, Lepidus threw in his lot with Antonius. He announced his betrayal of the Republic in a despatch couched in hypocritical language, with pointed advice in conclusion and a reference to his "dignitas."[25] On June 30, the Senate declared Lepidus a public enemy. Cicero at last had the chance to let out his long dislike of Lepidus and his pent-up anger—and also, no doubt, to name the parent, in proper detestation. A grammarian happens to preserve two fragments of *Philippics* XVI. One of them mentions Juventius Laterensis, that officer in the army of Lepidus who committed suicide in protest.[26]

With Cicero denouncing the public enemy, the confrontation between present and past was now complete. None of which was lost on Sallust. The later *Philippics* must have imposed admiration, much as he disapproved those excesses of partisan spirit that bring a commonwealth to ruin.[27]

As the historian moved forward, passing from Lepidus and Sertorius to the war against Mithridates, fortune conspired to enact further dramatic scenes for his advantage. First, the campaigns in the East, with great battles and long marches to evoke Lucullus. In 40 the Parthians saw their chance. Their horsemen

---

[23] V. 38 ff.

[24] XIII. 14 ff. Cf. the stronger tone of his letter to Lepidus (*Ad fam.* X. 27).

[25] *Ad fam.* X. 35. 2: "quod si salutis omnium ac dignitatis rationem habueritis, melius et vobis et rei p. consuletis."

[26] "Laterensis ne vestigium quidem deflexit" (cited in Schöll's edition of Cicero's *Fragmenta* (Teubner IV. 2 [1927], 467).

[27] *Jug.* 42. 4.

crossed the Euphrates, overran the provinces of Syria and Asia, and reached the coast of the Aegean. Antonius, as soon as the pact of Brundisium freed his hands, sent Ventidius against them. Ventidius, an expert in supply and transport, swept the invaders out of Asia and defeated them utterly in two battles.

Ventidius celebrated his triumph in November of 38. Chance preserves a precious fact. Sallust wrote the oration for Ventidius.[28] Sallust had no liking for the new system of rule and its upstart generals. He may have acknowledged some personal reason for gratitude, however, towards Ventidius.[29]

Most of the better men in the Caesarian party stood by Antonius, disdaining Caesar's heir; and the Republican survivors had joined him after the Battle of Philippi. If a man honoured the memory of Cato, he might observe among the admirals of Antonius a nephew and a grandson—the young Ahenobarbus and the young Calpurnius Bibulus.

An oration for Ventidius—but Sallust refused to insert in his *Historiae* any rhetorical laudation of Roman victories over oriental adversaries. Instead, the letter in which Mithridates warns the Parthian monarch of the fate in store for his crown and realm, such being the habit of the Romans in their ruthless and methodical aggression. The letter is placed after a great victory of Lucullus. It is sharply relevant (before, during, or after) to the expedition which everybody expected and which Antonius, preparing for two years, launched in 36.[30]

Antonius marched through Armenia, invaded Media, and laid siege to Phraaspa. Failing to take the place, he retreated, a long and arduous march, with much loss and damage to his prestige. Meanwhile, Caesar's heir had been occupied with the son of Magnus on the coasts and seas of Italy. The Triumvirs came to an ac-

---

[28] Fronto p. 123 N = II. 136 (Haines). Cf. O. Hirschfeld, *Kleine Schriften* (1913), 780 ff.

[29] That Sallust was an Antonian partisan in 38 has been suggested, on the basis of this oration, by W. Allen, *Studies in Philology* LI (1954), 11. For what it is worth may be registered the allegation that Antonius' relations with Ventidius cooled off after his great victories (Plutarch, *Antonius* 34; Dio XLIX. 21. 1). And one will observe the language used about the Triumvir's parent (*Hist.* IV. 2 f.).

[30] E. Bikermann, *Rev.ét.lat.* XXIV (1946), 131.

commodation with Sextus Pompeius in 39, but it was quickly disrupted. Strenuous naval warfare ensued. Sextus manned his ships with slaves and foreigners. And, distrusting his Roman partisans, he depended for admirals on the freedmen of his father, among them former pirate chieftains from Cilicia. His adversaries duly designated Sextus himself as a pirate. Slaves and pirates, that was a large portion in Sallust's theme. He recorded the maritime operations of M. Antonius, with terms of no amenity applied to the Triumvir's father: "nocentior piratis." [31] Spartacus and the Servile War were amply narrated; and he would be expecting before long to reach Magnus and the pacification of the Mediterranean coasts.

In the late summer of 36 Octavianus at last defeated Sextus Pompeius and conquered Sicily. A clash arose with Lepidus, or was contrived, and his troops were artfully seduced from their allegiance. Lepidus, all his "dignitas" forfeit, was spared to live on ignominious.[32]

Sallust before death took him enjoyed a double spectacle: one Triumvir discarded and humiliated, the second failing in Media. The third stood as a startling document to the caprice of fortune. The first march on Rome in November of 44, the War of Mutina, Philippi and the extreme peril of the Perusine War—Octavianus had survived, by luck, skill, and resolution to achieve full parity with the great Antonius. The events of 40 proclaimed it. Private armies of veterans, special commands extorted in emergency (a senior consular helping), and the consulate achieved by arms or armed pressure, everything sharpened the parallel with the early career of Pompeius Magnus. If Sallust, aspiring to write a history of his own times, modified his plan and decided to go back to the year of Lepidus and Catulus for his inception, Caesar's heir may be one of the reasons.

Recent transactions called up the seventies, and Sallust in the paucity of good written sources needed much personal information. Of the consuls in the decade after Sulla, many had been old men already, with no long survival, and the Civil War produced

---

[31] *Hist.* IV. 2.
[32] Velleius II. 80. 4: "spoliata, quam tueri non poterat, dignitas."

numerous gaps. Cicero early in 43 boasted that there had been ten consulars in the camp of Pompeius.[33] Cicero was the last survivor of that company.

Though so many of their coevals and their juniors had perished, the consuls of 53 lived on, destined to length of days: Domitius Calvinus and Messalla Rufus. Calvinus after his second consulship in 40 was absent for several years, governing Spain for Octavianus. But Messalla was available, now in retirement which he dignified by composing books on family history and on the science of augury.[34] He had been coöpted into the college of augurs by Sulla in 81, as a young man.[35]

Other persons were extant who had been on the fringe of great events or knew the *arcana* of political leaders. Cornelius Balbus, the man of Punic Gades, earned the Roman citizenship for services rendered in the Sertorian War. At first an adherent of Pompeius, he was won over by Caesar; and, last heard of in November of 44, he reëmerges suddenly as consul suffect in 40, with no activity on record to explain it. There was also Pomponius Atticus, bland and helpful as ever, on terms of amity with the masters of Rome and in constant correspondence with Antonius at the end of the world. Atticus died on March 31, 32 B.C. At his bedside stood old Balbus, also Vipsanius Agrippa, the son-in-law.[36]

Varro's powers showed no diminishment: at the age of eighty he indited the books *De re rustica*. Atticus, an Epicurean, may have discovered common tastes and interests with Sallust, easily. His own bent was strongly historical—not only annals and chronology but noble families.[37] Varro, however, had no use for his Sabine compatriot.

The conversation of elderly ladies had an especial charm, for it reflected an old-fashioned purity of speech. Daughters of the nobility and relics of consuls could impart entertainment of superior value, for they were often repositories of secret history. Terentia, whom Cicero divorced in 46 to marry Publilia, a young

---

[33] *Phil.* XIII. 29 f. Not wholly veracious, cf. *Rom.Rev.* (1939), 45.
[34] Pliny, *NH* XXXV. 8; Gellius XIII. 14 ff.
[35] Messalla Rufus was augur for fifty-five years (Macrobius I. 9. 14).
[36] Nepos, *Vita Attici* 21. 4.
[37] ib. 18.

girl who had been left as his ward, reached the age of a hundred and three (so it is alleged).[38] Mucia, the third wife of Magnus, outlived her son Sextus.[39] Clodia, the widow of Metellus Celer, was furnishing political information in 49;[40] and she is attested as late as 45.[41] Further, that Caecilia Metella (Creticus' daughter and wife to the elder son of Crassus), whose mausoleum stands on the Via Appia, may have prolonged her existence into the next age.[42]

The historian's own survival, surmounting the hazards of war and revolution, enhanced his sense of isolation. His generation had been almost wiped out. Of a dozen sons of consular families, taken for example, born between 90 and 80, only Antonius and Lepidus were left.[43] Again, the youth and fashion of the fifties, the friends of Clodius, the poets and orators of promise: most of them had gone with Caesar in preference to Pompeius and the oligarchs.[44] The casualties were numerous, among them Scribonius Curio at the head of an army, Caelius Rufus perishing in an abortive revolutionary movement, Helvius Cinna torn to pieces by the mob at Caesar's funeral, Q. Cornificius killed in Africa.

Some younger men, not yet of senatorial age when the wars began, survived to recall that brilliant group. They rose high. Asinius Pollio, who held the Cisalpina for Antonius at the time of the Perusine War, mediated between the dynasts at Brundisium. After his consulship Pollio governed Macedonia, celebrated a triumph and reverted to literature, composing tragedies. Gellius Poplicola and Sempronius Atratinus found employment commanding fleets for Antonius.[45] The former opened the year 36 as con-

---

[38] Pliny, NH VII. 158.

[39] Mucia went on a mission to Sextus, and she was still alive in 31 (Dio XLVIII. 16. 3; LI. 2. 5).

[40] Ad Att. IX. 6. 3; 9. 2.

[41] Cicero was thinking of purchasing her gardens (Ad Att. XII. 38a. 2, etc.), cf. D. R. Shackleton Bailey, Towards a Text of Cicero: AD ATTICUM (1960), 95 ff.; L. Pepe, Giorn.it.di fil.class. XIII (1960), 22 ff.; 97 ff.

[42] ILS 881.

[43] P. 21.

[44] Rom.Rev. (1939), 62 f.

[45] Gellius Poplicola, a half-brother of Messalla Corvinus, married the sister of Atratinus (IG II². 866).

sul, with M. Cocceius Nerva as colleague. The latter, noted for great eloquence in his early youth, was to follow not far behind (*suff.* 34).

Sempronius Atratinus is in fact the son of Calpurnius Bestia, who was tribune of the plebs in 62 and a partisan of Antonius in 43.[46] Sallust's treatment of Bestia is not exempt from malice.[47] It may be noted that other sons of Catilinarian characters were about—Cn. Piso, a pertinacious Republican, and Autronius Paetus, on his way to a consulship (*suff.* 33).[48] P. Sulla, whom Sallust came to know in 47, if not earlier, died at the end of 46. He had a son by his marriage with Pompeia, the sister of Magnus. That son survived his father but leaves no trace in history.[49]

Eloquence found no scope in public any more, but a smooth talent might earn employment in the secret negotiations of high diplomacy. A notable adept was Munatius Plancus, one of whose brothers had been an ally of the tribune Sallust in 52. Plancus was the last survivor of Caesar's legates in the Gallic War—and the most elegant among the correspondents of Cicero. His dexterity (to give it no other name) carried him into the next age as the senior consular, and ease after many hazards in the cool shade of his native Tibur.

Novi homines like Plancus had no monopoly of opportunism. Indeed, they were outdone by aristocrats alert to retrieve their fortunes and refurbish the "dignitas" of their houses. The young men surviving from the party of Brutus and Cassius, such as Messalla Corvinus, looked to Antonius in preference. But, after a time, Octavianus was able to attract adherents of noble birth.[50] The narrative of the Sicilian War discloses Ap. Claudius Pulcher in his company, and Paullus Aemilius Lepidus, the nephew of the

---

[46] His parentage is shown by *ILS* 9491.

[47] P. 132.

[48] Cn. Calpurnius Piso, *suff.* 23 (*PIR²*, C 286); L. Autronius Paetus, *suff.* 33 (A 1680).

[49] *Ad. Q. fratrem* III. 3. 2, cf. Ch. VII, n. 88. He is presumably the parent of L. Sulla (*cos.* 5). There was also the stepson of P. Sulla, C. Memmius: perhaps the *suffectus* of 34.

[50] *Rom.Rev.* (1939), 237.

Triumvir. What is known of the former might be conjectured of the latter—a variegated allegiance hitherto. Neither Pulcher nor Paullus hold command by sea or land. Nor was there any Scipio or Metellus to recall by their exploits the ancient struggle for Sicily. The generals and admirals of the Triumvirs are *novi homines* in heavy preponderance.

Though consuls are now more numerous (*suffecti* a normal practice), the promotions of the Triumvirs include hardly any *nobiles*. In 36 the ranks of the "principes civitatis" number only one Claudius and one Cornelius of the patrician houses, but no Fabius or Manlius, and no Valerius (except old Messalla Rufus, living in retirement). As for the plebeian *nobilitas*, no Metelli, Licinii, Junii, Cassii or Calpurnii.

Instead of the historic names, a fearsome collection of adventitious consuls, many of them patently non-Latin by their type of nomenclature, and a document to posterity if scholarly enquirers cared to take a look at the *Fasti*. With Caesar, two defeated causes rose again: confederate Italy and the party of Marius and Cinna. The Triumvirs suitably inaugurated their regime with new consuls by appointing C. Carrinas and P. Ventidius for a brief tenure at the end of 43. Carrinas was the son of a Marian general. Ventidius had been captured as an infant at Picentine Asculum and led or carried at the triumph of Pompeius' father.

Various other consuls are patently municipal. Thus, from the Umbrian border of the Sabine country C. Calvisius Sabinus (of Spoletium) and the Cocceii (of Narnia). Calvisius was one of the two senators who tried to protect Caesar from the assassins.[51] His "pietas" had a proper reward and commemoration from the Triumvirs (consul in 39). The Cocceii first turn up as partisans of Antonius, earning two consulates (39 and 36).

Men and towns of the Sabine country suffered various vicissitudes. Varro was not the only owner of large estates to be put on the lists of the proscribed. Several names on casual record can be supposed Sabine.[52] One family, the Ligarii (three brothers, so it

---

[51] Nicolaus, *Vita Caesaris* 26. 96. An inscription at Spoletium suitably honours his "pietas" (*ILS* 925).

[52] For example, T. Vinius (Appian, *BC* IV. 44. 187, cf. Dio XLVII. 7. 4): there is an *octovir* at Amiternum in the time of Augustus called T. Vinius

appears) was destroyed through a pertinacious adherence to lost causes.[53] Tisienus Gallus, after defending Nursia in the Perusine War, escaped to take service with Sex. Pompeius in Sicily.[54] However, a certain T. Peducaeus stood in prospect of a consulship (*suff.* 35). The Peducaei were a reputable family, already senatorial in the last epoch of the Republic: Sabine, perhaps from Nursia.[55]

Roman prejudice and conventional language casts a heavy shadow on *novi homines*. On proper scrutiny the repellent upstarts are often found to belong to the ancient nobility of the towns. So it is with some of the Triumviral consuls. But no enemy needed to arraign, and no friend could cover, the obscure origins of M. Vipsanius Agrippa and Q. Salvidienus Rufus, the foundation-members of Octavianus' faction, whose generalship won the War of Perusia. Salvidienus began as a shepherd boy in the mountains, perhaps in the land of the Vestini, eastwards from Sabine Amiternum.[56] As for Agrippa, nothing could be ascertained about his parentage when it subsequently became safe to make enquiry.

Of the plebeian marshals, Ventidius stood out as the proverbial figure. Plancus and others called him a muleteer, and opprobrious lampoons hailed his consulship: Ventidius had in fact operated teams of mules, and he came to Caesar's notice as an organiser of transport.[57] Sallust had nothing against Ventidius. Like Asinius Pollio, Ventidius may have belonged to a dynastic family of confederate Italia.[58] Italy and the *municipia* had been defeated and punished by Sulla.

Rufus (*ILS* 3701). And, touching the proscribed Vettulenus (Appian, *BC* IV. 25. 104), observe the tribe "Quirina" of a senatorial Vettulenus not much later (*CIL* VI. 31773).

[53] For the Ligarii, F. Münzer, *R-E* XIII, 518 ff.

[54] Dio XLVIII. 13. 2; XLIX. 8. 1.

[55] A Sex. Peducaeus was a friend of C. Plotius of Nursia (*De finibus* II. 58). The rare *nomen* occurs there (*CIL* IX. 4582) and at Amiternum (4480 = I². 1874). Not elsewhere in *CIL* IX.

[56] Dio XLVIII. 33. 2. The name is portentously rare. Likewise "Salvidenus," of which the land of the Vestini shows two specimens, *liberti* of a Q. Salvidenus (*CIL* IX. 3496: Peltuinum; 3639 = I². 1813: Aveia).

[57] Gellius XV. 4. 3.

[58] P. 12.

Not all of the new marshals, however, will have been to Sallust's liking. As he says in the prologue of the *Bellum Jugurthinum*, they are not the traditional *novi homines*. They have risen through craft or violence.[59] Salvidienus and others of the brutal military illustrate and justify his repugnance. The base-born offended the social prejudices of the municipal aristocrat; and he was further repelled by the sight or notion of generals totally destitute of education. The speech he contrived for Marius hits off some of their vulgar features.[60]

Sallust himself entered the Senate at a time when, he implies, competition was severe.[61] Caesar, however, had augmented the Senate. Some of the new senators came of good municipal stock, but others, such as centurions and the sons of freedmen, were vulnerable to unfriendly criticism. The Triumvirs went further, and lower. The august assembly now numbered over a thousand.

Sallust had made his momentous decision several years earlier. Perhaps soon after his African proconsulate—but perhaps not until the winter of 44 and the War of Mutina. Then did sagacious men take alarm, and some could foresee no end to the renewed civil strife.[62] Nothing that had happened since proved them wrong. Sallust was in a stronger posture for negation when he wrote the second prologue.

Aversion from public life was already manifest and declared in the years after Sulla. Atticus by his wealth and connections might have aspired to the career of honours. Instead, he went to Athens and abode there for long years. Lucretius belonged to a good family of the municipal aristocracy, so it may be conjectured

---

[59] *Jug.* 4. 7: "furtim et per latrocinia potius quam bonis artibus ad imperia et honores nituntur." Cf. n. 12.

[60] ib. 85. Marius was equestrian, as Sallust well knew, not low class, as was later fabled (Pliny, *NH* XXXIII. 150; Seneca, *De ben.* V. 16. 2; Juvenal VIII. 245 ff.).

[61] ib. 4. 4: "qui si reputaverint et quibus ego temporibus magistratus adeptus sim et quales viri idem adsequi nequiverint." The author protests too much: he had not reached a curule magistracy while the Republic endured, only a tribunate.

[62] Thus the excellent Hirtius, "usque ad exitum non quidem civilis belli, cuius finem nullum videmus, sed vitae Caesaris" (*BG* VIII. 1. 2).

—nothing in his language towards his patron Memmius is in discrepance. Lucretius, contemplating the torments of ambition, the hazards and catastrophes and the play of chance in human affairs, passionately exhorts to a quiet life. And, at the lowest count, "quies et otium" is the conventional plea in defence of Roman knights usefully augmenting their patrimony.

The revulsion from politics derived new strength from war and revolution. It took various forms. Some longed to go away to some island of the Aegean, to end their days in studious leisure at Rhodes or Mytilene, or play the petty despot in a small city.[63] That could hardly happen now. The nearest approach was a proscribed consular, Aemilius Paullus, eking out his last years at Miletus.[64]

To active daring the East offered rewards in the service of Antonius and adventure in far lands. The Antonians were much to be envied. Those who stayed at home were exiles in their own country and prisoners, held fast by the generals, the soldiers and the veterans in their garrison colonies. Dignity and liberty had departed from life, also security and comfort. After the expropriations and bloodshed, Italy faced impoverishment and famine, the provincial revenues cut off, while the navies of Sextus Pompeius blockaded the coasts.

There were many signs and portents of doom. When a comet appeared after Caesar's death, it was interpreted to signify the end of an age in the system of the Etruscans.[65] And, when the Caesarian leaders entered Rome in November of 43, an Etruscan prophet proclaimed that the epoch of the ancient kings was come again.[66] On one calculation, the end of a *saeculum,* according to Roman observances, could be assigned to 40 or 39.[67] But it was hardly a season for *Ludi Saeculares*. A poet, it is true, was encouraged to acclaim the consulship of Pollio as the dawn of an age of gold. The occasion, it is plausibly conjectured, was the renewal of con-

---

[63] For Rhodes or Mytilene, cf. Cicero's words to an exile (*Ad fam*. VII. 3. 5). Previously C. Antonius (*cos*. 63), condemned in 59, had established a kind of lordship on Cephallenia (Strabo XII, p. 455).

[64] Appian *BC* IV. 37. 155.

[65] Servius on *Ecl*. IX. 47 (the haruspex Vulcanius).

[66] Appian, *BC* IV. 4. 15.

[67] M. P. Nilsson, *R-E* I A, 1710.

cord advertised by Caesar's heir and Antonius at Brundisium.
Those aspirations were premature.

In this atmosphere of oppression and fear, men turned for comfort to occult science and various mystical beliefs. Some sought
escape and relief in a pastoral Arcadia, others found the equivalent in far or fabled lands at the world's end. They yearned for
an ease and primeval felicity that knew nothing of trade, profit,
or warfare.

The appeal of the remote and exotic turns up where least expected, in an author who annexed for model the austere Thucydides. Sallust knew Africa (at least a small part of it), and his
earlier existence may have taken him to other provinces. When
he narrated the campaigns of the Roman *imperatores* in the age
after Sulla, geography had a claim, no less for variety than for
elucidation. That was in order. How explain the digression on the
Pontus, lavish in legend and erudition, how excuse the Isles of
the Blest? Oblivious or not caring, Sallust laid himself open to
blame from anybody thereafter. An unpretentious historian, who
lacked the advantages of a senator, saw his chance. He used mild
words of deprecation: one ought not to give way to the seduction
of "deverticula amoena." [68]

Those digressions of Sallust betray discomfort with the times
or a recollection of the poets. For others of the educated class who
refused to fall back on farming and hunting or vegetate in an
apathy dull or querulous, various avocations offered: literature,
scholarship, or the higher thought.

Varro had dedicated the second part of his vast *Antiquitates* to
Caesar the Dictator. It was concerned with religion. Varro deplored the decline of the old Roman worship and professed the
aim of bringing it back to credit, yet, such were the revelations
he made that in later ages some fancied that his secret purpose
was subversive.[69]

---

[68] Livy, IX. 17. 1.

[69] Servius on *Aen*. XI. 787: "ubique expugnator religionis." According to
Augustine he could not have produced more "ridenda contemnenda de-
testanda" if he were an "oppugnator" and a "destructor" (*De civ. Dei* VI. 2).
For a proper appraisal of Varro's religious beliefs see K. Latte, *Römische
Religionsgeschichte* (1960), 291 ff.

The official cult and system could not comfort or inspire. Varro himself had leanings towards the mystical doctrines that had gathered around the name of Pythagoras. He wrote on that subject, and he left directions that his interment be disposed in the Pythagorean fashion.[70]

The polygraph went on writing indefatigably. He produced a treatise De gente populi Romani. It was a strange blend of mythology and chronology, from the deluge of Ogyges to the consulate of Hirtius and Pansa. More significant were the four books De vita populi Romani, dedicated to Atticus.[71] Here he ventured on a kind of social history, in four sections: Rome of the Kings, the early Republic, the middle prime, and the epoch of decline and fall. Some of the sentiments expressed in Book IV would have been congenial to Sallust. Fragments show that Varro alluded to the detrimental results of wealth and prosperity and deplored the depopulation of Italian towns.[72] He also condemned the ambition of candidates for honours—people who cared not if the heavens fell, provided they got elected.[73]

Varro compiled a vast treasure of erudition, interlaced with philosophical fancies and ludicrous etymologies. His classic achievement deterred criticism and became pernicious in the sequel. There was need to bring severe and destructive enquiry against the ancient legends and the recent fabrications, before it was too late. Instead, the science of Varro served to propagate errors and foster the growth of sentimental romanticism about the Roman past.[74]

Varro, it is true, had made notable contributions to the history of the times, writing about Pompeius and about his own service abroad in various provinces.[75] He also produced an autobiography.

---

[70] Pliny, NH XXXV. 160. For contemporary Pythagoreanism, notably as connected with the name of Nigidius Figulus (pr. 58), cf. K. Latte, o.c. 289 f.

[71] On this work, see H. Dahlmann, R-E Supp. VI, 1243 ff.; B. Riposati, M. Terenti Varronis de vita populi Romani (1939).

[72] Varro, De vita p.R. IV, fr. 115 Riposati.

[73] ib. fr. 121 Riposati.

[74] cf. the eloquent indignation of Mommsen, The History of Rome V (1895), 495.

[75] C. Cichorius, Römische Studien (1922), 189 ff.; H. Dahlman, o.c. 1248 ff.

Nor will the *Logistorici* be neglected, a large collection of miscellaneous essays, the names which stood as titles indicating some relevance of the person to the theme.[76] *Curio de cultu deorum* reflects the known religious interests of the consul of 76. The *Laterensis*, it may be conjectured, dealt with honour and patriotism—for Juventius Laterensis was the exemplary officer in the army of Lepidus.[77] *Pius de pace* conveyed a political argument: to know its date would be important.[78] And who would not sigh for *Sisenna de historia?*

All types of history enjoyed assiduous favour in Rome of the Triumvirs, ranging from the safe and venerable past to recent transactions. Legal or religious antiquities were traditional and suitable occupation for a senator in retreat. Thus Messalla Rufus, writing on augury. Q. Aelius Tubero, who failed in his prosecution of the Pompeian Q. Ligarius (he had been on that side himself in Africa), turned for solace to the annals of the early Republic.[79] He also composed books on Roman law, in a style too archaic for the liking of later experts.[80] Tubero belonged to a family of the plebeian *nobilitas* now in decay (no Aelius consul for over a century). Another historian was the patrician C. Sulpicius Galba, whose disappointed parent had joined the conspiracy against Caesar: Galba happens to be cited for an incident of the seventies.[81]

More recent events were also treated, not without political purposes open or veiled. Among those who produced revelations about Caesar's early career was Tanusius Geminus.[82] It would be worth knowing precisely when he wrote. Caesar's memory was defended by Balbus and Oppius, that faithful pair.[83]

---

[76] H. Dahlmann, o.c. 1261 ff.

[77] P. 222.

[78] cf. further p. 278.

[79] H. Peter, *HRR* I² (1914), CCCLXVI ff. He is presumably the dedicant of Dionysius, *De Thuc.* and parent of the consul of 11 B.C., cf. *PIR²*, A 274.

[80] *Dig.* I. 2. 46.

[81] Orosius V. 23. 9. Galba may, however, be early Augustan rather than Triumviral.

[82] P. 96. The *nomen* is very rare. Observe Tanusia, the wife of the proscribed T. Vinius (Dio XLVII. 7. 4), cf. n. 52.

[83] H. Strasburger, *Caesars Eintritt in die Geschichte* (1938), 30 ff.

Political history was not a wholesome pursuit in Triumviral Rome. The aged Cornelius Nepos chose a safe theme for his industrious talents—an encyclopedia of biographies. One section comprised short lives of non-Roman generals. The work, written in a simple and unpretentious style, and perhaps designed for use in schools, was dedicated to his friend Atticus. Nepos also wrote a book *De latinis historicis*. The studies of Atticus in Roman family history excited his fervent admiration.[84] And something more. This modest compiler essayed a startling novelty, for he included a *Vita Attici*, when its subject was still among the living. A second edition and epilogue followed soon after his friend's decease. The biography of Atticus conveys a firm apologia for the man—and for the nonpolitical class.

Sallust by his ostentatious retreat reverted to that class. The second prologue voices their sentiments, in detestation of present conditions—and at the same time the author manages to import an attack on the Roman *nobiles*. The better sort in the *municipia* had to suffer much of the damage in Roman dissensions, proscribed or mulcted of their property. Birth often secured protection. Sulla did not wish to destroy the aristocrats in the party of Marius and Cinna. And, if the Triumvirs put on the lists the brother of Lepidus and the maternal uncle of Antonius, that was mainly for intimidation. Neither came to harm.[85] It was not blood or revenge that the Triumvirs wanted most, but money to pay the troops and land for the veterans after victory.

Sulla brought back the *nobiles*, with enormous enrichment for many decayed families. Partisans of low degree also benefited, freedmen and centurions. The evil precedent was a stimulus to adherents of Catilina—they had seen common soldiers become senators, or flaunt a royal opulence.[86] The oration of Lepidus duly

---

84 Nepos, *Vita Attici* 18. 4: "quibus libris nihil potest esse dulcius iis qui aliquam cupiditatem habent notitiae clarorum virorum."

85 Appian, *BC* IV. 37. 155 ff. (L. Aemilius Paullus and L. Julius Caesar).

86 *Cat.* 37. 6: "deinde multi memores Sullanae victoriae, quod ex gregariis militibus alios senatores videbant, alios ita divites ut regio victu atque cultu aetatem agerent." Observe the Sullan centurion and profiteer L. Luscius, condemned in 64—"amplius centies possederat" (Asconius 81).

registers creatures of Sulla, among them the ex-centurion Fufidius, in opprobrious terms.[87]

Most of the centurions rose from the ranks, and the legions were recruited from the proletariat. Marius began the practice, and the question of his motives evokes from Sallust an unfriendly comment on the lower classes.[88] Sallust also depicts in strong language the revolutionary attitude of the poor in 63 B.C.[89] They now had weapons in their hands. Odious language about the soldiers can be used in public discourse by an eminent consular.[90]

The propertied class in Italy was confronted by the alarming spectacle of vast proletarian armies. There was also the danger of the slaves, recalling Spartacus, or the older risings in Sicily. Many slaves had absconded to join Sex. Pompeius. After Octavianus' victory they were sent back to their owners or, failing such, put to death by impalement. The whole country was in a melancholy condition. The "vastitas Italiae" of the Ten Years War had come again, with campaigns and sieges and murderous local feuds renascent. During the Sicilian War disturbances broke out in Etruria. Brigandage was prevalent in many regions. In 36 the tried military man Calvisius Sabinus was instructed to clean up the countryside.[91] But, though order was now restored, the menace subsisted of another upheaval if Antonius returned, with the proscribed and the Republicans, clamorous for their estates, and a mass of veterans to be provided for.

The removal of Lepidus destroyed equilibrium. West and East, two rulers shared the Roman dominions—or, worse, divided them in a way that corresponded with history, geography, and language. The rivalry between the dynasts sharpened the division

---

[87] *Hist.* I. 55. 22. Cf. p. 211.

[88] *Jug.* 86. 3: "homini potentiam quaerenti egentissumus quisque opportunissimus, quoi neque sua cara, quippe quae nulla sunt, et omnia cum pretio honesta videntur."

[89] *Cat.* 37. 3: "nam semper in civitate, quibus opes nullae sunt, bonis invident malos extollunt, vetera odere nova exoptant, odio suarum rerum mutari omnia student."

[90] *Phil.* VIII. 9: "homines agrestes, si homines illi ac non pecudes potius."

[91] Appian, *BC* V. 132. 547.

and threatened to split the Empire apart. Otherwise a conflict, with Rome and Italy subjugated by a monarch coming out of the eastern lands.

In any event, monarchy was already there, and to stay. Power based upon army and plebs was now devising its forms and titles. In 38 the heir of Caesar, after a naval defeat, adopted a *praenomen* to outbid the "Magnus" paraded by his adversary. He now styled himself "Imperator Caesar." [92] And in 36 he annexed to his person the sacrosanctity of the tribunes.

Not only power, but the worship and adulation of power. Poets, to be sure, acclaimed the young Caesar as a "deus." [93] That was not much, for he was already "Divi filius." After the Sicilian War he earned a golden image in the Roman Forum, with an inscription proclaiming peace on land and sea; and the towns of Italy placed the statues of their benefactor and saviour in the temples of their gods. Policy worked on credulity as well as on gratitude. All manner of superstitions were now rampant, fostered by fear and insecurity. Alien creeds invaded every class, they even acquired official recognition.

There was something else, and most distasteful. Sober-minded men who in their homage to tradition had incautiously deplored the decline of the old religion now witnessed a disconcerting revival. Ancient legends were returning to favour, especially the myth of the founder of Rome. When the young adventurer entered the city to seize the consulate on August 19, 43 b.c., he saw in the sky the omen vouchsafed to Romulus, the twelve vultures, so it was alleged.[94] The allegation may well be a subsequent invention; but an odd item of the year 38 deserves interest—the *pontifices* engaged on some ritual or other at the straw-covered hut of Romulus, which caught fire and was destroyed.[95]

Earlier hints or precedents indicate some exploitation of the myth by military leaders. The statue of Caesar the Dictator was put in the temple of Quirinus (an old god now acquiring identity

---

[92] For this explanation of "Imp. Caesar" see *Historia* VII (1958), 172 ff.
[93] Virgil, *Ecl.* I. 6.
[94] Dio XLVI. 46. 2 f.
[95] Dio XLVIII. 43. 4.

238 THE TIME OF WRITING

with Romulus).[96] In 67, it is reported, the consul exclaimed that if
Pompeius behaved like Romulus, he would end like Romulus—
that is, assassinated by senators.[97] Sulla may have claimed to be a
new founder of Rome. In the oration of Lepidus he is denounced
as "scaevus iste Romulus." [98] Applying that phrase, the author may
have been influenced by the young Romulus of his own time.

Sulla, Pompeius, and Caesar prefigured the new despotism in its
various manifestations. The heir of Caesar, returning in victory
from the Sicilian War, announced that the Republic could be
restored before long.[99] Small comfort even to the credulous, and
men of understanding might divine what it meant: one more in
the sequence of "extraordinaria imperia," but comprehensive, with
authority nominally based on delegation from Senate and People
for the benefit of the ruler. The Triumvirate itself had been established by a law. The new system of government was now acquiring
stability and permanence. There could be no going back to political freedom.

The Republic of the Optimates showed itself incompetent to
manage the empire of the world. For a season, as Sallust points out,
the "res publica" was strong enough to carry the "vitia" of the governing order.[100] That season was long past. The "vitia" of Rome
had become too grievous to endure any longer—while the cure
and remedy was not easy to accept. That is the sombre opinion of
a contemporary.[101] The "remedium" could be briefly and sharply

---

[96] Hence the proper subject for a bitter joke—"eum σύνναον Quirini malo
quam Salutis" (Ad Att. XII. 45. 2).

[97] Plutarch, Pompeius 25.

[98] Hist. I. 55. 5.

[99] Appian BC V. 132. 548.

[100] Cat. 53. 5: "sed postquam luxu atque desidia civitas corrupta est,
rursus res publica magnitudine sua imperatorum atque magistratuum vitia
sustentabat." Cf. Cato's remark, "opulentia neglegentiam tolerabat" (52. 9).

[101] Livy, Praef. 9: "donec ad haec tempora quibus nec vitia nostra nec
remedia pati possumus perventum est." The passage was probably written
not long after the War of Actium. The reference is general, not (as often
believed) specific, to abortive marriage legislation, deduced from Propertius
II. 7. 1 f. See Harvard Studies LXIV (1959), 42. While "vitia" here has a

specified—the rule of one man. Such, according to a later historian, was the only means of abating Roman discords.[102] Sallust loved freedom. But Sallust and others wanted stability. It could only be had at the price of accepting centralised authority: "cum domino pax ista venit." [103]

The prospect was dark. The world would collapse in ruin or hold together in bondage. Sallust did not allow himself to be discouraged in the evil days. Gathering strength from his vocation, he might hope to prosecute his task to the end. Leisure and recreation rot the mind, but work keeps a man alive.

---

moral flavour, the term can also apply to political errors, as in *Cat.* 53. 5. Compare Horace, *Odes* II. 1. 2. Also Nepos, *Vita Attici* 16. 4: "de studiis principum, vitiis ducum."

[102] Tacitus, *Ann.* I. 9. 4: "non aliud discordantis patriae remedium fuisse quam ut ab uno regeretur."

[103] Lucan I. 670 (spoken by Nigidius Figulus).

XIV

HISTORY AND STYLE

Sallust was cut short. Only a brief span for his chosen vocation (about seven years), but it saw the rapid creation of a new idiom, potent and intoxicating. What he achieved for Latin letters is not in doubt. The quality of a historian is another matter. Style and the mastery of structure are not enough. One looks for accuracy, insight, integrity.

Furthermore, another aspect comes under debate. Must the historian be also a thinker? Are his ideas original, or at least coherent? At these questions, however, dubitation arises. Systems and doctrines decay or ossify, whereas poetry and drama live on, also style and narrative.

Sallust saw fit to preface his monographs with general disquisitions. The ideas developed in those prologues have not failed to capture the attention of scholarly investigators, with enormous discussion ensuing.[1] Some, it is true (but a minority), are content to dismiss the prologues as a collection of banalities, dreary and derivative.[2] A more friendly view concedes value to the truism when it is decently disguised or presented in a novel form, crisp and epigrammatic. Sallust, having made that effort, can evade censure.[3]

---

[1] For recent surveys of the sources (and, more important, the purpose) of the prologues, see A. D. Leeman, *Mnem.* VII[4] (1954), 323 ff.; VIII[1] (1955), 38 ff.; A. La Penna, *Maia* XI (1959), 23 ff.; 93 ff.; D. C. Earl, *The Political Thought of Sallust* (1961), 5 ff.

[2] E. Howald, *Vom Geist antiker Geschichtsschreibung* (1944), 146.

[3] G. Boissier, *Journal des Savants* 1903, 59 ff.

Sallust, it might seem, would have been better if bolder, refusing tribute to the higher thought and coming quickly to grips with his subject. Are the prologues necessary and relevant? A dark suspicion comes into play, suggested by a practice of Cicero. He had a whole supply of prefaces ready, and on one occasion nearly used the same piece twice over.[4]

Quintilian states that Sallust had recourse to prefaces not concerned with "historia." What does the critic mean? If "irrelevant to the subject-matter," the stricture is more or less valid.[5] If "irrelevant to history," Quintilian has missed the point. The prologues argue and defend the writing of history, discreet in the first monograph but explicit and aggressive in the second.[6]

The solution is easy and welcome. Not that it exhausts the problem. To track down the ideas of Sallust, to label them and classify, that is the task that many have found absorbing.[7] Sallust starts from the dualism of body and spirit and goes on to establish the sovereignty of the mind and the primacy of intellectual pursuits. As the origin of that doctrine, Plato occurs, inevitably; and it has been held that Sallust drew directly on Plato.[8] That view is not at all plausible. Ethical theory and commonplaces had been transmitted by a myriad of writers in the sequel. Among the recent exponents was the great Posidonius.[9]

The question is of subordinate value. Abstract thought among

---

[4] *Ad Att.* XVI. 6. 4.

[5] Quintilian, after mentioning epideictic prefaces as used by Isocrates and Gorgias, proceeds "quos secutus videlicet C. Sallustius in bello Iugurthino et Catilinae nihil ad historiam pertinentibus principiis orsus est" (III. 8. 9).

[6] F. Egermann, *Wiener S-B* CCXIV. 3 (1932), 23; V. Pöschl, *Grundwerte römischer Staatsgesinnung in den Geschichtswerken des Sallust* (1940), 28; A. D. Leeman, *Mnem.* VII[4] (1954), 337. A. La Penna, criticising Quintilian, points to previous defences of history-writing by historians (o.c. 26 ff.).

[7] A large number of the "borrowings" and "influences" are insignificant, their accumulation tedious. Compare the vigorous protest of A. La Penna, o.c. 89.

[8] F. Egermann, o.c. 27 ff.

[9] Arguing against Egermann, S. P. Thomas suggested Stoic sources (*Symb.Osl.* XV–XVI [1936], 140 ff.). That is to say, Posidonius in the forefront: cf., earlier, C. Wagner, *De Sallustii prooemiorum fontibus* (Diss. Leipzig, 1910).

the Romans cannot deny its Hellenic origins. None the less, while using and adapting Greek doctrines, the Romans could hardly fail to introduce the colouring of their own traditional morality—some perhaps inadvertent, but others in deliberate opposition to a foreign influence. That is what Sallust appears to have done, averse from the Greeks, from their recent imitators or translators, and from the new tendency summed up as "humanitas." [10] He took over words and idioms from the earlier writers of Rome—and something else, an attitude, consciously. The whole result is coherent. Sallust writes according to the spirit and categories of the past, parading as a renovated Cato.[11]

To postulate "old-Roman virtues" that can be isolated from Greek influences is hazardous. Yet "virtus" as conceived by Sallust seems to be something solid, distinct, and authentically native.[12] "Virtus" is not confined to narrow or abstract systems of moral dogma. The corresponding adjective appears to be "strenuus." Thus Cato, in Sallust's appraisal, "cum strenuo virtute . . . certabat." [13] Cato and Caesar each possess "virtus" though contrary in principle and behaviour. What is the common factor? "Virtus" is a dynamic quality.[14] The doctrines of the Stoics preached moral energy and encouraged participation in public life. As modified and interpreted by Panaetius, those doctrines were found congenial by the Roman governing class.

By contrast, the creed of Epicurus justified abstention, with emphasis on the private virtues of friendship and charity. Epicureanism in this age exercised a powerful appeal. For some, to be sure, a cloak for life at ease, an excuse for shunning the hazards and the expense of the public career. Atticus could have entered

---

[10] Sallust eschews the word "humanitas"—and shows no liking for Greek thought and Greek education.

[11] The same opinions are expounded in the two prologues—and recur in digressions and orations. That does not mean that Sallust's main purpose in writing is to exemplify an ethical doctrine.

[12] V. Pöschl, o.c. 12 ff.; D. C. Earl, o.c. 28 ff. In Cicero "virtus" is watered down and debased, all too frequently accompanied by suspect and conventional adjectives such as 'singularis' and 'incredibilis' (D. C. Earl, o.c. 37).

[13] *Cat.* 54. 6.

[14] V. Pöschl, o.c. 23; M. Rambaud, *Rev.ét.lat.* XXIV (1946), 115 ff. It will not be necessary to invoke the meaning of "virtus" in Tacitus.

the Senate if he wished. But senators also were Epicureans, in vigour and public spirit not behind the advocates of doctrines ostensibly more robust and salubrious. L. Piso, being the friend and patron of Philodemus, was vulnerable to cheap and easy defamation from Cicero. However, this Piso, consul, proconsul of Macedonia, and censor, comported himself admirably, a person of refined tastes and intervening more than once for concord and good sense when rash measures were proposed.[15] Nor did Cassius suffer his Epicurean tenets to inhibit the conspiracy to murder a despot.[16]

Caesar professed the creed, not hesitating to expound a cardinal tenet in his speech of December 5: there is nothing beyond the grave.[17] In Cicero's version, Caesar proclaims that the immortal gods have ordained death as a merciful release from human tribulation.[18] A public oration from Caesar might pay normal and verbal homage to the gods. Sallust leaves them out.

Sallust is insistent to denounce the pursuit of pleasure. That was the perversion of a reputable doctrine, annexed as cover by the vicious and slothful. Nothing forbids (and everything commends) the notion that Sallust himself inclined to a creed so widely diffused among the educated in every class: aristocrats or poets, senators, bankers, or the better sort in the towns of Italy. He may have known Lucretius, approving his style and the energy which achieved a work of epic grandeur. Each had made an escape to the "templa serena," Sallust from the turmoil and striving that Lucretius surveyed in contemplation,

> certare ingenio, contendere nobilitate
> noctes atque dies niti praestante labore.[19]

The old Roman poets no doubt came into Sallust's early education. Oratory and philosophy called for instruction from classic Greek models. Their trace has been assiduously sought in the

---

[15] cf. Rom.Rev. (1939), 135 f.

[16] For the Epicureans who turned against Caesar, cf. A. Momigliano, JRS XXXI (1941), 151 ff.

[17] Cat. 51. 20: "in luctu atque miseriis mortem aerumnarum requiem, non cruciatum esse; eam cuncta mortalium mala dissolvere; ultra neque curae neque gaudio locum esse."

[18] In Cat. IV. 7.

[19] Lucretius II. 11 f.

writings.[20] It is evident that he had read Plato's *Seventh Epistle*, which he adapts to his own apologia in the prologue of the first monograph.[21] Otherwise, except perhaps for the *Menexenus*, Plato is not much in evidence. Sallust owes something to Xenophon, who was much read by Romans in the period.[22] Also to Isocrates; but, among the orators, the influence of Demosthenes is most clearly perceptible.[23]

The school of Isocrates produced historians as well as speakers. It is not likely that Sallust had much use for Ephorus.[24] He might have been drawn to the biting and aggressive Theopompus, but there is no sign.[25] As for the dramatic and rhetorical historians in the age after Alexander, that is a question. Not direct use or imitation—and he wrote in deliberate revulsion from many of their characteristic features.[26] However, it will not be supposed that Sallust was immune from the general influence which those authors had already exercised on the prose of the Latins. Finally, he can hardly have neglected the recent works of Posidonius. The extent of his debt is another matter (perhaps not very large).[27]

---

[20] See especially K. Latte, *Neue Wege zur Antike* II. 4 (1935), 42 ff.; P. Perrochat, *Les modèles grecs de Salluste* (1949); W. Avenarius, *Symb.Osl.* XXXIII (1957), 48 ff. For a convenient and summary catalogue, K. Büchner, *Sallust* (1960), 431. Despite Sallust's claim, "multa legenti" (*Cat.* 53. 2), the range is restricted and suggests school texts subsequently reread (W. Avenarius, o.c. 86).

[21] Notably *Cat.* 3. 3, from Plato, *Epp.* VII, 324b, and *Jug.* 3 from 331 c-d. For the other passages deriving from that epistle see P. Perrochat, o.c. 49 ff.

[22] K. Münscher, *Philologus,* Supp. XIII (1920), 70 ff. According to Cicero, the memoirs of Scaurus were more instructive than the *Cyropedia* (*Brutus* 112).

[23] P. Perrochat, o.c. 73 ff.; W. Avenarius 78. The influence of *Olynthiacs* II. 17–20 on Sallust's oration of Lepidus, *Hist.* I. 55. 21–24, has been detected by D. Guilbert, *Les ét.class.* XXV (1957), 296.

[24] W. Theiler proposed to discover some Ephorus in the Sallustian orations of Caesar and Cato (*Navicula Chiloniensis* [1956], 144 ff.). Against, A. La Penna, o.c. 98; K. Büchner, *Sallust* (1960), 406 f.

[25] A. La Penna, o.c. 105. However, for the derivation of *Cat.* 14. 4 see K. Büchner, o.c. 329. Since, according to Dionysius, Theopompus had a genius for penetrating the arcana of ostensible virtue and concealed vice (*Ad Pompeium* 6), he ought to have appealed to this subversive writer.

[26] P. 51.

[27] It was long the fashion to overplay Posidonius. His influence was dis-

The personal experience of the Roman and the senator had a greater validity than early education or any author he read. With one exception—Thucydides.

The Athenian historian had come into sudden prominence in a paradoxical fashion, through polemics about oratory.[28] Other reasons commended him. For Sallust, it can be claimed, Thucydides was a recent discovery, congenial and exciting. Sallust responded. It took no great discernment to hail Sallust as a rival of Thucydides. That was quickly done, long before Quintilian's asseveration.[29] The Roman verdicts, however, are defective. Where explicit in the parallel, they bear on style; and indeed, no Roman critic attempts any proper estimation of Sallust from a historical standpoint.

Style, therefore.[30] But even that comparison might be challenged. For the rest, the two historians do not resemble each other very much on first inspection.[31] Set against the chronicle of a long war, elaborated through long years of patient enquiry and meditation, the pair of essays appears a rudimentary and pretentious lucubration. Sallust went on to compose a full-length narration, it is true. But argument is not easy from fragments, a few speeches, and the unverifiable.

Nevertheless, something can be said. The two writers take the

---

covered or postulated in three places—in the prologues, in the narration of the Jugurthine War, and in the notion of moral and political decline ensuing at Rome after the fall of Carthage. For the last item, see p. 249. Posidonius himself has now gone into a decline. Since he defended the cause of the Optimates, presumably Sallust must have joined issue with him (cf. K. Büchner, o.c. 348), but little of positive value can emerge.

Nor can anything be affirmed about Polybius. If Sallust studied him, it is strange that he should not betray any sign anywhere of the "mixed constitution."

[28] P. 52.

[29] Velleius II. 36. 2: "aemulumque Thucydidis Sallustium." Quintilian said "nec opponere Thucydidi Sallustium verear" (X. 1. 101).

[30] P. 260.

[31] Against the notion of their resemblance (let alone congeniality) observe C. Wachsmuth, *Einleitung in das Studium der alten Geschichte* (1895), 662; E. Howald, *Vom Geist antiker Geschichtsschreibung* (1944), 160; V. Paladini, *Sallustio* (1948), 62 ff.; E. Paratore, *Ann. della Scuola Normale Superiore di Pisa* XIX (1950), 158 f.; *Tacito* (1951), 26 f.

246

246   HISTORY AND STYLE

same view of human nature, and they are at one in their conception of how history should be written: concentrated, selective and
eschewing the trivial.[32] Politics is the theme, with a dramatic presentation and a psychological analysis. Thucydides produced a
masterpiece when he diagnosed the discord at Corcyra, showing
its effects on behaviour, and also on language. A single chapter so
captivated Sallust that he put it under contribution a dozen
times.[33]

Thucydides discarded the supernatural, and Sallust sees no moving force beyond human reason or passion, only chance. It is
"fortuna." Not "fatum," which occurs only once, in reference to
the Sibylline oracle about the destiny of the three Cornelii, which
encouraged the foolish Lentulus Sura.[34] Fortune is dominant
everywhere, dispensing fame or oblivion according to her "lubido."
That is the historian's comment on the injustices of history.[35]
And Caesar in the oration makes suitable allusion to "fortuna,
quoius lubido gentibus moderatur."[36] Sallust's belief coincides
with that of Caesar.

To acknowledge "fortuna" is not to deny courage and intelligence. Caesar and the historian are right. As old Philippus proclaims in a call to action, "fortuna meliores sequitur."[37] Other
ages have known that kind of confidence.[38]

Philippus lets fall a scornful remark about oracles.[39] Predictions
and premonitory signs were admitted by the Stoics. Hence a rein-

---

[32] E. Norden, *Die antike Kunstprosa* I (1898), 201; K. Bauhofer, *Die
Komposition der Historien Sallusts* (Diss. München, 1935), 137 ff.; H. Patzer,
Neue Jahrbücher N. F. IV (1941), 124 ff.; P. Perrochat, o.c. 3 ff.

[33] For the traces of Thucydides III. 82 see P. Perrochat, o.c. 17 f.; W. Avenarius, o.c. 51; K. Büchner, o.c. 432 (a list of fourteen items).

[34] *Cat.* 47. 2.

[35] ib. 8. 1: "sed profecto fortuna in omni re dominatur; ea res cunctas ex
lubidine magis quam ex vero celebrat obscuratque."

[36] ib. 51. 25. Cf. Sulla to Bocchus (*Jug.* 102. 9).

[37] *Hist.* I. 77. 21.

[38] The easy parallel is Machiavelli.

[39] *Hist.* I. 77. 3: "verbis et vatum carminibus." They were presumably to
be mentioned in the next year, for the consul Scribonius Curio sent to
Erythrae for the original Sibylline oracles (Lactantius, *Inst. Div.* I. 6. 14).

forcement of the state religion and of public credulity. A rational man could express his doubts. Even the much-vaunted "fatum" of the Stoics deserved to be held a superstition, an old wives' tale.[40]

Cicero in an oration to the People made lavish play with the portents manifested during his consulate and two years earlier. And he asseverated that the immortal gods in their providence guided him to the detection of the conspiracy.[41] When he spoke before the Roman Senate, he eschewed that adventitious aid.

Sallust has a curt and instructive comment: on the news of the rising in Etruria, "portenta atque prodigia" were reported, as was normal.[42] He refuses to go into detail. Instead, he enlarges on the state of opinion at Rome under the menace of war, and notes the emotional behaviour of distracted females—they forgot for once to be haughty and fastidious.[43]

Sallust eschews "numen." And he is not enamoured of the word "religio"—he uses it only to describe a cult or a superstitious usage.[44] The old Romans are designated "religiosissimi mortales," to be sure; and the historian duly registers "deos neglegere" among symptoms of decline.[45] That does not imply any personal belief. Nor is it significant that he says of Marius "credo, dis fretus."[46] Marius was also a prey to the superstitions of the vulgar. Again, no surprise that Sallust's writings contain appeals made to Heaven in conventional language, and often, as is natural, in orations. Cato concedes that the immortal gods have saved Rome from great peril

---

[40] *De div.* II. 19: "anile sane et plenum superstitionis fati nomen ipsum. sed tamen apud Stoicos de isto fato multa dicuntur." The speaker is Cicero himself.

[41] *In Cat.* III. 18 ff., cf. 22: "dis ego immortalibus ducibus hanc mentem voluntatemque suscepi atque ad haec tanta indicia perveni." For the religious beliefs of Cicero, see the cool appraisal of K. Latte, *Römische Religionsgeschichte* (1960), 285 f.

[42] *Cat.* 30. 2. Subsequent historians did not neglect them, cf. Obsequens 61 (from Livy).

[43] ib. 31. 3: "superbia atque deliciis omissis."

[44] *Jug.* 75. 9; *Hist.*, III. 50.

[45] *Cat.* 12. 3; 10. 4.

[46] *Jug.* 90. 1, cf. the "fretus dis" in the counsel of the *haruspex* at Utica (63. 1).

in the past. But he goes on to proclaim that prayer is of no use in an emergency. Only counsel, decision, and action avail.[47]

Disbelief and positivism does not, however, bring Sallust anywhere near Thucydides. He lacks the cool scientific appraisal. For Thucydides, the phenomena at Corcyra were likely to occur so long as human nature remains the same: Sallust speaks of the "vitium humani ingenii" when commenting on the earliest dissensions at Rome.[48] His intelligence is lucid but limited, destructive rather than sceptical.[49] He is carried away by his temperament, and perhaps by habits acquired in the practice of political oratory, hence exaggeration and a Roman dislike of evasive understatement. Nor could he escape from his own experiences and emerge to serene objectivity. Thucydides stated the facts about his own exile, without comment; and he asseverated the value of his task in monumental impersonality. Sallust presents an apologia, and also a counterattack.

As a historian of Rome, Sallust is variously defective. He knew little about the older Republic, and study would not have helped him. In the first monograph he succumbed to the normal idealisation—liberty and discipline prevailing, courage and justice down to the fall of Carthage. Then everything went wrong, "saevire fortuna ac miscere omnia coepit." [50] In the years of peace, greed for wealth and dominion arose. Similarly, in the central digression in the *Bellum Jugurthinum*.[51] The preface of the *Historiae*, however,

---

[47] *Cat.* 52. 29: "non votis neque suppliciis muliebribus auxilia deorum parantur: vigilando agundo bene consulundo prospera omnia cedunt. ubi socordiae te atque ignaviae tradideris, nequiquam deos inplores: irati infestique sunt." Similarly, but briefly, on the vanity of expecting help from the gods, Licinius Macer in his oration (*Hist.* III. 48. 15). When Cato himself uses "benignitas deorum" (*Ad fam.* XV. 5. 2) it is only a conventional phrase.

[48] *Hist.* I. 7. For a comparison between Thucydides on Corcyra and Sallust as revealed in his adaptations, see K. Büchner, o.c. 332 ff.

[49] Thucydides applied a powerful intellect to the elucidation of early Hellas, whereas Sallust discoursed upon a standard view of history; and Sallust, at least in the first monograph, seems hardly aware of the difficulty of establishing facts.

[50] *Cat.* 10. 1.

[51] *Jug.* 41. 1 ff.

shows a gain in penetration. Sallust recognised that the love of liberty and the love of power proceed from the same source in the nature of man.[52] Further, he put early Roman dissensions on record. In so doing he emphasised the fear of foreign enemies as a factor of domestic peace, finally and notably the "metus Punicus." [53]

It was axiomatic that public and private morality had gone downhill. Some supposed that the decline began even earlier than 146. They pointed to the influx of wealth from campaigns subsequent to the Hannibalic War, or the deleterious effects of peace and prosperity already apparent.[54] Sallust opted for the fall of Carthage.[55] How did the notion come to him? It is easy to invoke the inevitable Posidonius, and suspect.[56] The seductive explanation should have become current long before. It may have been hinted in Polybius, or expounded in the memoirs of a Roman consular, Rutilius Rufus. It derived, indeed, from a historical situation, not from theorising. Scipio Nasica in the famous dispute with Cato argued that Carthage should be allowed to subsist for the advantage of Rome.[57]

It is seldom permitted to assign a single cause or turning point in history without running into trouble—and also censure. Sallust is commonly blamed for importing moralistic standards.[58] Not

---

[52] *Hist.* I. 7: "nobis primae dissensiones vitio humani ingenii evenere quod inquies atque indomitum inter certamina libertatis aut gloriae aut dominationis agit."

[53] *Hist.* I. 11 and 12.

[54] Thus the return of the army of Manlius Vulso from Asia in 187 was invoked (Livy XXXIX. 6. 7). And Piso the consular annalist chose 154 (Pliny, *NH* XVII. 244).

[55] For Sallust's deliberate choice, going against a tradition, cf. D. C. Earl, o.c. 42 ff.

[56] The thesis of F. Klingner, *Hermes* LXIII (1928), 165 ff. Against, M. Gelzer, *Philologus* LXXXVI (1931), 271 ff. = *Vom römischen Staat* I (1943), 78 ff.; W. Steidle, *Historia,* Einzelschriften 3 (1958), 16 f.

[57] Diodorus XXXIV. 43, etc. But Gelzer's view perhaps makes too much of Nasica, cf. the arguments of W. Hoffmann, *Historia* IX (1960), 309 ff.

[58] He in fact has adopted the standard and fraudulent idealisation of the Roman tradition; on which cf. R. M. Henry, *Proc.Class.Ass.* XXXIV (1937), 7 f.; F. Hampl, *Hist.Zeitschrift* CLXXXIV (1957), 249 ff.; CLXXXVIII (1959), 497 ff.

always with justice, since he had to struggle with crude categories
and a vocabulary rebellious to fine distinctions. However, in this
instance he has his eye on political stability ("concordia"), and he
is influenced by the absence of civil strife at Rome between the
second war against the Carthaginians and the third. Hence his
emphasis on "metus Punicus," and on the removal of that restraint.[59] Other causes could have been discovered (if he had looked
and meditated) such as the Spanish wars, producing conflict in the
nobilitas, exacerbation, and dissension.

There was another aspect of deterioration, namely the foreign
and provincial policy of the government. For a long time, so it was
claimed, the Roman People made war only for just cause, in self-
defence or to protect clients and allies. Empire accrued, but it was
accepted as a kind of trusteeship, "patrocinium orbis terrarum."
If the facts no longer conformed, it was the fault of Sulla.[60] Such
was Cicero's explanation, welcome no doubt to Sallust. But Sallust
puts the change earlier.[61]

The Senate had direction of foreign affairs, with the nobilitas
intent to keep a monopoly of command, patronage, and profit. Enemies of the dominant clique sought to break that monopoly. "Populares" arraigned corruption, oppression, and incompetence, a
war mismanaged or a peace that offended the honour of the Populus Romanus. Sallust furnishes the arguments, through the mouths
of Roman tribunes. He also employs other agents. His Cato attacks
the governing class which failed to maintain the "iustum imperium" of ancestral days.[62]

There is something else. Not a class only but the imperial Republic is indicted for wars and conquest. Mithridates diagnoses the
cause—"cupido profunda imperi et divitiarum." The Romans are
brigands on a world scale, "latrones gentium." They know no limit
or scruple, they have won dominion "audendo et fallendo et bella

---

59 D. C. Earl, o.c. 47. Sallust is thus to be regarded not so much as a
partisan writer, but the victim of a generalised schema.
60 De off. II. 27.
61 Cat. 10. 6.
62 ib. 52. 21.

ex bellis serendo." [63] Further, it may be supposed that Gabinius in his oration, while evoking Rome's duty to her subjects and allies, did not refrain from stigmatising wars waged for ambition and greed, with a hint at Lucullus and some other generals of the Optimates.[64]

Dominion abroad and liberty at home, such was the happy lot of the Roman People, it could be asserted. There was another side, if the possession of empire produced anarchy at Rome or despotism. Thoughtful men like Marcus Brutus avowed the dilemma. It would be better, Brutus argued, to surrender empire than submit to monarchy.[65]

Empire brought out all that was worst in the *nobiles*. Sallust is unrelenting in his hostility. His exposition suffers, as has been shown, from schematism and defective terminology; and prejudice is manifest and pervasive. He does not allow for the difficulties confronting the government, for example in relation to Jugurtha;[66] he underestimates the strength of the aristocratic tradition, the energy and integrity of individuals; and he was blind to a great truth, that corruption can be a safeguard of political liberty.

Equity calls for a reappraisal. That is not easy. Fate and the "victrix causa" stand in the way. As the event showed, the *nobiles* were not able to maintain their predominance—hence, on a surface view, proved inferior to their ancestors; and the faction of the Optimates bore a heavy burden of guilt for the final catastrophe, having joined forces with Magnus to destroy the proconsul of Gaul.

Such was their political transgression. Personal and social reasons sharpened Sallust's enmity towards the whole class. The *nobiles* were unbearably arrogant in their comportment. Cicero bears witness. Metellus Celer read him a sharp lesson on the "dignitas" of

---

[63] *Hist.* IV. 69. 5; 22; 20. Compare Jugurtha's remarks to Bocchus, *Jug.* 81. 1: "Romanos iniustos, profunda avaritia, communis omnium hostis esse," etc. For the sources of Sallust in the Letter of Mithridates, see H. Fuchs, *Der geistige Widerstand gegen Rom in der antiken Welt* (1938), 16 ff.

[64] P. 197.

[65] Quoted in Quintilian IX. 3. 95: "praestat enim nemini imperare quam alicui servire."

[66] P. 194.

his house.[67] Friction and distasteful experiences were the lot of
Cicero, as of others, when they had dealings with Ap. Claudius
Pulcher. The Claudii were proverbial for inborn arrogance. Cicero
was moved to coin the word "Appietas."[68]

The new man, however excellent, was despised. They fancied it
a pollution if he acquired the consulate. That is Sallust's comment
on the candidature of Cicero. But, he adds sarcastically, the *nobiles*
being in danger had to abate their envy and their arrogance.[69]

Next to insane pride, their wealth and ostentation. The princes
of the Optimates amassed enormous riches. Sallust interrupts a
digression to evoke their mansions reared like great cities.[70] And
he goes on with his personal testimony. There are things not to be
believed if you have not seen them with your own eyes—a mountain levelled, the sea built over.[71] Sallust had seen the palace of
Lucullus on the Bay of Naples.[72] He had also seen the *nobiles* at
close quarters in their political operations.

In 54 when Ap. Pulcher and Domitius Ahenobarbus held the
fasces four candidates competed avidly, with lavish bribery and
versatile combinations of intrigue.[73] It was some satisfaction perhaps that all of them were condemned for *ambitus,* the first two
in 52.[74] For Aemilius Scaurus the memory of his father could not
avail, or the magnificent shows he exhibited when aedile. Scaurus
fades from record. C. Memmius went to Athens, where he is found
demolishing the house of Epicurus to erect a mansion suitable to
himself.[75] Though Domitius Calvinus and Messalla Rufus were

[67]*Ad fam.* V. 1. 1.

[68] ib. III. 7. 5. For "superbia," and its early emergence in relation to the
Claudii, see H. Haffter, *Stud.it.fil.class.* XXVII–XXVIII (1950), 135 ff.

[69] *Cat.* 23. 6: "sed ubi periculum advenit, invidia atque superbia post
fuere."

[70] ib. 12. 3.

[71] ib. 13. 1: "nam quid ea memorem quae nisi iis qui videre nemini
credibilia sunt, a privatis compluribus subversos montis maria constrata
esse." Cf. remarks of Catilina (20. 11).

[72] Which is clearly alluded to here, cf. Varro, *Res Rusticae* III. 17. 9;
Velleius II. 33. 4. For further details, M. Gelzer in *R-E* XIII, 411.

[73] P. 29.

[74] Appian, *BC* II. 24. 91 ff.

[75] *Ad fam.* XIII. 1. 2 ff.

elected at last in the summer of 53, both succumbed to prosecution two years later.[76]

Rejoicing in the feuds they incurred, Domitius Ahenobarbus and Ap. Pulcher, that intolerable pair, stood as champions of the oligarchy in its last hours and helped to bring on the catastrophe, Ahenobarbus stupid and stubborn, Appius exceedingly crafty. Appius excelled in ritual and casuistry. He was also addicted to necromancy.[77] This was the censor who had Sallust removed from the Senate.

Sallust had cause to know and assess the Aemilii Lepidi (the consul of 50 and his younger brother), and other members of ancient houses. The names of Scipio and Metellus stood for epochs in the history of Rome. The consul in Sallust's tribunate of the plebs was Metellus Scipio, of unmatched pedigree, but vain, debauched—and grossly ignorant about certain particulars in his ancestry.[78] Arrogance, rancour, and corruption in the *nobiles,* the reckoning seemed complete, but under Caesar and under the Triumvirs, subservience was added—no expedient too base to retrieve the "dignitas" of an ancient family.[79]

Sallust's attitude does not lack a plea of defence. In every age, talent has to contend with birth and privilege. The contest is often subdued or masked through fear, interest or deference. Sallust comes into the open. Other *novi homines* of the time were not so bold and ruthless. Though Cicero extols the "innocentia" and the "industria" of new men, especially in the period prior to his consulship, he abates that theme in the sequel and is at pains to avoid any public and generalised assault on rank and pedigree. Sallust, however, took over the old aristocratic ideal of "virtus" and restated it, to the detriment of the *nobiles,* in terms of personal achievement.[80]

Hostile to the predominance of the *nobilitas* and exultant in attack when he produces a tribune's harangue, Sallust in his own

---

[76] P. 217.

[77] *De div.* I. 132; *Tusc.Disp.* I. 37.

[78] *Ad Att.* VI. 1. 17. On his ancestry, *Brutus* 212 f.

[79] P. 217.

[80] D. C. Earl, o.c. 30 ff.; 39. As that scholar suggests (119 f.), Sallust may have found this notion in Cato.

reflections shows no whole-hearted enthusiasm for champions of
the People. Sundry comments in the *Bellum Jugurthinum* are instructive;[81] and, in the earlier monograph, describing conditions
after 70, he is against both sides—Senate or People, those were only
the specious pleas, the "honesta nomina." [82] Similarly and more
outspoken in the preface of the *Historiae*, he extends his condemnation backwards in time, to the aftermath of the Third Punic
War: the "honestum nomen" again, veiling the struggle for personal power.[83]

No illusion therefore about "populares." Like others of his class,
Sallust feared the plebs, the poor, and the veterans. Sulla or the
Triumvirs, the same outcome: the better sort in Italy were the
victims of spoliation and murder. Caesar had avoided proscriptions and had been able to provide lands for his veterans without
recourse to expropriation. Caesar did his best to abate the worst
excesses of war between citizens. He proclaimed clemency and put
an end to party strife. Sallust detests cruelty, and in solemn language utters a warning against party spirit, the ruin of great nations.[84]

Even if Sallust conceived some disappointments about Caesar,
the Dictator became embellished in retrospect, under the rule of
the Triumvirs. How then does Sallust stand towards Caesar, and
the central problem of the Roman Commonwealth? Stability and
concord was the ideal of Sallust (and of most people). But concord
was not to be had without central control and the primacy of one
man. There lies the dilemma.[85] It is not faced and answered in
Sallust's writings. Only negations seem to emerge. The historian
is not the advocate of any party or policy. He evades label and
definition, save through his dislikes.

A senator's experience endowed him with a keen and unfriendly insight into human behaviour, a flair for hypocrisy and

---

[81] *Jug.* 40. 3; 5; 73. 5.
[82] *Cat.* 38. 3.
[83] *Hist.* I. 12: "dum pauci potentes, quorum in gratiam plerique con-
cesserant, sub honesto patrum aut plebis nomine dominationes adfectabant."
[84] *Jug.* 42. 4: "quae res plerumque magnas civitatis pessum dedit," etc.
[85] A. La Penna, *Stud.it.fil.class.* XXXI (1959), 53 ff.

fraudulence in all their varied manifestations; and from life in a highly refined society he took on the habit of coining sharp epigrams about the powerful or the pretentious. Not for him the conventional notion of the plain bluff man—Sallust duly discloses the unlovely aspects of Marius. Noble professions are torn apart and comforting platitudes turned upside down. He is alert all the time for the contrast between the words and the facts, with an especial delight in orations designed to demolish the speaker.[86]

The behaviour of language draws his interest, provoked or sharpened by study of Thucydides. Cato's oration expounds the central axiom of a novel and exciting science. Protesting against the phrase "mansuetudo et misericordia," Cato explains that the true meanings of words have been perverted. Giving away the property of others is now called generosity, while criminal audacity is manly courage.[87] In like strain the tribune Licinius Macer. He warns his hearers not to modify the "nomina rerum" and describe as peace what is really enslavement.[88]

Various terms took their colour from partisan interpretation. The "boni" were so styled because they stood for the existing order;[89] and "amicitia" can have another name, "factio."[90] It is to be regretted that the historian did not go further in exemplification. He might have declared in "potentia" the pejorative synonym of "auctoritas." [91] And, according to persons and circumstances, "dignitas" and "superbia" could be interchangeable.[92]

Acutely aware of political connotations, colour and odour, Sal-

---

[86] P. 198.

[87] *Cat.* 52. 11 f., cf. p. 117.

[88] *Hist.* III. 48. 13: "neu nomina rerum ad ignaviam mutantes otium pro servitio appelletis." Cf. Tacitus, *Hist.* I. 37. 4: "falsis nominibus"; IV. 17. 2: "miseram servitutem falso pacem vocarent"; 73. 3: "libertas et speciosa nomina."

[89] ib. I. 12: "uti quisque locupletissimus et iniuria validior, quia praesentia defendebat, pro bono ducebatur."

[90] *Jug.* 31. 15: "sed haec inter bonos amicitia, inter malos factio est."

[91] cf. *Tacitus* (1958), 413.

[92] As was no doubt apparent to enemies of Caesar. For interchangeable terms, cf. *Pro Marcello* 31: "quae enim pertinacia quibusdam, eadem aliis constantia videri potest."

lust is selective and discriminatory.[93] The enemy of the dominant
clique eschews "optimates," nor is "populares" admitted (in the
political sense).[94] He refuses to invest any individual with the impressive quality of "auctoritas."[95] The "dignitas" which Caesar
so assiduously advertised is denied him (the other applications of
the word are instructive); while "clementia" (vulnerable term) is
banished from the great debate and its context.[96] "Felix" is allowed, but not "felicitas." Further, the author is sparing with
"pius" and "pietas,"[97] now already on the way to an almost complete metamorphosis and debasement. Aping the Metelli, Pompeian loyalists in Spain seized on "pietas" as their watchword; the
consul L. Antonius during the troubles in 41 proclaimed firm allegiance to his brother by parading "pietas" as *cognomen;* the
younger son of Pompeius adopted the nomenclature "Magnus
Pompeius Pius"; and "pietas" was the plea of Caesar's heir, taking
up arms to avenge the murder of his parent.[98]

Sallust falls into place in a recognisable tradition of historiography, linking Thucydides and Tacitus.[99] He belongs to the
company of searching and subversive writers, preoccupied with
power and the play of chance in human affairs, finding their delec-
tation in disillusionment.

In Sallust the grim and truculent manner derives from the
theme as well as from the author's personal experience. If, as one
historian avows, a man's thoughts take on an antique hue when
he writes of the venerable past,[100] recent or contemporary transactions can transmit a deeper dye.

---

[93] In which matter he found a disciple who did not need to learn, cf.
Tacitus (1958), 412 ff.; 754 ff.

[94] P. 18.

[95] The word "auctoritas" can be insidiously attached to a group of
"homines nobiles factiosi" (*Jug.* 28. 4).

[96] P. 119.

[97] One example of "pius," two of "pietas."

[98] cf. *Rom.Rev.* (1938), 157.

[99] E. Norden, o.c. 201: "er bildet mit Thukydides und Tacitus die Trias
der σεμνοί. Developing this theme, A. La Penna observes that "la grande
corrente del pessimismo storiographico" has been sadly neglected (*Stud.it.fil.-
class.* XXXI [1959], 154; *Maia* XI [1959], 114).

[100] Livy XLIII. 13. 2: "mihi vetustas res scribenti nescio quo pacto
antiquus fit animus."

In style as in sentiments, the determinant in Sallust is opposition and revulsion. Above all, perhaps, his distaste for a certain type of political eloquence, notably in its newest manifestations. The appeal to noble ideals and vulgar emotion had been strained and perverted by Cicero in his last and fatal efforts, supporting the cause of the Republic in the ambiguous alliance of Caesar's heir against the Caesarian party. Among other claims, Cicero asserted that there was a "consensus Italiae" on his side. The truth was different—acts of coercion and the reverse of unanimity.

Sallust eschews "consensus" altogether. The word might have seemed innocuous enough. But Sallust carries his aversions far beyond the province of the overtly political. "Gravitas" and "constantia," unimpeachable Roman virtues, it should seem, are lavishly distributed by Cicero. In Sallust, no instance of "gravitas." And only one of "constantia"—applied to Cato, who also has the monopoly of "integritas."[101] Again, the rhetorical and meaningless epithet. In Cicero anybody can become unique for some quality or other. Thus L. Aemilius Paullus, "singulari virtute civis."[102] That adjective is absent from Sallust; "infinitus" occurs only once; and "incredibilis" is not frequent.[103] Similarly, the superlative in "-issimus" is not favoured, unless for convinced emphasis and in orations (generally for blame).

Narration by its nature demands a style divergent from oratory and persuasion. Yet Sallust, it will be observed, extends his peculiar and wilful style to speeches. He can be characterised as anti-Ciceronian both in sentence structure and in vast tracts of his vocabulary. Not only notable avoidances of the conventional and "classical," but numerous words and turns not admitted by Cicero (or by Caesar). But there are other features that defy any single and simple definition.[104]

---

101 *Cat.* 54. 2 f.

102 *Pro Milone* 24. The word "singularis" occupies 4½ columns in Merguet's *Lexikon zu den Reden Ciceros.*

103 Sallust has "infinitus" only once (*Cat.* 11. 13), "incredibilis" three times in *Cat.*, twice in *Jug.* Tacitus' treatment of the three adjectives will be no surprise.

104 On the style and vocabulary of Sallust, see S. L. Fighiera, *La lingua e la grammatica di C. Crispo Sallustio* (1896); E. Norden, *Die antike Kunstprosa*

The ancient estimates are good as far as they go. Quintilian registers the brevity and the "immortalis velocitas." [105] Brevity, he says, and the "abruptum sermonis genus" are sheer delight for the cultivated reader. But, he is careful to add, detrimental in forensic practice: taste is not often found in jurymen.[106] The neatest verdict is perhaps that of Seneca—truncated phrases, words coming before expected, and obscure brevity. To describe and convey the fashion, he coins a Sallustian expression, "fuere pro cultu." [107]

Men duly noted the main components that went to make the style—Cato and Thucydides. Archaism held a constant appeal for Romans, not confined to any one form of stylised discourse. It lent dignity and resonance. It might even be admitted with cautious discrimination, in oratory. Cicero confessed that he would hardly have the heart to ban "proles" and "suboles," or "qua tempestate." [108]

The archaic and the poetical sometimes coincided. Poetry emerged before history at Rome, with the *Bellum Punicum* of Naevius and the *Annales* of Ennius preceding the *Origines* of Cato; and history, in the view of Quintilian is close kin to

---

I (1898), 200 ff.; W. Kroll, *Glotta* XV (1927), 280 ff.; E. Löfstedt, *Syntactica* II (1933), 290 ff.; K. Latte, *Neue Wege zur Antike* II. 4 (1935); E. Skard, *Symb.Osl.*, Supp. XV (1956); R. Syme, *Tacitus* (1958), 353 ff.; 728 ff.

Sallust being so wilful a writer, his choice of words, and his avoidances, are highly significant. Statistics can be a useful clue. Those adduced in the present chapter depend in the main on the Index of R. Dietsch's edition (1859)—which is defective. Therefore some estimates of frequency will be qualified with "about" or "at least."

[105] Quintilian X. 1. 102.

[106] ib. IV. 2. 45, cf. X. 1. 32: "itaque, ut dixi, neque illa Sallustiana brevitas, qua nihil apud aures vacuas atque eruditas potest esse perfectius, apud occupatum variis cogitationibus iudicem et saepius ineruditum captanda nobis est."

[107] Seneca, *Epp.* 114. 17: "sic Sallustio vigente amputatae sententiae et verba ante exspectatum cadentia et obscura brevitas fuere pro cultu."

[108] *De oratore* III. 153: "neque enim illud fugerim dicere, ut Caelius "qua tempestate Poenus in Italiam venit," nec "prolem" aut "subolem" aut "effari" aut "nuncupare" aut, ut tu soles, Catule, "non rebar" aut "opinabar"; aut alia multa, quibus loco positis grandior atque antiquior oratio saepe videri solet." The context shows that Cicero means archaisms in oratory, not "in the highly artificial language of historiography," as argued by E. Fraenkel, *JRS* XLI (1951), 194.

poetry.[109] It is not an idle search to look for a poetical infusion in annalists before or subsequent to Sallust.[110]

Cornelius Sisenna exhibited a freedom in word creation like that of the old poets. Further, according to Cicero, he had theories about word forms and paraded as an "emendator sermonis usitati." [111] It is to be regretted that no continuous passage survives. However, the fragments are useful through the oddities they register, notably a proliferation of adverbs ending in "-tim." [112] There are sundry other inventions, some too extreme for Sallust. Also several archaic words that Sallust happens to eschew.[113] Comparison can be instructive.[114]

Sisenna's *Historiae* ran to at least a dozen books. He had achieved great ease of composition. That was the trouble. In history as in his forensic eloquence he was averse from taking pains. A number of his sentences show redundance.[115]

Cicero equated him with Clitarchus and thought his history childish.[116] Sallust, however, gives him credit for care and accuracy.[117] But the style was not good enough. Sallust, it may be supposed, made his own selection of the old-fashioned, going back to Cato, and perhaps to some of the orators like C. Gracchus. It

---

[109] Quintilian X. 1. 31.

[110] E. Skard, *Symb.Osl.*, Supp. XV (1956), 45 ff. That author sometimes finds too much of the poetical, cf. A. Dihle, *Gnomon* XXIX (1957), 592 ff. And it is no secret that the archaic is often prosaical, cf. B. Axelson, *Unpoetische Wörter* (Lund, 1945), 27 ff.

[111] *Brutus* 259. He insisted on the form "adsentio" (Varro in Gellius II. 25. 9).

[112] Gellius XII. 15. 1 = Sisenna fr. 2 (in H. Peter, *HRR* I² (1914). See J. Schaffner-Riman, *Die lateinischen Adverbien auf -tim* (Diss. Zürich, 1958), 17 f.

[113] Thus "apiscor" (fr. 94), "dispalor" (35; 134), "protelo" (27; 69).

[114] He has "claritudo" (49), but Sallust did not care to take over his "crebritudo" (122), nor did anybody else. The peculiar adjectives in "-bundus" can be instructive, cf. M. Niedermann, *Mélanges Meillet* (1902), 97 ff. Sisenna has "populabundus" (55 f.), Sallust, however, "praedabundus" (once) and "vitabundus" (four times).

[115] Sisenna 28; 35; 50; 115. He was called diffuse by Fronto, p. 114 N = II. 48 Haines.

[116] *De legibus* I. 7.

[117] *Jug.* 95. 2.

was his aim to achieve gravity and concentration, to make the writing of history tighter and fiercer. To that end, and to introduce a much needed infusion of mature and masculine intellect, he had recourse to Thucydides.

What struck ancient literary critics in Thucydides was the deliberate and wilful creation of a style like that of no man, from first to last in his long labours turning everything upside down, filing and shaping without cease. The product was a strange old-fashioned idiom, so Dionysius of Halicarnassus avers.[118] He proceeds to classify the devices employed by the historian. They are four in number: poetical language, variety of grammatical turns, disharmony, rapidity. Further, the qualities that emerge—the writer is hard and tight, bitter and austere, majestic, vehement and terrifying, and above all dramatic.[119]

Though Sallust falls short of Thucydides' achievement, the devices which he in his turn adopted present a genuine resemblance, notably the selective vocabulary ("poetical" and old-fashioned), the abnormal grammar, the broken structure, the impatient omission of words or ideas.[120] Quintilian characterised Thucydides as "densus et brevis et semper instans sibi." [121] The phrase could be transferred without impropriety to his Roman emulator. To reproduce Thucydidean effects in Latin, Sallust strives for a noncontemporary style, as was that of his model: he uses and develops the resources of the older language, plain, vigorous, and majestic. The phenomenon does not lack a close parallel—Lucretius rendering a Greek doctrine in diction remote from the poetical idiom favoured in his own day. The two writers have many things in common.

The style of Sallust is peculiar but in no way enigmatic. What he was trying to do is clear enough. None the less, an estimate wholly aberrant was for a long time in fashion. Certain features

---

[118] Dionysius, *De Thuc*. 24.

[119] For the wilfulness of Thucydides, see the fine appreciation by E. Norden, o.c. 96 ff.

[120] For the actual stylistic imitations, see K. Latte, o.c. 16 f.; P. Perrochat, 23 ff.

[121] Quintilian X. 1. 73.

of old Latin survived at Rome in the speech of daily life, especially among the lower orders. It was therefore supposed that the historian, in concordance with his political opinions, was deliberately composing in a kind of "democratic Latin." [122] Let it pass that Sallust was anything but a democrat in politics or society.[123] As a writer, he is alert, subtle, and sophisticated. Intent as he is to avoid the conventional or tainted language of contemporary eloquence, he would be no less on guard against the vulgar or colloquial.[124] That can be proved in a significant instance. The brief letter of Lentulus Sura to Catilina had expressions belonging to ordinary speech. Sallust is careful to modify them in his version.[125]

Archaism is the hall-mark of the Sallustian idiosyncrasy, patent and avowed. It is manifest in all manner of ways—vocabulary and structure, syntax and accidence, orthography.[126] Also in the meanings of words. The charge was early made that Sallust had looted Cato.[127] Rare specimens prove it: "torpedo," "prosapia," "dehortor," "strenuissimus," and whole phrases have been adopted.[128] Other antique words, less obtrusive, are unmistakable, for example "memoro," "patro," "reor." [129]

The author betrays a predilection for certain types of verbs— the picturesque inchoative ("gravesco," "pavesco," "torpesco"), and the emphatic frequentative, from "agito" (about fifty times) by "ducto," "imperito," and others down to the rare "missito." The weighty terminations of certain nouns suggested ancient majesty. C. Gracchus in speeches had used "dedecoramentum" and "inhonestamentum." [130] Sallust produces "dehonestamentum"—which

---

[122] E. Wölfflin, *Philologus* XXXIV (1875), 137 ff.

[123] S. L. Fighiera, developing Wölfflin's thesis, credited Sallust with "vivo amore alla plebe" (o.c. 18).

[124] W. Kroll, *Glotta* XV (1927), 280, cf. XXII (1934), 21.

[125] *Cat.* 44. 5 compared with *In Cat.* III. 12., cf. p. 72, and K. Latte, o.c. 19 f.

[126] K. Latte, o.c. 11 ff.

[127] Suetonius, *Divus Aug.* 86; *De gramm.* 15.

[128] For the Catonian influence, S. L. Fighiera, o.c. 11 f.; E. Skard, o.c. 75 ff.

[129] For a list of typically Sallustian words, W. Kroll, *Glotta* XV (1927), 301 ff.

[130] Isidorus, *Orig.* II. 21. 4.

enjoyed a fortune with posterity.[131] He has three other new words of this type.[132]

According to Gellius, nouns ending in "—tudo" lent "dignitas." [133] They were in high favour with the old tragedians. Some, it is true, were of standard usage in contemporary prose, such as "amplitudo" and "turpitudo." Not, however, "claritudo," which Sallust takes over from Cato and from Sisenna: the subsequent history of "claritudo" is to be noted.[134]

The idiosyncrasy of a stylist often comes out most clearly in what he avoids. Sallust has no liking for abstracts ending in "-itas." [135] To "cupiditas" (three times only) he prefers "cupido" and "lubido" (about twenty and thirty-five times respectively); and "crudelitas" soon gives place to the more select "saevitia." Further, "veritas" is admitted once, in praise of a Roman historian.[136] And no examples of "caritas," "claritas," "gravitas," "honestas." Instead, for vigour and solidity, the adjectives "carus," "clarus," "gravis," "honestus." Their frequency deserves statistical commemoration.[137]

Sallust achieves effects of power with plain phrases such as "clarus atque magnus" or "clari magis quam honesti." [138] And, not unmindful of Thucydides, he extends the use of the neuter adjective. He has other devices against the abstract, notably the words "facinus," "negotium," "res," "artes." Above all, a predilection for

---

[131] cf. *TLL*. Sallust has "dehonestamentum" twice (*Hist*. I. 88; 55. 21), Tacitus four times.

[132] For the first time occur in Sallust "hortamentum" (*Jug*. 98. 7), "inritamentum" (ib. 89. 7), and "turbamentum" (*Hist*. I. 55. 25); but "delenimentum" (*Hist*. III. 48. 21) did not lack precedent, in Afranius and in Laberius, cf. *TLL*.

[133] Gellius XVII. 2. 19 (discussing "sanctitudo"). Cato preferred "duritudo" to "duritia."

[134] P. 294. And cf. *TLL*.

[135] cf. App. I.

[136] The reference to the "veritas" of Fannius occurs in Victorinus, cited by Maurenbrecher under *Hist*. I. 4.

[137] The statistics are approximately: "carus" (20), "clarus" (20), "gravis" (34), "honestus" (25). Also "verus" (30).

[138] *Cat*. 53. 1; *Jug*. 8. 1.

the simple verbs "ago," "facio," "habeo." [139] Sallust's aversion from
the normal and contemporary can be documented by other prefer-
ences, such as "miseriae" against "calamitas," "facundia" against
"eloquentia," "saevitia" against "crudelitas." His exacting taste
confirms various phenomena in Latin semantics. Thus "culpa," but
never "culpo," and "repente," not "subito." He employs "fluvius"
and "amnis" only once. In other particulars Sallust suggests problems of no small interest. Since he likes simple and concrete verbs,
why does he keep off "celo," "carpo," "surgo," "tango?"

Sallust's dealings with the technical terms of Roman public life
need occasion no surprise.[140] He goes in for studious variation,
thus "designati consules," "senatus princeps," "sociorum et Latii."
Further, the order of consecrated phrases is turned back to front.
He produces "maria terraeque" or "ad occasum ab ortu solis." [141]
Again, "militiae et domi." [142] And, while everybody spoke of
"bonum publicum," Sallust almost alone among the Latins has
"malum publicum." [143] Similarly, most instructive for Sallust's attitude or his psychology, "malae secundaeque res." [144]

The writer is ambitious and anxious all the time in his zeal for
dignity and majesty. It is strange that he should not have hit upon
certain elevated words of subsequent fame in the historical idiom
of the Latins. Preoccupied with the antique, he is blind to "priscus" and "vetustus"; he neglects the archaic "apiscor"; he has
"glisco" only once; and he might have found a use for others of
the strong and vivid, like "egenus," "ingruo," "turbator." [145]

So pervasive are the choice locutions that a single sentence can
sometimes exhibit several items.[146] Many rare words now emerge

---

[139] For "habeo" cf. S. L. Fighiera, o.c. 68 ff. Other simple verbs in predilection are "gero," "peto," "teneo," "traho," "valeo."

[140] W. Kroll, o.c. 299.

[141] Cat. 10. 1; 36. 4.

[142] Hist. I. 1.

[143] ib. I. 77. 13, cf. IV. 51: "boni aut mali publici." The plural, "mala
publica" is not a rarity in historical writers.

[144] ib. II. 47. 1. Cf. Thucydides II. 41. 4: μνημεῖα κακῶν τε καὶ ἀγαθῶν.

[145] cf. Tacitus (1958), 731.

[146] Jug. 38. 1: "quasi vitabundus per saltuosa loca et tramites exercitum
ductare." Cf. Tacitus (1958), 731. Quintilian attests 'ducto' as typical of Sal-

for the first time in Latin, some of them to be found seldom or
never again, such as "properantia," "desenesco," or the horrid "discordiosus." [147]

Sallust ranked as a notable inventor, "novator verborum," for
so was he described by the critic Valerius Probus, who wondered
whether he did not use "loquentia" instead of "eloquentia." [148]
The word "novator" happens to be suitably rare and exquisite.

There is a danger of exaggerating Sallust's innovatory operations. So much of Latin prose has perished. Moreover, other
writers, and not historians only, were bold and free in producing,
for example, an agent noun in "-tor," or an adjective in
"-osus." [149] And new compounds with "per" and "prae" arose in
all periods of the language.

Sallust's procedure is best and conveniently put on show through
his vocabulary. It also comes out in his syntax. That would demand
a lengthy exposition. Let it suffice to notice sundry indubitable innovations, such as a new type of ablative absolute ("comperto,"
"audito"), or the gerundive of purpose.[150] He extends the parti-
tive genitive from examples like "extremum diei" to "omnia op-
pidi." The latter instance is modelled on Greek usages. Quintilian
detected Grecisms in Sallust.[151] He is right. One can point to the

---

lust (VIII. 3. 44); and "saltuosus" and "vitabundus" make their first appearance in Latin with this author.

[147] "Discordiosus" (*Jug.* 66. 2) is taken up by late fanciers—Cyprian (2),
Augustine (8), Sidonius (2); "desenesco" (*Hist.* I. 145) is unique; while
"properantia" (*Jug.* 36. 3) recurs only in Tacitus (*Ann.* XII. 20. 1) and in
two authors of late antiquity (cf. *Eranos* LV [1957], 174).

[148] Gellius I. 15. 18. Gellius also notes his "novandi studium" (IV. 15. 1).

[149] For the creation of agent nouns in "-tor" and "-sor," observe in Seneca
"adrisor" and "adrosor" (*Epp.* 27. 7), which are unique, as may be "lapida-
tor," which comes in a string of six in Cicero, *De domo* 13. And cf. the words
of warning in *Tacitus* (1958), 723. Adjectives in "-osus" are a large and instructive theme. Historians had already been creating them, "bellosus"
(Coelius Antipater fr. 5), "facundiosus" (Sempronius Asellio fr. 10). Set beside
the "detrimentosus" of the purist Caesar (*BG* VII. 33. 1), Sallust's "discordiosus" (*Jug.* 66. 2) appears not such a "monstruosum" after all.

[150] E. Löfstedt, o.c. 291. For the gerundive of purpose note *Hist.* I. 77. 10.

[151] Quintilian IX. 3. 17.

adjective governing the noun, to the locutions "volenti esse" or "in maius celebrare." [152]

Next to vocabulary and syntax, the structure of sentences. Sallust could write an admirable period, if he wished. There are examples.[153] But Sallust is out to destroy balance and harmony. The perpetual antithesis of his thought is expressed in the composition, abrupt, with changes of subject and parataxis. Hence the effect of rapidity, of alertness—and of sincerity, disdaining conventional parallelism. His "inconcinnitas" is a pseudo-negligence, a deliberate refinement. It comes in useful to reinforce an antithesis or, more subtly, to reproduce the ambiguity of mixed motives.[154] "Inconcinnitas" is not noticeably present in Sisenna.[155] Sallust learned from Thucydides, with the added exploitation of his own temperament.

Sallust is hostile to the smooth and the redundant. Anything can be sacrificed for brevity and for concentration. It would be a poor compliment to catalogue his brachylogical devices. Nor does his "velocitas" stand in need of exemplification, when the military narrations are there—a swift sequence of historic infinitives or a series of short sentences, with simple active verbs.[156]

The plain style of the ancient Romans conveyed weight and majesty. Sallust, who eschews the word "gravitas," achieved a "seria et severa oratio," so one critic called it.[157] Sallust's manner is exhibited to perfection when he makes Caesar refer (not without a thought of Caesar himself) to persons of rank and dignity—"qui . . . in excelso aetatem agunt, eorum facta cuncti mortales novere." [158]

---

[152] *Jug.* 84. 3 ("volenti"); 100. 4 ("volentibus"); 73. 5 ("in maius"). For Sallust's Grecisms see E. Löfstedt, o.c. 412 ff.; K. Latte, o.c. 15 ff.

[153] *Cat.* 45. 3; *Jug.* 13. 7; 31. 19 f.

[154] For the different types of "inconcinnitas" see W. Kroll, o.c. 287 ff.

[155] Sisenna has one specimen, "occulte tacitique" (fr. 25).

[156] Thus *Jug.* 53 f., with a mass of simple verbs, in the present tense, against few compound verbs or passives. For rapid historic infinitives, cf. 101. 11: "sequi fugere, occidi capi."

[157] Gellius XVII. 18 (registering Varro's allegation touching the wife of Milo).

[158] *Cat.* 51. 12.

Narration or oration, the style is uniform. No attempt, for example, to reproduce Caesar by his vocabulary. The Sallustian Caesar duly employs Sallustian words and expressions—"lubido," "saevitia," "miseriae," "aetatem ago," and others.[159] The speeches, as might be expected, show a more flowing style, with some relaxation of the concision and abruptness. Thus Philippus in his senatorial oration is suitably balanced and harmonious. Again, features like initial "igitur" are avoided, and there is an abatement of the inconcinnity.[160] But, a strange phenomenon: the speeches in the *Historiae* exhibit a number of startling or archaic words not elsewhere found in Sallust, such as "musso," "torpedo," "turbamentum." [161]

Sallust achieved his individual style with the first monograph, audacious and challenging. That is not the end of the matter. Inspection reveals constant experimentation. After the *Bellum Catilinae* he leaps forward, innovating or rejecting, with a remarkable enhancement of his devices.[162]

The novelties in syntax registered above will be found to occur for the first time in the *Bellum Jugurthinum* and the *Historiae*. Likewise the form "quis" instead of "quibus." The vocabulary becomes more rigorous and selective. Significantly, the author discards "crudelitas," "cupiditas," and "turpitudo." "Formido" rises sharply, and "metuo" wins the advantage over "timeo." As for frequentatives, "occulto," "prolato," and "sustento" advance, while "imperito," "ostento," and "tutor" make their first appearance. Again, new and poetical words emerge, such as "aequor" and "sonor." [163]

---

[159] H. Schnorr von Carolsfeld, *Über die Reden und Briefe bei Sallust* (1888), 34 ff.; 79 ff. He registers the following, all frequent in Sallust, never in Caesar: aetatem ago, dissero, divitiae, lubido, miseriae, profecto, saevitia, saevus, strenuus, verum.

[160] For examples of inconcinnity, *Cat.* 51. 6: "et in pace et per indutias"; *Hist.* I. 77. 15: "per fidem aut periurio."

[161] "Musso" (*Hist.* I. 77. 3; III. 48. 8); "torpedo" (I. 77. 19; III. 48. 20; 26); "turbamentum" (I. 55. 25). Also "delenimentum" (III. 48. 21) and "proles" (I. 55. 2). Tacitus by contrast is more normal and temperate in his orations.

[162] See especially A. Kunze, *Sallustiana* III. 1 (1897). His results are briefly summarised by E. Löfstedt, o.c. 290 ff.

[163] cf. the lists in App. I.

To document the change, the less obtrusive are the more remunerative. "Propter" now recedes in favour of the more stylish
"ob," while "ceterum," three times in the first monograph, has
about fifty occurrences in the second. "Ergo" is new, likewise
"quamquam" and "quando." [164]
The various phenomena disclose conscious effort and a wilful
enhancement. The author has become more acutely aware of his
own idiosyncrasy and resources. His taste refined—and in the
process he became a better historian. Care for words does not always entail the neglect of facts; and a bold style reflects an independent mind.
Literary skill was already there, in the first monograph. Caesar's
oration is a masterpiece of reason and logic. The speaker begins
quietly, deprecating appeal to emotion; he supports his case with
arguments drawn from history, he puts emphasis on the dignity of
an imperial people and the honour of the high assembly. The consul designate D. Silanus is addressed in graceful terms; and, in
gentle irony, the orator points out that there is no cause for fear,
thanks to the military preparations made by the consul. Again, he
can have recourse to parody. He reproduces with relish the conventional and alarmist rhetoric that other speakers indulged in:
"rapi virgines, pueros . . . fana atque domos spoliari, caedem in-
cendia fieri," etc.[165]
Curiosity asks what was the fashion and quality of Sallust's own
eloquence. As exhibited in the year 52, it must have been vigorous
and violent. Other virtues may be surmised from the orations in
his works, notably a firm architecture. The man whom Caesar
put in charge of transport and supply during the African campaign
was not devoid of organisatory talent. That quality comes out in
his writing.

When Sallust turned to the strong latinity of Cato, he found
something more than verbal aid in his warfare against the diffuse
and the debased; and those who emulate a style may acquire an

---

[164] This is only a brief selection from the observations of A. Kunze. One
of the strangest phenomena is the eclipse of "tametsi" after *Jug.* 38. 9, while
"quamquam" first appears in that monograph (A. Kunze, o.c. 20 f.).

[165] *Cat.* 51. 9. The allusion is to rhetoric like that of *In Cat.* IV. 2; 11 f.

affinity. The author of the first history in the native tongue was a man of action, with a gift for business organisation, a keen and ruthless innovator. When censor he might have dedicated temples to the ancient gods. He preferred to create a banking centre in the Roman Forum, the Basilica Porcia.

Cato was combative in his oratory, asserting personal merit, with a sharp edge against the pretensions of noble birth. When he wrote history he spoke for Italy as well as Rome; and he left out the names of aristocratic generals when he recounted the "gesta populi Romani." [166]

The exordium of his *Origines* carried a firm pronouncement, valid for ever: a man who has earned renown in the service of the Commonwealth ought to have something to show for the use of his free time.[167] Sallust in his prologues condemns those who neglect the things of the mind and surrender to sloth or vice or idle recreation. By that doctrine, Sallust endorses the great advocate of energy—and perhaps in the phrasing, could it be known.[168]

Sallust is in his own person a document of concentrated energy and controlled violence. In his scale of estimation, "virtus" is paramount, and he preaches a dynamic gospel. The good man is "strenuus" or "intentus";[169] "cura" and "labor" occur frequently; and the author has a predilection for terms condemnatory of sloth and inaction, notably "ignavia" and "socordia."[170] But "virtus" cannot always command "gloria." It is liable to be corrupted by ambition, with energy diverted into criminal paths, as in Catilina

---

[166] Nepos, *Vita Catonis* 3. 3.

[167] *Pro Plancio* 66: "clarorum hominum atque magnorum non minus otii quam negotii rationem exstare oportere."

[168] There might be Catonian language in *Cat.* 4. 1: 'non fuit consilium socordia atque desidia bonum otium conterere," and in *Jug.* 2. 4: "per luxum et ignaviam aetatem agunt, ceterum ingenium . . . incultu atque socordia torpescere sinunt."

[169] Sallust has "strenuus" fourteen times, "intentus" twenty-three times. Note also the verbs expressing effort or endurance: certo (22), exerceo (18), fatigo (14), nitor (18), tolero (18).

[170] cf. App. I. Indeed, for emphasis Sallust couples "socordia" with "ignavia" three times (*Cat.* 52. 29; 58. 4; *Jug.* 31. 2), also with "desidia," "incultus," and "mollitia" (*Cat.* 4. 1; *Jug.* 2. 4; 70. 5). The oration of Marius has "ignavia" five times.

and in the Numidian prince. For such personalities Sallust betrays
an insight verging on sympathy. His curiosity is drawn infallibly
to characters in whom evil mingles with good, inextricably, like
Marius and Sulla.

Sallust puts the individual at the centre of the stage and portrays
him acting under the sway of the passions. The words for desire
and fear abound, notably "cupido" and "lubido," "formido," and
"metus." [171] Also the expressions denoting force and fraud, power
and pride, greed and rapacity.

Sallust's keen interest in the psychology of ambition and violence provokes a question about his own temperament. How far
can one argue from the author to the man?

The theme of the writing justified a harsh presentation. Sallust
adopts a moral tone, censorious and bitter. That owes something
to a tradition, and it inspires a doubt. When Roman writers use
the language of ancient virtue, as when Roman politicians make
appeal to ancestral custom, the "mos maiorum," it is time to pause
and look again. Sallust himself pounces on the eternal contrast between the name and the thing, and he has a gift for portraying
duplicity or demolishing pretence.[172]

The grave austere habit cannot prove him a true Roman of the
old time, a stranger in a new and alien world. On the contrary.
Nor is a taste for plain bare words always the sign of a simple
character. Literary artifice is patent, and much contriving. A further step, but not legitimate, is to dismiss Sallust as a hypocrite
and a pretender.

Sundry allegations about the private life of the historian came
into currency, and later ages deplore or enjoy the contradiction
between ethical language and reprehensible conduct. The allegations do not stand up well to scrutiny. If Sallust committed adultery with Milo's wife, or with other matrons, that does not suffice
to prove him a scandalous exception in Rome of the day. He was
expelled from the Senate. Cassius Dio, who records the expulsion,
gives no hint of any such delinquencies.[173]

---

[171] cf. App. I.

[172] Sallust's technique of "double demolition" is displayed in the orations
of politicians, notably that of the consul Lepidus.

[173] Dio XL. 63. 4, cf. p. 34 and p. 290. Many scholars have found it hard

More serious the charge of peculation in Africa—and some will point to Sallust's obsession with greed and rapacity as a suspicious feature, or an involuntary self-disclosure.[174] The measure of the proconsul's transgression defies estimate.[175] The service of the State was a normal method of enrichment. Equity might adduce many a man who did well out of war and revolution, not least the lucky or illustrious, such as Messalla Corvinus and Asinius Pollio.[176]

In the prologue of the Bellum Catilinae the historian condemns his past ambitions and congratulates himself on his liberation "ex multis miseriis atque periculis," without specifying any details. An edifying document of conversion, since he confessed his error, so some are tempted to maintain. They annex him as a worthy pupil of Plato (who likewise suffered disillusionment and was not afraid to say so), or enroll him among the Stoics.[177]

Almost anybody of the Roman writers is liable to be labelled a Stoic. With Sallust, that notion would not take one very far or very deep. However, the question of Sallust's conduct and personality is bound up with his performance as a historian. Estimates have shown a wide range, all the way from the crafty author of pamphlets to the grave moralist.[178] The fancy has even emerged that Sallust was a bookish and unworldly character.[179]

---

to break free from the "tradition." Thus Maurenbrecher—"C. Sallustius Crispus maiore aetatis parte improbe peracta ad res scribendas se contulit et quo turpior in vita fuerat ganeo lurcoque, eo acerbior in scriptis exstitit morum censor" (Prol. [1891], 1). It can still be profitable to read the firm defence of Sallust by F. Kritz in the Prolegomena to his edition (1856), 5 ff.

[174] E. Howald, o.c. 162.

[175] P. 39. Further, the question of Dio's source should be raised (p. 291). M. Gelzer seems to accept the full bill of the proconsul's misdeeds (Caesar⁶ [1960], 250); and M. L. W. Laistner discounts "the probity of the reformed burglar who has turned policeman" (The Greater Roman Historians [1947], 48).

[176] Adduced by anonymous speakers in Tacitus, Ann. XI. 7. 2.

[177] E. Skard, Symb.Osl. IX (1930), 93; 95; K. Vretska, Eranos LIII (1955), 41 ff. Indeed, W. Schur termed the historian "ein stoischer Sittenprediger" (Sallust als Historiker [1934], 83).

[178] For a review of opinion subsequent to the momentous and misguided paper of Eduard Schwartz in 1898, see A. La Penna, Stud.it.fil.class. XXXI (1959), 1 ff.; K. Büchner, Sallust (1960), 369 ff.

[179] H. Oppermann, Neue Jahrbücher XI (1935), 47 ff.

If Sallust were purely a literary artist, it might be legitimate
to waive biography and let the writings speak for themselves—
and they breathe the spirit of independence. But Sallust had been
a senator before he became a historian. What can be known or
divined of his life, actions and allegiance—that is all relevant.

A politician's apologia can be admitted without much of either
rigour or compassion. Sallust's public career exhibited a wide gap
between aspiration and the achievement. That is clear. Some lay
emphasis on conflict and discord in his nature. What comes out
beyond doubt or disguise is a general spirit of negation and defiance. Sallust stands in sharp reaction from his whole environment, literary, social, and political. His style is novel and aggressive; he is against the aristocracy (personal experience no less than
political conviction), and also against the Triumvirs. Dislikes and
disharmonies, so much the better. A powerful will prevails, imposing a uniform colour and manner.[180]

The writings exhibit men and governments in dark colouring
or hostile portrayal. Mankind is corrupt, life devoid of meaning,
nothing stable or secure, no hope anywhere, time and change the
only constant factor. Such, it is affirmed, is Sallust's conception
of history.[181]

The author himself is by no means a prey to universal pessimism. One marks his firm asseverations. Men make complaint, he
says, about their condition—fragile, brief in duration, and doomed.
They are wrong. On the contrary, no cause to surrender to fatalism
or indolence. Spirit and energy find a way out, however evil the
times.[182]

The prologue to the first monograph advertised a fierce disdain
for the pastimes of hunting and agriculture.[183] Nor would Sallust
seek an escape in mystical aspirations, strange religions, or occult
science. Sallust has no use for religion or the supernatural. Like
so many among his contemporaries, he may have been drawn to
the teaching of Epicurus. That creed was something more than

---

[180] K. Latte, o.c. 47; V. Pöschl, o.c. 8 f.
[181] K. Latte, o.c. 46.
[182] *Jug.* 1 f. (paraphrased on p. 214).
[183] *Cat.* 4. 1; cf. p. 43.

an excuse for retreat or self-indulgence. It had not always pre-
cluded a career in war and government.

Sallust chose the writing of history. Not for comfort. Not from
any antiquarian curiosity about the remote past, or as relief from
the tribulations which the age witnessed through long years.[184]
He goes to recent history, alive, challenging, recalcitrant.

The theme was sombre and murderous. Historians sometimes
profess distaste when depicting scenes of violence and disintegra-
tion. Their professions need not always be taken seriously. Let it
be asked, what compelled them, if not talent and ambition? Sallust,
as he found his way in authorship, may have grown resilient and
robust, the more menacing the present or the future. He had
survived and come out of the turmoil, now able to parade as a
censor, passing judgment on the dead. Revenge for past disappointments—and he could deal sharp blows at the rulers of Rome.

Misfortune or banishment can be the making of a historian.
And, if a man has not encountered calamity, he may be able to
play upon a grievance or behave like an exile in his own environment, estranged wilfully and for advantage as a writer.

Sallust, who had been a failure more times than one in his career
as a senator, enjoyed luck and a supreme felicity. His vicissitudes
were benefit in the end; and he exploited the flaws and limitations
of his own temperament, transmuting ambition into literary excellence. History was waiting to be claimed and conquered, exalted and adorned. Sallust came in the right season. He discovered
style and subject congenial to his nature, and he wrought his will
on the Latin language, imperiously.

Two monographs and the incomplete *Historiae,* Sallust took
the rank of a classic, with a new idiom valid ever after. Sallust was
a slow composer, so tradition averred. And, the judicious Quintilian adds, effort is patent in what he wrote.[185] The reward was
commensurate. As the historian Tacitus observes when condemn-

---

[184] cf. Livy, *Praef.* 5: "ut me a conspectu malorum quae nostra tot per
annos vidit aetas tantisper certe, dum prisca illa tota mente repeto, avertam."
[185] Quintilian X. 3. 8: "sic scripsisse Sallustium accepimus, et sane mani-
festus est etiam ex opere ipso labor."

ing a fluent facile orator, it is style that endures, and the effort of style—"meditatio et labor in posterum valescit." [186]

Warfare, the governing of the nations and the contest for public honours, that was the supreme good of the Romans: writing was no proper compensation for the active life. Sallust appeals to Roman tradition—and subverts it. Proud and insistent, he puts literary excellence equal with the service of the State, or superior. Birth has been found wanting, anybody can be consul, it is better to write history.[187]

---

[186] *Ann.* IV. 61. The historian is condemning the fluent Haterius—and asserting the claim of his own style.

[187] *Jug.* 4. 8: "proinde quasi praetura et consulatus atque alia omnia huiusce modi per se ipsa clara et magnifica sint ac non perinde habeantur ut eorum qui ea sustinent virtus est."

XV

THE FAME OF
SALLUST

Sallust was born in the first era of tribulation, when Marius attained his seventh consulship, in the midst of the Ten Years War. The second lasted longer, twenty years in round figures. That is the estimate of Tacitus, expressed (as was suitable) in exquisite Sallustian language.[1] The first era showed no benefit to Latin letters, but the second engendered a great historian, and much writing besides.

Periods in the development of literature are a normal device, questionable but not easy to dispense with, useful when not slavishly obeyed. It is expedient to know where to make the cut. The standard categories are "Ciceronian" and "Augustan," not always exempt from confusion or error. Most manuals deposit Sallust in the "Ciceronian age." A curious inadvertence. Something might be said for a "Triumviral period," from the extinction of Cicero down to the sixth consulate of Caesar Augustus (28 B.C.). That year can be accorded emphasis, as it was by Tacitus, marking the new dispensation of "pax et princeps" (the fact that the young Caesar had discarded the name and title of Triumvir several years previously is irrelevant).

Fifteen years can seem a great space of time, especially in ages of disturbance and rapid change. This period produced a remarkable flowering, both original genius and novel types of

---

[1] Tacitus, *Ann.* III. 28. 1: "exim continua per viginti annos discordia, non mos non ius: deterrima quaeque impune ac multa honesta exitio fuere."

writing: Sallust, Horace with *Epodes* and *Satires* (also several *Odes* already, it might be surmised), and Virgil, after the *Eclogues,* his verse and manner mature in the *Georgics.* Virgil finished the *Georgics* in 29. More was expected of him—an epic poem glorifying the new Romulus.

Not every poet was disposed to forget the evil deeds of the Triumvirs. With Propertius, elegiac poetry blossomed suddenly. His first book probably came out in 28. It conveys no sign that Rome and Italy have been rescued from the menace of Antonius and the foreign queen, no word for the saviour and hero. A man from Perusia has the dedication, and the closing poem evokes the fate of his city, "Italiae duris funera temporibus." [2]

The recent disturbances might repel or attract. In any event, they were dangerous to narrate. The lava was still hot and glowing beneath the ashes of the eruption. Not to be deterred, the consular Asinius Pollio went to work. His was a given theme, to recount the fall of the Republic, in continuation of Sallust. Parallel by the season of its inception, but in nothing else, stands the vast enterprise of Livy, who may have begun as early as 30 or 29. Actium, the fall of Alexandria and the end of the civil wars concluded an epoch in the history of Rome. The triple triumph which Caesar's heir held in 29 indicated a suitable goal and a culmination. [3]

Sallust died without issue. There was a grandson of his sister, who inherited the name—perhaps not until the historian's decease, through testamentary adoption. [4] If Sallust had owed obligation to any of the Triumvirs, it may have been to Antonius. His grandnephew was a partisan of Antonius who deserted before it was too late (it would be worth knowing when). His name stands, along

---

[2] Propertius I. 21. 4. Tullus, the poet's friend, was a nephew of L. Volcacius Tullus (*cos.* 33).

[3] For that notion, cf. *Harvard Studies* LXIV (1959), 38. It can be supposed that the last nine books, covering the "Republic of Augustus" from 28 to 9, were an epilogue.

[4] Tacitus, *Ann.* III. 30. 1: "Crispum equestri ortum loco C. Sallustius, rerum Romanarum florentissimus auctor, sororis nepotem in nomen adscivit."

with those of Dellius and the Cocceii, on the list of the friends
whom Caesar Augustus had recruited from the camps of his adversaries.[5]

The second Sallustius Crispus receives emphatic commemoration in an ode of Horace, the second of Book II. The poem is
neatly placed in a set of three. Crispus comes after Asinius Pollio,
whose *Historiae* are described and praised, vividly, and before
Dellius, whom the poet exhorts to keep an equal mind in adverse
fortune, and also in prosperity.

Q. Dellius stood in need of no such admonition. He was proverbial for balance and agility. Messalla Corvinus, whose changes
of side were protected by birth and principle, called him by an
unfriendly appellation.[6] Dellius left Antonius shortly before the
decision at Actium: Messalla had discerned the better cause several years earlier. Dellius, it happens to be known, wrote history
or memoirs, narrating Antonius' invasion of Media in 36, if no
other transactions of warfare and diplomacy (he had been much
in demand for confidential missions).[7]

Pollio, Crispus, and Dellius, all three had come safely through
the hazards of war and revolution—and each with profit. Dellius
is reminded by Horace that death will take everything away, the
estates he purchased and his mansion beside the yellow Tiber. As
for Crispus, the poet, covering himself by a compliment to begin
with (Crispus is against money unless put to good use), goes on to
praise the generosity of another man (Proculeius, one of Augustus'
equestrian friends and counsellors), and, proceeding insidiously to
admonishment, warns Crispus against the temptations of wealth
and cupidity.[8]

---

[5] Seneca, *De clem.* I. 10. 1.

[6] Seneca, *Suas.* I. 7: "quem Messalla Corvinus desultorem bellorum civilium
vocat."

[7] *PIR*[1], D 29 (dropped without cause from the second edition). His writing
of history is attested by Strabo XI, p. 523; Plutarch, *Antonius* 59.

[8] Horace, *Odes* II. 2. The poem presents a problem, and a test. Some,
reproducing the scholiast Porphyrio, are content to see praise for the generosity and munificence of this person (cf. Crinagoras, *Anth.Pal.* XVI. 40). But
there is a clear note of criticism, cf. W. H. Alexander, *TAPA* LXXIV (1943),
196. That scholar failed to exploit the theme properly. Horace is ironical. He
evokes against Crispus the historian's condemnation both of "avaritia" and

The historian forfeited any chance of a consulship from the Triumvirs, his heir did not require the honour. When Maecenas fell from power, Sallustius Crispus slipped into his place in the counsels of the ruler. Of his services in the secret politics of the dynasty, no record until the decease of Caesar Augustus. It was he who transmitted to a tribune of the Guard the order to kill Agrippa Postumus. The ultimate source and validity of the order was and is an enigma (but probably an injunction from the dead ruler). When the deed was done, the minister warned Livia about the dangers of publicity, with suitable maxims of statecraft.[9] Livia did not need to be told.

Sallustius Crispus died in A.D. 20. Tacitus is careful to furnish an obituary (the earliest in the *Annales,* and otherwise exceptional, for the man was not a senator and consul). He drew the parallel with Maecenas—both luxurious in their way of living, but subtle and alert, far excelling through secret power the men who paraded consulates or triumphal *insignia*. But neither kept the favour of his master till the end—such is ever the fate of "potentia." [10]

Like the historian, his heir stands in an enigmatic isolation—no wife known, no kinsfolk named.[11] And Crispus had no male issue either. He adopted the son of L. Passienus Rufus, a new man of some oratorical talent, consul and proconsul of Africa. The heir, who was a wit and an orator, rose high: consul under Tiberius, consul again under Claudius, as *ordinarius* in A.D. 44, but not long surviving that honour.[12] He made resplendent marriages—two princesses. The first was Domitia, a granddaughter of Marcus Antonius and Octavia. Divorcing Domitia, Passienus Crispus married

---

[9] Tacitus, *Ann.* I. 6. 3.

[10] ib. III. 30, cf. *AJP* LXXIX (1958), 20.

[11] The way in which Horace adduces C. Proculeius (*Odes* II. 2. 5 ff.) might suggest a link between Crispus and a powerful nexus. Proculeius (*PIR* 1, P 736) was the brother-in-law of Maecenas.

[12] *PIR* 1, P 109. By his full style "C. Sallustius Crispus Passienus" (*AE* 1924, 72: Ephesus). The article in *R-E* XVIII 2097 f. is variously defective. Passienus must have died before 47—and his obituary notice stood in a portion of the *Annales* not now extant, cf. *AJP* LXXIX (1958), 21.

her sister-in-law, Agrippina, widow of Cn. Domitius Ahenobarbus, who brought with her an infant son. Agrippina, it is said, was after his wealth, and she compassed his death. Passienus had the honour of a public funeral; and the widow was still available, providentially, when a new consort had to be found for Claudius Caesar.

Such was the fortune that attended upon a new family from the Sabine country. The historian's name being perpetuated by persons of consequence, there is a chance that family papers or details of an authentic tradition were preserved and transmitted. The elder Seneca, it will be noted, refers to speeches of Sallust, but without interest or enthusiasm: they find readers but only as a tribute to his historical works.[13] Seneca was an expert, but he does not quote those orations. He is citing a famous practitioner among the orators, namely Cassius Severus. Further, Seneca's son was a close friend of Passienus Crispus.[14]

None the less, fable might come into circulation as well as fact, at an early date. Before seeking the first impact of Sallust on the literature of the time it will be expedient to cast a brief glance on certain allegations about his life and habits.

Sallust, so Varro asserted, had been taken in adultery by Annius Milo, scourged and let go on payment of money.[15] The assertion stood in a pamphlet entitled *Pius aut de pace*. That is important. Which Metellus Pius is meant—the consul of 80 B.C., or Metellus Scipio, his adoptive son, consul in 52? And further, when was the pamphlet written?

Metellus Scipio in fact exchanged missives with Caesar about terms of peace in 48.[16] In 46 he held command in Africa, on the

---

[13] Seneca, *Controv.* III, *praef.* 8: "orationes Sallustii in honorem historiarum leguntur." See also p. 297.

[14] Seneca, *NQ*, IV, *praef.* 6.

[15] Gellius XVII. 18: "M. Varro, in litteris atque vita fide homo multa et gravis, in libro quem inscripsit *Pius aut de pace* C. Sallustium scriptorem seriae illius et severae orationis, in cuius historia notiones censorias fieri atque exerceri videmus, in adulterio deprehensum ab Annio Milone loris bene caesum dicit et, cum dedisset pecuniam, dimissum."

[16] Caesar, *BC* III. 57.

other side from Sallust, and committed suicide after the defeat. His end, with the proud words "imperator se bene habet" passed into fame and literature.[17] Varro's pamphlet might have been composed soon after.[18] If so, it was highly polemical. A later date is not excluded. Even if named after Metellus Scipio, the work might have been evoked by Sallust's treatment of Metellus Pius in the *Historiae*—and perhaps did not see the light of day before the historian's decease.[19]

However that may be, it is perhaps relevant that the guilty wife is not named in Varro's fragment as cited. If Varro in fact omitted the name, deliberately (craft, not scruple) he was on easy ground. Who would fail to identify her as the notorious Fausta? And, be it added, who could essay a refutation, so numerous being the cohort of this lady's paramours?[20]

Sulla's daughter engrossed anecdotes. One parallel story might be enough to arouse disquiet about the testimony of Varro. There happen to be two. First, Horace mentions her lover Villius, who was caught and manhandled.[21] This person is patently Sex. Villius Annalis, attested as a friend of Milo.[22] Second, Valerius Maximus in a brief catalogue of mishaps in adultery, registers a certain L. Octavius, whom C. Memmius punished—that is, Fausta's first husband, the praetor of 58.[23]

No kind of criterion can here avail; and there is no need to invoke the silence of Asconius in his commentary on *Pro Milone*. It was time long since to dismiss the problem and let Varro's

---

[17] Livy, *Per.* CXIV.

[18] H. Dahlmann and R. Heisterhagen, *Abh.der Mainzer Ak.* 4 (1957), 159 ff.

[19] C. Cichorius, *Römische Studien* (1922), 228 ff., followed by H. Dahlmann, *R-E*, Supp. VI, 1266. A dating subsequent to the *Historiae* can be maintained, even if the phrase "scriptorem seriae illius . . . exerceri videmus" belongs (as it surely does) to Gellius, not to Varro.

[20] Macrobius II. 2. 9.

[21] Horace, *Sat.* I. 2. 64 ff.

[22] *Ad fam.* II. 6. 1.

[23] Valerius Maximus VI. 1. 13. The praenomen "Lucius" is not common among Octavii. This man might be a son of L. Octavius of Reate *(Brutus* 241). But Lanuvium, the home town of Milo, can produce a homonym *(CIL* I². 1429).

allegation go where it belongs. Who can tell, and who cares? [24]

Another enemy of Sallust eschewed names, so far as known. Pompeius Lenaeus the freedman, angered at what stood about his patron in the *Historiae,* attacked Sallust for his writings and his morals: not only denouncing an inept plagiarist of Cato, but "lastaurum et lurconem et nebulonem popinonemque appellans." [25] Choice terms in the vocabulary of invective, but one would prefer documentation.

However, the name "Sallustius" crops up in the *Satires* of Horace, and with it a problem that has not been properly handled by commentators ancient and modern. The poem (the second in Book I) is a clear, vigorous, and spirited piece of work. The general theme is the avoidance of extremes in sexual behaviour, and the special injunction, didactically enounced in solemn and archaic language is "desine matronas sectarier" (78).

Three passages have to be borne carefully in mind—and kept separate. First, the various mishaps that can befall the pursuer of married women are set forth, without any names for exemplification (41 ff.). Next, freedwomen (it follows) are a safer commodity, but excess in this matter is as bad as adultery.

> tutior at quanto merx est in classe secunda,
> libertinarum dico, Sallustius in quas
> non minus insanit quam qui moechatur [47 ff.]

If this man listened to reason, he could be generous to the girls, "bonus atque benignus," without harming estate and reputation —"nec sibi damno/ dedecorique foret." But no, Sallustius cloaks his conduct with the one defence—"matronam nullam ego tango" (54). Third, a little further down, the poet reverts to the subject of matrons and adultery. He adduces the sorry plight of Villius, the lover of Sulla's daughter Fausta, who suffered physical maltreatment, "pugnis caesus ferroque petitus" (66).

As for the interpretation, one thing is clear. Sallustius is not an adulterer. On the contrary, he conforms to Horace's own maxim

---

[24] For strong scepticism about the whole story, G. Funaioli, *R-E* IA, 1916 f.; F. Münzer, XVII, 1820. Later, however, Funaioli held that it was not a mere invention, taken up by Varro out of partisan spirit (*Studi di letteratura antica* II. 1 [1947], 56 f.).

[25] Suetonius, *De gramm.* 15.

and practice of avoiding matrons, as revealed towards the end of the poem, "parabilem amo venerem facilemque" (119), as reinforced by appeal to the authority of Philodemus, the Epicurean philosopher and poet (120 ff.). The trouble is that Sallustius went too far in his predilection for freedwomen. If in fact the name of a Sallustius was attached to a known and notorious case of adultery, the poet would be fogging the issue, and guilty of sheer incompetence. That is not Horace's way.

Touching the characters introduced by the satirist, a rule has been promulgated at first sight unexceptionable: they are either dead or unimportant.[26] How does the rule stand in this instance? The name "Sallustius" is rare, and now prominent. Employed at Rome in the thirties, to whom can it apply but the historian, be he dead or alive? If not, there is only one way out—the historian's adoptive son, the partisan of Antonius. It would have to be supposed that the young man's addiction to freedwomen was so flagrant and scandalous that no doubt or confusion could exist.

The dilemma is patent.[27] It has a bearing on the date of this *Satire,* which is generally held among the earliest and assigned to 39 or 38 B.C.[28] Also a bearing on the licence the poet permitted himself when alluding to persons whose nomenclature was distinctive, their identity obvious.

Literary chronology comes into the question. When Horace wrote the poem is relevant—but there is another factor, the date at which Book I of the *Satires* was made public. That might have been in 35 or 34, as most suppose.[29] There is nothing against 33. The historian was now dead—and, while he lived, he cannot have been regarded with favour and indulgence by the rulers of Rome.

A neglected item could be brought into play. If, as may well be,

[26] E. Fraenkel, discussing the names in *Sat.* I. 3 (*Horace* [1957], 88). The criterion is here valuable and valid, for example, in scouting the idea that "Alfenus vafer" could be P. Alfenus Varus (*suff.* 39).

[27] It is therefore to be regretted that Fraenkel does not deal with this person and incident in his full discussion of the poem (o.c. 76–86). And there is only a perfunctory mention in the study of names in the *Satires* by N. Rudd, *CQ* X[2] (1960), 163.

[28] Thus in the commentary of Kiessling-Heinze (ed. 5, 24, reprinted 1957). Cf. E. Fraenkel, o.c. 76.

[29] E. Burck in Kiessling-Heinze (1957), 385.

Sallust's heir was adopted by testament, he did not acquire the name "Sallustius" until the decease of the historian in 35. Before that, being the grandson of a sister, the young man must have borne some other *gentilicium*. Furthermore, after an adoption the original name tended to persist and prevail in common usage. Thus T. Pomponius Atticus, although his legal style had changed when he was adopted by the testament of his uncle Q. Caecilius.

So far the testimony of Horace and the hazards in its interpretation. No help can be expected by any prudent man from the ancient commentators. Annotating the first of the three passages referred to above (the catalogue of anonymous mishaps), the scholiast adduces Sallust, caught with Fausta the wife of Milo and beaten up by the outraged husband. This item, he says, was reported by Asconius Pedianus in his *Life of Sallust*.[30] It is much to be regretted that this interesting document is not cited anywhere else in antiquity. If Asconius in fact wrote about Sallust and recorded the allegation, it cannot be taken as certain that he gave it credence. A double measure of caution is requisite. According to a Virgilian scholiast, Asinius Gallus (the son of Pollio) told Asconius that he, Gallus, was really the miraculous child heralded by the *Fourth Eclogue*.[31] There is no sign that Asconius believed him.

As for the second passage, the scholiast produces an explicit statement. Sallust in the Senate affirmed that he was a pursuer of freedwomen, not of matrons, whereupon and for which reason he was expelled by the censors.[32] The third passage, however, which names Milo's wife and her paramours, carries no mention of the historian—and is wholly inept.[33]

It will be relevant to observe that the scholiast betrays no aware-

---

[30] Pseudo-Acro on *Sat.* I. 2. 41: "quod Q. Asconius Pedianus in vita eius significat." The other occurrence of the story may be noted. Discussing "quique ob adulterium caesi" (*Aen.* VI. 612) Servius says that if "caesus" means "killed" the reference is to Aegisthus, if not, to Sallust.

[31] Servius on *Ecl.* IV. 1.

[32] Pseudo-Acro on *Sat.* I. 2. 49. It is a pity that this passage, as well as the note on l. 41, is not even mentioned in Kiessling-Heinze.

[33] The scholiast Porphyrio foolishly says "Villius pro Annio dixit" and then goes on to explain that Annius Milo was the husband of the adulterous Fausta.

ness of the younger Sallustius. Further, the commentator on the ode which Horace dedicated to that eminent person is ignorant, conflating him with the historian.[34] That being so, the note attached to another passage in the *Satires* need not detain, though it may well excite curiosity. The voluptuary Nomentanus had a cook called Dama who was hired for a large fee by the historian Sallust.[35]

Sallust, it is a plausible conjecture, was sympathetic to the precepts of Epicurus. But Sallust denounced ease and luxury, and nothing proves him lavish in his way of living. That was the mark and label of Sallustius Crispus, the peer and successor of Maecenas. His wealth stands on various and abundant record. The *Horti Sallustiani* were monumental in opulence.[36] If first acquired by the proconsul of Africa Nova, the palace and gardens near the Colline Gate may have been developed, extended and conspicuously adorned by his heir. As Tacitus attests, Crispus was "per cultum et munditias copiaque et adfluentia luxu propior."[37] There is a chance (and something more than a chance) that ignorance or malice has transferred to the historian the tastes and habits of the Augustan minister.[38]

To conclude. There is no support in Horace for the story about adultery. On the contrary, only a fancy for freedwomen which the satirist condemns not for itself but because carried to excess, so

---

[34] Pseudo-Acro says "Sallustium Crispum adloquitur, historiographum, equitem Romanum, Augusti amicum."

[35] Porphyrio on *Sat.* I. 1. 102, supplying the name of Dama, slave of L. Cassius Nomentanus. For problems about Nomentanus, cf. F. Münzer, *R-E* XVII, 820; N. Rudd, *CQ* X² (1960), 167.

[36] Platner-Ashby, *A Topographical Dictionary of Ancient Rome* (1927), 271 f.; P. Grimal, *Les jardins romains* (1943), 135 ff. Crispus bequeathed the *Horti* to Tiberius Caesar, not to his adopted son Passienus Crispus, as may be deduced from *ILS* 1795.

[37] Tacitus, *Ann.* III. 30.2.

[38] A universal persuasion gives the historian the credit (or the blame) for the *Horti Sallustiani*. It seems to have escaped notice that the sole testimony is "Cicero," *In Sallustium* 19: "hortos pretiosissimos, villam Tiburti C. Caesaris, reliquas possessiones." There is no evidence for a Tiburtine villa of Caesar. If Sallust owned a princely palace, his strictures on "domos atque villas" in *Cat.* 12. 3 (cf. 20. 11) would show a singular measure of inadvertence or hypocrisy.

he alleges. Indeed, and precisely, Horace is arguing that Sallust's conduct proves him not a genuine Epicurean. That is all, and it is a solution.[39] Otherwise it will have to be maintained that the Sallustius of Horace is not the historian, but his grandnephew.[40] Slight and suspect, such is the evidence on which is based the standard notion of the historian's morals, the sorrow or the censure evoked by the contrast between life and writings.

Credulity or invention was not confined to defamation. One of the Church Fathers transmits an engaging and ridiculous fabrication. Jerome asserts that Terentia, divorced by Cicero, married Sallust, on whose decease she transferred herself to the orator Messalla Corvinus.[41]

So much for anecdote or fable. The earliest impact of Sallust's writings can probably be detected in Horace. The *Sixteenth Epode,* as its exordium proclaims, is emphatically dedicated to the second era of Roman tribulation,

> altera iam teritur bellis civilibus aetas
> suis et ipsa Roma viribus ruit.

The poem is instinct with sombre premonitions of doom. There is no way out. Ironically the poet addresses his fellow citizens as "vos quibus est virtus"; and, ironically, he proposes a solution

---

[39] A welcome solution, given Horace's appeal to Philodemus on the perils and the folly of adultery (120 ff.). It can be argued on other grounds that Sallust was an Epicurean.

[40] It is the general assumption that Horace must be referring to the grandnephew. Thus Kiessling-Heinze on *Sat.* I. 2. 47 ff.; G. Funaioli, *R-E* I A, 1916; W. H. Alexander, *TAPA* LXXIV (1943), 192 ff. And some scholars inadvertently disclose their reason—because the historian is excluded, being notoriously adulterous with the matron Fausta. That is a perverse and illicit type of argument: one must inspect Horace without prejudice. B. L. Ullman suggests that the remarks, generalised, about adultery in *Sat.* I. 2. 41 ff. are intended to foreshadow the emergence of the name of Sallust in 1. 48 (*AJP* LXXI (1950), 410). But, on that argument, Sallust (i.e., the historian) is both an adulterer and a fancier of freedwomen—which is not the thesis of Horace.

[41] Jerome, *Adv.Iovinianum* I. 48. Accepted by E. Meyer, *Caesars Monarchie und das Principat des Pompejus*³ (1922), 164; L. Pareti, *La congiura di Catilina* (1934), 204.

that is impossible—a voyage out of the known world to seek the Isles of the Blest.[42]

The reference is clear—to the story about Sertorius' yearning to escape from war and tyranny.[43] And something more. Where did the poet find the story, if not in Sallust?[44] Before that notion is dismissed or denied, it would be well to look for other clues pointing to Sallustian themes. Among the past enemies of Rome, Spartacus is chronicled in the opening lines of the poem. Next after Spartacus, and more significant,

"novisque rebus infidelis Allobrox."

Horace cannot be alluding to any wars or rebellions of that tribe.[45] He means the Conspiracy of Catilina ("novae res") which, through Sallust's monograph, brought the name of the Allobroges into Latin literature.[46]

A valuable consequence follows. It concerns a problem long in dispute among the learned: which is earlier in date, Horace's *Epode* or the *Eclogue* in which Virgil commemorated the consulship of Asinius Pollio (40 B.C.)? Various arguments support the priority of the *Eclogue*.[47] If the allusion in Horace to Sallust's *Historiae* be conceded, the question is settled.

The episode of Sertorius was narrated in Book I. How did it come to the poet's knowledge? Through recitation? That is not certain. Asinius Pollio was the first of all the Romans to give recitals from prose writings.[48] Nor could it with safety be assumed

---

[42] For this interpretation cf. E. Fraenkel, *Horace* (1957), 49 f.

[43] Sallust, *Hist.* I. 100 ff., cf. Plutarch, *Sertorius* 8.

[44] Sallust is widely believed the source, cf. G. Schörner, *Sallust und Horaz über den Sittenverfall und die sittliche Erneuerung Roms* (Diss. Erlangen, 1934), 42 ff. The notion does not require the support of the scholiast on l. 41 of the poem. E. Fraenkel is agnostic—"it is possible, but not provable, that Horace remembered the story of Sertorius" (o.c. 49).

[45] An Allobrogic War in 61 is adduced by Kiessling-Heinze, ad loc.

[46] This point has been neglected by G. Schörner (o.c.)—and by most other writers.

[47] The convincing case was put by B. Snell, *Hermes* LXXIII (1938), 237 ff. Cf. E. Fraenkel, o.c. 51. Yet some still argue for the priority of the *Epode*, thus K. Büchner, *R-E* VIII A, 1204.

[48] Seneca, *Controv., praef.* 2.

that Book I was issued separately. If *Historiae* I-III came out together, that could hardly be earlier than 37 or 36. But again, Sallust may not have published any portion of the *Historiae* when
death overtook him in 35, Book V not yet finished.[49]

After Horace, Virgil, who was writing the *Georgics* between 37
and 29. A phrase in Book III where he describes a cattle plague
may reflect something in the *Historiae*.[50] However, the poet's conspicuous tribute to the historian is of another order. The *Shield of
Aeneas* exhibits Catilina in everlasting torment, and Cato in the
other place, a legislator among the blessed dead.

"Secretosque pios, his dantem iura Catonem." [51] Virgil left it
to be guessed where Caesar belonged—Caesar who, according to
Cato in the oration, dismissed the belief that the good and the bad
have separate habitations in the hereafter.[52]

Sallust was a partisan of Caesar who had lapsed, sullen and recalcitrant against the Caesarian party, while others steadily loyal
or with necessary shifts of allegiance went on to help the cause to
victory, to support, commend, and adorn the new order of Caesar
Augustus. That man had no cause to honour Sallust's memory;
and the *nobilitas* soon renascent in the alliance of the monarchy
must have found his opinions detestable.

Like Sulla and like Caesar, the ruler had a strong predilection
for the oldest families of all, irrespective of talent or energy. Dull
and numerous, the Cornelii Lentuli tend to acquire frequent con-

---

[49] If, as is here argued, *Epode* XVI reflects Sallust, *Hist.* I (the allusion
to Sallust being reinforced through the mention of the Allobroges), there
are consequences (and clashes) in Horatian chronology. Early dating of the
Epode, to 41 or 40, is excluded: A. Rostagni, to be sure, both put the *Epode*
in 41 and argued precise derivation from Sallust (*La letteratura di Roma
repubblicana ed augustea* [1939], 271). How far down one should go, that is
a question. E. Fraenkel (who appears to dismiss Sallust) is both precise and
vague—"in the spring of 38 B.C. or somewhat later" (o.c. 53). A. La Penna
opts for 38 (*Maia* XIII [1961], 99).

[50] Servius on *Georgics* III. 482 produces *Hist.* I. 43: "ne simplici quidem
morte moriebantur." Note also in the vicinity Servius on 469 and 475,
whence *Hist.* V. 1; II. 40.

[51] Virgil, *Aen.* VIII. 670.

[52] *Cat.* 52. 13: "credo falsa existumans ea quae de inferis memorantur:
diverso itinere malos a bonis loca taetra inculta foeda atque formidulosa
habere."

sulships in seasons of peace—five in the last epoch of the Republic, six under Caesar Augustus. No Lentulus yet had been signalised by victory in warfare foreign or civil. Sallust, when he invented the notorious label for Lentulus Clodianus,[53] was mocking not an individual only, but a family and a class. The *nobilitas* he attacked had been a ruling aristocracy still, proud and combative, though menaced in its predominance. Now, however, birth in its own right had more prestige than ever before, conveying the *nobilis* along a smooth path to public honours by support and patronage of Caesar Augustus.

The historian had also done his best to demolish Pompeius Magnus. In vain, so it turned out. No long time elapsed before the dynast was transmuted and embellished: it suited nobody to be reminded that Magnus had once been the enemy of the Optimates, the true and authentic precursor of Octavianus. Instead, he was paraded as a defender of the "res publica."

Moreover, there survived an important cluster of "Pompeiani." Cicero, however, had never been the leader of a party, and his fame was at a double disadvantage. Republicans accorded scant recognition; and, through subservience to despotism, many were eager to speak ill of him.[54] Sallust had not been of that company. No writer of antiquity implies that Sallust's portrayal of Cicero in the *Bellum Catilinae* was in any way malicious or unfair. On the contrary, and it is clear enough, the historian essayed a quiet and firm defence of the consul's actions.[55] That showed courage and independence in the year 42. Not to the liking of the Triumvirs—and Cicero's name continued unpopular in the family and entourage of Caesar Augustus.[56]

The notion flourished that Sallust was an enemy of the orator, it is true. For a reason not political perhaps but literary. It was not a certain episode of Sallust's tribunate (few recalled it), or even Sallust's allegiance in the Civil War, but rather the historian's deliberate creation of an anti-Ciceronian manner. Nobody missed

---

[53] *Hist.* IV. 1, cf. p. 209 and p. 300.
[54] Quintilian XII. 10. 13.
[55] P. 110.
[56] cf. the anecdote in Plutarch, *Cicero* 49.

that, and fervent admirers of Cicero among the rhetoricians and educators exploited the contrast.

Various reasons thus conspired to the disparagement of Sallust in the next generation. There was a powerful counterweight. Sallust praised and exalted Cato. That ensured his credit with serious men and won the suffrages of the whole educated class. Caesar Augustus conformed, alert and astute. He annexed Cato as a conservative statesman.[57]

Sallust had devised a fine demolitionary technique—but no skill or desire to use it on the Roman tradition. He took over conventional views about the past. That idealisation was now acclaimed and enhanced by crafty men, or credulous (more the latter). The laudation of ancient virtue and frugality was congenial to this prosperous age; and the government had a policy of social regeneration which was advocated by many who did not allow it to interfere with their way of living.

However, it was not Sallust's opinions that evoked praise or censure, but his style. Disapprobation or silence is often the first welcome of a bold innovator in letters. Asinius Pollio came out with a whole treatise, condemning Sallust for inordinate archaism.[58] Pollio, who inherited Sallust's literary counsellor, Ateius Philologus, alleged that Sallust had employed that scholar to make a collection of old-fashioned words. The charge seems petulant, as Suetonius points out, for Pollio had reason to know the precepts of Ateius—plain and normal speech. Ateius himself blamed Sallust's obscurity and bold metaphors.[59]

Pollio for once was in concordance with Caesar Augustus. The charge of archaism also occurred in a polemical epistle attacking Antonius for his oratorical style (or rather styles): Octavianus

[57] Macrobius II. 4. 18 (Augustus' answer to Seius Strabo).

[58] Suetonius, De gramm. 10. This may, or may not, be the same as his letter to Munatius Plancus (Gellius X. 26. 1). For Pollio's style, see p. 55. According to Gellius, it was Sallust's "elegantia" and his "novandi studium" that got him disliked: "cum multa prorsus invidia fuit" (IV. 15. 1).

[59] ib. According to Suetonius, Ateius furnished Sallust with a "breviarium omnium rerum Romanarum." Ateius, it is worth noting, had been the tutor of the brothers of P. Clodius and accompanied them on their provincial governorships (ib.).

there alludes to words like those culled by Sallust from the *Origines* of Cato.[60]

Livy for his part disapproved of orators who had recourse to "verba antiqua et sordida." [61] Further, he went out of his way to decry one of Sallust's adaptations of a Greek phrase. According to the elder Seneca, who reports the particular, Livy was unfair, Sallust's rendering being admirable.[62] Sallust, he adds, can beat Thucydides on his own ground and with his own weapon, brevity.[63]

Historians could be censured for their use of digressions or orations. A later writer, an epitomator, reports some criticism of Sallust's indulgences;[64] and Livy has an observation about the abuse of the picturesque excursus in historians.[65] Further, Pompeius Trogus blamed both Sallust and Livy for their orations. Direct discourse, he argued, was an illicit device.[66] Trogus took it upon himself to demonstrate how the thing should be done. Not Sallust's letter of Mithridates to the Parthian, but a harangue to his army when invading Asia (rendered in indirect speech), with a lengthy indictment of Roman imperialism.[67] Trogus, it should be added, betrays influence from Sallust in his style.[68]

Nor could Livy be wholly immune. However, certain common features in the early books, especially archaic and poetical expressions, belong to the common stock and derive from Livy's predecessors. Livy continues the annalists, and supersedes them. For this reason, and for a Ciceronian redundance in his style, it is not unfitting to describe him as the last of the Republican writers.[69] Sallust by contrast heralds the Empire.

---

[60] Suetonius, *Divus Aug.* 86. 3.

[61] Seneca, *Controv.* IX. 2. 26.

[62] ib. IX. 1. 13. Livy criticised "secundae res mire sunt vitiis obtentui" (*Hist.* I. 55. 24). In fact from Demosthenes XI. 13, not Thucydides as assumed by Livy, or by Seneca (or by both).

[63] ib. "hac eum Sallustius vicit et in suis illum castris cecidit."

[64] Granius Licinianus p. 43 Bonn: "Sallustium non ut historicum scribunt sed ut oratorem legendum," etc.

[65] Livy IX. 17. 1, cf. p. 232.

[66] Justin XXXVIII. 3. 11.

[67] ib. 4. 1–7. 10.

[68] M. Rambaud, *Rev.ét.lat.* XXVI (1948), 171 ff.

[69] E. Norden, *Die antike Kunstprosa* I (1898), 234 ff.

Fervent in admiration for the eloquence and the ideals of Cicero, Livy regarded Sallust's views of men and government with extreme distaste. It is not fanciful to detect revulsion in his *Praefatio*.[70] Livy proposed to write a history that should be patriotic and edifying—as were, it can be conjectured, certain of the recent annalists, such as Valerius Antias.

When Livy in the course of his long labours came to the period treated by Sallust, much time had elapsed since the Battle of Actium and the inception of the work. Caesar's heir had quickly lost interest in Julius Caesar, proconsul and Dictator. He had the halo, as "Divi filius," the rest was superfluous, or rather deleterious. Livy responded. He expressed a doubt—was Caesar's birth a blessing to the world?[71] He also extolled Pompeius. That did not offend Augustus either.[72] Literary critics praised Livy for his "candor." That propensity to benevolence sometimes led him astray. He was capable of omitting or toning down episodes discreditable to the Romans in their dealings with other peoples. Sallust's revelations about Roman imperialism would not be at all to his liking; and, eager no doubt to refute Sallust, he expurgated actions of violence or treachery in the early career of Pompeius Magnus.[73]

To narrate the Jugurthine War, Livy used other sources beside Sallust, to his detriment.[74] Likewise in the campaigns of Lucullus, where he imported fictions and material inaccuracies.[75] Cassius Dio is extant from a point in 69, after the Battle of Tigranocerta. It appears that he went back to Sallust. How closely he followed Livy after the *Historiae* break off is a question in debate. Dio's summary account of the subversive movement at Rome in 66–65 does not bring in the name of Caesar. That may, or may not, reflect Livy's version.[76]

Dio reports Sallust's expulsion from the Senate, without incrimination of any sort; and he has a brief reference to Sallust's

---

[70] L. Amundsen, *Symb.Osl.* XXV (1947), 31 ff.
[71] Seneca, *NQ* V. 18. 4.
[72] Tacitus, *Ann.* IV. 34. 3.
[73] P. 202.
[74] P. 154.
[75] Th. Reinach, *Mithridate Eupator* (1890), 434.
[76] P. 92.

mishap with the mutinous soldiers in 47.[77] About the governorship
of Africa Nova, however, he is explicit—extortion and a province
looted.[78] He adds hostile comment: Sallust incurred discredit, after
what he had written, after his bitter censure on the exploiters of
provinces. Dio is guilty of anachronism. He makes a careless assumption which reflects his own epoch rather—authors becoming
magistrates and governors. His comment may be entirely his own.
However, if Dio was following Livy, he may have found in his
source something more than the alleged facts about Sallust's pro-
consulship. Either way, a suspicion arises that somebody has enhanced the misdemeanours of Sallust.

Despite various and manifold detraction, Sallust could not be
denied his fame. Sallust and Livy were soon acclaimed as the classic
pair, "pares magis quam similes." That is the epigram of the consular historian Servilius Nonianus.[79] Livy dealt with recent and
contemporary transactions as well as the safe and standard legends
of the Roman past. There was a pertinent question which members of the governing class cannot have failed to put: how can a
man write the history of Rome if he is not a senator?

Asinius Pollio discovered "Patavinitas" in Livy. Quintilian, it
appears, understood Pollio's objection to apply to local words and
idioms.[80] Alluding to Patavium, that smug and prosperous *municipium*, the disdainful consular may have had something deeper in
mind, and a graver reproach than the mere solecisms of Transpadane Italy.[81] History is not an improving subject. Benevolence and
noble aspirations were not enough. A man had to be penetrating
and ruthless.

When the excellent L. Arruntius (*cos.* 22 b.c.) was impelled to
narrate the First Punic War, he adopted and outdid the manner
of Sallust. Arruntius had been in Sicily with Sextus Pompeius, and
he later commanded a part of the Caesarian fleet at Actium.[82] Well

[77] Dio XL. 63. 4; XLII. 52. 1 f.
[78] ib. XLIII. 9. 2.
[79] Quintilian X. 1. 102. Since Nonianus himself was "minus pressus quam
historiae auctoritas postulat" he cannot have been a close imitator of Sallust.
[80] ib. I. 5. 56, cf. VIII. 1. 3.
[81] cf. *Rom. Rev.* (1939), 485 f.; *Harvard Studies* LXIV (1959), 76.
[82] *PIR*², A 1129.

might he fancy that he possessed the proper and traditional equipment of a Roman annalist of the better sort.

Seneca furnishes a number of citations from Arruntius to illustrate the ravages of a Sallustian mania.[83] Exaggeration could not
outmode Sallust or detraction impair. His fame mounted steadily.
Martial and Quintilian concur in awarding the palm. For Martial
he is "primus Romana Crispus in historia." [84] Quintilian quietly
points out that whereas Livy is useful for the education of boys,
Sallust is the greater historian.[85]

"Rerum Romanarum florentissimus auctor," such is the tribute
of Cornelius Tacitus, who, like Sallust, is not prone to the laudatory superlative.[86] The conventional epithet might appear ironical,
were not the admiration patent and profound. A careful contriver,
Tacitus uses the necrological notice on Sallustius Crispus, the
grandnephew, to introduce the compliment; and he concludes the
item with a maxim on the transience of power in bare Sallustian
language. Elsewhere he evokes his predecessor when asserting the
diligence of his own historical researches—"nobis pleraque digna
cognitu obvenere, quamquam ab aliis incelebrata." [87] The word
"incelebratus" occurs nowhere else in Latin save in Sallust's rebuke
to the historians who grudged the fame of Sertorius.[88]

Like Sallust, Tacitus began with two monographs, but, less cautious than the great precursor, he announces at the outset, when
commemorating Agricola, the project of a future history. Though
the *Agricola* is ostensibly a biography, it had a theme of deep
political import with a sharp contemporary relevance; and the
military and geographical portions demanded a Sallustian tech-

---

[83] Seneca, *Epp.* 114. 17 ff. He registers a passion for phrases with "facio";
also for the verb "hiemo," as in "tempestas hiemavit" and two other instances (modelled on "hiemantibus aquis" in *Jug.* 37. 4). And he notes
"ingentes esse famas de Regulo," from *Hist.* I. 90: "inter arma civilia aequi
bonique famas petit."

[84] Martial XIV. 191. 2.

[85] Quintilian II. 5. 19: "Livium a pueris magis quam Sallustium; et hic
historiae maior est auctor, ad quem tamen intellegendum profectu opus sit."
Nor is his comment on "illa Livii lactea ubertas" (X. 1. 32) meant for praise.

[86] Tacitus, *Ann.* III. 30. 1.

[87] VI. 7. 5.

[88] Sallust, *Hist.* I. 88.

nique. There was also, to recall the *Letter of Mithridates,* an oration from a Caledonian chieftain denouncing the Romans for greed, injustice and perfidy. Nor could the *Germania* disavow its model (it resembles an extended excursus on lands and peoples).

How Tacitus employs Sallust in his *Historiae* can be succinctly demonstrated in his portrayal of Licinius Mucianus, who is thrown into strong and proper emphasis by the first character sketch in the whole work. After noting the vicissitudes of Mucianus' early life, the author describes this enigmatic and blended character in a series of short antithetic phrases, lacking connectives.[89] Later, when the season comes to proclaim an emperor in the East, Mucianus delivers a Sallustian oration, encouraging Vespasian. In the exordium it closely imitates Mithridates' letter of advice (which in its turn had been modelled on Thucydides).[90] Further, the speaker reinforces his argument with a series of bold and paradoxical maxims. Empire, he explains, is the only refuge now; to inspire fear is renown enough; war is safer than peace, to talk of rebelling is already to have acted.

The *Historiae,* however, betray a strong Livian infusion—colour, eloquence, and even a certain redundance. It is only with the *Annales* that Tacitus achieves his mature idiom, his concentrated majesty—and his perfect assimilation of Sallust.[91] The archaic manner comes out most clearly in the first six books, which is appropriate. Tiberius Caesar was an old-fashioned ruler, a link with the Republic, and there still subsisted "quaedam imago rei publicae." Nero could not be depicted thus.

Resemblances of person or episode are brought out by stylistic devices to suggest the classic original.[92] Thus the rebel Tacfarinas with African warfare to recall Jugurtha. When L. Piso is assassinated by a native in Hispania Citerior, the reader is compelled to think of the fate of Cn. Piso in the same region.[93] Sejanus borrows the criminal features of Catilina, and the seductive Poppaea Sabina comes on the scene like a second Sempronia.

---

[89] Tacitus, *Hist.* I. 10. 2.
[90] II. 76. 1. Cf. Sallust, *Hist.* IV. 69. 1, from Thucydides I. 32. 1.
[91] E. Löfstedt, *Syntactica* II (1933), 276 ff.; R. Syme, *Tacitus* (1958), 340 ff.
[92] cf. *Tacitus* (1958), 353 ff.; 728 ff.
[93] *Ann.* IV. 45, cf. *Cat.* 19.

Those examples are unmistakable. There are many others. Praising Marcus Lepidus, Tacitus has recourse to Sallust on Metellus (the form "comperior" marks it).[94] The short oration he devises for Lepidus exhibits Sallustian language.[95] Likewise the obituary notice which recapitulates the mixed fame of the Aemilii, "genus fecundum bonorum virorum et qui eadem familia corruptis moribus inlustri tamen fama egere." [96] Or again, the whole digression on legislation, which advances to the period of which Sallust wrote (not omitting a reference to the consul Lepidus), gives a hostile presentation of the dynast whom Sallust disliked, and, passing from Magnus to Caesar Augustus, describes in curt detestation the twenty years of tribulation.[97]

Sallust can often be surmised through the subject matter—geography and warfare, character sketches and obituaries, digressions and orations. The idiom confirms: syntax, archaic forms, vocabulary, wilful disharmony. Tacitus illuminates his predecessor in various and sometimes startling ways. There are close parallels in their stylistic evolution.

To begin with, both furnish a negative avowal by the words they avoid or discard. Like Sallust, Tacitus has no liking for what is typical of Ciceronian eloquence. Thus "singularis" never, "infinitus" hardly ever.[98] Above all, the ethical terms that had been diluted by orators and debased by politicians before they were annexed by the Caesars. Tacitus' treatment of "auctoritas," "pietas," "felicitas," and others is variously instructive.[99]

Tacitus insists on strong, archaic, and majestic language. From *Historiae* to *Annales* there is a visible enhancement.[100] "Claritudo" prevails over "claritas," and "cupido" expels "cupiditas" utterly; and "cognomentum," once in the *Historiae,* occurs seventeen times in the *Annales.* The second work admits a number of words not

---

[94] IV. 20. 2: "hunc ego Lepidum temporibus illis gravem et sapientem virum fuisse comperior." Cf. *Jug.* 45. 1 (p. 158).

[95] III. 50.

[96] VI. 27. 4.

[97] III. 26 ff.

[98] *Tacitus* (1958), 344. For Sallust, cf. p. 256.

[99] ib. 413 ff., cf. p. 257.

[100] ib. 340 f.; 716 f

employed previously. Among them the Sallustian are clear and notable.[101] At the same time, however, he gives up some which had been admitted to the *Historiae,* such as "torpedo," "hortamentum," "turbamentum." His sure taste found them too ornamental now, or too archaic.

Developing the idiosyncrasy, Tacitus exploits Sallust in subtle and manifold ways. To describe the pitiless shores and the pathless steppe, he evokes the author of *De situ Ponti,* transferring thither the language Sallust used about Numidia.[102] And he can improve on Sallust, as in the striking phrase about the fish at Byzantium—"vis piscium immensa Pontum erumpens." [103]

It is no mere matter of imitation or neat allusion. Tacitus goes on to create new "Sallustian" types for derision, such as the prosecutor, the sinister court buffoon, the treacherous philosopher.[104] Perhaps his mastery is best shown by specimens of free composition in the plain archaic manner (where nothing happens to be extant for parallel in Sallust). When L. Arruntius (the son of the historian) resolves to end his life, the comment is "documento sequentia erunt bene Arruntium morte usum." [105] And what could equal Poppaea Sabina—"huic mulieri cuncta alia fuere praeter honestum animum"? [106] Not even the master and model.

Tacitus found a classic and surpassed him. To begin with, the manner was congenial. The affinity grew. Tacitus absorbed the sentiments of his predecessor, and some of his prejudices. Sallust preserved him from any temptation to promote the idealisation of Pompeius Magnus. In the *Historiae* Tacitus dismissed Magnus as "occultior non melior" in the line of the dynasts who destroyed the Republic.[107] In the *Annales,* when the legislation of his third consulate comes in for mention, Pompeius Magnus is condemned

[101] ib. 731. For these words in Sallust, cf. App. I.

[102] *Ann.* XII. 20, cf. *Tacitus* (1958), 730. The passage has the portentously rare word "properantia" (from *Jug.* 36. 3).

[103] XII. 63. 2, cf. Sallust, *Hist.* III. 66: "qua tempestate vis piscium Ponto erupit."

[104] III. 66. 4; XV. 34. 2; XVI. 32. 3.

[105] VI. 48. 3.

[106] XIII. 45. 2.

[107] *Hist.* II. 38. 1.

as "suarum legum auctor idem ac subversor"; his predominance rested on force, and he lost it in war.[108]

Another fashion had been pushed to delusive extremes: the worship of the Republic, Cato and Brutus being the saints and heroes. Tacitus, it will be observed, never praises Cato in his own person (the name occurs only in orations). Further, and all but unique among the Latin writers, he insists on the order "Cassius et Brutus." [109] Sallust would have approved that exhibition of anti-suggestibility.

Each elected a theme of decline and fall. With the one, the destruction of the Republic through dissension and civil war. With the other, liberty and dignity perishing in the years of peace, ground down by the dynasty of the Caesars, themselves a progressive degeneration from Tiberius to Nero.

Each has a propensity to the darker side, a senator's suspicious insight into men and governments. Tacitus shares Sallust's predilection for crime, violence and dissimulation; and, like Sallust, he delights in characters compounded of evil and good. Sallust writes in unmitigated revulsion from the present. Not that he is in danger of being taken for a genuine old Roman. And Tacitus can be deceptive. The tone is sombre, giving no encouragement to hope or ease or happiness. Fear and discord overshadow his landscape. None the less, the author, it can be claimed, is robust and resilient. Like Sallust, he values energy above all, and the individual. Each stands in proclaimed hostility to despotism, but Tacitus enjoyed paradoxical advantages of condemnation deriving from Rome's long and bitter experience under the Caesars. Tacitus saw that he must speak out for freedom of speech since political liberty had passed away; and he enhances a Roman's contempt for servility and adulation. At the same time, Tacitus had something else denied to Sallust—humour, tolerance, and a measure of optimism. Protesting against conventional beliefs, and quietly subverting a consecrated delusion, he affirms in a masterly understatement that not all things were better in the old days.[110]

---

[108] *Ann.* III. 28. 1.

[109] cf. *Tacitus* (1958), 557.

[110] *Ann.* III. 55. 5: "nec omnia apud priores meliora, sed nostra quoque aetas multa laudis et artium imitanda posteris tulit."

The idiom of Sallust cast its spell on historians, with emulation pushed almost to parody, as evinced by the early example of L. Arruntius. Classic fame and a distinctive style also encouraged the production of spurious works. Not always with intent to deceive, still less for crafty and political ends. It was a normal method in education—speeches or letters composed for training or diversion, and sometimes for malice.[111]

Speakers hostile to the manner and memory of Cicero were active in the Augustan schools of rhetoric, eagerly supplying orations that had been lost, or never delivered. Cicero thought of defending Catilina in 65.[112] One historian believed he had done so.[113] On what grounds? Some parodist may have come out with a *Pro Catilina*. Speeches of Catilina and of C. Antonius were in circulation, to illustrate the electoral contest of 64.[114] One notorious practitioner wrote a counterblast to *Pro Milone*.[115] And the *Philippics*, it seems, were controverted in a scurrilous invective, ostensibly from a consular on the side of M. Antonius.[116]

Sallust's hostility towards Cicero would tend to be exaggerated or antedated, for various reasons.[117] If nothing survived of the tribune's speeches in 52, anonymous talent may have been ready to fill the gap. It can be noted as relevant but inconclusive that Cassius Severus had a poor opinion of Sallust's orations.[118] And further, that Asconius in his careful and detailed commentary on *Pro Milone* refers to the tribune's harangues but does not cite them.

---

[111] See the fundamental remarks of Quintilian on "prosopopoeiae" (III. 8. 49 ff.). These impersonations, he says, are not easy—"namque idem illud aliter Caesar aliter Cicero aliter Cato suadere debebit." But, he says, they are valuable for poets and future historians, indispensable for orators.

[112] *Ad Att.* I. 2. 1.

[113] Namely Fenestella, quietly and firmly refuted by Asconius 76.

[114] Asconius 84.

[115] Quintilian X. 5. 20 (Cestius Pius).

[116] A source, it is presumed, of the oration of Fufius Calenus in Dio XLVI. 1 ff. Cf. F. Millar, *Mus. Helv.* XVIII (1961), 19.

[117] P. 287.

[118] Seneca, *Controv.* III, *praef.* 8. Bogus orations of this type would not necessarily discredit the speech for Ventidius reported by Fronto, p. 123 N = II 136 (Haines).

There was another factor. After a time men grew curious about the early years of authors who had obtained classic rank. Hence the discovery or invention of biographical material. Likewise *juvenilia*. That is the explanation of the Virgilian *Culex*.[119] There were also elegiac verses of Horace and a petition to Maecenas.[120]

Augustus instituted public libraries. A check and guarantee against *pseudepigrapha*, it might seem.[121] Yet perhaps not. The cupidity of dealers or librarians will be taken into account. Would they have resisted *curiosa* like the erotic letters of Dellius to the Queen of Egypt?[122] Books were banned from the public collections, on political grounds, but none, so far as recorded, merely for dubious authenticity.[123]

Some frauds could be rejected out of hand, for reasons of style. Suetonius dismissed the Horatian letter to Maecenas, for it was obscure: not a fault to which Horace was liable.[124] Literary critics, however, sometimes lacked penetration. Quintilian was taken in by the *Invective against Cicero*. He assumed it to be Sallustian.[125] He also cited a speech of C. Antonius.[126] That is disturbing. Asconius had peremptorily damned the speeches of Antonius and Catilina.[127] Asconius was in the habit of using historical criteria. His *Life of Sallust* would have been worth having, if it existed— which is not likely.[128]

---

[119] As demonstrated by E. Fraenkel, *JRS* XLII (1952), 1 ff.

[120] Suetonius, *Vita Horatii*.

[121] The thesis of E. H. Clift, *Latin Pseudepigrapha. A Study in Literary Attributions* (1945). On which, cf. *JRS* XXXVII (1947), 198 ff.

[122] Seneca, *Suas.* I. 7: "hic est Dellius cuius epistulae ad Cleopatram lascivae feruntur."

[123] cf. *JRS* XXXVII (1947), 202.

[124] Suetonius, *Vita Horatii:* "nam *Elegi* vulgares, epistola etiam obscura, quo vitio minime tenebatur."

[125] Quintilian IV. 1. 68; IX. 3. 89. For this pamphlet see App. II.

[126] ib. IX. 3. 94.

[127] Asconius 84: "feruntur quoque orationes nomine illorum editae, non ab ipsis scriptae sed ab Ciceronis obtrectatoribus: quas nescio an satis sit ignorare."

[128] The only "evidence" is Pseudo-Acro on Horace, *Sat.* I. 2. 41, on which cf. p. 282. If Asconius wrote biographies of the Roman historians, it is unfortunate that no trace should survive of his *Life of Livy,* a fellow townsman.

In due course there was produced a Ciceronian *Invective against Sallust*.[129] Not a useful piece of work in any respect. Its allegations can be dismissed, for a good reason. The author was not aware of an authentic and damaging fact—Sallust tribune of the plebs in 52 as an adherent of P. Clodius.

Quintilian knew that Caesar's position in the Roman state lent itself to rhetorical exercises. He cites an appropriate line of argument—when we advise Caesar to assume the monarchy, we will affirm that the "res publica" cannot subsist if there be not one man to rule.[130] But neither Quintilian nor other writers in classical antiquity betray any awareness of the *Epistulae ad Caesarem senem* (suspicious entitlement), purporting to be works of Sallust.[131]

It would be more than peculiar that one and the same author should try his hand twice at this sort of thing. That is not the worst. The second of those *Suasoriae* (in the manuscript order) appears to expand and imitate the first. But the historical situation it presupposes is earlier. Therefore it cannot be contemporaneous with the events. And not by Sallust. The natural assumption is separate authorship—and no compulsion to believe that the first *Suasoria* is Sallustian either.

The authors of these two pamphlets know the idiom which Sallust with much contriving invented for the writing of history. Perhaps they know it too well. They can reproduce the surface—but not the bite and vigour of Sallust, not the constructional power and concentric argument that is exhibited, for example, in Caesar's oration or the prologue of the *Bellum Jugurthinum*.

The author of the second letter is in the worse posture—he betrays familiarity with passages in Sallust's historical works. This is not the place to go into the detail of his various transgressions. One sentence consigns his fate, in double damnation. The fellow has the face to assert his profound conviction that all human life is

---

[129] The author was a certain Didius, cf. Diomedes in *GL* I. 387K. A number of its allegations have crept into the modern "tradition" about Sallust's life.

[130] Quintilian III. 8. 47: "et C. Caesari suadentes regnum adfirmabimus stare iam rem publicam nisi uno regente non posse."

[131] For detail about these documents, see App. II.

watched over by divine Providence—"divino numine invisier." [132]
That is too much. Not Sallust's view of the universe, not Caesar's
either. And the expression would have dismayed Caesar no less
than the idea. The form of the passive infinitive, "invisier," is not
conceivable in prose of the time.

If the epoch of the Antonines exhibited fervour for anything,
it was old writers and the style of Sallust. The historian was imitated, debated and commented without end, by a prince and his
tutor, by orators, philosophers, and grammarians. Impostors arose
as well as experts, for fashion engenders hypocrisy and fraudulence
in every age. Gellius reports from youthful memories a delightful
scene in the book market at Rome. Among the company gathered
for scholarly converse was a pretentious person, a "iactator et venditator Sallustianae lectionis." [133] Not for him the mere surface
and epidermis, he got into the blood and marrow of Sallust, "san-
guinem quoque ipsum ac medullam." Sulpicius Apollinaris put his
claims to the test, gently asking him to elucidate the phrase describing Lentulus Clodianus, "perincertum stolidior an vanior." [134]
After a vague and shambling attempt the fellow slunk away.

Fronto was the great arbiter of taste and especial ornament of
the age. Fronto proclaimed that history ought to be written "splen-
dide." [135] Passing from precept to example, he composed a treatise
to celebrate the military exploits of L. Verus in the Parthian War.
The product is adulatory and dismal. Fronto cites Sallust frequently, and he admires the old annalists. Fronto and the others
never even mention the consular historian who assimilated and
perfected the manner of their paragon. Tacitus was ignored and
disliked. For good reasons, which went beyond their general dispraisal of imperial authors. Tacitus wrote about dynasties in decline, armed proclamations and civil war, and tyranny once again.
His main preoccupation is the life of senators under despotism.
That was disturbing and noxious, better forgotten. Men wanted

---

[132] "Sallust," *Epp.* II. 12. 7.

[133] Gellius XVIII. 4. 1. The word "venditator" happens to be very rare:
elsewhere only in Gellius V. 14. 3; Tacitus, *Hist.* I. 49. 3.

[134] *Hist.* IV. 1, cf. p. 209.

[135] Fronto, p. 126 N = II. 142 (Haines).

to believe that the evil past could never come back. Sallust is a subversive writer, but the theme was remote, the praise of ancient virtue salubrious.

The fame of Sallust endured to the end. The whole range of literature in late antiquity acknowledges his spell, from Ammianus to the *Historia Augusta,* from Church Fathers to the lowly tribe of grammarians and scholiasts. Despite a doubt here and there subsisting about the integrity of the historian's life,[136] he is valued for his ethical pessimism by edificatory writers and can also be acclaimed as "nobilitatae veritatis historicus." [137] Only Cicero and Virgil surpass him in estimation.[138]

---

[136] Lactantius, *Inst. div.* II. 12. 12; Symmachus, *Epp.* V. 68. 2; Macrobius III. 13. 9.

[137] Augustine, *De civ. Dei* VII. 3.

[138] For the literary influence of Sallust, down to the modern age, see E. Bolaffi, *Sallustio e la sua fortuna nei secoli* (1949). For the various estimates of the man and the historian since the Renaissance, F. Schindler, *Untersuchungen zur Geschichte des Sallustbildes.* (Diss. Breslau, 1939); K. Büchner, *Sallust* (1960), 362 ff.

APPENDIXES

I

THE EVOLUTION OF
SALLUST'S STYLE

At first sight the Sallustian idiom is as uniform as it is distinctive. Inspection shows a sharp advance after the *Bellum Catilinae,* prosecuted on several fronts.

The change can be documented through statistics. Not without extreme caution. The field is narrow: forty pages for the first monograph, seventy-seven for the second (in old-Teubner pagination). Nor will the difference in subject matter be ignored (the vocabulary of warfare and geography must be excluded). And the *Historiae* present a difficulty, since what survives is heterogeneous: the speeches and letters (fifteen pages), and the fragments which comprise for the most part citations from grammarians. Maurenbrecher's edition of the *Historiae* is equipped with a glossary, but there exists no *Lexicon Sallustianum.* The Index to the edition of R. Dietsch (1859) is useful but defective. Hence some of the figures here adduced are subject to error.

The advance after the first monograph is manifested in various ways (cf. p. 266). First, innovations in syntax, with several Grecisms. Second, change and selectiveness in the use of a number of small and unobtrusive words: conjunctions, prepositions, adverbs. These aspects were investigated in an exemplary fashion by A. Kunze, *Sallustiana* III. 1 (Leipzig, 1897): for a convenient summary, see E. Löfstedt, *Syntactica* II (1933), 290 ff. Third, vocabulary. It is easy to establish the historian's ambitious enhancement of his manner, eschewing the "classical" or indistinctive, striving ever to be strong, archaic, and impressive.

A development along that line is patent in Sallust's great emulator as he moves from *Historiae* to *Annales,* with startling parallels in detail. Each shows an increasing predilection for the same words, or types of words. For example, the following verbs:

imperito, memoro, patro, polleo, reor, sustento, tutor.

Next, in Tacitus a new crop of typically "Sallustian" words. Thus,

antevenio, consultor, inquies, insuesco, praemineo, praeverto, prolato, satias, vecordia.

These words, and others, are conspicuously on show in the first hexad of the *Annales* where the historian achieves his mature grandeur of diction (cf. *Tacitus* [1958], 719; 731). And some fade in the sequel.

Appended are five lists. List *A* comprises some Ciceronian words absent from Sallust.[1] The other four will illustrate in selective and summary fashion the trend taken by Sallust's vocabulary. Apart from the restricted area, various warnings are enjoined for preface. How discriminate between the deliberate, the unconscious, the fortuitous?

Negative indications can be helpful. From the outset, Sallust had his marked avoidances (p. 262). Further, the reasons for some of his discards are not mysterious. Thus the dropping of "crudelitas" and "turpitudo." All manner of phenomena concur; and it may be surmised, for example, that the author knew what he was doing when he gave up "malevolentia" (*Cat.* 3. 2; 12. 1) for "malitia" (*Jug.* 22. 2).

Compound verbs tend to be thrown over. Thus "committo," "commoror," "communico" (each twice in *Cat.*).[2] Hence no surprise about the statistics for "immuto" (*Cat.:* 5; *Jug.:* 1; *Hist.:* 0) and "muto" (4; 16; 12).[3]

Other aversions are perhaps enigmatic at first sight—"exopto" and "vexo" (4 times each in *Cat.* but never again).[4] And Sallust drops "formidulosus" (4 times in *Cat.*).

On the other side, the author knew that he needed to enrich his vocabulary in all sorts of ways. Many of the accessions are wilful and ornamental, telling their own story. Others are puzzling—or acciden-

---

[1] Those marked by asterisk occur in the *Epistulae ad Caesarem senem.*

[2] The figures for Tacitus are instructive: "committo" (*Germ.:* 1; *Dial.:* 1; *Hist.:* 1), "commoror" (never), "communico" (*Agr.:* 1).

[3] Tacitus has "immuto" only four times.

[4] "Exopto" is not in Tacitus, and he recedes from "vexo" (*Dial.:* 6; *Hist.:* 1; *Ann.:* 1).

tal. Thus, after "laetitia" and "laetor" arrives "laetus" (9 times in *Jug.*). Indeed, a whole collection of verbs can be registered that appear for the first time in the *Bellum Jugurthinum:*

cogo (20), conor (2), demo (1), gaudeo (1), iuvo (4), laedo (3), noceo (1), posco (4), suadeo (2), taceo (2).

The usage of Sallust, like that of Tacitus, brings up a number of problems in Latin semantics, some not beyond a conjecture, others subtle and not yet explained.[5] Observe, for example, that "opinor" is absent from his works, "cogito" occurs only in the letter of Lentulus Sura (*Cat.* 44. 5, cf. Cicero, *In Cat.* III. 12), and "arbitror" is found only twice (*Jug.* 69. 1; *Hist.* III. 48. 2): but "existimo" about 37 times.[6] Again, "oboedio" is admitted only in the present participle (*Cat.* once, *Jug.* 3 times).[7] And why do "rarus" and "recens" have to wait until the *Historiae* (twice and 5 times, respectively)?

List *B* is designed to show rising frequency from the first monograph to the second. It exhibits certain archaic or stylish words, such as "facundia," "opulentus," "polleo," "reor." At the same time, however, it includes some of the less decorative, which also illustrate Sallust's predilections ("pergo," "nitor," "tempto") or his growing sensitivity (such as the sharp rise of "metuo" and "metus"). Lists *C* and *D* are restricted, for the most part, to the rare or ornamental words that are first on show in the *Bellum Jugurthinum* and the *Historiae* respectively (these specimens do not exhaust the count of first appearances). Some are portentously rare.[8] And it may be noted in passing that certain words that look more or less ordinary such as "antecapio" and "antevenio" happen to occur seldom in Latin.[9] Compare "antehabeo" (only in Tacitus, *Ann.* I. 5. 8; IV. 11. 3). Further, "favor" and "taedium" appear to be neologisms in the time of Sallust.

List *E* registers some synonymous nouns. It can serve to exemplify Sallust's growing aversion from certain types of words. Observe, for example, the eclipse of "cupiditas," the augmentation of "cupido."

---

[5] cf. *Tacitus* (1958), 726.

[6] For "arbitror" cf. B. Axelson, *Unpoetische Wörter* (Lund, 1945), 64.

[7] That verb is shunned by the Latin poets, cf. B. Axelson, o.c. 65. Note therefore "Sallust," *Ep.* II. 10. 6: "oboedit"; 11. 7: "oboediendum."

[8] cf. p. 264.

[9] "Antecapio" (*Cat.*: 3; *Jug.*: 2) occurs, once each, in Cicero (*De nat.deorum* I. 43) and in Tacitus (*Hist.* IV. 66. 1).

The words denoting "sloth" and "fear" will be found instructive on various counts. As for the rise of "metus," compare "metuo" (once in *Cat.*, 12 times in *Jug.*). It is strange that the author was not aware from the start how superior "metuo" is to "timeo." Similarly, while eschewing "claritas," he did not at once light upon the archaic and impressive "claritudo."

Sallust extols the men and the morality of the old time. It is perhaps disconcerting to find that he has "antiquus" only once (*Hist.* I. 92), "priscus" and "vetustus" [10] never. But those phenomena, and many others of choice or avoidance in this fastidious writer, would take one on distant and devious paths.

A   Words not in Sallust

abundo	cogitatio	delenio
accommodo	cognitio	demens
addubito	commoneo	*deminuo
adhortor	conatus	demonstro
adicio	*concilio	denuntio
adminiculum	*confundo	descisco
affirmo	congrego	desidiosus
*amarus	*congruo	deligo
*amens	consensus	dimico
*amplifico	consentio	*distineo
amplitudo	consequor	distinguo
*ango	consocio	dominatus
angor	conspiro	excello
appareo	contamino	excogito
blanditia	corroboro	excuso
blandus	*corruo	exhibeo
*candidus	debello	exiguus
caritas	debilito	eximius
carpo	decerto	*expio
castigo	degenero	exprimo
celo	dego	exsequor
claritas	delecto	exstinguo

---

[10] Observe in Tacitus "priscus" (*Hist.:* 1; *Ann.:* 18) and "vetustus" (6: 29).

facultas
fastidiosus
fastidium
felicitas
firmamentum
*fluctuo
fortuitus
fraudo
furiosus
gratiosus
gravitas
honestas
humanitas
indignatio
indignitas
*indulgeo
indulgentia
infamia
intellegentia
inveterasco
lenitas
*meditor
mitigo
mitis
momentum
*numen
*obsequor
*obsum
*obtrecto
*occupatio
odiosus
offensio
opinor
ornamentum
otiosus

*pauper
pellicio
*penetro
percipio
periclitor
perspicio
persuasio
*pervado
piger
pigritia
pondero
praecaveo
praecipuus
praeparo
praepono
priscus
*proclivis
profero
*prospicio
prudentia
punio
rapidus
reconcilio
recordatio
recreo
redintegro
reduco
reformido
regno
reicio
relaxo
renuntio
reparo
repono
reservo

respuo
retardo
*ritus
robur
robustus
sanitas
sano
sanus
servo
singularis
*stabilio
*stupor
suavis
subtilis
subtraho
*succumbo
suffragor
summitto
supersum
suppedito
surgo
suscenseo
tango
torpor
turbulentus
*vaco
*vastatio
verecundia
versor
*versutus
vetustus
vexatio
*vigilantia
violentus
vitupero

B   From *Cat.* to *Jug.*

aerumnae	1	4	occulto	1	5
agito	13	34	opulentus	1	8
anxius	1	8	patro	3	6
certo	6	12	pergo	1	16
cupido	5	14	polleo	1	6
facundia	1	4	pravus	1	5
fatigo	2	9	reor	4	22
formido	1	10	reputo	1	8
ignavia	4	13	socordia	3	9
metuo	1	12	sustento	1	3
metus	9	30	tempto	4	23
nitor	3	15	vecordia	1	4

C   Words first in *Jug.*

aevum
antefero (2)
anteo
antepono
antevenio (5)
augesco
claritudo (2)
comperior (2)
consultor (3)
defenso (2)
dehortor (2)
dictito
diffidentia (2)
discordiosus
extorris
facundus

favor (2)
grassor (2)
hortamentum
imperito (5)
impiger (5)
incolumis (4)
infensus (2)
inritamentum
intestabilis
laetus (9)
ludificor (2)
missito
negito
opulens (2)
ostento (8)
ostentus

palor (4)
pavesco
perniciosus (5)
pessum (2)
pollicitatio (2)
praedoceo
praegredior
praepedio
praevenio
properantia
prosapia
segnis (2)
socors
taedium
tutor (8)
vitabundus (3)

D   Words first in *Hist.*

aequor	ignorantia	praemineo
coepto (2)	in cassum	praeverto
cognomentum (2)	incelebratus	prodigo
dedecor	inclutus (4)	proles
dehonestamentum (2)	incuriosus (2)	rarus (2)
delenimentum	inquies (4)	recens (5)
desenesco	musso (2)	repertor
despecto	obsequentia	satias
dilargior	obtentus	scaevus
excidium (2)	obtrecto	segnitia
festinus	occipio (2)	senectus (*adj.*)
formido (*verb*)	penso	sonor (2)
glisco	perdomo	stolidus (3)
gnaritas	perincertus	torpedo (3)
gnarus (4)	permulceo	turbamentum
gravesco	perquiro	turbo

E   Some Synonyms

	Cat.	Jug.	Hist.
aerumnae	1	4	1
calamitas	2	1	0
miseria	5	7	3
crudelitas	3	0	0
saevitia	2	4	2
cupiditas	3	0	0
cupido	5	14	4
lubido	17	17	2
desidia	3	0	0
ignavia	4	13	4
inertia	2	3	0
socordia	3	9	5
eloquentia	2	0	0
facundia	1	4	2
formido	1	10	7
metus	9	30	20
pavor	0	0	1
terror	0	3	5
timor	4	8	1

APPENDIX

II

THE FALSE SALLUST

A sad thing, so it seemed, if nothing can be known for certain about the personality and opinions of Sallust before he wrote the first monograph. It was therefore a temptation to redeem and revalue certain pamphlets of dubious authenticity. The last fifty years have seen an enormous effort lavished on those documents. Men like and approve them. By contrast, the historical works suffer obscuration. And there are other bad results.[1]

I

First, the short pamphlet in the form of an oration attacking Cicero. The *Invective* is not devoid of merit, being swift and vivid, alert and scurrilous.[2] In style this diatribe bears no resemblance to the historical writings of Sallust, nor would that be expected, the genre being different. However, it happens to be vouched for. Quintilian twice quotes from it as a work of Sallust (IV.

---

[1] See the Teubner texts of A. Kurfess, *Appendix Sallustiana*. I. *Epistulae ad Caesarem senem de re publica* (ed. 5, 1959); II *Invectivae* (ed. 3, 1958). They are equipped with bibliographies. And (after the writing of this Appendix) appeared the erudite and elaborate study of K. Vretska, *C. Sallustius Crispus. Invektive und Episteln*. I. Einleitung, Text und Übersetzung. II. Kommentar, Wortindex zur Invektive (1961). Add further A. Ernout, *Pseudo-Salluste. Lettres à César, Invectives* (Budé, 1962).

[2] cf. A. Ernout, *Salluste* (Budé, 1941), 34: "elle a du reste de la chaleur, du mouvement."

1. 68; IX. 3. 89). The *Invective* appears to reflect the political situation in the autumn of 54, after Cicero's defence of Vatinius, but before he was induced (or compelled) to come out as the advocate of Gabinius whom he had recently reviled. It carries no subsequent items to the discredit of Cicero. Therefore the dramatic date is clear. That seemed a safe starting point.

A further and fatal step was taken. Is not the *Invective* the most welcome of testimonies, nothing less than a contemporaneous oration, delivered in the Roman Senate? It remained to cast about for the real author. Not Sallust perhaps: he might more plausibly be identified as the consular L. Piso, making a brief, sharp, and damaging retort to the elaborate denunciations of his enemy Cicero.[3] Other scholars, however, felt no inhibitions. They were ready to concede Sallustian authorship, and they went on to extol the pamphlet as a source of useful information.[4]

The *Invective* purports to be the reply of a Roman senator who has been reviled by Cicero. It begins "graviter et iniquo animo maledicta tua paterer, M. Tulli." At once, an impediment. The year being 54, how can C. Sallustius Crispus be the author? Quaestor perhaps the year before, this "senator pedarius" is hardly in a position to excoriate the eminent consular.

Ingenuity finds a way out. The product is still contemporary. Not a senatorial speech but a pamphlet, and still the composition of Sallust. Two explanations have recently been devised. Sallust wrote the piece because he was moved by a sense of justice and by sympathy for Gabinius after Cicero had denounced that person in September of 54.[5] Or again, Sallust wrote as a partisan of Crassus: he recalled the famous

---

[3] R. Reitzenstein and E. Schwartz, *Hermes* XXXIII (1897), 87 ff. Accepted by E. Meyer, *Caesars Monarchie und das Principat des Pompejus*[3] (1922), 163 f.; J. Carcopino, *Histoire romaine* II (1936), 754. According to Vretska, "an der Piso-Hypothese hält Syme I 135, 3 fest" (o.c. I, 14). That scholar missed the negation implicit in the phrase of *Rom.Rev.* he was referring to —"it demands faith to believe that 'Sallust,' *In Ciceronem* . . . was written by Piso."

[4] According to E. Bolaffi, Sallustian authorship was disputed only by "voci isolate di critici" (*Sallustio* [1949], 95). It was accepted by Funaioli, Rostagni, M. Gelzer, L. R. Taylor, to name only a few.

[5] F. Oertel, *Rh.Mus.* XCIV (1951), 46 ff., followed by K. Vretska (o.c. 21 ff.).

altercation of 55 between Crassus and Cicero, and he was revolted by their subsequent and ostensible reconciliation.[6]

Sallust in a pamphlet vindicating either Gabinius or Crassus, such are the pleas now put out by the advocates of authenticity at all costs. Each on the surface perhaps vaguely plausible, but in fact remedies of faith or despair.

Sallust or somebody else in 54, it was one and the same assumption of contemporaneity. That turns out to be a deception. A searching enquiry came to the help of common sense and demonstrated that the *Invective* betrays clear anachronisms.[7] It cannot be a senatorial oration of the year 54. Let it be thrown over, cheerfully. No plea can avail for defence or salvage.

Enough, it might seem, if a fraud be exploded and mocked out of existence. Yet it might prove variously instructive to establish the nature and purpose and date of literary forgery. To what end was the *Invective* composed?

Patent propaganda, so it has been asserted. The unknown author used his pen in the service of Caesar's heir, about the year 33.[8] His aim was to discredit the memory of Cicero, and he contrived the attack with diabolical skill and subtlety. He got damaging material from various speeches of Cicero; he may have drawn on Sallust; and he produced a mosaic of defamation.

The notion is ingenious and superfluous.[9] Cicero, dead ten years before, belonged to a past already remote, so rapidly had events moved, so fundamentally was the political argument transformed. In this late season, Cicero could neither help nor harm anybody. His failures, treacheries and inadequacies were known—or forgotten. Other issues

---

[6] K. Büchner, *Sallust* (1960), 36: "der Crassianer der Invektive ist der Crassianer Sallust."

[7] G. Jachmann, *Misc.Ac.Berolinensia* (1950), 235 ff. See further R. G. M. Nisbet, *JRS* XLVIII (1958), 30 ff. Kurfess, after a review of hypotheses, concluded: "post mortem Sallustii publicatam esse hodie inter omnes constat" (ed. 3, Teubner [1958], VII).

[8] O. Seel, *Klio*, Beiheft XLVII (1943). Described by A. Kurfess as "sein methodisch mustergiltiges Buch" (*Aevum* XXVIII [1954], 230). Kurfess went on to suggest, however, that the *Invective* might be an extract from Pollio's *Historiae*.

[9] cf. *JRS* XXXVII (1947), 200 f., in review of E. H. Clift, *Latin Pseudepigrapha* (1945).

dominate the polemical interchanges between Octavianus and Antonius on the eve of Actium. That is clear. Nor, to bring in another
matter, can Octavianus have fancied that it would profit his cause if
he induced Pomponius Atticus to unmask Cicero by publishing his
correspondence.[10]

A simple solution offers. When speeches or pamphlets in depreciation of Cicero were produced in the days of Caesar Augustus, their
authors being aware that the memory of the great orator was not congenial to the ruler of Rome, the intent had, however, little bearing on
any political issue. The dispute was rather one of style and fashions.
And, it will be conjectured, some wrote for the fun of the thing, in
the spirit of parody.[11] Artful compositors were at work, the choice
products of intensive education in the schools of rhetoric. They could
not fool everybody, as the elder Seneca shows, condemning a speech
alleged to be the work of his friend Porcius Latro (*Controv.* X, *praef.*
12). But a librarian might be taken in, avid for a curious and revealing document, or, in a later age, even a careful literary critic such as
Quintilian.

The *Invective* therefore falls into its proper place and category. It
is an impersonation or "prosopopoeia," precisely of the type which
Quintilian himself has elsewhere defined (III. 8. 49).

Who then is being impersonated? It might be L. Piso, as some have
suggested.[12] The impudent and flagrant dishonesty of *In Pisonem* cried
out to be controverted. Or perhaps some other enemy of Cicero,
thereby equitably accorded a posthumous revenge, such as Gabinius,
or even Clodius.[13]

There is another notion. The author might be passing himself off
as Sallust. The style of an invective could not be the same as that of
the historical writings. Yet hints and echoes of Sallust can with propriety be adduced.[14] What follows? There is no authentic tradition

---

[10] The thesis of J. Carcopino, *Les secrets de la correspondance de Cicéron*
(1947).

[11] *Mus.Helv.* XV (1958), 47.

[12] *JRS* XXXVII (1947), 201. And, in a detailed enquiry, G. Jachmann,
o.c. 262.

[13] For Clodius, J. Hejnic, *Rh.Mus.* XCIX (1956), 255 ff.

[14] Thus R. G. M. Nisbet in App. VII of his edition of *In Pisonem* (Oxford,
1961). He cites "iniquo animo paterer" (1. 1); "neque modus neque modestia"
(1. 1); "fortunas suas venales habeat" (1. 1); "collibuisset" (1. 2); "parum quod

that Sallust was hostile to Cicero in 54. The *Invective* attests the beliefs and practices of rhetoricians in the age of Caesar Augustus, for there it can find an easy resting place.

II

The *Invective* carried a certain appeal to curiosity about Sallust's earliest emergence in the arena of Roman politics, and that no doubt explains why Quintilian in a later generation accepted the attribution with ease or without thinking. There is something more pernicious than the *Invective*—the *Epistulae ad Caesarem senem*, as they are entitled.[15]

This pair of *Suasoriae* appeals to edification. The two letters of counsel to Caesar have enjoyed an enormous vogue among men of good will and salubrious aspirations, for they seemed to exhibit a new and attractive Sallust. Not the failed politician or rancorous party hack, but a man who, for all his personal devotion to Caesar, chose that allegiance because of high ideals and was urgent to encourage the Dictator in the task of social and political reform. Ambition and opportunism is a deplorable and unworthy explanation of Sallust. One wanted men, and documents, of this reassuring type.[16]

The first *Epistula* (in the order of the manuscript) is not the first in ostensible date. It presupposes Caesar victorious in civil war and ready to turn his efforts to peace and stability. When was that? After the Battle of Thapsus in the early summer of 46, such is the consensus of scholarship.[17] Perhaps premature. Thapsus and Cato's suicide marked

---

impune fecisti" (3. 6). Add the words "opulentia" and "miseriae" (2. 4). It is worth observing that this "color Sallustianus" fades out soon after the exordium of the pamphlet.

[15] They are transmitted (without name of author) by *Cod.Vat.lat.* 3864 in a miscellany which includes the speeches and letters culled from the authentic works of Sallust.

[16] And so perhaps did Caesar, promptly after *Ep.* I entrusting Africa Nova "dem idealistischen Mahner," so Meyer suggested (o.c. 587). As Funaioli says, "in questo giovane è un idealista." And further, "si contemplano le cose dall' alto, siccome da Platone nelle lettere politiche" (*Studi di letteratura antica* II (1947), 50 f.).

[17] K. Vretska, o.c. 48: "kein Zweifel."

and consecrated the defeat of the Republican cause, it is true. If that consummation is what the author had in mind, he gives no sign, or any hint of a war against the Republicans that had been prosecuted after the Battle of Pharsalia. He refers to something different, to Caesar's victory over Pompeius Magnus—"bellum tibi fuit, imperator, cum homine claro, magnis opibus, avido potentiae" (I. 2. 1). And Pompeius is named twice (I. 2. 7; 4. 1).

An important conclusion follows. The "dramatic date" of *Epistula* I should belong in the autumn of 48, after Pharsalia and the murder of Magnus on the Egyptian shore. Those events must have appeared decisive to men at the time. It was not at once evident that the wars should go on. (This conclusion, be it noted in passing, could be exploited on the side of authenticity.)

More puzzling in every way is *Epistula* II. It reflects an earlier situation. How much earlier, that is the question.[18] A number of scholars have put this *Suasoria* in 49, in the first weeks of the Civil War; and a historian argued for the summer or autumn of the year.[19] However, the pamphlet betrays no sign that fighting has begun. One thorough investigation argues for 51.[20] Recently a consensus has emerged in favour of 50.[21] That year had a further attraction if the open letter to Caesar were supposed to belong after Sallust was expelled from the Senate.[22]

In view of the alleged note of vivid and urgent contemporaneity, the divergence seems not a little disturbing: 51, 50, 49, these were years in which issues changed and events moved quickly.

III

So far the ostensible dates. Next, authenticity, which had long been denied on general grounds and

---

[18] For a summary of opinions, K. Vretska, o.c. 49.

[19] E. Meyer, o.c. 572.

[20] G. Carlsson, *Eine Denkschrift an Caesar über den Staat* (Lund, 1936). Followed by L. R. Taylor, *Party Politics in the Age of Caesar* (1949), 185 f.

[21] That was the date advocated long ago by M. Gelzer. See now his *Caesar* (ed. 6, 1960), 166 ff.

[22] Thus K. Vretska, o.c. 51.

because of suspicious items of matter or language.[23] To demonstrate
that the two *Suasoriae* are not only contemporary documents but genuine products from the pen of a known person, C. Sallustius Crispus,
separate and converging arguments were adduced.

First, the historical argument. The pamphlets, it was asserted, have
the stamp and flavour of immediacy.[24] No conceivable rhetorician in
any later age possessed the knowledge or grasp of affairs. Only a politician of the day, a partisan of Caesar, and literate. Who but Sallust?

Or again, if to some sympathetic enquirers the author's approach
seemed a little unworldly, that was no impediment: Sallust was com-
paratively young and inexperienced. Or further, if the counsels im-
parted to Caesar are not all of the most clear and compelling, if the
exposition is weak in structure, an explanation was to hand. Caught
up in the turmoil of action, Sallust was pressed for time: otherwise
he could have made a better showing.[25]

Second, the opinions about history and politics as disclosed in the
Suasoriae appeared to concord admirably with the historical writings
—while at the same time (which was welcome and credible) allowing
a development in the author's thought, not yet come to full maturity.[26]

Third, the style. No doubt, it is Sallustian. All was clear. The *Suasoriae*, if a contemporary document (as the matter seemed to asseverate
and prove), must be held authentic, for Sallust's manner is all his
own.[27] Exhaustive studies of grammar, vocabulary and usage confirmed what nobody was impelled to doubt: the *Suasoriae* are "Sallustian" in style.[28] A lexicon has been compiled in support.[29] Finally,

---

[23] Since H. Jordan, *De Suasoriis quae ad Caesarem senem de Re Publica
inscribuntur commentatio* (1868).

[24] G. Funaioli, *R-E* II A (1920), 1937; E. Meyer, o.c. 587.

[25] W. Kroll, *Hermes* LXII (1927), 376.

[26] For the criterion of "Zeitechtheit" and personality, cf. K. Vretska,
Wiener Studien LXX (1957), 306 ff.

[27] H. Dahlmann, *Hermes* LXIX (1934), 389: "sind aber die Briefe aktuell,
dann sind sie von Sallust."

[28] cf. the commentary of B. Edmar, *Studien zu den Epistulae ad Caesarem
de re publica* (Lund, 1931); M. Chouet, *Les lettres de Salluste à César* (1950).
Also the long list of "congruentiae Sallustianae" appended to the Teubner
edition of A. Kurfess (21–28).

[29] E. Skard, "Index verborum quae exhibent Sallustii Epistulae ad
Caesarem." *Symb.Osl.*, Supp. III (1930).

therefore, style and sentiments so intimately fused, the personality that comes through and vindicates his own earliest productions is none other than the historian Sallust.[30]

By these paths argument converged, a persuasion hardened, dogma took shape. Not only a renovated Sallust, but fresh light on Caesar, and much else besides. The new doctrine invaded and infested the high road of Roman history. And it seemed permissible and profitable to widen the enquiry. Were the *Epistulae* ordered by Caesar, or a spontaneous approach? Were they designed for publicity? How much knowledge was vouchsafed to the author about Caesar's designs for the welfare of the Roman State? How far was he bold and free in the tendering of advice? And so on.[31]

Both weight and numbers were on show. The "literature of the subject" grew, and grows. A bibliography published in 1950 registers (from 1918 to 1948) no fewer than forty-four items in favour, only four against.[32] At first sight, a formidable company: heterogeneous, but embracing some of the names most illustrious in the study of Latin literature.[33] Also, historians. Confident language was used.[34] Meanwhile, however, dissent had been lifting its head. The ranks began to waver. Perhaps the rout has begun.[35]

---

[30] F. Arnaldi, *Stud.it.fil.class.* VI² (1928), 307 ff. And many others.

[31] M. Chouet, o.c. 105 ff. See now K. Vretska, o.c. 52 ff.

[32] M. Chouet, o.c. XV ff. (items XI–LVIII). The negative items are Last (two papers), Fraenkel, and Salmon. The list suffers from omissions, notably the important contribution of K. Latte, *JRS* XXVII (1937), 300 (reviewing G. Carlsson); also M. L. W. Laistner, *The Greater Roman Historians* (1947), 169 f. And there should have been an entry for A. Ernout (Budé, 1941), 33 ff. Further, for the history of the question down to 1923, cf. H. M. Last, *CQ* XVII (1923), 87 ff.—whose arguments were largely ignored on the Continent.

[33] As Funaioli noted, "erst der Historiker Pöhlmann hat die Frage von allen Seiten gründlich bearbeitet (S.-Ber.Akad.Münch. 1904) und den Philologen den rechten Weg gezeigt" (*R-E* IA, 1936). Latinists followed that fatal path. Thus (to name only the deceased), Norden, Kroll, Löfstedt, Funaioli, Rostagni.

[34] K. Büchner, *Lateinische Literatur und Sprache* (1951), 83: "so glaubt man jetzt, soweit die Meinungen sich öffentlich exponiert haben, allgemein an die Echtheit"; L. O. Sangiacomo, *Sallustio* (1954), 43: "le ricerche puramente filologiche . . . hanno cosí portato a risultati direi quasi matematici di certezza."

[35] The veteran Kurfess felt a shock—"nunc haesito, postquam Eduardus Fraenkel (*JRS* XLI, 1951, 192–4) et A. Dihle (*Mus.Helv.* XI, 1954, 126–130)

Not deterred, two champions have recently come into the open, firm and convinced.[36] In default of clear proof to the contrary, it is sound and legitimate, they assert, to start from the axiom that the two *Suasoriae* were written in 50 and in 46—and written by none other than the Caesarian partisan C. Sallustius Crispus (*tr. pl.* 52).

IV

That being the obdurate posture of defence, how should one proceed to impugn the *Epistulae ad Caesarem senem?* A single potent challenge might compel the whole edifice to collapse. The talisman may exist. It is worth looking for. Meanwhile, an assault on all fronts is expedient.[37] Since Sallust is in cause, it is suitable to treat the business "quam paucissumis."

Preface can likewise be brief. First of all, one author or two? The documents exhibit parallel passages. The list is instructive.[38] On a candid inspection, *Ep.* II seems both to imitate *Ep.* I and to expand it. That is peculiar. The dramatic date of *Ep.* II (taken to be 50) is earlier than that of *Ep.* I (46, or better, 48). Hence, at the very least, different authors, whoever they be.[39] That conclusion can be supported on other grounds. Therefore *Ep.* I might still be kept as a genuine work of Sallust, but *Ep.* II has to be dropped.[40]

If this point be not conceded, no matter. The argument can go on,

---

nos docuerunt eas post Sallustii opera historica demum conscripta esse a Sallustio personato." Such was his avowal in his *Appendix Sallustiana*[4] (1955), IV. But in the next edition (1959) he inserted the words "at v. Dietz p. XI." He is referring to the unpublished Freiburg dissertation of G. Dietz, *Sallusts Briefe an Caesar* (1956).

[36] Namely, K. Büchner, *Sallust* (1960) and K. Vretska in his definitive work (1961, cf. above, n. 1). And it will not escape notice that M. Gelzer briefly defends the position he reached long ago, cf. *Caesar*[6] (1960), 166 f.

[37] That a resolute attack might well succeed was indicated by H. Fuchs, *Mus.Helv.* IV (1947), 189.

[38] H. Jordan, o.c. 1 ff.; H. M. Last, o.c. 152.

[39] As assumed in Schanz-Hosius, *Gesch. der r. Literatur* I[2] (1898), 235. The notion was quietly discarded in ed. 4 (1927).

[40] The thesis of H. M. Last, o.c., with his concluding note on *Ep.* I in *CQ* XVIII (1924), 83 f.

first to style, thence to substance, in a declared and honourable design to discredit both *Suasoriae* at the end.[41]

Their language is Sallustian. That carried conviction, it seemed the strongest plea.[42] By paradox, style debilitates the whole case. First, it is a style that belongs to history, not to homiletic letters. Second, and more important, that style was an innovation, contrived for the writing of Roman history, with pains and much deliberation. Nobody, not even Sallust, knew that idiom as early as 50.[43]

What manner was suitable and permissible when a man composed political pamphlets in the last age of the Republic, that is perhaps a question. Few Romans could resist the appeal of the Roman past. Archaism was a normal and natural phenomenon in the historians. Furthermore, as Cicero attests in *De oratore* (III. 153), a speaker might adopt a manner or devices that suggested an earlier generation, without incurring dispraisal. Cicero was referring to past practitioners, it is true. But some orators of the Attic tendency risked archaic words for effect (p. 55).

Therefore it is not beyond credence that the author of a political pamphlet might seek advantage by posing as a plain serious old-fashioned sort of person. Let that be granted. It does not help. The manner of the *Epistulae* is not merely archaistic—it is patently "Sallustian." Now that which is "Sallustian" is the invention of the man who, after renouncing the career of honours, decided to become a historian. The ancient critics knew that his style was an artefact; they recognised the ingredients; it was not only archaistic but innovatory (p. 264).

V

The politician is deemed to know and employ the idiom which the historian created. That is disturbing.

---

[41] The brief and sporadic treatment of the *Epistulae* in *Rom.Rev.* (1939) was inconsistent and unsatisfactory, as is indicated in *Mus.Helv.* XV (1958), 55. For a clear statement of negation, *JRS* XXXVII (1947), 201.

[42] W. Kroll, o.c. 385.

[43] K. Latte, *JRS* XXVII (1937), 300 (reviewing G. Carlsson); E. Fraenkel, *JRS* XLI (1951), 192 ff. (reviewing M. Chouet). Fraenkel had briefly stated disbelief in *Deutsche Literaturzeitung* 1936, 884, reviewing E. Löfstedt, *Syntactica* II (1933).

The defence must put on a bold face. No imitator, they say, was capable of so perfect a performance.

That is a large postulate. The ancients were familiar with impersonation in speeches and letters as a useful and indeed necessary part of literary training. Quintilian testifies warmly (III. 8. 49 ff.). There must have been some neat practitioners.

Nor should the later ages be neglected, when translation into the languages of Hellas and Rome was in some countries enjoined or imposed. Or, better no doubt, the practice of free composition on the model of classic authors. That can serve for guidance. Also parody and pastiche, wherever the study of polite letters still obtains.

Most seductive and most remunerative is a writer with a novel manner all his own. The Romans conceived a passion for Sallust—fervent, recurrent, and enduring to the last days. He was also adored in Italy of the Renaissance, with various and notable manifestations. For example, the book of Rucellai, *De bello Italico,* narrating the French invasion of 1494. An ambitious emulation, and it succeeds. The book is worth inspection—and worth reading.[44]

Or, for that matter, observe the procedure of Cornelius Tacitus. He assimilates the thought as well as the manner. Not merely small vivid vignettes or isolated patches. He can essay a long Sallustian tract, such as the digression on the history of law, from "vetustissimi mortalium" to "multa honesta exitio fuere" (*Ann.* III. 26. 1—28. 1). And elsewhere Tacitus improves on his model.

Therefore, a new line of approach might cut a sharp clean swathe. If a man tried his hand at writing letters of advice to Caesar, how would he set about it? Where is he likely to succeed, and how will he fall in?

The general recipe is obvious. Addressing Caesar, the aspirant will promptly bring on "Fortuna" and her "lubido" (I. 1.1; II. 1.2). It is suitable to invoke Caesar's "dignitas" (II. 1. 4; 4. 2) and his "munificentia" (II. 1. 6). But it is elementary to eschew "clementia" if one purports to be writing before the outbreak of the Civil War—and in

---

[44] B. Oricellarius, *De bello Italico* (published for the first time by R. Brindley, London, 1724). Politian's account of the conspiracy at Florence in 1478 began quite well, but he could not keep up the Sallustian manner (*Pactianae conjurationis Commentarium,* first published at Basel in 1553). That tends to happen with imitations and impersonations, in any age.

fact the word occurs only in the *Epistula* ostensibly later in date (I. 3. 3; 6. 5).[45]

The tone must be aggressive and moralising, with plenty of gnomic utterances. Energy and integrity will be praised, sloth and corruption castigated. In style the author knows that he has to be bold and harsh, not shunning the obscure or the precious. A Grecism will be in place, such as "non peius videtur" (I. 8. 8); and the use of Plato's *Seventh Epistle* is a potent device (I. 8. 2).[46] And, naturally, the dullest pupil cannot fail to assert brevity, "quam paucissumis" (I. 8. 7; II. 13. 8), whatever the redundance he is perpetrating.

Nobody can neglect phrases built up with "facio" and "habeo." Frequentative verbs offer, such as "certo" and "sustento." And "agito" above all, which Sallust used a little too often (about 50 times). The verbs "memoro," "patro," and "reor" will be adopted, for they are old-fashioned. Similarly, those expressing effort or energy, such as "exerceo," "fatigo," "nitor." And vigorous adjectives appeal—"acerbus," "asper," "ferox," "praeceps," "saevus," "strenuus."

To emulate the plain old-fashioned manner, there should be frequent recourse to "artes," "facinus," "negotium." Then "mortales" is demanded, often. And it is good to follow Sallust in avoiding a number of abstract nouns with the ending "-itas." Thus no case of "caritas" or "claritas." After the first monograph Sallust dropped "crudelitas" and "cupiditas." Hence use of the more select "saevitia" (II. 6. 1) and "cupido" (II. 7. 4; 12. 4). Alert adepts will naturally be lavish with "lubido" (*Ep*. I: 4 times; *Ep*. II: 6 times).

The terms condemnatory of sloth are on conspicuous show in Sallust: "desidia," "inertia," "ignavia," "socordia." For strong emphasis, he links "socordia" with "ignavia" (*Cat*. 52. 29; 58. 4; *Jug*. 31. 2). An imitator will conform (II. 6. 2; 10. 9).

It is good to have certain distinctively Sallustian words that occur seldom or never in Cicero and in Caesar such as "munificentia" and

---

[45] For "clementia" in Sallust, used only of the imperial people (*Jug*. 33. 4; *Hist*. I. 55. 1), see p. 119. As for "clemens" (*Ep*. I. 1. 4), Sallust avoids employing it in the political sense.

[46] cf. Plato, *Ep*. VII. 326b. As A. Dihle demonstrates, *Ep*. I uses Plato directly, not so *Ep*. II (*Mus.Helv*. XI [1954], 129). E. T. Salmon, impugning *Ep*. II, had argued that its echoes of Greek writers derive precisely from Sallust's writings (*CP* XXXII [1937], 72 ff.).

"opulentia," "strenuus" and "saevus." Also "consultor" used to mean an adviser *(Jug.:* 3 times; *Hist.* 3 times).

Now there are a number of words that look "Sallustian" but happen not to be attested in the writings as extant. It is strange that Sallust did not employ some that crop up in Tacitus, in patently Sallustian sections.[47]

The *Suasoriae* supply several more or less plausible specimens of this type.[48] There is "incuria" (I. 1. 3), which anybody might easily take to be Sallustian:[49] he has "incuriosus" twice *(Hist.* II. 42; IV. 36), and both words are in favour with Tacitus. Sallust exhibited the portentous "dehonestamentum" *Hist.* I. 88; 55. 21). *Ep.* II comes out with "honestamenta pacis" (II. 13. 2): the word is very uncommon, first registered in Seneca *(Epp.* 66. 2), then in Gellius and Apuleius (not in Tacitus). *Ep.* II also has "additamentum" (II. 9. 4; 11. 6), which occurs in Cicero *(Pro Sestio* 68), next in Seneca and in Apuleius (it is eschewed by Livy and by Tacitus). The verb "adiuto" might seem at first sight unobjectionable—frequent in Plautus and Terence (but again, not in Livy or Tacitus). Next, the rare "dispalor," in the form "dispalatus" (II. 5. 6): twice in Sisenna (35; 134). Finally, a writer preoccupied with the theme of power might well be drawn to the solemn and solid "rerum potiri" (II. 6. 5), cf. Lucretius II. 13. A coeval of Sallust has "qui rerum potiuntur" (Caelius in *Ad fam.* VIII. 14. 2); and Tacitus in the *Annales* is happy to use the phrase no fewer than eleven times. Similarly, at first sight, "rerum potentes" (I. 1. 5), cf. "reges rerumque potentes" (Lucretius II. 50; III. 1027). Perhaps from Ennius, perhaps too poetical. The nearest that Tacitus ventures is "Iovem ut rerum omnium potentem" *(Hist.* IV. 84. 5).

Not only choice locutions. An imitator shows his flair by attention to the less ornamental and less obtrusive words. "Tametsi" is characteristic of Sallust—at least to begin with. It disappears abruptly after *Jug.* 38. 9, to be replaced at once by "quamquam." There are five

---

[47] cf. *Tacitus* (1958), 731.

[48] They are discussed, with the plea for authenticity, by A. Holborn-Bethmann, *De Sallustii epistula ad Caesarem senem de re publica* (Diss. Berlin, 1926), 26 ff.

[49] At least, observe the mistake committed in *Mus.Helv.* XV (1958), 51: "the typically Sallustian *incuria.*"

instances of "tametsi" in *Ep.* II—which may seem all to the credit of that author.[50]

Sallust was dominated by contrasts and by the impulsion to "varietas," morbidly. "Bonum publicum" is the standard phrase. Who among the Latin classics has "malum publicum"? A rarity, save in Sallust (*Cat.* 37. 7; *Hist.* I. 77. 13; IV. 51). "Mala publica," that is "public calamities," is normal Latin; "malum publicum," however, denotes harm done to the Commonwealth.[51] Commentators have not been alert to this refinement. The authors of the *Suasoriae* are able to produce "malum publicum" (I. 7. 2; II. 5. 8; 11. 1).

Laudation would be premature. Both pamphlets lapse into a peculiar lingo from time to time. A number of their expressions evoked sharp censure from students of Latin usage. Not good, they argued, not conceivable in this age, but only to be understood on the hypothesis of a late date, perhaps in the Flavio-Antonine period.[52] Among them stand "multo multoque asperius" (I. 1. 8); "magis aut minus" (II. 7. 4; 10); "multipliciter animus . . . fatigatur" (II. 10. 5); "quae per mortaleis avide cupiuntur" (I. 1. 1); "ut . . . concordia . . . coalescat" (II. 7. 2). Some of the objections have been contested, it is true: is there enough Latin available for comparison?

The phenomena in question were taken to deny authorship in "classical" times. Another explanation may avail. Not perhaps late or defective Latinity, but sure stigmata of deliberate and wilful affectation.

VI

With pastiche in any age the temptation is to develop, exploit, and overdo the manner. That was a failing of the excellent Arruntius in his history of the Punic War: a plethora of expressions with "facio," and abuse of the Sallustian verb "hiemo." Seneca bears witness. As he observes, "quae apud

---

[50] For "tametsi," see A. Kunze, *Sallustiana* III. 1 (1897), 20 f. To Löfstedt this item spoke powerfully for authenticity (*Syntactica* II [1933], 292).

[51] The article in *TLL* fails to draw the distinction.

[52] H. Jordan, o.c. 23 ff.; H. M. Last, o.c. 94 f.

Sallustium rara fuerunt, apud hunc crebra sunt et paene continua"
(*Epp.* 114. 18).

The authors of the *Suasoriae* cannot escape. Sallust himself is a
monotonous writer, prone to repetition or obsession. More so the
two pamphlets, in proportion to their bulk. Taken together, they are
between a quarter and a third as large as the *Bellum Catilinae*; while
Ep. II by itself is between a fourth and a fifth.

For a number of typical Sallustian words, the *Epistulae* equal or
even exceed the total of occurrences in the first monograph. Thus
"agito" (*Epp.* 12: *Cat.* 13); "asper," metaphorically (8: 5); "clarus"
(9: 9); "exerceo" (8: 8); "mortales" (12: 13); "socordia" (5: 3). Also
"parentes" in collocation with "patria": twice in *Cat.*, but three times
in *Ep.* II alone (II. 8. 4; 13. 1; 13. 6).[53]

Notable is the supine of "facio" with an adjective. The first monograph has "facilia factu" (*Cat.* 3. 2; 14. 1) and "optumum factu" (*Cat.*
32. 1; 55. 1; 57. 5). The imitators, from "optumum factu" (I. 3. 1), go
on to "difficile atque asperum" (II. 1. 1), "haud difficile" (II. 12. 2),
"haud obscurum" (I. 8. 4), "utilia" (II. 4. 5), "utilissima" (II. 13. 8).

Similarly, "vera via" in the first monograph (*Cat.* 11. 2). The imitators, in addition to "vera atque simplex via" (I. 5. 8) are able to produce "ardua" (II. 7. 9), "patens" (I. 5. 1), "prava" (I. 5. 6) and
"melior" (I. 8. 10).

Sallust has a predilection for "bonae artes" (*Cat.* twice; *Jug.* 5 times);
and the use of the phrase in later authors is significant (Livy twice,
Tacitus 12 times, *Pan. vet.* once, Augustine once). The opposite is
"malae artes" (*Cat.* 3. 4; 13. 5; *Jug.* 41. 1) or "pessumae artes" (*Jug.*
85. 43). No emulator could be heedless. Hence "bonae artes" (I. 1. 8;
II. 7. 4; 13. 2), and "malae artes" (II. 1. 3).

That is not all. Why not go further? The author of *Ep.* I has
"firmanda res publica . . . pacis bonis artibus" (I. 1. 8). The expression cannot be defended by appeal to "vir facundus et pacis artibus"
(Tacitus, *Hist.* I. 8. 1). Also, and worse, "pravas artes malasque libidines" (I. 6. 4). Sallust came to like the adjective "pravus" (*Cat.* once;
Jug. 5 times; *Hist.* 3 times). The authors of the *Epistulae* are alert—
both here and with "prava via" (I. 5. 6) and "prava consilia" (II. 1. 2).

---

[53] Well worth quoting is the peculiar exhortation in *Ep.* II. 13. 1: "quod
si tecum patria atque parentes loqui possent, scilicet haec tibi dicerent.
o Caesar, nos te genuimus fortissimi viri, in optima urbe."

But the expression "pravae artes" can be matched in no Latin writer. Nor can one feel happy about "malae libidines." Prone as is Sallust to "lubido" (at least 36 instances), he nowhere descends to "malae lubidines." Indeed, he nowhere attaches an adjective to "lubidines." Not an attractive locution, therefore. And, for other reasons, a doubt will arise about "bona lubido" (II. 13. 6).

Indeed, in various other unobtrusive phrases a clear and wilful deviation can be detected from the usage of Sallust. *Ep.* II employs "malum facinus" no fewer than three times (II. 6. 2; 12. 7; 13. 3). Not in Sallust, who has "mala facinora" (*Cat.* 16. 1) and "pessumum facinus" (*Cat.* 18. 8). In the matter of choice and taste, Tacitus confirms. His writings exhibit "mala facinora" (twice), "pessimum facinus" (4 times)—and never "malum facinus." Fortified by this phenomenon, as by "malae lubidines," one therefore begins to wonder about a number of expressions which, similarly, nobody would think of challenging otherwise.

Three examples. First, "laeta omnia et candida visa" (I. 3. 2). But Sallust does not employ "candidus." Next, "virtus amara atque aspera est" (II. 7. 7). Not "amarus" either. Third, "omnia in proclivi erunt" (II. 8. 6). Not in Sallust, but in Plautus and Terence: the nearest in Tacitus is "tanto proclivius est" (*Hist.* IV. 3. 2).

These performers, it becomes clear, force and pervert the Sallustian idiosyncrasy. It was the historian's habit to modify normal phraseology or technical terms. Once again, the adepts show their hand. "Facinus facere" ought not to be absent. Thus "praeclara facinora fecit" (II. 2. 4). But what is to be said about "praeclara facinora egisti" (II. 13. 2)?[54] As for "adversa res" (II. 10. 7), that might be claimed to be patently in the manner of Sallust.[55] The phrase is on record (Plautus twice, Publilius once, Livy 3 times), but nowhere in Sallust. That author prefers the plural, or the neuter plural "adversa."

Another variation. One lights upon "magis clarum magisque acceptum" (II. 7. 6). Sallust has the phrase "carus acceptusque" (*Jug.* 12. 3; 70. 2; 108. 1). The manuscripts read, it is true, "clarus acceptus-

---

[54] Vretska in his commentary refers to *Pro Caelio* 54: "quod per ignotos actum," etc., where "facinus" has been used in the previous sentence. Hardly a parallel—and, indeed, "facinus" does not here have to be understood under "quod."

[55] As by B. Edmar, ad loc.

que" in *Jug.* 70. 2, as also in Tacitus, *Ann.* XII. 29. 1. Examination of both contexts will show that doubt is legitimate, that emendation is preferable, even though the distorted formula be retained by the latest editors.

Finally, "cum paucis senatoriis" (II. 11. 6). The standard term is "vir senatorii ordinis." No example of "senatorius," meaning "a senator," can be dug up, even from the lowest levels of late Latinity.[56]

Sallust likes to couple pairs of words for emphasis (e.g., "socordia atque ignavia"), sometimes with the added art of alliteration, thus "flagitiis atque facinoribus" (*Cat.* 23. 1) or "fluxa atque fragilis" (*Cat.* 1. 4). Hence a certain redundancy in this fanatic of brevity. But would Sallust have chosen to write "saeva atque crudelia" (I. 4. 2)? Discovering the superior value of "saevus," he eschews "crudelis" almost entirely (once in *Jug.* after 11 times in *Cat.*).

Synonyms or redundancy import a kind of old-fashioned simplicity, which is appropriate. But who will tolerate "quanti et quam multi mortales" (I. 2. 7), or "multam magnamque curam" (II. 1. 3)? It is vain to bolster the latter specimen with "multis et magnis tempestatibus" (*Cat.* 20. 3) and "multis magnisque praesidiis" (*Jug.* 62. 9). The passages are not parallel.[57]

As emerges in various ways, imitators cannot help exaggerating. The historian was notorious and blamed for his "audacia in translationibus" (Ateius Philologus in Suetonius, *De gramm.* 10). The adepts respond with strained metaphors, preciosity, obscurity. Thus "hostem adversum deprimere" (II. 7. 2), or "alios praegressus" (I. 1. 2): Sallust has "praegredior" only in the literal sense (*Jug.* 94. 2; *Hist.* IV. 66).[58] *Ep.* I exhibits "gratiam gratificans" (I. 7. 5). The expression lacks attestation anywhere in Latin, and the verb is probably taken over by the other pamphlet—"quodsi tibi bona lubido fuerit patriae parentibusque gratificandi" (II. 13. 6). Sallust has "gratificor" for the first and last time in *Jug.* 3. 4.

---

[56] cf. *Mus.Helv.* XV (1958), 54, on information supplied by the Direction of *TLL*. The defence is to take "senatoriis" not as a noun but as an adjective, supplying "hominibus" from the preceding "homines nobiles" (K. Vretska, ad loc.).

[57] Those passages are adduced, but not quoted, by Kurfess in his catalogue of "congruentiae."

[58] Other words, in Sallust only in the literal sense, are "coaequo" (II. 8. 2; 11. 3), "communio" (II. 4. 4), "conglobo" (I. 5. 2).

"Dispalor" is a very rare verb. One observes "multitudo . . . in artis vitasque varias dispalata" (II. 5. 6). The next and solitary use as metaphor is in Ammianus (XVI. 12. 1); and, for that matter, Sallust avoids the plural of "vita." Another metaphor, "hebeti atque claudo sc. animo" (I. 8. 2). Surely excessive, although the later Sallust can go as far as "lamed by sloth"—"nihil socordia claudicabat" (*Hist.* fr. inc. 23 in Maurenbrecher p. 204). Justification from the developed style of the *Historiae* cannot avail. On the contrary.

One might expect to find some perverse and obscure play with the inevitable "agito." Enquiry is rewarded richly. Observe "asperius magisque anxie agitat" (II. 10. 5); "super omnes mortales gloriam agitabis" (II. 13. 6). And "fatigo" is put to hard labour—"nam vivos interdum fortuna, saepe invidia fatigat" (II. 13. 7).

To go further and lower. "An illa . . . oblivio interfecit" (I. 4. 1), or "id quod factu haud obscurum est" (I. 8. 4). Recourse has been had to the art of emendation, easily enough (reading "intercepit" and "absurdum").[59] That may only obscure the truest explanation.

Oddities of style and language pile up (not all are here adduced). They betray. The *Suasoriae* can therefore serve a useful turn. They exemplify what Quintilian calls "mala affectatio." As the critic defines the thing, "tumida et pusilla et praedulcia et abundantia et arcessita et exultantia sub idem nomen cadunt" (VIII. 3. 56).

Other tests of aptitude confront an impersonator. One is the feel for the "sanguis ac medulla" of the authentic Sallust. It is perhaps strange that both authors neglect "facundia," "fluxus," "miseriae," "occulto," "ostento," "vecordia." [60] Again, never "tempto" or "tolero" (18 and 32 times in Sallust). The area for comparison is narrow; and it will be recalled that Sallust's own selections or omissions often baffle explanation (cf. App. I). Nor is it worth bothering about words absent from Sallust such as "concilio" (II. 6. 2), "confundo" (II. 8. 1), "congruo" (II. 5. 6) or "stabilio" (I. 6. 5; II. 4. 4; II. 11. 1).[61]

---

[59] Gronovius proposed "intercepit," H. Jordan "absurdum." Neither change is adopted in the texts of Kurfess and of Vretska.

[60] It must be emphasised that those items are not here adduced as though to disprove authenticity.

[61] For the full list, M. Chouet, o.c. 21 f. See also the items marked by asterisk in App. I, Table A ("Ciceronian" words). A warning is in place—these words are not adduced as any kind of proof in themselves. It could

Let that pass therefore. It is enough to demonstrate that the imitators overdo things. There is something else, the evolution of a style. Large and heavy items of condemnation are to hand.

If a man proposed, for example, to render Tacitus or parody him, caution is requisite. There are different types of the Tacitean style. The manner of the *Historiae* is vivid, and eloquent—and not a little in debt to Livy.[62] By contrast, the mature and often Sallustian first hexad of the *Annales*. He who composes a pastiche ought to know what he is doing. Now Sallust himself had gone through a process analogous to that which can be established in Tacitus—towards the archaic, concentrated, and evocative.

That process was not detected and studied by the two imitators. Lured and taken by the choice and decorative, they succumb to words of which Sallust, when he wrote the first monograph, had not discovered the value, the colour or the resonance. The prime examples are "consultor" (II. 1. 1), "defenso" (II. 10. 5), "imperito" (I. 1. 5; 1. 6; II. 5. 5; 11. 7). That being so, there is no point in citing a number of less distinctive words from the *Suasoriae* which in Sallust happen to be first attested in the *Bellum Jugurthinum*.[63]

Next, that which first emerges in the *Historiae*. "Excidium" (I. 5. 2) is revealing, or the verb "formido" in the form "formidatur" (I. 1. 4). Or again, the stylish "obtentui erit" (II. 11. 5): "obtentui," registered in *Hist.* I. 55. 24, recurs in Tacitus (3 times, and once "obtentum habebat," *Ann.* XII. 7. 3). Also perhaps worth noting are "disturbo" (II. 2. 4; 6. 5) and "everto" (II. 3. 7; 4. 2; 13. 3). Finally, and most significant, "torpedo," from Cato. Sallust lit upon the word and used it three times in orations in the *Historiae* (I. 77. 19; III. 48. 20; 26). Tacitus tried it once (*Hist.* III. 63. 2). He dropped it thereafter, rightly. "Torpedo" is on show in *Ep.* II. 8. 7. By itself, it ought to explode that pamphlet.

---

easily be contended that Proto-Sallust used a number of words which (in the next stage) the author of the first monograph discarded, many of them deliberately. That would miss the point. What excites alarm is the cohabitation and amalgam of Proto-Sallust with Deutero-Sallust (i.e., the developed author of *Jug.* and *Hist.*).

[62] *Tacitus* (1958), 197; 200 f.; 340; 350; 733 f.

[63] e.g. "deformo," "demo," "depono," "desidero," "desino." Yet "demo" is of some interest—three times in each pamphlet.

Small drab words can be no less destructive. "Mox," "ergo," and
"ferme" do not happen to turn up before the second monograph. But
Ep. I has "mox" (I. 6. 5) and "ergo" (I. 1. 9; 5. 6), *Ep.* II "ergo" (II.
7. 10) and "ferme" (II. 10. 2). Similarly the preposition "adversus"
(*Jug.*: 17 times; *Hist.*: 4 times). *Ep.* I, however, has two instances (I. 1.
8; 4. 3). Next "ceterum" (thrice only in *Cat.* but about fifty times in
Jug.): *Ep.* I can present one specimen (I. 1. 3), *Ep.* II no fewer than
four (II. 4. 5; 5. 7; 8. 4; 13. 8). Finally, "quis" instead of "quibus."
No case in the first monograph, but *Ep.* I has "ex queis" (I. 2. 6).
Hence, though alert to "tametsi" (cf. above), the *Suasoriae* fall down
repeatedly on words characteristic of the historical style.

To state the matter succinctly. The ostensible Proto-Sallust manages
to anticipate the evolution of the historian in his habits and predilections, manifest and manifold.

It would be an entertaining pastime (but idle and superfluous) to
confront the two impostors and compare them in detail. The second
(it is no surprise) imitates the first. Their subject matter, however,
is not identical, and only the second exhibits "factio" (7 times),
"factiosus" (2), "nobilis" (5) and "nobilitas" (5). Other divergences in
vocabulary might rather excite curiosity—"accido" (0: 5), "ago" (0: 5),
"beneficium" (0: 4), "civitas" (1: 10), "dignitas" (0: 6), "everto" (0: 3),
"facinus" (0: 7), "gloria" (0: 9), "gratia" (1: 5), "honestus" (0: 3), "inertia" (0: 4), "opulentia" (0: 4), "patria" (1: 8), "probo" (0: 5), "restituo" (0: 5), "valeo" (0: 3). Contrariwise, only the first *Epistula* has
"attingo" (3 times), "compono" (5), and "gero" (5).[64]

A question abides. What of their literary quality?[65] Some merit
may be conceded, if only as a consolation to the faithful. Exercise in
the plain concentrated style yields clear profit here and there. Thus
"victores praedam petunt, victi cives sunt" (I. 1. 8); "orta omnia
intereunt" (I. 5. 2); "magnae curae magna merces est" (I. 7. 1);

[64] If it were one author, "ago" (0: 5) and "gero" (5: 0) are indeed peculiar.
[65] W. Kroll held them genuine, but not good (o.c. 376). For G. Jachmann,
"ein politisches Phrasengewäsch" (o.c. 253). As A. Ernout justly observes,
"on n'y trouve ni la fermeté, ni la vigueur, ni la rapidité de Salluste."
Salluste [1941], 35, cf. *Pseudo-Salluste* [1962], 16). On the other side,
M. Chouet—"le style est sobre, sévère et vigoureux, il fuit la banalité sans
blesser l'harmonie" (o.c. 125). That author has an especial note of praise
for the metaphors, the "fortes images" (42): among them is "oblivio interfecit"
(I. 4. 1).

"plerique mortales ad iudicandum satis ingenii habent aut simulant" (I. 8. 9). Nor can eloquence be denied—"qua tempestate urbi Romanae fatum excidii adventarit" (I. 5. 2).[66] But poverty of thought lurks everywhere. They are too long for what they have to say, notoriously the second pamphlet.

Their "sententiae" have been scrupulously catalogued by serious enquirers, as though for praise.[67] Some are deliciously revealing, such as II. 10. 4 (quoted below), or II. 8. 3: "nam perinde omnes res laudantur atque adpetuntur ut earum rerum usus est." Whether or no the Antonine experts (cf. Gellius XVIII. 4, discussed on p. 330) would have been taken in is a vain question; and there is no compulsion to set a high value on the intelligence of Cornelius Fronto. But would even Fronto have said of this specimen "gnomas egregie convertisti, hanc quidem, quam hodie accepi, prope perfecte, ut poni in libro Sallustii possit" (p. 48 N = I.12 Haines)?

To sum up: some scholars have taken the *Suasoriae* to be a cento or mosaic of Sallustian phrases.[68] The lists so ingeniously compiled in the support and persuasion of authenticity reinforce that opinion. The authors, however, go further than that. They are pretentious, varying Sallust and trying to outdo his manner. They therefore fall under Quintilian's condemnation of "mala affectatio." The surface of a style may be copied or exaggerated. Not so easily the personality, with the tension, the vigour, and the structural power. The *Suasoriae* are diffuse and incoherent. To harp a monotonous theme: if good Sallustian is looked for, look to Cornelius Tacitus.

VII

So far the argument from language. Is it valid and peremptory?

Some who cling fast to the thesis that the *Epistulae* are genuine will offer, as an amiable concession, to waive the whole business of the Sallustian style, so strong is their conviction that the documents

---

[66] cf. Tacitus, *Hist.* IV. 13. 3: "rei publicae cura, cui excidium adventabat."
[67] Observe the "conspectus sententiarum" in Kurfess' edition (20 f.).
[68] H. Jordan, o.c. 1.

are true to the historical situation.[69] Perhaps they do well to re-
nounce. However, let the argument go on to dates and facts. What
will be said if the *Suasoriae* can be induced to disclose flagrant
anachronisms, of more kinds than one?

It is best to concentrate on *Ep.* II, the more vulnerable, if only
because it is longer and wordier. The author seems to betray an
acquaintance with definite passages in the historical writings of Sallust.

The consul Cotta proclaims "multa cura summo imperio inest"
(*Hist.* II. 47. 14). The *Suasoria* has the "sententia" in a diluted and
debilitated form—"equidem ego sic apud animum meum statuo:
cuicumque in sua civitate amplior inlustriorque locus quam aliis est,
ei magnam curam esse rei publicae" (II. 10. 4).[70] Again, Philippus in
his oration says "ubi malos praemia secuntur, haud facile quisquam
bonus est" (*Hist.* I. 77. 9). The *Suasoria* presents "malitia praemiis
exercetur: ubi ea dempseris, nemo omnium gratuito malus est" (II.
8. 3).[71] Which is the original? Surely the former. The copyist may, or
may not, have got the notion of "gratuito malus" from *Cat.* 16. 3:
"scilicet ne per otium torpescerent manus aut animus, gratuito potius
malus atque crudelis erat." Anyhow, he seems to be exploiting and
perverting the gnomic utterance in the *Historiae*.

Again, Sallust speaks of the new men "qui antea per virtutem
soliti erant nobilitatem antevenire" (*Jug.* 4. 7). *Ep.* II can produce
"nobilis ignobilem anteibat" (II. 5. 3) and "virtute anteire alius alium
properabit" (II. 8. 2). Unexceptionable, at first sight. Yet one wonders.
Is there not adaptation and variation? And Sallust happens not to
use the verb "anteo" in the first monograph.

These items may not convince everybody. No matter. There is a
single sentence that no plea or artifice can rescue. It occurs in the
exordium. Brief exegesis of the whole context may prove variously
instructive.

Scio ego, quam difficile atque asperum factu sit consilium dare regi aut
imperatori, postremo quoiquam mortali, quoius opes in excelso sunt, quippe
cum et illis consultorum copiae adsint neque de futuro quisquam satis cal-

---

[69] W. Steidle, *Hermes*, Einzelschriften 3 (1958), 100 f.

[70] The parallel is not registered in Vretska's commentary.

[71] Sallust happens to have "malitia" only in *Jug.* 22. 2. As for "demo" (a
favourite of the imitators), the figures are: *Cat.*: 0; *Jug.*: 1; *Hist.*: 4.

lidus satisque prudens sit. quin etiam saepe prava magis quam bona consilia prospere eveniunt, quia plerasque res fortuna ex libidine sua agitat. sed mihi studium fuit adulescentulo rem publicam capessere, atque in ea cognoscenda multam magnamque curam habui.

First, some small points. "Scio ego," thus does Marius begin (*Jug.* 85. 1, from Cato). Sallust has "nihil tam asperum neque tam difficile" (*Cat.* 40. 4), but never "asperum factu" (cf. above). "Postremo" in the sense of "denique" is Sallustian, but "mortalis" in the singular crops up first in *Jug.* 72. 2; 92. 2. "Consultor" is characteristic, but of the later Sallust (*Jug.* 3; *Hist.* 3). As for "multam magnamque curam," that, as suggested above, looks like an attempt at archaic naïveté.

It is right and proper to have at the outset an allusion to the "lubido" of Fortuna (cf. *Ep.* I. 1. 1): here the word "agito" is dragged in. And, in relation to Caesar, "in excelso" appears sheer felicity. In the Sallustian speech Caesar refers with disdain to persons of low degree "qui demissi in obscuro vitam habent" and goes on to mention by contrast "qui magno imperio praediti in excelso aetatem agunt" (*Cat.* 51. 12).

The phrase is worth attention. It means "elevated and conspicuous." Thus, in the literal sense, "iusserunt simulacrum Iovis facere maius et in excelso conlocare" (Cicero, *In Cat.* III. 20); "in excelso autem Tigranocerta" (Pliny, *NH* VI. 26), contrasted with "in campis iuxta Araxen Artaxata." But, used metaphorically, it is very rare. Perhaps only in Seneca, who, in reference to "beatae vitae magnitudo," says "scies illam in excelso, sed volenti penetrabilem" (*Epp.* 64. 5).

It is therefore a compelling inference that the author knows the passage in Sallust. And, typically, he twists it, not in the better way. Sallust's Caesar speaks of persons "in excelso." The imitator has "postremo quoiquam mortali cuius opes in excelso sunt." [72] Not felicitous. If anybody cared, it could perhaps be defended (but hardly commended) by recourse to Valerius Maximus on Pompeius—"opes privato fastigio excelsiores" (I. 6. 12).

And now, at last, the deciding point. Sallust in the first monograph made allusion to his political career—"sed ego adulescentulus initio sicuti plerique studio ad rem publicam latus sum, ibique multa mihi

---

[72] Vretska's rendering is "überhaupt jeglichem Menschen, der auf der Höhe seiner Macht steht." Not quite correct for "in excelso," which signifies an elevation above other people.

advorsa fuere" (*Cat.* 3. 3). The historian, writing in 42, in his middle forties, is looking back a long way, to an earlier and totally different phase of his existence. The impostor innocently takes over the phrase and produces "sed mihi studium fuit adulescentulo rem publicam capessere" (II. 1. 3). If Sallust wrote that in 50, he was still close to his début, and absurd.

For a valid comparison, the exordium of the *Dialogus* can be cited. Reporting a conversation he had heard in A.D. 74 or 75, Tacitus says that he was then "admodum adulescens" (*Dial.* 1. 2). Absurd, if Tacitus were writing (as some have fancied) only a few years later, in A.D. 80.

It is a dismal reflection that the significance of this item escaped notice through long years and exhaustive investigations. It has only recently been detected and put to proper use.[73] After this patent and inept imitation of the *Bellum Catilinae,* nothing more should remain to be said.

None the less, faith appears to persist.[74] It is necessary to go on. Next, therefore, anachronism in the use of political terminology.

VIII

Sallust links the notions of "nobilitas" and "factio" again and again, obsessively. Even at the foreign town of Lepcis there has to be a "homo nobilis factiosus" (*Jug.* 77. 1). According to Sallust, "nobilitas factione magis pollebat" (*Jug.* 41. 6). However, so it happens, he nowhere admits "factio nobilitatis." That locution occurs twice in the pamphlet (II. 2. 4; 8. 6). If it was congenial to Sallust as early as 50, how did he manage to keep off it later on?

After several sallies against the *nobiles,* the author rises to a climax and denounces the leaders of the "factio," Bibulus, Ahenobarbus and Cato (II. 9. 1–3). Then follows a description of the rest of the party, with two names as typical:

---

[73] A. Dihle, *Mus.Helv.* XI (1954), 126 ff.

[74] W. Steidle contests the imitation and argues against any close resemblance between the two passages (o.c. 101 f.); but he does not face the chronological absurdity in the *Epistula.* His view is accepted, summarily, by K. Büchner (o.c. 389); and it is developed by K. Vretska in his commentary, with appeal to the unpublished dissertation of G. Dietz.

reliqui de factione sunt inertissimi nobiles, in quibus sicut in titulo nihil est additamenti. L. Postumii M. Favonii mihi videntur quasi magnae navis supervacuanea onera esse: ubi salvi pervenere usui sunt; si quid adversi coortum est, de illeis potissimum iactura fit quia pretii minimi sunt (9. 4).

The passage calls for careful scrutiny.[75] Favonius is the faithful friend and adherent of Cato, a name preserved for praise or blame in history and letters. Postumius is another matter: a minor character, albeit something of an orator and a strong partisan at the beginning of the Civil War (if he is to be held identical with the T. Postumius of *Brutus* 269). The name of Postumius has seemed sure guarantee of a good source, indeed contemporaneous.[76] Yet, it will be suitably re-called, late, inferior or fraudulent writers can transmit items of great value about persons seldom or never on record in the extant literature. For example, the *Historia Augusta*.[77] And, for that matter, Postumius and Favonius occur together in a letter of Cicero in 49 (*Ad Att.* VII. 15. 2).

There is something else. As the passage runs, the two men appear to be comprised in the group of "inertissimi nobiles": the rest of the "factio," mere passengers of no substance who can easily be jettisoned. Now Favonius is a municipal man, from Tarracina.[78] He cannot be styled *nobilis*. The term, though not legal or technical, is restricted to the descendants of consular families.[79]

That looks bad. Most commentators or translators clearly reckon Favonius and Postumius among the *nobiles*.[80] Some scholars, it is true, the difficulty now emerging to notice, are disposed to wonder whether the context irretrievably imposes the conclusion.[81] Yet there

---

[75] For the argument here summarised, see *Mus.Helv.* XV (1958), 50 ff.; XIX (1962), 177 ff. It is accepted by A. Ernout, *Pseudo-Salluste* (Budé, 1962), 12.

[76] E. Meyer, o.c. 573; L. R. Taylor, o.c. 185 f.; 234.

[77] *Tacitus* (1958), 796.

[78] *ILS* 879 (Tarracina), cf. *Mus.Helv.* XV (1958), 53.

[79] Disputed by W. Steidle (o.c. 101), with appeal to H. Strasburger, *R-E* XVIII, 786 f.—whose views do not support him. On the contrary.

[80] e.g., H. Jordan, o.c. 26 f.; E. Meyer, o.c. 571; G. Carlsson, o.c. 61; L. R. Taylor, o.c. 156.

[81] E Malcovati, *Athenaeum* XXXVI (1958), 176; D. C. Earl, *Mus.Helv.* XVI (1959), 152; M. Gelzer, *Caesar*[6] (1960), 167; K. Büchner, o.c. 389; K. Vretska ad loc.; D. R. Shackleton Bailey, *CQ* X[2] (1960), 256; L. Ferrero, *Riv.fil.* XXXIX (1961), 438.

would appear to be only one remedy. It is a change in the text, proposed long ago by Orelli, but admitted by only one editor in the recent age.[82] Orelli read "in quibus sicut in titulo nihil est. additamenta L. Postumii M. Favonii mihi videntur," etc. That might be supported by a passage later on in the *Suasoria*, "homines nobiles cum paucis senatoriis, quos additamenta factionis habent" (II. 11. 6). Compare also Cicero, *Pro Sestio* 68: "Ligus iste nescio qui, additamentum inimicorum meorum."

On this showing, however, the "reliqui de factione" are left anonymous: Postumius and Favonius belong to a new category, outside it, introduced abruptly. That is to say, the emendation is illicit, for it clashes with the whole context. The author is talking about the "factio nobilitatis" (8. 6). At first in general terms (8. 7), but then he proceeds "sed quid ego plura quasi de ignotis memorem?" (9. 1). The names follow, first of all the three leaders. The author gives no sign that he is proposing to furnish names and details about persons not comprised in the "factio."

Moreover, there is a clear sequence of thought linking the two sentences. In the first are described "inertissimi nobiles," who contribute nothing—"in quibus . . . nihil additamenti est." The second exemplifies the class, with the names of Postumius and Favonius, who can be thrown overboard because they are of no value—"quia pretii minimi sunt."

Emendation has sometimes been invoked, be it noted, to save the other author from "oblivio interfecit" (I. 4. 1) and "factu haud obscurum" (I. 8. 4). If it were to be conceded here, perhaps the objection falls, the fellow is redeemed.[83] But not for long. Enquiry brings up anomalies in the use of political language.

A pair of telling examples has recently been put on record.[84] The author furnishes a clear case of "gloria" used in a bad sense—"ubi gloria honorem . . . vincit" (II. 7. 6). That lacks parallel in the language of the time, as does the use of "auctoritas" in the expression "ergo in primis auctoritatem pecuniae demito" (II. 7. 10).

This path is promising. The author addresses the proconsul of

---

[82] viz., V. Paladini in 1952. Accepted with conviction by A. Rostagni, *Riv.fil.* XXXVI (1958), 102 f.

[83] It will be noted that Vretska does not accept the emendation.

[84] D. C. Earl, o.c. 154 ff.

Gaul as "imperator" (II. 6. 6; 12. 1)—and nobody seems to mind. The matter is worth looking into.

In the common usage of this age, "imperator" develops as a normal designation for holders of *imperium* abroad.[85] Various distinctions can be drawn. Thus, in the first instance, "imperator" with an epithet. Catullus ironically hails Caesar as "imperator unice" (29. 11); and Cicero, likewise not in a friendly way, interpellates the proconsul of Macedonia, "praeclare imperator" (*In Pisonem* 91). And, in this *Suasoria*, there is no call or need to challenge "te oro hortorque ne clarissimus imperator, Gallica gente subacta . . . patiaris" (II. 12. 5).

The vocative standing by itself is another matter. It is natural and normal from a soldier or centurion to his general, as in Caesar (*BC* III. 91. 3), or in the *Bellum Africum* (35. 4), or in later writers. So the loyal soldiers who knew Tiberius of old, "videmus te, imperator" (Velleius II. 104. 4), or the Caesarian veteran in an anecdote, "meministi, inquit, imperator" (Seneca, *De Ben.* V. 24. 1). It is also appropriate when the envoys of the insurgent Manlius make humble appeal to Marcius Rex, the commander of an army—"deos hominesque testamur, imperator" (*Cat.* 33. 1).

So far so good. But what, be it asked, is the decent form of address when one of the better sort (whether or no he has just forfeited a seat in the high assembly) indites a missive to a proconsul, be it private or destined for wide publicity? The superscription of a genuine document might run "C. Caesari imp.": compare Cicero in a letter that was meant to be more than a letter, "M. Cicero s.d. Lentulo imp." (*Ad fam.* I. 9). But Sallust (or another), in exhortation of the proconsul, would say "C. Caesar," not "imperator."

In contrast, the insensitive impostor—"quo tibi, imperator, maiore cura fideique amici et multa praesidia paranda sunt" (II. 6. 6); "forsitan, imperator, perlectis litteris desideres" (12. 1).[86] These passages have nothing to do with war or conquest; and the author does not conceive of himself as being with Caesar in the field.

If this objection be held cogent, a question arises. Why was not the impropriety seen and scourged? Sobering thoughts occur. The author of the *Suasoria* is out of focus. So are many other people,

---

[85] cf. *Historia* VII (1958), 180.

[86] For "perlectis litteris," cf. *Cat.* 47. 3—in reference not to a letter but to letters.

misled by conventional beliefs and prone to accept a predestinate and monarchic Caesar or acclaim in Sallust a fervour of personal devotion that no normal Roman would have felt for the proconsul of Gaul.

IX

Next, absurdity or anachronism in the historical situation. The author vouches for an unusual view of Sulla. He did not kill many people, "paucis interfectis ceteros beneficio quam metu retinere maluit" (II. 4. 1). Praise of Sulla on any count, let alone mercy, is rare and paradoxical anywhere in Latin literature. Some take it without qualms, others essay a forced defence.[87] In vain. The author betrays himself. Where did he get the notion, if not from Caesar's speech? When Sulla after his victory killed Damasippus and some other scoundrels, "quis non factum eius laudabat" (*Cat.* 51. 32)?

But, Caesar continues, the time for joy was short. General massacre followed, "neque prius finis iugulandi fuit quam Sulla omnis suos divitiis explevit."

The author's recollection of the classic text is hasty and defective. And, not content with his asseveration of a beneficent and compassionate Sulla, he at once goes on to draw a contrast between Sulla and the oligarchic leaders. Forty senators, he says, and besides, "multi cum bona spe adulescentes," were massacred by Cato and Domitius Ahenobarbus and the rest of the "factio"—"sicutei hostiae mactati sunt." [88] The passage has been much under discussion.[89] One defence argues a metaphorical use of "mactati," as not inappropriate to the

---

[87] M. Chouet, o.c. 93: "il n'est point exclu qu'un césarien ait cherché à préparer la voie à son chef en éveillant une certaine sympathie pour l'ancien dictateur." He continues "on le voit: l'auteur de la lettre II s'y connaît en histoire." No comment.

[88] There is a question, whether to read "a M. Catone" (Mommsen) or "M. Catoni" (Orelli). After preferring the former, Kurfess in recent editions has come round to the latter, and he is followed by Vretska.

[89] For a vigorous assault on this passage, cf. H. M. Last, o.c. 96 ff. The figure of forty senators was a difficulty—they recall the forty proscribed by Sulla (Appian, *BC* I. 95. 422). Vretska (ad loc.) has an involved explanation. He argues that the dative in "M. Catoni L. Domitio . . . mactati sunt" is deliberately ambiguous—not only "by" but "for the advantage of": hence a link between Sulla and the contemporary oligarchs.

victims of a judicial reign of terror in 52.[90] Many approve. Yet the
context does not conform to that interpretation. The comparison is
between murders—otherwise the contrast is nonsensical.[91]

The next mention of Cato and Domitius Ahenobarbus lumps them
with Calpurnius Bibulus as the leaders of the "factio" (II. 9. 1–3).
Bibulus comes first. Does he deserve that prominence? Since the summer of 51 Bibulus had been away from Rome, proconsul of Syria. In
December of 50 it was known that he had left his province, and it
was not expected that his return journey would be rapid (*Ad Att*. VII.
3. 5). In fact, he did not reach Italy until the Civil War was well
under way (ib. IX. 9. 2).

Not Bibulus, therefore. The man to denounce was the great Ap.
Claudius Pulcher, highly vulnerable, who in his own person symbolises
the combination that formed against Caesar: one of his daughters was
married to the elder son of Pompeius Magnus, another to Brutus,
the nephew of Cato (*Ad fam*. III. 4. 2). The author has missed his
cue.[92] Ap. Pulcher is the censor who expelled Sallust from the Senate.

As for Cato, there is tribute of a kind—"unius tamen M. Catonis
ingenium versutum loquax callidum haud contemno." But, he proceeds, Cato is a pupil of the Greeks, and the Greeks are no good—
"virtus vigilantia labor apud Graecos nulla sunt." The Greeks cannot teach an imperial people anything.

Now Cato, for all his addiction to abstract studies, is not to be
explained by them (cf. p. 115). The author's conception is a malicious
perversion of the literary and posthumous image—the philosopher
extolled at the expense of the practical politician. Sallust knew better.
No Roman of the time could have denied to Cato "virtus vigilantia
labor."

Various other phenomena dispel the fancy that the pamphlet is
contemporaneous. The author calmly assumes that Caesar will be in a
position to order the Roman State at his will. That is to say, is he not
presupposing the war, victory, total predominance?[93]

He proffers sundry pieces of advice. Touching the Senate, a dual
proposal, both augmentation and the secret ballot:

[90] G. Carlsson, o.c. 42 ff.

[91] A. Dihle, *Mus.Helv.* XI (1954), 130.

[92] As pointed out in *Mus.Helv.* XV (1958), 52.

[93] H. M. Last, o.c. 99.

igitur duabus rebus confirmari posse senatum puto, si numero auctus per tabellam sententiam feret. tabella obtentui erit quo magis animo libero facere audeat: in multitudine et praesidii plus et usus amplior est (II. 11. 5).

The purpose of the secret ballot is explained: to give the inferior senators a chance of speaking their mind, not under pressure from the powerful minority of the *nobilitas* and their hangers-on. At first sight, an unimpeachable motive, with negative confirmation. Oligarchs were hostile to *leges tabellariae* whether in the popular assemblies at Rome or in the *municipia* (*De legibus* III. 42).

Popular voting is one thing, the procedure of business in the Senate another. The whole notion of such a change is alien to Roman thought in this age, abhorrent to the "dignitas" of a "senator populi Romani." It reeks of the imperial epoch.

Even then, when the Senate elects magistrates and has the function of a high court of justice, the vote is open and personal, by "discessio." Observe the full and clear account of the prosecution of a proconsul (Pliny, *Epp.* II. 11). For some purposes the secret ballot was conceivable.[94] It was tried under Trajan, temporarily, for the elections to the lower magistracies. Not a success, it appears (Pliny, *Epp.* III. 20; IV. 25).

As a suspicious parallel and commentary to this proposal it can be noted that secret voting crops up in a speech of advice to an emperor, namely Maecenas to Augustus in the pages of Cassius Dio (LII. 33. 4). In that context, however, the ballot is recommended as a useful device which enables the ruler (he will be in control of the mechanism) to ascertain the true opinions of his counsellors.

No obvious connection exists between secret voting and that increase in the Senate's membership which the author promulgates in one and the same formulation. He reverts briefly to the latter proposal but eschews detail—"forsitan, imperator, perlectis litteris desideres quem numerum senatorum fieri placeat" (II. 12. 1). Nor does he bother to furnish any general plea of justification.

That is to say, a larger Senate is casually slipped in as the most natural thing in the world. Was it? One needs the facts. How and when did an enlargement of the high assembly become a subject of plausible speculation, earnest public debate, or active and political contention?

---

[94] Mommsen, *R.Staatsrecht* III (1887), 992 ff.

That subject emerged in an early season, if credit be given to
proposals which some ancient sources assign to C. Gracchus and
M. Livius Drusus. Defenders of the *Suasoria* duly make appeal to that
evidence.[95] Their enterprise is hazardous.

First, C. Gracchus according to Livy. The epitomator of Book LX
reports a law of C. Gracchus which enjoined an addition of six
hundred knights to a Senate of three hundred. The text is explicit,
doubly so—"id est ut equester ordo bis tantum virium in senatu
haberet." What is to be made of this statement? Some take it to be
the original proposal of the tribune, a mild measure (they suggest),
after opposition to which he proceeded to take the law courts from
the Senate, transferring them to equestrian jurymen.[96]

The proposal and the interpretation of it are alike repugnant to
good sense. The Roman Senate was recruited from ex-magistrates.
Why should its size be abruptly trebled? That is monstrous. An easy
explanation avails. Either Livy or his epitomator is guilty of a gross
misconception—the proposal of C. Gracchus envisaged mixed jury
courts (part senators, part knights) not an augmentation of the Roman
Senate.[97] Next, Livius Drusus in 91. The account of Appian clearly
implies an increase in the size of the Senate (*BC* I. 35. 158, cf. *De
viris illustribus* 66). But Appian may not be right. Perhaps it is only
the combined jury courts recurring once again.

However that may be, Sulla the Dictator brought the total of the
Senate to six hundred. And, for normal supplement in consonance
therewith, twenty quaestors each year. There is no hint in the next
age of anybody advocating a further increase. When that came, it
was in the direct consequence of civil war.

In 47 Caesar enrolled new senators. It was to fill the gaps caused
by casualties, so Cassius Dio states explicitly (XLII. 51. 5). Hitherto,
be it noted, Caesar's adherents came in by standing for magistracies.
Further adlections are reported by that historian under 46 and 45
(XLIII. 27. 2; 47. 3). After the revision of the rolls in 45, the total
stood at nine hundred, so Dio says (XLIII. 47. 3). That round figure, a
conventional multiple, may or may not be correct. Perhaps a little too

---

[95] Thus K. Vretska, o.c. I, 68 f.

[96] Notably H. M. Last, *CAH* IX (1932), 52 f.

[97] Plutarch, *C. Gracchus* 5, cf. *Compar.* 2.

high.[98] The inflated and utterly scandalous Senate of the Triumvirs is said to have exceeded a thousand (Dio LII. 42. 1; Suetonius, *Divus Aug.* 35. 1).

Why the increase beyond six hundred? In the first place, to reward partisans. No need to play down that motive. But the Dictator was thinking of the future. Hence forty quaestors instead of twenty. Also a doubling of the praetors, sixteen for 44 and for 43. When Sulla arranged things there were ten provinces. In the meantime, apart from Caesar's conquest of Gaul, three more had accrued by 50. The Dictator was providing for still more, for a system of two consular and sixteen praetorian provinces.[99]

These provisions are coherent and intelligible, the product of events, not somebody's forecast or project. Caesar, if concord held, may have had a programme of legislation for his second consulship. No trace of it emerges in the public debates of 51 and 50, or in any writings. Nor does Caesar in the books *De bello civili* let drop a hint or advance any claims about reforms thwarted by the malice and folly of his adversaries.[100] All that he has to say in an interchange with Metellus Scipio in 48 is "quietem Italiae pacem provinciarum salutem imperii" (*BC* III. 57. 4).

Whatever the proconsul of Gaul may in secret have meditated, whatever the aspirations of his various adherents, an increase of the Senate above six hundred can have had no place. To enlarge the Senate was invidious—and not then seen to be in any way desirable. Caesar Augustus in a reorganized State was able to manage with the old total.

For the author of the hortatory epistle, the consequence is damaging and damning. He starts from the presupposition that Caesar will be in complete control of the Roman State; and, taking it for granted that the Senate is to be augmented, he betrays foreknowledge of what happened as the sequel of war and dictatorship. That is enough.

By introducing projects, this "Sallustius personatus" goes beyond the normal run of open letters to rulers. Those documents are generally

---

[98] cf. *BSR* Papers XIV (1938), 11.

[99] ib. 9.

[100] As firmly argued by J. H. Collins, *AJP* LXXX (1959), 118.

confined to the enunciation of truths that all men know and concede. It is idle to complain. And it would be frivolous to observe that the advice which Caesar needed in 50 is also of the most obvious—how to avoid either political extinction or a civil war.[101]

This *Suasoria* (so many have believed) reflected, faithful and vivid, ideas and aspirations of the year 50, the issues and the personalities. That turns out a delusion. On various counts the pamphlet betrays a later date. It knows and uses the writings of the historian Sallust; it sins against the political terminology of the time; and, under guise of counsel to Caesar, it puts out proposals that no senator could ever have entertained.

X

What manner of man is the author? It is worth observing how he presents himself. He adopts a conventional role, as one of those who furnish counsel "regi aut imperatori" (II. 1. 1). His attitude is that of a scholar or thinker. About which, he makes a profession or avowal—"postquam mihi aetas ingeniumque adolevit, haud ferme armis atque equis corpus exercui, sed animum in litteris agitavi" (II. 10. 2). Further, he goes on to extol the fruits of his studies—"atque ego in ea vita multa legendo atque audiendo ita comperi, omnia regna, item civitates et nationes," etc. (II. 10. 3).

The counsellor thus parades a contrast between himself and the man of action and power. What is one to make of the admission "haud ferme armis atque equis"? Not every aspirant to the senatorial career in the last age of the Republic claimed (or indeed required) much in the way of military training. But who of the Romans would think of advertising a deficiency in that field? [102]

A senator's previous experience with the armies of the Roman

---

101 The difficulties of composing to order an "open letter" to Caesar were borne in upon Cicero in 45. He refers to addresses of Aristotle and of Theopompus to Alexander—"sed quid simile?" (*Ad Att.* XII. 40. 2, cf. further XIII. 27. 1; 28. 2 f.). He clearly had no Latin model before him. Hence, to be sure, an argument that the *Suasoriae* had not been published by their author Sallust (cf. K. Vretska, o.c. I, 73).

102 For the ineptitude of the author in relation to Caesar, cf. H. M. Last, o.c. 96.

People often emerges only in a casual fashion. Thus Cicero's service in the *Bellum Italicum* (*Phil.* XII. 27). Other persons of equestrian origin, lacking resplendent gifts of eloquence, or such a plenitude of "gratia" as is credibly attributed to Atticus (Nepos, *Vita Attici* 6. 2), would do well not to neglect the various benefits accruing from the military tribunate, from a post on the staff of a proconsul, or from a quaestorship in one of the armed provinces. Thus, illustrating all three, Cn. Plancius of Atina (p. 28). Sallust was put in charge of a legion in 49 (Orosius VI. 15. 8). Not, perhaps, his first sight of Roman soldiers.

Essaying to tender useful advice to the conqueror of Gaul, no man in his senses would deprecate "arma et equi," or claim merit from the reading of books. And there were other things to avoid.

When appealing to Caesar, the author duly makes his bow to Fortuna at the outset—"plerasque res fortuna ex libidine sua agitat" (II. 1. 2). That is Sallust's doctrine, and Caesar's (p. 246). Moving towards his conclusion, however, he divagates and retracts. He uses portentous and menacing language, and calls down insanity on Caesar as a punishment should Caesar neglect his duty to Rome—"profecto, si id accidat, neque tibi nox neque dies curam animi sedaverit quin insomniis exercitus furibundus atque amens alienata mente feraris" (II. 12. 6).[103] What is it that emboldens him to this dire vaticination? He explains it at once. It is his faith in divine providence—"namque mihi pro vero constat omnium mortalium vitam divino numine invisier" (II. 12. 7).

There is worse in this passage than a failing of tact or the assertion of a novel and contradictory doctrine. What is to be made of the form "invisier"? Some scholars are silent. Others find a way out. The phrase might be a quotation from one of the old dramatists.[104] Who can tell? Better, an archaist going over the edge.

---

[103] The "insomnia" are sleeplessness, not dreams, cf. K. Vretska ad loc. Is not the author drawing on Sallust's picture of Catilina—"namque animus impurus, dis hominibusque infestus, neque vigiliis neque quietibus sedari poterat" (*Cat.* 15. 4)? Sallust has "furibundus" once only, describing him (31. 9). But "amens" is not Sallustian; and "alienatus" with the meaning "insane" happens not to be attested before Livy X. 29. 2; "veluti alienata mente."

[104] W. H. Friedrich, *Hermes* LXXVI (1941), 118.

Sallust avoids "numen." Also, be it added, "fatum," except when he reported the oracle about the destiny of the three Cornelii (*Cat.* 47. 2). Now the author of this *Suasoria* makes play with it—"si morbo iam aut fato huic imperio secus accidat" (II. 13. 6). The other fellow had contemplated "fatum excidii" for Rome (I. 5. 2).

Not Sallust, therefore. Where, then, shall these impersonators be lodged?

Sallust was all the rage in the time of Fronto and Gellius, with a plethora of admirers, adepts and experts (p. 300). That might be the season. Some of the linguistic phenomena induced critics to deny an origin as early as the epoch of Caesar Augustus. But, as has been indicated above, there is another explanation. They may derive from the intention of writers who wanted to be strange and wilful, as Sallust was. Such is the habit of pastiche, and its nemesis is to overdo the manner.

The *Suasoriae* stand outside time, except that they must have been fabricated later than the *Historiae* of Sallust. Nothing therefore forbids an ascription to the period of Augustus or Tiberius for the first pamphlet (in the manuscript order). Possibly for the second as well.

Bogus speeches of Cicero were circulating in the schools of rhetoric. Why not also some speeches or letters of Sallust? At least, the *Invectiva in Ciceronem* probably belongs about this time. Cassius Severus had no high opinion of Sallust as an orator, according to the elder Seneca (*Controv.* III, *praef.* 8). Perhaps he was influenced by products he unconsciously took to be genuine.

XI

Reverting to the *Invective*, the argument comes full circle. A passage in that pamphlet denouncing Cicero is found to stand, almost word for word, in the second *Suasoria*. As follows:

In Ciceronem 3. 5: "cuius nulla pars corporis a turpitudine vacat, lingua vana, manus rapacissimae, gula immensa, pedes fugaces: quae honeste nominari non possunt, inhonestissima."

Ep. II. 9. 2: "an L. Domiti magna vis est, quoius nullum membrum a flagitio aut facinore vacat? lingua vana, manus cruentae, pedes fugaces: quae honeste nominari nequeunt, inhonestissima."

At once a problem of priority arises—or rather, no problem at all for a convinced champion who is persuaded that each document is true to its ostensible date, that both were composed by Sallust. He will claim that each confirms the other. They stand or fall together.[105]

To salvage the *Suasoria*, it might have been wise and easier to jettison the *Invective*. Perhaps it is now too late for that sacrifice to be of any use. Attention has recently been drawn to a third parallel passage.[106] It comes from a lost speech of the orator Lycurgus, and it is preserved in Rutilius Lupus, a rhetorician of the early imperial age.[107] As follows:

cuius omnes corporis partes ad nequitiam sunt appositissimae: oculi ad petulantem lasciviam, manus ad rapinam, venter ad aviditatem, membra quae non possumus honeste appellare ad omne genus corruptelae, pedes ad fugam.

The confrontation is instructive and damaging. Both "Sallustian" passages go back ultimately to Lycurgus—why not by the channel of Rutilius Lupus? If so, both go down together.

As concerns priority, that hardly matters. Authenticity is the question. However, it seems pretty clear that the author of *Ep.* II is copying the *Invective*. He makes it more Sallustian by duly substituting "nequeunt" for "non possunt" and "flagitio aut facinore" for "turpitudine." [108] As has been shown, this writer was in the habit of improving on Sallust himself.

Even without Rutilius Lupus, those of the faithful who yoked together *Invective* and *Suasoria* were in for tribulation. Only Gibbon can do justice. Discussing the "defence of two obsolete legions, the least absurd of which staggered the well-disciplined credulity of a Franciscan Friar," he observes "Moyle wishes no greater penance to the believers of the Thundering Legion than that they may also believe the Martyrdom of the Thebaean Legion." [109]

---

[105] K. Büchner, o.c. 30: "Echtheit des Briefes und der Invektive hängen eng miteinander zusammen." Let it be so.

[106] R. G. M. Nisbet, *JRS* XLVIII (1958), 30 ff.

[107] Rutilius I. 18 (*Rhet.lat.min.*, ed. Halm, p. 11).

[108] R. G. M. Nisbet, o.c. 31.

[109] E. Gibbon, *Miscellaneous Works* II (1796), 613. For "legions" read "legends."

XII

The *Invective* helps to drag down
Ep. II. What then is to be said about *Ep.* I? On a first inspection, its
matter discloses nothing flagrant or absurd. The author has done well
not to spread himself on detailed advice to Caesar. Apart from much
verbiage about moral regeneration, his only definite proposals concern military service and provision for veterans (I. 8. 6). There might
be a temptation to keep this document.[110]

To what end and benefit—and with what degree of confidence? The
author conceives of Caesar's position as absolute, he equates him with
"rerum potentes" (I. 1. 5 f.), he addresses him as "imperator" (I. 2. 1).
Nor can adaptation of a Sallustian passage escape notice—"orta omnia
intereunt" (I. 5. 2), from "omniaque orta occidunt" (*Jug.* 2. 3).[111]
Further, in common with the other adept, he exhibits a number of
those preciosities, strained locutions, or perverse Sallustianisms that
tell their own story.

Nothing therefore precludes applying the primary and negatory
argument—the date and origin of the style which Sallust devised for
the writing of history. Let the two go out together, to plague and
molest no more.

Caesar and monarchy, that was a theme in the schools of rhetoric,
and men knew what plea and tone to adopt when they were to speak
"C. Caesari suadentes regnum" (Quintilian III. 8. 47). The earlier
dictator was also put to good employ,

> consilium dedimus Sullae, privatus ut altum
> dormiret (Juvenal I. 16 f.).

It is unfortunate that no letter or oration of the historian Cornelius
Sisenna should be extant, imparting sage counsel to his political leader
(whether he urged abdication or continuance in the supreme power).

---

[110] Thus H. M. Last, having demolished *Ep.* II, made a firm pronouncement about the other pamphlet in postscript—"the evidence in its favour,
which to me appears almost conclusive" (*CQ* XVIII [1924], 84). That was
abated later, cf. the indication of "greater scepticism" about *Ep.* I in
Mélanges Marouzeau (1948), 357.

[111] A. Dihle, o.c. 128. Contested (it was to be expected) by the faithful,
e.g., W. Steidle, o.c. 102 f.; K. Vretska, ad loc.

The document might have carried novel views about Roman history, or items foreshadowing the destiny of Pompeius or of Caesar with a remarkable precision. Hence a welcome confirmation of certain anecdotes in biography or legend.[112] The old-fashioned style would likewise appeal. Archaism coupled with devotion to Sulla, who would be so obtuse as to deny?

Pseudo-Sisenna might not have been easy to unmask.[113] Next to nothing exists for confrontation. Sallust's style and language condemns the pair of impostors. They may continue to afford pleasure, but only to fanciers of the spurious; and they retain a modest utility as texts to illustrate the art of pastiche and impersonation.[114] For the rest, "quod vides perisse perditum ducas." [115]

---

[112] For dubious items about the young Pompeius and the young Caesar, see p. 185.

[113] For the "spurcum additamentum" in Apuleius, rashly claimed as a piece from the *Historiae Milesiae* of Sisenna, see E. Fraenkel, *Eranos* LI (1954), 152 ff.

[114] There was less of literary fraud among the Romans than among the Greeks. A. Gudeman suggested the reasons—much of Latin literature is imitation anyhow, the Romans were sober and practical, and their efforts went to the embellishment of their national history (*TAPA* XXV [1894], 140 ff.). That scholar dismissed the *Suasoriae* in one sentence.

[115] In the recent age "Sallustforschung," so it is said, has been "eine eigentlich deutsche Angelegenheit" (H. Fuchs, *Mus.Helv.* IV [1947], 185). That is not quite fair to Italy. Scholars and publicists in both countries have been assiduous, notably in urging the claims of *Invectiva* and *Suasoriae* (and, meanwhile, no proper edition of the monographs, scant understanding for the *Historiae*). "Quo usque tandem?"

If the arguments that have been advanced in this Appendix, pertinaciously, but from honest conviction and from respect for the virtues of C. Sallustius Crispus, senator and historian, were to be held valid, the consequences would have a general application. They concern the various criteria of authenticity—language and style, an author's personality, the historical context. Also, an enormous mass of writing about Sallust (exact erudition no less than woolly edification) may go "with hideous ruin and combustion down/to bottomless perdition."

BIBLIOGRAPHY

BIBLIOGRAPHY

The standard manual is A. D. Leeman, *A Systematical Bibliography of Sallust* (1879–1950), published at Leyden in 1952. Further, one will note the items registered in the Teubner edition of A. Kurfess (ed. 3, 1957, XVI ff.; 199 f.); also the selective "Fachbericht" on 1945–1956 of H. Dieterich, *Gymnasium* LXIV (1957), 533 ff. For Pseudo-Sallust, *Invectiva* and *Suasoriae*, see especially the annotation to Appendix II.

In these days the superfetation of bibliography often tends to obscure the ancient texts, with doxology and "the history of the problem" instead of the direct approach to the author. Sallust has suffered especial damage—the bulk of writing is enormous, and much of it has been concerned with the *Suasoriae*. If modern works are to be cited, "for use and not for ostentation," there ought to be strict selection, and the reader deserves some help. The following list comprises, with name and date and title, the writings cited in the footnotes. That is to say, articles in learned journals, in collected papers and the like (whatever the subject), also books and dissertations on Sallust—but not the general works on Roman history and Latin literature.

In the footnotes, when the sign "o.c." occurs, it stands for a title previously furnished in the same chapter at its first citation; and publications by the author of this volume are generally referred to without his name.

Afzelius, A. "Das Ackerverteilungsgesetz des P. Servilius Rullus." *Class. et Med.* III (1940), 214.

——. "Die politische Bedeutung des jüngeren Cato." *Class. et Med.* IV (1941), 100.

Alheit, L. "Charakterdarstellung bei Sallust." *Neue Jahrbücher* XLIII (1919), 17.

Alexander, W. H. "*Nullus argento color* (Horace, *Odes* 2. 2. 1–4)." *TAPA* LXXIV (1943), 192.

Allen, W. "Caesar's *Regnum* (Suet. *Iul.* 9. 2)." *TAPA* LXXXIV (1953), 227.

——. "Sallust's Political Career." *Studies in Philology* LI (1954), 1.

Amundsen, L. "Notes to the Preface of Livy." *Symb.Osl.* XXV (1947), 31.

Arnaldi, F. "L'autenticità delle due Epistole Sallustiane ad Caesarem." *Stud.-it.fil.class.* VI² (1928), 307.

Avenarius, W. "Sallust und der rhetorische Schulunterricht." *Rendiconti Inst.lomb.* LXXXIX–LXC (1956), 343.

———. "Die griechischen Vorbilder des Sallust." *Symb.Osl.* XXXIII (1957), 48.

Badian, E. "P. Decius P. f. Subulo." *JRS* XLVI (1956), 91.

———. "Caepio and Norbanus." *Historia* VI (1957), 318.

———. "The early career of A. Gabinius (*Cos.* 58 B.C.)." *Philologus* CIII (1959), 87.

———. "From the Gracchi to Sulla (1940–1959). *Historia* XI (1962), 197.

———. "Waiting for Sulla." *JRS* LII (1962), 47.

Baehrens, W. A. "Sallust als Historiker, Politiker und Tendenzschriftsteller." *Neue Wege zur Antike* IV (1926), 35.

Bailey, D. R. Shackleton. "The Roman Nobility in the Second Civil War." *CQ* X² (1960), 253.

Balsdon, J. P. V. D. "The Ides of March." *Historia* VII (1958), 80.

Bauhofer, K. *Die Komposition der Historien Sallusts.* Diss. München, 1935.

Bennett, W. H. "The Death of Sertorius and the Coin." *Historia* X (1961), 459.

Berve, H. "Sertorius." *Hermes* LXIV (1929), 199.

Bikermann, E. "La lettre de Mithridate dans les *Histoires* de Salluste." *Rev.ét.lat.* XXIV (1946), 131.

Bloch, G. "M. Aemilius Scaurus. Étude sur l'histoire des partis au VII° siècle de Rome." *Univ. de Paris, Bibliothèque de la Faculté des Lettres* XXV (1909), 1.

Bloch, H. "The Structure of Sallust's *Historiae:* the Evidence of the Fleury Manuscript." *Didascaliae.* Studies in Honor of Anselm M. Albareda (1961), 61.

Boissier, G. *La conjuration de Catilina* (1905).

———. "Les prologues de Salluste." *Journal des Savants* 1903, 59.

Bolaffi, E. *Sallustio e la sua fortuna nei secoli* (1949).

Bonnet, M. "Les *Histoires* de Salluste: quels en devaient être le sujet et l'étendue?" *Rev.ét.anc.* II (1900), 117.

Bosselaar, D. E. *Quomodo Sallustius historiam belli Jugurthini conscripserit.* Diss. Utrecht, 1915.

Broughton, T. R. S. "Was Sallust fair to Cicero?" *TAPA* LXVII (1936), 34.

———. "More Notes on Roman Magistrates." *TAPA* LXXIX (1948), 63.

Büchner, K. "Der Aufbau von Sallusts Bellum Jugurthinum." *Hermes,* Einzelschriften, Heft 9 (1953).

———. *Sallust* (1960).

Calabi, I. "I commentarii di Silla come fonte storica." *Mem.Acc.Lincei*⁸ III. 5 (1950), 247.

Calder, W. M. "Irony in Horace *Carm.* 2. 2: *nullus argento color est avaris.*" *CP* LVI (1961), 175.

Carcopino, J. "Le culte des Cereres et les Numides." *Rev.hist.* CLVIII (1928), 1 = *Aspects mystiques de la Rome païenne* (1941), 13.

Carlsson, G. *Eine Denkschrift an Caesar über den Staat* (Lund, 1936).

Carney, T. F. "Once again Marius' Speech after Election in 108 B.C." *Symb.Osl.* XXXV (1959), 63.

———. "Cicero's Picture of Marius." *Wiener Studien* LXXIII (1960), 83.

Carolsfeld, H. Schnorr von. *Über die Reden und Briefe bei Sallust* (Leipzig, 1888).

Chantraine, H. *Untersuchungen zur römischen Geschichte am Ende des 2. Jahrhunderts v. Chr.* (Kallmünz, 1959).

Charlier, R. "La Numidie vue par Salluste. Cirta Regia, Constantine ou Le Kef?" *L'ant.class.* XIX (1950), 289.

Chouet, M. *Les lettres de Salluste à César* (1950).

Cichorius, C. "Das Offizierkorps eines römischen Heeres aus dem Bundes-genossenkriege." *Römische Studien* (1922), 130.

———. "Historische Studien zu Varro." Ib. 189.

Clausen, W. "Notes on Sallust's *Historiae.*" *AJP* LXVIII (1947), 293.

Collins, J. H. "Caesar and the Corruption of Power." *Historia* IV (1955), 445.

Courtois, C. "La Thala de Salluste." *Recueil des notices et mémoires de la soc.arch.de Constantine* LXIX (1955–1956), 55.

Dahlmann, H. "Sallusts politische Briefe." *Hermes* LXIX (1934), 380.

——— and R. Heisterhagen. "Varronische Studien I: Zu den Logistorici." *Abh.der Mainzer Akademie* 4 (1957).

De Sanctis, G. "Sallustio e la guerra di Giugurtha." *Problemi di storia antica* (1932), 187.

Dihle, A. "Zu den epistolae ad Caesarem senem." *Mus.Helv.* XI (1954), 126.

———. "Analogie und Attizismus." *Hermes* LXXXV (1957), 170.

———. Review of E. Skard, *Sallust und seine Vorgänger* (1956). *Gnomon* XXIX (1957), 592.

Douglas, A. E. "*Clausulae* in the *Rhetorica ad Herennium* as Evidence of its Date." *CQ²* X (1960), 65.

Drexler, H. "Sallust." *Neue Jahrbücher* IV (1928), 390.

———. Review of K. Büchner, *Sallust* (1960). *Gnomon* XXXIII (1961), 567.

Earl, D. C. "Political Terminology in Epistula ad Caesarem II." *Mus.Helv.* XVI (1959), 152.

———. *The Political Thought of Sallust* (1961).

Edmar, B. *Studien zu den Epistulae ad Caesarem senem de re publica* (Lund, 1931).

Egermann, F. "Die Prooemien zu den Werken des Sallust." *Wiener S-B* CCXIV. 3 (1932).

Ehrenberg, V. "Sertorius." *Ost und West. Studien zur geschichtlichen Proble-matik der Antike* (1935), 177.

Ferrero, L. Review of K. Büchner, *Sallust* (1960). *Riv.fil.* XXXIX (1961), 438.

Fighiera, S. L. *La lingua e la grammatica di C. Crispo Sallustio* (Savona, 1896).

Fraccaro, P. "Scauriana." *Rend.Ac.Lincei*⁵ XX (1911), 169 = *Opuscula* II (1957), 125.

Fraenkel, E. Review of E. Löfstedt, *Syntactica* II (1933). *Deutsche Literaturzeitung* 1936, 884.

——. Review of M. Chouet, *Les lettres de Salluste à César* (1950). *JRS* XLI (1951), 192.

——. "The Culex." *JRS* XLII (1952), 1.

——. "A Sham Sisenna." *Eranos* LI (1954), 151.

Franke, J. "Der Angriff des M. Lepidus und M. Brutus auf das Reformwerk Sullas." *Jahrbücher für cl.Phil.* XXXIX (1893), 49.

Friedrich, W. H. "Zur altlateinischen Dichtung." *Hermes* LXXVI (1941), 113.

Frisch, H. "The First Catilinarian Conspiracy." *Class. et Med.* IX (1947), 10.

Fritz, K. von. "Sallust and the Attitude of the Roman Nobility at the Time of the Wars against Jugurtha." *TAPA* LXXIV (1943), 134.

——. "Die Bedeutung des Aristoteles für die Geschichtsschreibung." *Histoire et historiens dans l'antiquité*. Fondation Hardt, Entretiens IV (1958), 85.

Fuchs, H. "Rückschau und Ausblick im Arbeitsbereich der lateinischen Philologie." *Mus.Helv.* IV (1947), 147.

——. "Eine Doppelfassung in Ciceros Catilinarischen Reden." *Hermes* LXXXVII (1959), 463.

Funaioli, G. "C. Sallustius Crispus." *R-E* IA (1920), 1913.

——. "Nuovi orientamenti della critica Sallustiana." *Studi di letteratura antica* II. 1 (1947), 45.

Gabba, E. "Le origini della Guerra Sociale e la vita politica romana dopo l'89 a.c." *Athenaeum* XXXII (1954), 41; 293.

Gagé, J. "Hercule-Melqart, Alexandre et les Romains à Gadès." *Rev.ét.anc.* XLII (1940), 425.

Gebhardt, O. *Sallust als politischer Publizist während des Bürgerkrieges*. Diss. Halle, 1920.

Gelzer, M. "Nasicas Widerspruch gegen die Zerstörung Karthagos." *Philologus* LXXXVI (1931), 261 = *Vom römischen Staat* I (1943), 78.

——. "Hat Sertorius in seinem Vertrag mit Mithradates die Provinz Asien abgetreten?" *Phil.Woch.* 1932, 1129.

——. "War Caesar ein Staatsmann?" *Hist.Zeitschr.* CLXXVIII (1954), 449.

Gudeman, A. "Literary Fraud among the Romans." *TAPA* XXV (1894), 140.

Guilbert, D. "Salluste *Oratio Lepidi consulis* et la II° Olynthienne." *Les ét.class.* XXV (1957), 296.

Guillemin, A. "La lettre de Cicéron à Lucceius." *Rev.ét.lat.* XVI (1938), 96.

Haffter, H. "Superbia innenpolitisch." *Stud.it.fil.class.* XXVII–XXVIII (1956), 135.

Hampl, F. "Stoische Staatsethik und frühes Rom." *Hist.Zeitschr.* CLXXXIV (1957), 249.

——. "Römische Politik in republikanischer Zeit und das Problem des Sittenverfalls." *Ib.* CLXXXVIII (1959), 497.

Hands, A. R. "Sallust and *Dissimulatio*." *JRS* XLIX (1959), 56.

Hanell, K. "Bemerkungen zur der politischen Terminologie des Sallust." *Eranos* XLIII (1945), 263.

Hardy, E. G. "The Catilinarian Conspiracy in its Context: a restudy of the evidence." *JRS* VII (1917), 153. Reprinted (Oxford, Blackwell, 1924).

———. "Some Notable *Iudicia Populi* on Capital Charges." *Some Problems in Roman History* (1924), 1.

———. "The Agrarian Proposal of Rullus in 63 B.C." Ib. 68.

Heitland, W. E. "A Great Agricultural Emigration from Italy?" *JRS* VIII (1918), 34.

Helm, R. "Hieronymus' Zusätze in Eusebius' Chronik und ihr Wert für die Literaturgeschichte." *Philologus,* Supp. XXI. 2 (1929).

Henderson, M. I. *"De Commentariolo Petitionis." JRS* XL (1950), 8.

Hendrickson, G. L. "The *Memoirs* of Rutilius Rufus." *CP* XXVIII (1933), 153.

Henry, R. M. "The Roman Tradition." *Proc.Class.Ass.* XXXIV (1937), 7.

Heurgon, J. "La lettre de Cicéron à P. Sittius (Ad fam., V, 17)." *Latomus* IX (1950), 369.

Hejnic, J. "Clodius Auctor. Ein Beitrag zur sog. Sallust Invective." *Rh.Mus.* CXIX (1956), 255.

Hirschfeld, O. "Dellius ou Sallustius?" *Kl.Schr.* (1913), 780.

Hoffmann, W. "Die römische Politik des 2. Jahrhunderts und das Ende Karthagos." *Historia* IX (1960), 309.

Holborn-Bethmann, A. *De Sallustii epistula ad Caesarem senem de re publica.* Diss. Berlin, 1926.

Holroyd, M. "The Jugurthine War. Was Marius or Metellus the Real Victor?" *JRS* XVIII (1928), 1.

Howald, E. "Sallust." *Vom Geist antiker Geschichtsschreibung* (1944), 140.

Jachmann, G. "Die Invektive gegen Cicero." *Misc.Ac.Berolinensia* (1950), 235.

John, C. "Sallust über Catilinas Candidatur im Jahre 688." *Rh.Mus.* XXXI (1876), 401.

———. "Der Tag der ersten Rede Ciceros gegen Catilina." *Philologus* XLVI (1888), 650.

———. "Die Entstehungsgeschichte der catilinarischen Verschwörung." *Jahrbücher für cl.Phil.,* Supp. VIII (1876), 703.

Jordan, H. *De suasoriis quae ad Caesarem senem de re publica inscribuntur* (1868).

Klingner, F. "Über die Einleitung der Historien Sallusts." *Hermes* LXIII (1928), 165.

Kornemann, E. "Thucydides und die römische Historiographie." *Philologus* LXIII (1904), 148.

Kroll, W. "Die Sprache des Sallust." *Glotta* XV (1927), 280.

———. "Sallusts Staatsschriften." *Hermes* LXII (1927), 373.

———. "Die Entwicklung der lateinischen Schriftsprache." *Glotta* XXII (1934), 1.

Kunze, A. *Sallustiana* III (Leipzig, 1897).

Kurfess, A. "Die Invektive gegen Cicero." *Aevum* XXVIII (1954), 230.

Lämmli, F. "Sallusts Stellung zu Cato, Caesar, Cicero." *Mus.Helv.* III (1946), 94.

Laistner, M. L. W. "Sallust." *The Greater Roman Historians* (1947), 45.

La Penna, A. "L'interpretazione Sallustiana della guerra contro Giugurtha." *Annali della Scuola Normale Superiore di Pisa* XXVIII (1959), 45; 243.

———. "Il significato dei proemi Sallustiani." *Maia* XI (1959), 23; 89.

———. "L'interpretazione Sallustiana della congiura di Catilina." *Stud.it.fil.-class.* XXXI (1959), 1; 127.

———. "La lirica civile di Orazio e l'ideologia del principato." *Maia* XIII (1961), 83.

Last, H. M. "On the Sallustian *Suasoriae.*" *CQ* XVII (1923), 87; 151.

———. "A Note on the First Sallustian *Suasoria.*" *CQ* XVIII (1924), 83.

———. "Sallust and Caesar in the 'Bellum Catilinae.'" *Mélanges de philologie, de littérature et d'histoire anciennes offerts à J. Marouzeau* (1948), 355.

Latte, K. "Sallust." *Neue Wege zur Antike* II. 4 (1935).

———. Review of G. Carlsson, *Eine Denkschrift an Caesar über den Staat* (1936). *JRS* XXVII (1937), 300.

Lauckner, C. *Die künstlerischen und politischen Ziele der Monographie Sallusts über den Jugurthinischen Krieg.* Diss. Leipzig, 1911.

Leeman, A. D. *A Systematical Bibliography of Sallust (1879–1950).* (Leyden, 1952).

———. "Le genre et le style historique à Rome." *Rev.ét.lat.* XXXIII (1955), 183.

———. "Sallusts Prologe und seine Auffassung von der Historiographie." *Mnemosyne⁴* VII (1954), 323; VIII (1955), 38.

———. "Aufbau und Absicht von Sallusts Bellum Iugurthinum." *Med.der Kon.Ned. Ak. van Wetenschappen* XX. 8 (1957), 200.

Löfstedt, E. "Reminiscence and Imitation. Some Problems in Latin Literature." *Eranos* XLVII (1949), 148.

———. "A Roman Publicist and Historian." *Roman Literary Portraits* (1958), 93.

Malcovati, E. "Rassegna di studi Sallustiani." *Athenaeum* XXXVI (1958), 171.

Meier, C. "Pompeius' Rückkehr aus dem Mithridatischen Kriege und die Catilinarische Verschwörung." *Athenaeum* XL (1962), 103.

Millar, F. "Some Speeches in Cassius Dio." *Mus.Helv.* XVIII (1961), 11.

Momigliano, A. Review of B. Farrington, *Science and Politics in the Ancient World* (1939). *JRS* XXXI (1941), 149.

Moravski, C. "De oratione Philippi apud Sallustium." *Eos* XVII (1911), 135.

Münscher, K. "Xenophon in der griechisch-römischen Literatur." *Philologus,* Supp. XIII (1920).

Neumann, K. J. "Zu den Historien des Sallust, 2. Die Rede des Licinius Macer und der Principat." *Hermes* XXXII (1897), 313.

Neunheuser, J. *M. Aemilius Lepidus.* Diss. Münster, 1902.

Nisbet, R. G. M. "The *Invectiva in Ciceronem* and *Epistula Secunda* of Pseudo-Sallust." *JRS* XLVIII (1958), 30.

———. "The *Commentariolum Petitionis:* Some Arguments against Authenticity." *JRS* LI (1961), 84.

Oertel, F. "Sallusts Invektive gegen Cicero, mit einem Anhang zu Sall., Ep. ad Caes. II 4." *Rh.Mus.* XCIV (1951), 46.

Ogilvie, R. M. "Livy, Licinius Macer and the *Libri Lintei.*" *JRS* XLVIII (1958), 40.

Oppermann, H. "Das heutige Sallustbild." *Neue Jahrbücher* XI (1935), 47.

Pais, E. "M. Emilio Scauro." *Dalle guerre puniche a Cesare Augusto* I (1918), 91.

Pajk, J. "Sallust als Ethiker." *Program Wien* I (1892).

Paladini, V. *Sallustio* (1948).

Paratore, E. "Rassegna di Studi Sallustiani." *Annali della Scuola Normale Superiore di Pisa* XIX (1950), 155.

———. Review of K. Büchner, *Hermes,* Einzelschriften, Heft 9 (1953). *Maia* VII (1955), 69.

Pareti, L. *La congiura di Catilina* (Catania, 1934).

Passerini, A. "Caio Mario come uomo politico." *Athenaeum* XXII (1934), 10; 257.

Patzer, H. "Sallust und Thukydides." *Neue Jahrbücher,* N. F. IV (1941), 124.

Pepe, L. "Gli horti di Lesbia." *Giorn.it.di fil.class.* XIII (1960), 22.

———. "Lesbia madre suocera e Pompeiana." *Ib.* 97.

Perrochat, P. *Les modèles grecs de Salluste* (1949).

Pöschl, V. *Grundwerte römischer Staatsgesinnung in den Geschichtswerken des Sallust* (1940).

Rambaud, M. "Les prologues de Salluste et la démonstration morale dans son oeuvre." *Rev.ét.lat.* XXIV (1946), 115.

———. "Salluste et Trogue-Pompée." *Rev.ét.lat.* XXVI (1948), 171.

Reitzenstein, R., and E. Schwartz. "Pseudo-Sallusts Invective gegen Cicero." *Hermes* XXXIII (1898), 87.

Rostagni, A. "Cronache e commenti." *Riv.fil.* XXXVI (1958), 102.

Rudd, N. "The Names in Horace's *Satires.*" *CQ²* X (1960), 161.

Salmon, E. T. "Concerning the Second Sallustian Suasoria." *CP* XXXII (1937), 72.

———. "Notes on the Social War." *TAPA* LXXXIX (1958), 159.

Sangiacomo, L. O. *Sallustio* (1954).

Schindler, F. *Untersuchungen zur Geschichte des Sallustbildes.* Diss. Breslau, 1939.

Schörner, G. *Sallust und Horaz über den Sittenverfall und die sittliche Erneuerung Roms.* Diss. Erlangen, 1934.

Schur, W. *Sallust als Historiker* (1934).

Schwartz, E. "Die Berichte über die Catilinarische Verschwörung." *Hermes* XXXII (1897), 554 = *Ges.Schr.* II (1956), 275.

Seel, O. *Sallust von den Briefen ad Caesarem zur Coniuratio Catilinae* (1930).

——. "Die Invektive gegen Cicero." *Klio,* Beiheft XLVII (1943).

Skard, E. "Sallust als Politiker." *Symb.Osl.* IX (1930), 69.

——. "Marius' Speech in Sall. Jug. 85." *Symb. Osl.* XXI (1941), 98.

——. "Sallust und seine Vorgänger." *Symb.Osl.,* Supp. XV (1956).

Snell, B. "Die 16. Epode von Horaz und Vergils 4. Ecloge." *Hermes* LXXIII (1938), 237.

Stahl, W. *De bello Sertoriano.* Diss. Erlangen, 1907.

Steidle, W. "Sallusts historische Monographien." *Historia,* Einzelschriften, Heft 3 (1958).

Strasburger, H. "Cäsar im Urteil der Zeitgenossen." *Hist.Zeitschr.* CLXXV (1953), 225.

Syme, R. "Caesar, The Senate and Italy." *BSR Papers* XIV (1938), 1.

——. "The Allegiance of Labienus." *JRS* XXVIII (1938), 113.

——. Review of M. Gelzer, *Caesar der Staatsmann*[3] (1941). *JRS* XXXIV 1944), 92.

——. Review of E. H. Clift, *Latin Pseudepigrapha* (1945). *JRS* XXXVII (1947), 198.

——. "Missing Senators." *Historia* IV (1955), 52.

——. "A Fragment of Sallust?" *Eranos* LV (1957), 171.

——. "Obituaries in Tacitus." *AJP* LXXIX (1958), 18.

——. "Pseudo-Sallust." *Mus.Helv.* XV (1958), 46.

——. "Imperator Caesar. A Study in Nomenclature." *Historia* VII (1958), 172.

——. "Livy and Augustus." *Harvard Studies in Classical Philology* LXIV (1959), 27.

——. "Bastards in the Roman Aristocracy." *Proc.Am.Philosophical Soc.* CIV (1960), 323.

——. "The Damaging Names in Pseudo-Sallust." *Mus.Helv.* XIX (1962), 177.

——. "Two Emendations in Sallust." *Philologus* CVI (1962), 300.

Theiler, W. "Ein griechischer Historiker bei Sallust." *Navicula Chiloniensis* (1956), 144.

Thomas, S. P. "The Prologues of Sallust." *Symb.Osl.* XV–XVI (1936), 140.

Timpe, D. "Herrschaftsidee und Klientelstaatenpolitik in Sallusts Bellum Jugurthinum." *Hermes* CX (1962), 334.

Tolkiehn, J. "Zur Behandlung Ciceros durch Sallust." *Phil.Woch.* 1925, 1404.

Treves, P. "Sertorio." *Athenaeum* X (1932), 127.

Ullman, B. L. "History and Tragedy." *TAPA* LXXIII (1942), 25.

——. "Psychological Foreshadowing in the Satires of Horace and Juvenal." *AJP* LXXI (1950), 408.

Ullmann, R. "Essai sur le Catilina de Salluste." *Rev.phil.* XLII (1918), 5.

——. *La technique des discours dans Salluste, Tite-Live et Tacite* (Oslo, 1927).

Veith, G. "Zu den Kämpfen der Caesarianer in Illyrien." *Strena Buliciana* (1924), 267.

Vitelli, G. "Note ed appunti sull' autobiografia di L. Cornelio Silla." *Stud.- it.fil.class.* VI (1898), 353.

Vretska, K. "Der Aufbau des Bellum Catilinae." *Hermes* LXXII (1937), 202.

——. "Zur Chronologie des Bellum Iugurthinum." *Gymnasium* LX (1953), 339.

——. "Sallusts Selbstbekenntnis (*Bell. Cat.* 3, 3–4, 2)." *Eranos* LIII (1955), 41.

——. "Studien zu Sallusts Bellum Jugurthinum." *Wiener S-B* CCXXIX. 4 (1955).

——. "Zur Methodik der Echtheitskritik (Epistulae ad Caesarem senem)." *Wiener Studien* LXX (1957), 306.

Wagner, C. *De Sallustii prooemiorum fontibus.* Diss. Leipzig, 1910.

Walbank, F. W. "History and Tragedy." *Historia* IX (1960), 216.

Wickert, L. "Sertorius." *Rastloses Schaffen.* Festschrift für Friedrich Lammert (Stuttgart, 1954), 97.

Williams, G. W. Review of K. Büchner, *Hermes,* Einzelschriften, Heft 9 (1953). *JRS* XLIV (1954), 158.

——. Review of W. Steidle, *Historia,* Einzelschriften, Heft 3 (1958). *Gnomon* XXIII (1960), 509.

Wirz, H. "Die stoffliche und zeitliche Gliederung des bellum Jugurthinum des Sallust." *Festschrift Zürich* (1887), 1.

Wirtz, R. *Beiträge zur Catilinarischen Verschwörung.* Diss. Bonn. 1910.

Wölfflin, E. "Bemerkungen über das Vulgärlatein." *Philologus* XXXIV (1875), 137.

Wohleb, L. "Zur Abfassungszeit der Monographien Sallusts." *Phil.Woch.* 1928, 1242.

INDEX OF
PERSONAL NAMES

INDEX OF
PERSONAL NAMES

Persons are registered by their *gentilicia*, except for Latin authors and for Caesar, Catilina, Cato, Cicero. Further, the Index takes in certain items from the footnotes and from Appendix II.

110; letter to Pompeius, 62, 90; attacked by tribunes, 132;
 he defends Bestia, 132; relations with Crassus, 103 f., 315 f.; defends
Vatinius, 315; Gabinius, 30, 315; Milo, 32; in relation to S., 32, 33 n.;
 his policy towards Octavianus, 216, 221, 257; against Antonius, 220 ff.;
proscribed, 121; posthumous repute, 110, 121 n., 287, 297;
 his orations, often dishonest, 84, 89 f.; the *In toga candida,* 70 n., 74, 84,
89; *Pro Murena,* 76 n., 89; *Catilinarians,* 73, 74, 78 f., 89, 105 f., 107, 109;
Pro Sulla, 89 ff., 101, 113; *Philippics,* 63, 220 ff.;
 his *De oratore,* 46; *De r.p.,* 11, 18, 46; *De legibus,* 46 f.; *Brutus,* 52 ff.;
Orator, 53; *Cato Maior,* 45 f.; *De officiis,* 62, 124; interchangeable prologues, 241;
 the letter to Lucceius, 57; to Atticus about Brutus' *Cato,* 106; the *Cato,*
61; an abortive *suasoria* to Caesor, 346 n.; writings about his consulship,
73; *De consulatu suo,* 104; *De consiliis suis,* 62 ff., 73, 93, 104, 107;
 his style, 50, 52, 257; on archaism, 258, 323; on Caesar's style, 50; R. historiography, 46 ff.; Cato, 45, 55 f.; Macer, 47; Sisenna, 48; Greek historians,
49; on Thuc., 52 ff.; historical monographs, 57; the *Empedoclea* of Sallustius, 10;
 opinions about religion, 247; R. imperialism, 250; agriculture, 45;
"optimates," 18; *nobiles,* 251 f.; "populares," 18 n., 62;
 on Marius, 163, 176 n.; Sulla, 124 f., 177, 250; Catilina, 23, 84 f., 89 ff.;
Vatinius, 6, 89; Caesar, 62, 74 n., 119, 120; Cato, 115; Brutus, 106; Octavianus, 122 n., 221; Lepidus, 221 f.;
 as portrayed by S., 80, 105 ff., 110 f., 121, 211, 222, 287; not alluded to
in *Jug.* 3. 4, 216; probably mentioned in *Hist.,* 211; attacked in *Invective,*
314 ff.; the *In Sallustium,* 3n., 283n., 299; other bogus orations, 297.
Claudia, wife of M. Brutus, 35, 61.
Claudii, their origin, 7; *clientela,* 24; party politics, 171; arrogance, 252.
Claudius Nero, Ti., his motion, 108, 130.
Claudius Nero, Ti. (*pr.* 42), his notable actions, 130 f.
Claudius Pulcher, Ap. (*cos.* 79), his campaigns, 188; relatives, 208.
Claudius Pulcher, Ap. (*cos.* 54), stays with Q. Axius, 9; his brothers, 24 f.;
 sisters, 25; as consul, 24, 29 f., 252; censor, 33 ff.; his political importance,
34 f., 253, 343; arrogance, 252; religious interests, 253; not in Pseudo-S., 342.
Claudius Pulcher, Ap. (*cos.* 38), 227.
Claudius Pulcher, C. (*pr.* 56), 24.
Clitarchus, Greek historian, 47, 259.
Clodia, wife of Metellus Celer, 25; her survival, 226.
Clodius Pulcher, P. (*tr. pl.* 58), his early career, 24, 213; associates, 24 f., 226;
 political allegiance in 52, 31; his death, 31; partisans, 32; his widow, 134 f.
Cocceii, 228, 276.
Coelius Antipater, historian, 46, 258 n.
Cornelia, daughter of Cinna, 159.
Cornelii Lentuli, 286 f.
Cornelius, C. (*tr. pl.* 67), 87, 190 n., 209.

oligarchic consuls, 158 f., 208 ff.; tribunes, 126, 156, 166 f., 169 f., 209 f.; the
Triumvirs, 121 ff., 214 ff.; R. knights, 173, 175 f.; political ladies, 26, 210;
the lower classes, 163, 235 f., 254;

 his quality as a historian, 1, 83, 104 f., 123, 136 f., 186, 240, 248 ff., 272 f.,
288; his personality, 67, 111, 120 f., 212, 213, 239, 254 f., 267 ff., 287, 318;
morals, 26, 38 f., 269 f., 278 ff., 291; the *Horti Sallustiani,* 283;

 the first echoes of his writings, 284 ff.; posthumous fame, 288 ff.; Pseudo-
Sallust, 3, 298 ff., 313 ff.

Sallustii, 9 f., 275 ff.

Sallustius, Cn., friend of Cicero, 10 ff.

Sallustius Crispus, C., grand-nephew of S., 275 ff., 281, 284; his luxurious
tastes, 284; adoption and nomenclature, 281 f.; the Tacitean obituary, 277,
292.

Sallustius Crispus Passienus, C., (*cos. suff.* A.D. 27), 277, 278.

Salvidienus Rufus, Q. (*cos. des.* for 39), 218, 228.

Scaurus, *see* Aemilius.

Scipio, "Lepidi f.," 134 n., 183 n.

Scipiones, their predominance, 171.

Scribonius Curio, C. (*cos.* 76), his campaigns, 189; interest in religion, 193 n.,
246 n.; survival, 207; value of his testimony against Caesar, 96; his eccentric
deportment, 208.

Scribonius Curio, C. (*tr. pl.* 50), 24, 135, 226.

Sempronia, as depicted by S., 25, 125; the digression on her, 69; its purpose,
133 f.; her identification a problem, 134 f.

Sempronia, "Tuditani f.," 134 f.

Sempronii, *see* Gracchi.

Sempronius Asellio, Roman annalist, 149, 154.

Sempronius Atratinus, L. (*cos. suff.* 34), 25, 133 n., 226 f.

Sempronius Gracchus, C. (*tr. pl.* 123), 168, 173; alleged proposals about the
Senate, 344; perhaps imitated by S., 259, 261.

Sempronius Gracchus, Ti., (*tr. pl.* 133), 171.

Seneca, the Elder, 278; vindicates S., 289; on bogus speeches, 317.

Seneca, on the style of S., 258; on Arruntius, 292, 327 f.

Septimii, Sabine, 13 n.

Sergii, decayed patricians, 118.

Sergius Catilina, L. (*pr.* 68), *see* Catilina.

Sertorius, Q. (*pr.* ? 83), his origin, 12, 58; early career, 187, 188, 203; his wanderings, 193 f.; campaigns in Spain, 187, 204, 211; negotiations with Mithridates, 204 f.; his end, 190, 204; its date, 190 n.; no oration in *Hist.,* 196; as
treated by S., 203 ff.; exaggerated posthumous fame, 205; alluded to in
Horace, 285.

Servilia, mother of Brutus, 25; mistress of Caesar, 70 n.

Servilius Nonianus, M. (*cos.* A.D. 35), historian, 291.

Servilius Rullus, P. (*tr. pl.* 63), his agrarian bill, 98.

Servilius Vatia, P. (*cos.* 79), his relatives, 208; as proconsul of Cilicia, 66 n.,